A Toolbox for Economic Design

Dimitrios Diamantaras

with

Emina I. Cardamone, Karen A. Campbell,
Scott Deacle, and Lisa A. Delgado

D. Diamantaras dedicates this book to the memory of his father
Yannis Diamantaras and his former teacher Jeff Banks,
who left this world much too early.

First published in 2009 by
PALGRAVE MACMILLAN®
in the United States - a division of St. Martin's Press LLC,
175 Fifth Avenue, New York, NY 10010.

Where this book is distributed in the UK, Europe and the rest of the world,
this is by Palgrave Macmillan, a division of Macmillan Publishers Limited,
registered in England, company number 785998, of Houndmills,
Basingstoke, Hampshire RG21 6XS.

Palgrave Macmillan is the global academic imprint of the above companies
and has companies and representatives throughout the world.

Palgrave®and Macmillan®are registered trademarks in the United States,
the United Kingdom, Europe and other countries.

ISBN-13: 978–0–230–61060–6
ISBN-10: 0–230–61060–9

Library of Congress Cataloging-in-Publication Data is available from the
Library of Congress.

A catalogue record of the book is available from the British Library.

Design by Dimitrios Diamantaras

First edition: April 2009

10 9 8 7 6 5 4 3 2 1

Printed in the United States of America.

Contents

Figures

Tables

Preface

Economics has always been about designing better ways to organize our activities. When Adam Smith was writing *The Wealth of Nations*, he wanted to influence British laws in the direction of freeing up trade. His accomplishments are great, but he would have achieved more had modern game theory already been invented before he wrote. Economists have been more fortunate in the past 35 years or so. Not only do we have game theory now, but we know how to use it to design economic and other institutions that achieve our objectives by taking account of the incentives of participants. An early pioneer of this research was Leonid Hurwicz, who was honored with the Nobel Prize in economics in 2007, along with Eric S. Maskin and Roger B. Myerson, for the development of the theory of mechanisms. Nobel laureates John F. Nash, Reinhard Selten, John C. Harsanyi, James Mirrlees, and William Vickrey also contributed toward the foundations of the theory. This theory is our topic in this book. It is an important topic that has revamped all of microeconomics. It has found applications in many areas, such as auction design for the FCC auctions that raised billions of dollars, the design of electricity markets, the design of methods for the efficient provision of public goods, the matching of kidney donors to recipients and of medical residents to hospitals, and many more.

The topic is generally called mechanism design. However, within this field, there is a distinction between mechanism design and implementation theory, which we discuss in this book. We have chosen the more general term economic design to describe what the book is about. To describe economic design theory in plain terms, let us say that it is the study of how an economic institution works via the incentives it creates in its participants, so we can fine-tune it to make it work as well as possible. We do not explain this statement more here, as the whole book is dedicated to this task.

Reading the literature in any field requires knowing the specialized language of that field. The field of economic design is no exception and, in fact, has a language that is not easily accessible to a new student. Although good books on and surveys of the field exist, we are not aware of any source that presents the language and content of economic design as methodically and comprehensively as this book does. We know that most students of economic design either find the language too abstract and daunting or they spend enormous amounts of time figuring out basic elementary steps simply because the notation and techniques are unfamiliar. This book seeks to provide the necessary stepping stones in order to facilitate the diffusion and adoption of this powerful tool for studying incentive structures. It is a book written with graduate students for graduate students and advanced undergraduates. It will also be useful for economists, other social scientists, computer scientists and mathematicians who want an introduction to the subject. The graduate student authors are close enough to the graduate school experience to remember where the missing steps are that hinder understanding, while the lead author is a scholar and teacher in the field.

Although we employ a significant amount of mathematical notations and techniques, we have taken pains to lower the barriers against absorbing this material. We explain every mathematical symbol and derivation we present. We rely on research papers, monographs, and surveys for our material, as all books like ours must, but we explain concepts and proofs with more patience than our sources. We present a number of examples, both theoretical and real-life. We also have a chapter that samples the literature that tests mechanisms away from the blackboard, in laboratories and the real world.

The creation of this book has been unique, as far as we know. It originated as a class project for a graduate economics course that the lead author, Dimitrios Diamantaras, taught at Temple University. During and after two offerings of the course, the other authors contributed to the final product, which you hold in your hands. Their contributions have earned them full coauthor credit.

For up-to-date information on this book, including how to report typos, a list of errata, and online sources on mechanisms, please visit the Web page http://astro.temple.edu/~dimitris/page5/page5.html.

Acknowledgments

We are grateful to Nurgul Ukueva for her contributions at an early stage of this project. We were fortunate to receive excellent comments from anonymous reviewers, Charles E. Swanson of Temple University, and William Thomson of the University of Rochester. They are to blame neither for any deficiencies that remain in the book, nor for any omissions in coverage which are due solely to our limitations. We are grateful to Robert P. Gilles of Virginia Tech for suggesting a very helpful reference we did not know about. We owe a large debt of gratitude to the many creators and developers of the theories we present in this book: Leonid Hurwicz, Eric S. Maskin, Roger B. Myerson, Jean-Jacques Laffont, Alvin E. Roth, David Schmeidler, Jerry Green, Allan Gibbard, Mark Satterthwaite, Thomas R. Palfrey, Sanjay Srivastava, John O. Ledyard, John Moore, Rafael Repullo, Matthew O. Jackson, Dilip Abreu, Arunava Sen, Roberto Serrano, Rajiv Vohra, Hervé Moulin, William Thomson, Yves Sprumont, Tatsujoshi Saijo, Simon Wilkie, and many others. Special thanks go to William Thomson, Matthew O. Jackson, David Austen-Smith, Jeffrey S. Banks, Philip J. Reny, and Roberto Serrano, whose expositional writings have helped us tremendously. We also thank Don Campbell and David Austen-Smith for some very useful comments on the manuscript. Two Microeconomics II Ph.D. classes at Temple University suffered through early versions of parts of the book, and we are grateful to them for pointing out mistakes and unclear explanations; among them, special thanks go to Samuel Braithewaite, Adam Ozimek, Andrew Kish, and Hilary Lin for finding errors.

Marianne Miserandino offered support to Dimitrios Diamantaras over the years it took to prepare this book and helped with the creation of the index. But her support to him went well beyond spousal duties and editorial help. As she also provides the central meaning in his life, he cannot express his appreciation well enough. The hoary "I couldn't have done it without her" applies with double force. Dimitrios is also indebted to many friends in the United States, his adopted country, for emotional sustenance during some very trying times over the years. Suzanne DuPlantis, Jill Westbrook, Charles Swanson, Tenley Bank and Paul Diefenbach, Dominique Gaherty, Rob Gilles, Reiko and Troy Finamore, Eileen Kim, Philip and Ann Jones, and Rick Arras, thank you!

Karen Campbell is grateful to her teachers from elementary through graduate school who sparked her curiosity in the world and showed her how to satisfy that curiosity.

Emina Cardamone would like to thank her husband, Mike, for his tremendous love, support, and sense of humor, especially during the past few years while working on this project and getting through graduate school.

Scott Deacle would like to thank his wife, Sarah, for her support and sacrifice of time together as he worked on the project. His dog, Reggie, deserves praise and treats for urging him to take walks and play with toys. It helped keep things in perspective.

Lisa Delgado would like to thank her husband, Rich, for all his support and helping her make time for work. She also thanks her son, Braden, for sometimes listening when told "let mommy work."

Chapter 1

Introduction

1.1 A Story from Ancient Athens

During the Classical Period in Athens (479–322 BCE) direct government taxation was not feasible, and the city-state of Athens resorted to the private provision of some important public goods, such as the fleet necessary for the defense of the city.[1] The Athenians devised the *liturgical* system to deal with this, a system that deserves to be much better known especially in the world of economics.

The *New Oxford American Dictionary* offers this as its second entry for the word *liturgy:* "(in ancient Athens) a public office or duty performed voluntarily by a rich Athenian." At the center of the liturgical system was the *trierarchy,* which meant the "command, outfitting, and maintenance of a war ship for one year" (Kaiser, 2007, page 445). The war ship this refers to is the *trireme,* a fast galley with three banks of oars that proved very effective in the Battle of Salamis against the Persian Navy, which Persian king Xerxes had to watch being destroyed from a nearby hill in 479 BC. This battle was decisive in repelling the Persian threat to what is now mainland Greece, and it is no accident that the Classical Period is taken to start in the year of the Battle of Salamis.

The intrigue that the trierarchy holds for us is not the same as for history buffs. It was a remarkable institution that maintained a high level of support for the Athenian fleet by wealthy Athenians for a long time by giving them the right incentives.

The burden and honor of the trierarchy fell on the members of the landowning classes. These individuals had visible wealth, self-proclaimed wealth, and actual wealth, to use categories relevant for the trierarchy. There was a strong incentive to hide part of one's wealth. This could easily allow wealthy citizens to shirk their liturgical duties. The institution of trierarchy was an early example of a mechanism, a concept we discuss in this chapter and formally define in section 2.1. Its purpose was to make the true wealth of citizens become apparent so they would not be able to shirk their duties.

Athens was governed then by the *boulē*, a council chosen randomly from the population of citizens. The council did not observe the true wealth of citizens, it only observed visible

---

[1]This section draws on Kaiser (2007).

wealth, such as land holdings, slaves, and mines. Once it identified the wealthiest citizens, it imposed trierarchy duties on them. If an individual was assigned such a duty, he[2] could either perform the duty or attempt the *antidosis* challenge. This challenge meant that the citizen charged with the trierarchy duty could point his finger to another citizen and say that the latter is wealthier and hence more fit to carry out the duty than himself. The challenged citizen had three options: (a) agree that he is wealthier than the challenger and take on the trierarchy duty; (b) disagree that he is wealthier than the challenger and offer to swap his visible wealth for the challenger's visible wealth so that the challenger would perform the duty but with the challenged individual's wealth at his disposal; or (c) disagree that he is wealthier than the challenger and let the court decide, based on the court's subsequent investigation of the wealth of the challenger and the challenged.

This system had a purpose: in modern economic terms, it was aimed at securing the efficient provision of the public good of national defense. It was also sophisticated in that it took account of the incentives of individuals to free-ride, and actively counteracted them. The study of social goals and institutionalized incentive systems to achieve the goals is at the heart of this book. We turn now to a more general discussion of social goals and incentives embodied in institutions as an introduction to our methodical investigation of the topic in the rest of the book. Rest assured that we will return to the fascinating *antidosis* challenge system for the trierarchy when we have developed enough of the necessary theoretical tools to see how it provided incentives for people to perform their duties.

1.2 Institutions and Economics

Economics studies the arrangement of social affairs and how it affects the welfare of people. Adam Smith's foundational treatise inquires about the *Nature and Causes of the Wealth of Nations* in its very title (Smith, 1998). How society is organized is a fundamental cause of wealth, and one we still are trying to understand deeply.

The organization of society has been a source of interest and conflict since before the start of recorded history. Achieving any societal goals requires organized cooperation and inevitably leads to conflicts. Dictatorial methods were tried early and were prevalent for a long time and over many geographical areas. Having an individual control society certainly simplifies social decision-making, but is not the only way to go about it, and certainly not the best.

The seemingly chaotic system of voluntary trading in marketplaces was a late discovery of humanity. It took human society away from authoritarianism. It has led to a fantastically complicated division of labor across nations. Some call the division of labor it has led to the *great experiment,* as it has improved the lot of a vast number of people but

---

[2]Only free men could be Athenian citizens.

still is not guaranteed to survive as the dominant method for humans to interact with other humans, most of them strangers (Seabright, 2004). Economics textbooks extol this multifaceted, seemingly miraculous, division of labor. They laud the market system for bringing us unprecedented prosperity and freedom. They sing its praises for bringing us closer to an efficient allocation of resources.

To understand what makes markets tick, economic theorists have used the tools of game theory. This methodology provides a framework into which the entire social organization fits naturally. In this viewpoint, the allocation of resources is a special case of the organization of society, and market exchange is a special case of the allocation of resources. This general framework is the *mechanism design* framework, and this book gives an introduction to it. Its development, far from marginalizing the study of markets and competitive equilibrium, has given the study of markers better context. Thus it gives us deeper insight into markets at the same time as it teaches economists how to design economic institutions that go beyond markets in an effort to achieve better outcomes for society. The framework of mechanism design has proved capable of handling a wide variety of institutions, not only economic but also political and legal. We adopt a general viewpoint that encompasses institutions of all these kinds.

Mechanism design is about the creation and shaping of institutions. Institutions can evolve over time, or can be deliberately designed and created. Since we focus on deliberate institution design, we will not emphasize those institutions that have evolved over time, such as the general framework of property rights and economic exchange in marketplaces. The theories we will present often point out cases where evolved institutions function well and cases where the design of new institutions to complement them is necessary and useful. We should remember, however, that designing new institutions is not the solution to all ills. Thinking that it is so can easily lead to failed social experiments on a grand scale, such as communism. Indeed, the best use of the knowledge in this book is to apply it to piecemeal social engineering. It is also good to keep in mind that the assumptions of the theory we will present are not always applicable, so our results may be limited in their reach. Furthermore, the evolution of institutions over untold centuries has accumulated a vast store of hard-earned wisdom to which theory-based institutional design does not have easy access. All theories are limited and should be applied with care; the theories we explain here are no different.

It is time to define the institution concept. A succinct description of the principal meanings of the term is given in Schotter (2001, page 5), which we now summarize. An **institution** can be seen as (i) a set of unenforced conventions, such as tipping in restaurants, that society has developed to help solve repetitive economic problems or as (ii) a set of enforced rules to govern behavior. Enforcing is a matter of degree; what we mean is that the police do not chase us if we do not tip at the restaurant, but they do when we rob the restaurant of its receipts at gunpoint. The first meaning fits better with an evolutionary approach, such as the one the previous paragraph suggests. The second meaning bears more directly to the conscious choice of the rules of human interaction. We have adopted the second meaning in this book.

The design of rules to govern economic behavior has always been very much in the spirit of mainstream economics, although the techniques we will study here reached the mainstream rather recently. Economists are always looking to improve the functioning of society. The advantages of the economic design framework are that it gives us tools to understand and implement institutional improvements and it allows us to do this across many economic environments. Economies with private goods, economies with private and public goods, economies with externalities, auctions, and voting, are some examples of environments which fall under the umbrella of economic design.

We should pause to consider the much-used term "decentralization" at this point. Traditionally, this term referred to the second fundamental theorem of welfare economics, which is the result that says: if you want to get to any Pareto efficient allocation of resources in an economy with private goods, then make some necessary changes to agents' initial endowments and then unleash free markets. Perfectly competitive markets will reach the Pareto efficient allocation as a competitive equilibrium allocation, provided market participants have good information and you reallocate initial endowments exactly right at the beginning. This result not only has much renown but also many limitations not always explicitly acknowledged: (a) it relies on some central auctioneer to operate the competitive markets without considering what incentives this auctioneer has; (b) it assumes a complete set of perfectly competitive markets and so no externalities or public goods; (c) it assumes a staggering amount of information processing capability on the part of economic agents and even more so on the part of the auctioneer; and (d) it neglects the incentives that agents may have to manipulate markets even when all markets are set out to be competitive. By the time you have read most of this book, you will have an improved notion of what decentralization means. We start by looking at The Big Picture.

1.3 Getting the Big Picture

Mechanism design operates in what we call environments, which come from *domains*. Some examples will help clarify these concepts.

1. Let X be a set of alternatives from which a given set of individuals is to choose one. For instance, each alternative may be a candidate to be elected to a political office or as chairman of the board of a corporation. Each individual has a personal ranking of all alternatives, which is information not available to the central authority that organizes the social choice. We denote the list of all rankings by θ and the set of all allowable such lists by Θ. The information in θ is supposed to be the only basis on which to choose an alternative. The environment is θ and the domain is Θ. Society

has a given *social choice function, f*, which tells us which choice $f(\theta)$ from X is the best, if only θ could be known to the central authority so that it could implement $f(\theta)$. We take the criterion of goodness embedded in f as given; we do not question the origin of social choice functions in this book, but we will make it gradually quite clear what some of the common criteria for good alternatives are.

2. Let X be a description of the allocation of an object that is up to be sold at auction among the seller and the bidders, along with a complete description of the payments that are to take place among these people. Each individual has a valuation for this object, which is her private information, unavailable to the auctioneer. Here the environment θ is the list of the valuations, and the set of all allowable valuation lists is the domain, Θ. The social choice function f, as before, chooses $f(\theta)$ from X, based on θ; one prominent example considered in auction theory is the social choice function f that maximizes the expected revenue of the seller. Another is the f that chooses an efficient allocation of the object among the individuals, no matter what θ happens to be.

3. Let X be a set of feasible allocations of n commodities among a given set of individuals. Each individual has a utility function that encodes her preference relation over the consumption bundles she may receive in an allocation from X. This information is private to her, unavailable to the auctioneer who tries to lead the group to an allocation. Here the environment θ is the list of utility functions and the domain Θ is the set of all such lists that satisfy certain assumptions (for instance, that each utility function is increasing in every commodity). A social choice function here gives an allocation $f(\theta)$ of the commodities for each utility list θ. A popular one embodies Pareto efficiency; we will see several others later.

The main idea of mechanism design is captured in a venerable diagram shown in figure 1.1, called the Reiter Diagram in honor of its originator, Stanley Reiter. The relevant features of society are depicted as members of some domain Θ. A member θ of Θ is a description of such things as individuals' preferences and information and technological constraints, as in the examples we have just seen. As the examples make clear, the exact information encoded in θ varies with the application we want to make. A very important feature of θ is that the information it contains is distributed among the members of the society in such a way that each individual has a part of θ as her *private information*. For instance, each individual's preferences are accessible only to that individual; all others can only ask the individual about her preferences or try to infer the individual's preferences from the individual's behavior.

In the top right corner there is the set X of the objects of choice for the society, as seen in the examples. This is the set of all societal arrangements that can be made if there is information available to a central authority about the society, as encoded in any particular θ. The central authority may or may not exist in reality; in the theory, it serves as an idealization of what could be potentially coordinated centrally, in principle.

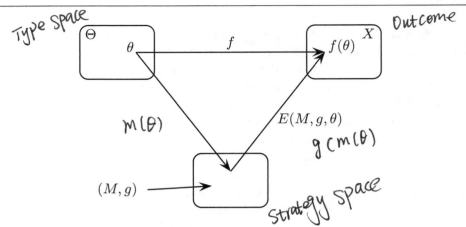

Figure 1.1: The Reiter Diagram

This framework allows us to study many social decision problems in addition to that of allocating resources, which is the staple of economics.

Now suppose that there is some way of operating on the information in θ to get a specific social arrangement x in X. Let us call this way of operating a *social choice function,* and denote it by f. For instance, the problem may be the choice of how much of a public good to provide. The social choice function f might amount to asking the society members their marginal willingness to pay for various levels of the public good, then using this information to find efficient levels of the public good and the efficient distribution of taxes to pay for it.

But what are we to do about people who will try to minimize the amount of tax they have to pay? In the public good example and many others, the members of society might misrepresent their preferences to try to get the social choice function f to result in an outcome more favorable to themselves. We have a name for this kind of behavior in the public good provision case: *free riding.* It has been a long-recognized reason why the voluntary contribution method of providing public goods will result in their inefficient under-provision.

In short, society wants to use the social choice function f to make its choice, because society likes the features of f, but it needs the agents' private information, embodied in θ, to compute $f(\theta)$. This is where mechanism design theory comes into its own. Society *devises a game for the agents to play* by means of a mechanism. Agents play this game and the outcome of the game coincides with the target, $f(\theta)$. We then say that this mechanism *implements* the social choice function f on the domain Θ. (More precise statements of all these definitions and claims are in the remainder of the book.)

A mechanism has two parts: M, a set of strategies for all participants, and g, a function that associates an alternative in X to each strategy combination. When we add to (M, g) the information about the preferences of the participants, who are the members of the society as encoded in θ, we have a *game* as defined in game theory. To this we add a theory of how participants play the game. For instance, we may assume that a combination of strategies m from M is an equilibrium if each player plays a strategy that is a best response to anything the others could play. This is known as dominant strategy equilibrium. Or we may assume that the participants play strategies that are mutual best responses. This is known as Nash equilibrium. There are yet other interesting variations, as we will see later, but now you have an idea of what *equilibrium* means in this context.

In the diagram, $E(M, g, \theta)$ denotes the equilibrium of the game that arises once the mechanism (M, g) has been designed and society members, endowed with their private information θ, participate in the mechanism.

A mechanism could be a dynamic procedure, as complicated as we want to imagine. After all, strategies in the normal form of a game can be derived by starting with an extensive form (as complicated as we like) and deriving the strategies that this extensive form implies. But it is time for an example.

1.4 Example: An Auction

Suppose that ten people are gathered to participate in an auction for a single item. The auction works as follows: the auctioneer starts with a ridiculously high price and gradually lowers it until one of the participants raises her hand to indicate a bid. The auction terminates at this point, and the bidder who made this bid receives the item and pays the amount of the bid. If you are wondering about these strange details, well, this is how the auctions for flowers have been conducted in The Netherlands for centuries.

Dutch auction

In this example the society members are the bidders and the owner of the item being auctioned. Only the bidders actually get to play by making bids. The owner as the auctioneer gets to *choose the game they play* by choosing the exact procedure for the auction to proceed. The procedure we described is one of an infinite number of potential procedures that can be imagined. Is it good?

This question is imprecise. Good for what or for whom? Let us say we mean "good for the owner of the auctioned item." Then the question becomes whether the auction procedure we described yields the highest possible expected revenue from the auction.

Note here that the social choice function in this case is not very social in spirit. We did not say it had to be, but the name "social choice function" suggests it should be. We start with an example in which the social choice function benefits just one member of society to make clear that the social choice function need not be in the best interest of all members of society, even if such a concept could be made unambiguous. (If the auction is conducted by a government, it is possible that it will have a more "socially minded" social choice function.)

The question is still imprecise. We need to make some reasonable assumptions about the preferences of the bidders. For the sake of this simple example, let us make some really basic assumptions on these preferences. Assume that each bidder is willing to pay up to some randomly determined amount v^i. Assume also that the random variables of the bidders are statistically independent of each other, are identically distributed across bidders, and that each bidder may have a value for v^i from zero to some common upper bound V. Finally, assume that each bidder is risk-neutral.

In terms of the Reiter Diagram, the social choice function here aims to maximize the expected revenue from the auction. The particular auction procedure we described is one mechanism out of many that can be used to try to implement this function. It can be shown, however, that this particular mechanism does not implement the social choice function. There is a different way of running the auction that yields the highest possible expected revenue under our assumptions. The point here is not to go into the details of this result. Rather, it is to show mechanism design in action by hinting at what it can really do. We do not assume the existence of a market for the good and search for the intersection of truthfully revealed supply and demand curves. The mechanism design approach requires us to specify the information and strategies available to the players. Based on more assumptions about the players' preferences and their rationality, we determine the outcome that will result from this auction. We will show the optimal auction design for a class of auctions that includes the one in this example in a subsequent chapter. (Yes, we like building suspense. It is our mechanism to encourage you to keep reading. The social choice function we have in mind involves you getting the maximum knowledge and fun from this book.)

1.5 A Taste of Social Choice Theory

The most general domain for the study of mechanism design is the social choice domain. All other domains are special cases. Social choice theory is also where the central concepts of mechanism design first emerged and were developed. This section provides an introduction to social choice theory in a simple social choice domain with a finite set of alternatives.

Imagine you are a member of a committee that has to decide on one out of a number of options. Perhaps the options are how to allocate office space to members of a business department. Perhaps the options are which candidates will be elected as officers of an organization. Perhaps the committee is the U.S. House of Representatives, and the options are different versions of a piece of proposed legislation. Perhaps the committee contains all voters in the electorate, and the options are different candidates for president in a direct election. The possibilities are endless, as this framework of choice by groups of people can accommodate just about any situation of group choice we can imagine.

Now suppose that each member of the committee has a ranking of all the alternative options. How will the committee come up with a ranking that synthesizes all these individual rankings? Less ambitiously, how will the committee choose an alternative that is in some meaningful way the best choice given the individual rankings? These are the questions of social choice theory. Soon after giving them serious thought, scholars found themselves thinking about the incentives facing the committee members. For instance, if the process for aggregating individual rankings involves voting, would it sometimes make sense for some agent to vote for her second or third choice if it meant that she avoids her bottom choice's election? Such questions are the province of the next chapter.

Kenneth Arrow introduced the systematic investigation of how society makes choices in *Social Choice and Individual Values* (Arrow, 1951). The topic had been studied before, but in a fragmentary fashion. Social choice is the foundation of all of economic design, and we will give it here a brief but serious look. We explain notation as it is introduced, and all notation in this book is collected in a chapter at the end of the book for easy reference. You can get the flavor of the main results of social choice theory without delving into the proofs, but there is simply no way to do justice to the material without the mathematics. We offer proofs at the end of this chapter.

We now start our brief survey of social choice theory. Naturally, a lot of relevant material is not even mentioned here, as it is not possible to include all the interesting work that has been done on this topic in a single book, let alone a chapter. Our presentation borrows some notation and structure from the superb microeconomics textbook by Mas-Colell et al. (1995).

1.5.1 Arrow's Impossibility Theorem

There are I individuals, whom we call **agents.** There is a philosophical reason for this name. It is intended to emphasize that these individuals are agents of their own fate.

The agents have to choose an element of a non-empty finite set X of social alternatives. If X has only two elements, the majority voting procedure works well. Things get more difficult with three or more elements. Indeed, with three or more alternatives, it is possible that no alternative receives a clear majority over all the others, so majority rule does not work.

Each agent i has a preference relation R^i on X. The meaning of $x \, R^i \, y$, for any $x, y \in X$, is "x is at least as good as y according to agent i." The strict preference relation, P^i, is defined by the statement: for all $x, y \in X$, $x \, P^i \, y$ if and only if $x \, R^i \, y$ and not $y \, R^i \, x$. This defines the statement "x is strictly better than y" as equivalent to the conjunction of the statements "x is as good as y" and "y is not as good as x." The indifference relation, I^i, is defined by the statement: for all $x, y \in X$, $x \, I^i \, y$ if and only if $x \, R^i \, y$ and $y \, R^i \, x$. This defines the statement "x is indifferent to y" as equivalent to the conjunction of the statements "x is as good as y" and "y is as good as x."

We assume the following three conditions hold for every agent $i \in \mathcal{I}$.[3]

---

[3]Our assumptions are the standard ones imposed on *homo economicus*, and they make high demands of

Completeness For each pair of alternatives $x, y \in X$, either $x\ R^i\ y$ or $y\ R^i\ x$. (For any two alternatives x and y, if you ask any agent i whether one of them is at least as good as the other, then you must receive an answer. The agent must be able to choose a preferred alternative. This property may be difficult to satisfy if some pairs of alternatives contain very different options, or if the alternatives in X are very complicated, such as legal systems or insurance policies.)

Reflexivity For each alternative $x \in X$, we have $x\ R^i\ x$. (Any alternative is considered at least as good as itself. This needs to be stated, although it is hard to imagine how it can be violated.)

Transitivity For each triplet of alternatives $x, y, z \in X$, if $x\ R^i\ y$ and $y\ R^i\ z$, then $x\ R^i\ z$. (This is fairly obvious, unless we have a very confused agent: if i thinks that x is at least as good as y and y at least as good as z, then she must also think that x is at least as good as z.)

A preference relation that satisfies these properties is called a preference ordering. Not-so-trick question: can you see how Completeness implies Reflexivity? We have nevertheless chosen to keep these distinct in our presentation, as Reflexivity brings out a specific aspect of Completeness.

The set of complete and transitive preference relations on X is denoted by $\mathcal{R}$. The proper subset of $\mathcal{R}$ which contains preference orderings that do not admit indifferences is denoted by $\mathcal{P}$. Thus a preference ordering that says for some pair of alternatives $x, y \in X$ that x is indifferent to y, belongs to $\mathcal{R}$ but not to $\mathcal{P}$.

In the definitions, axioms, and results to come we often refer to a list of preference orderings $(R^1, R^2, \ldots, R^I)$, one preference ordering per agent; such a list is called a **preference profile.** To make our life considerably easier, and the book easier to read, we use the shorthand ρ for such a preference profile. Write $\mathcal{R}^I$ for the I-fold Cartesian product of $\mathcal{R}$ by itself.

Definition 1.1 (Social Welfare Functional). Let $\mathcal{S} \subseteq \mathcal{R}^I$ be given. A **social welfare functional** is a map $R : \mathcal{S} \to \mathcal{R}$ that assigns to every profile of preference orderings $\rho = (R^1, \ldots, R^I) \in \mathcal{S}$ a preference ordering $R(\rho)$ in $\mathcal{R}$.

A social welfare functional takes a list of preference orderings of individuals and returns a preference ordering for society.

Note: Following standard mathematical practice, we have shown the domain of R as any subset $\mathcal{S}$ of the set of all conceivable preference ordering profiles $\mathcal{R}^I$. When we want to have some R be defined on only a particular subset of $\mathcal{R}^I$, such as the set of all strict preference orderings $\mathcal{P}$, all we will have to do is apply the same definition for R and set $\mathcal{S} = \mathcal{P}^I$.

the cognitive capacities and preference consistency of *homo economicus*. Although a more psychologically sophisticated approach to the material of this book, along the lines of the badly named "behavioral" economics, would be great to have, it does not exist yet. Perhaps you can help build it.

$R(\rho)$ is society's preference ordering. We have left the question of the details of its construction unanswered. This way we can study all social welfare functionals at once and discover unexpected results about their properties.

Given a profile of preference relations $\rho = (R^1, \ldots, R^I)$ and a social welfare functional R, we write $P(\rho)$ for the strict preference relation derived from $R(\rho)$. The derivation is as before: for any $x, y \in X$, $x\, P(\rho)\, y$ if and only if $x\, R(\rho)\, y$ and not $y\, R(\rho)\, x$. For $x\, R(\rho)\, y$ we say "x is socially at least as good as y" and for $x\, P(\rho)\, y$ we say "x is socially preferred to y" (in both cases we are to understand that "according to the social choice welfare functional R" is implied).

We focus only on the cases where $\mathcal{S}$ is $\mathcal{R}^I$ or $\mathcal{P}^I$.

The first property most economists would think of requiring of a social welfare functional is that it should rank Pareto efficient alternatives highest. The following axiom is a precise formulation of the weakest imaginable form of this requirement.

Axiom (Pareto Property). The social welfare functional $R : \mathcal{S} \to \mathcal{R}$ has the **Pareto property** if, for all x, y in X and for all $\rho = (R^1, \ldots, R^I)$ in $\mathcal{S}$, if for every i we have $x\, P^i\, y$, then $x\, P(\rho)\, y$.

This says that the social welfare functional respects unanimous strict rankings of pairs of alternatives. If every agent agrees that an alternative x is strictly better than y, then the social welfare functional R must also agree and rank x as strictly better than y.

Example 1.1. The Borda Count. This social welfare functional was proposed in the eighteenth century by Jean-Charles de Borda, an early French theorist of democracy and fighter in the American War of Independence on the American side, who was also a "mathematician, engineer, astronomer and naval hero" (Saari, 2001, page 43).[4] The Borda Count is defined when X is a finite set. Consider an agent i and an alternative $x \in X$. Given the agent's preference relation R^i, assign a number of points $p_i(x)$ to x by the following rule. If no two alternatives in X are indifferent to each other according to R^i and x is ranked nth from the top according to R^i, set $p_i(x) = n$. If indifference happens according to R^i, then set $p_i(x)$ equal to the average rank of x according to R^i. For instance, if there are three alternatives, x, y, z, and x is ranked top while y and z tie in the second rank, then $p_i(x) = 1$ and $p_i(y) = p_i(z) = 2.5$. Now, take any profile $\rho = (R^1, \ldots, R^I)$ in $\mathcal{R}^I$ and define $R(\rho)$ by the rule: $x\, R(\rho)\, y$ if $\sum_i p_i(x) \le \sum_i p_i(y)$. This method ranks the alternatives higher if they have fewer points. We now show that this social preference relation is complete and transitive and that it has the Pareto property.

To prove that it is complete, suppose that x, y are any two alternatives in X. Since all agents are assumed to have complete preference orderings, for each i there exist two positive rational numbers $p_i(x)$ and $p_i(y)$. Therefore, the sums $\sum_i p_i(x)$ and $\sum_i p_i(y)$ are

---

[4]Borda wrote down the eponymous election rule first in 1770 and published it in 1781.

well-defined. Because these sums are rational numbers, one of the following three size relations has to hold: $\sum_i p_i(x) \leq \sum_i p_i(y)$, $\sum_i p_i(x) = \sum_i p_i(y)$, or $\sum_i p_i(x) \geq \sum_i p_i(y)$. It follows that the social preference relation defined by the Borda count is complete.

To prove transitivity, suppose that $x, y, z \in X$ are three alternatives with $x\ R(\rho)\ y$ and $y\ R(\rho)\ z$. By the definition of the Borda Count, these two social rankings mean that $\sum_i p_i(x) \leq \sum_i p_i(y)$ and $\sum_i p_i(y) \leq \sum_i p_i(z)$; but this implies immediately, by the transitivity of rational numbers, that $\sum_i p_i(x) \leq \sum_i p_i(z)$. Finally, this implies by definition that $x\ R(\rho)\ z$, which proves the transitivity of the Borda Count.

To prove that the Borda Count has the Pareto property, suppose that x, y in X are two alternatives such that for every i we have $x\ P^i\ y$. By definition of the $p_i(x)$ and $p_i(y)$ numbers, it follows that for every i we have $p_i(x) < p_i(y)$. Therefore, $\sum_i p_i(x) < \sum_i p_i(y)$, which implies, by the definition of the Borda Count, that $x\ P(\rho)\ y$, which proves the Pareto property.

Note that we could have written the Borda Count procedure by giving more points to higher ranked alternatives rather than fewer (we would not call such points penalty points, of course). You will recognize the school grading system's calculation of a GPA (grade point average, used in the United States) of A, B, C, D, and F as a Borda Count. The highest alternative, A, gets 4 points in this case, the second-highest, B, gets 3 points, and so forth. ◇

The next property that we consider desirable for a social welfare functional to satisfy is a little lengthy, but important.

Axiom (Pairwise Independence). The social welfare functional $R : \mathcal{S} \to \mathcal{R}$ has the **pairwise independence property** if, for all pairs x, y in X, and for all preference profiles $\rho = (R^1, \ldots, R^I) \in \mathcal{S}$ and $\overline{\rho} = (\overline{R}^1, \ldots, \overline{R}^I) \in \mathcal{S}$ such that for each $i \in \mathcal{I}$ $x\ R^i\ y$ if and only if $x\ \overline{R}^i\ y$ and $y\ R^i\ x$ if and only if $y\ \overline{R}^i\ x$, we have that $x\ R(\rho)\ y$ if and only if $x\ R(\overline{\rho})\ y$ and $y\ R(\rho)\ x$ if and only if $y\ R(\overline{\rho})\ x$.

Pairwise Independence is also often called Independence of Irrelevant Alternatives. It applies if something should happen to change the social choice situation. Maybe an alternative suddenly becomes unavailable, or some preference orderings change for other reasons. In such a case, if the change did not affect how any agent ranks a particular pair of alternatives relative to each other, then it should not affect how society ranks these two alternatives relative to each other.

Pairwise independence simplifies the social choice problem. It is particularly appealing when the alternatives it treats as irrelevant are indeed irrelevant. This depends on the context more than is desirable for such a general theory. One context in which pairwise independence is appealing is that of an election. If one candidate in an election dies just before the election is held, there seems to be no reason for the ranking of the remaining candidates to be upset.

The Borda Count does not satisfy pairwise independence. This is fairly obvious, as the ranking of each alternative depends on the ranking of every other alternative. An explicit example where the Borda Count violates pairwise independence is easy to create. Here is one from Saari (2001, page 44). There are eleven agents and three alternatives, x, y, and z. Five of them have the preference ordering $x \ P^i \ y \ P^i \ z$ and the other six have the ordering $y \ P^i \ x \ P^i \ z$. As you can see easily when applying the Borda Count, it ranks y highest for this society. Now change the preference ordering of the first five agents to $x \ P^i \ z \ P^i \ y$. Note that after this change every agent still ranks x versus y as before, so Pairwise Independence says that the Borda Count should still rank y highest. However, after the change of preferences of the five agents, the Borda count ranks x highest.

If we want to adhere to pairwise independence, one way is to simply focus on socially ranking pairs of alternatives, ignoring any other alternatives. As we have mentioned, the majority rule voting social choice functional works well with two alternatives. Can it be extended to work with more than two? The answer has been known since the time of the French Revolution.

Example 1.2. The Condorcet Method and Condorcet Paradox. With three or more alternatives, the majority rule is not well defined. What happens if no alternative is ranked best by a majority of the agents? We can try to arrange sequential votes among pairs of alternatives, with the loser in each vote eliminated from the set of alternatives, until only one alternative remains, which we call the **Condorcet winner**. This is the **Condorcet method.** But it does not always work, as Condorcet[5] showed with a famous example. Suppose there are three alternatives, $X = \{x, y, z\}$. The preferences of the three agents are as follows:

$$x \ P^1 \ y \ P^1 \ z.$$
$$z \ P^2 \ x \ P^2 \ y.$$
$$y \ P^3 \ z \ P^3 \ x.$$

Now the pairwise majority rule is fruitless, as it depends on which pair is chosen to be ranked first. You can see this by asking yourself who wins if x is first paired with y and the winner then paired with z, and so on for every possible order of pairings. You will discover that which pairing you start with determines the ultimate winner. If there were a person who controlled the agenda (the order of pairings), that person effectively would be the dictator. This example shows that a Condorcet winner does not always exist.   ◊

---

[5]Marie-Jean-Antoine-Nicolas Caritat, Marquis de Condorcet, criticized Borda's method and introduced his own approach to voting. He was a "mathematician, philosopher, and politician." (Saari 2001, page v.)

So Condorcet's method does not show us a way of constructing a social welfare functional with desirable properties. Is there any such social welfare functional? Arrow proved in *Social Choice and Individual Values* that it is very hard to find a satisfactory solution. Before discussing Arrow's theorem, we state another property a social welfare functional may have, this time one that most people consider highly undesirable.

Axiom (Dictatorial Social Welfare Functional). A social welfare functional R is **dictatorial** if there is an agent $d \in \mathcal{I}$ such that, for any x, y in X and any profile $\rho = (R^1, \ldots, R^I)$ in $\mathcal{S}$, we have that $x \, P(\rho) \, y$ if and only if $x \, P^d \, y$.

The agent d can be considered a dictator, because society ranks any alternative above any other if and only if d does.

Theorem 1.1 (Arrow's Impossibility Theorem). *Assume that there are at least three alternatives and that the domain of admissible individual preference profiles, denoted $\mathcal{S}$, is either $\mathcal{S} = \mathcal{R}^I$ or $\mathcal{S} = \mathcal{P}^I$. Then every social welfare functional that satisfies the Pareto property and pairwise independence is dictatorial.*

We present a proof of this theorem in an appendix to this chapter. This is certainly a disheartening result. Does it mean that democracy is impossible? No. It does mean that a group of individuals cannot hope to have as coherent social preferences as a single agent can have individual preferences unless they appoint a dictator or have one forced on them. It also means that the institutional details and political procedures surrounding social decision-making are very important for the final outcome, as there is no social welfare functional that will work well under all preference profiles that can arise.

The original name of this theorem was the "general possibility theorem." Arrow chose this name because the theorem shows that for any method of aggregating individual preference profiles that satisfies the Pareto property and pairwise independence and is not dictatorial, it is possible to find a particular preference profile that renders the outcome of the method intransitive. In particular, this means that any given social aggregation method will work for many (but not all) possible preference profiles. Note well how this comment mitigates the negative force of the theorem. Note also how important for the theorem is the assumption that preference profiles are unrestricted. This assumption is somewhat hidden in the statement that "the domain of admissible individual preference profiles, denoted $\mathcal{S}$, is either $\mathcal{S} = \mathcal{R}^I$ or $\mathcal{S} = \mathcal{P}^I$."

1.6 Social Choice Functions

As we saw, a social welfare functional takes a list of preference orderings of individuals and returns a preference ordering for society. From Arrow's theorem we know that we should not expect social welfare functionals to satisfy a number of desirable axioms. Is this because the very concept of a social welfare functional is too ambitious?

At first sight, this appears plausible. When we aggregate individual preference orderings, our ultimate aim is to enable society to choose an alternative in some way that respects these orderings. We can use a social welfare functional for this task. Once it gives us the social preference ordering, we can simply say that society ought to choose the alternative that ranks highest in this ordering. But this is overkill. Once we know a top-ranking alternative, we do not really need to know information such as which alternative occupies the 117th position in the ranking. May we expect the aggregation of preferences to satisfy the kinds of axioms we would like it to if we modify what we expect the aggregation to do? If we are humble enough to just ask it to give one recommended alternative, will we succeed in this quest? Here is a formal presentation of what we mean by this aggregation of preferences.

Definition 1.2 (Social Choice Function). Let $\mathcal{S} \subseteq \mathcal{R}^I$ be given. A **social choice function** is a function $f \colon \mathcal{S} \to X$ that assigns to every profile of preference orderings $\rho = (R^1, \ldots, R^I)$ in $\mathcal{S}$ an alternative $f(\rho)$ in X.

A social choice function delivers a specific alternative to be chosen, once it is fed the preference orderings of all agents. What axioms might we want to require of it? It turns out we can consider very close relatives of the same axioms we discussed in relation to social welfare functionals.

Axiom (Pareto Property of a Social Choice Function). The social choice function $f \colon \mathcal{S} \to X$ has the **Pareto property** if, for all x in X and for all $\rho = (R^1, \ldots, R^I) \in \mathcal{S}$, if for every i we have that for all $y \in X$, $x\,R^i\,y$, then $f(\rho) = x$.

This version of the Pareto property says that if an alternative x is at the top of every agent's preference ordering, then it should be selected by the social choice function.

Axiom (Monotonicity). The social choice function f is **monotonic** if, for all profiles $\rho = (R^1, \ldots, R^I)$ in $\mathcal{S}$ and $\tilde{\rho} = (\tilde{R}^1, \ldots, \tilde{R}^I)$ in $\mathcal{S}$, if $f(\rho) = x$ and for every y in X, if $x\,R^i\,y$ for every i then $x\,\tilde{R}^i\,y$ for every i, then $f(\tilde{\rho}) = x$.

Assuming monotonicity means that if a social choice function initially selects alternative x, and then preferences change so that no other alternative y climbs higher than x in any agent's ranking, the social choice function still selects x. We will see in the Nash implementation chapter that a close cousin of this axiom is central in that subject.

Finally, let us state formally what dictatorship means for a social choice function.

Axiom (Dictatorial Property of a Social Choice Function). The social choice function f is **dictatorial** if there is an agent d such that, for every profile $\rho = (R^1, \ldots, R^I)$ in $\mathcal{S}$, $f(\rho) = x$ if and only if x is at the top of d's preference ranking.

And what happens if we want to have a social choice function that has the Pareto and Monotonicity properties? The next theorem shows that such a social choice function must be dictatorial. Monotonicity is a necessary condition for a social choice function to not give any agent the opportunity to misreport his preferences in order to manipulate the society's choice to something better for him. So the next theorem is disappointing as it implicitly shows that only dictatorial social choice functions have impeccable incentive properties. The Gibbard-Satterthwaite theorem that we cover right after the Muller-Satterthwaite theorem packages the same statement in starker form.

Theorem 1.2 (Muller and Satterthwaite, 1977). *Assume that there are at least three alternatives and that the domain of admissible individual preference profiles, denoted $\mathcal{S}$, is either $\mathcal{S} = \mathcal{R}^I$ or $\mathcal{S} = \mathcal{P}^I$. Then every social choice function $f : \mathcal{S} \to X$ that has the Pareto property and the Monotonicity property is dictatorial.*

We close this section with a classic result, the Gibbard-Satterthwaite Theorem, independently proven by its two namesakes, Allan Gibbard and Mark Satterthwaite (see Gibbard, 1973 and Satterthwaite, 1975). It talks about social choice functions that cannot be manipulated. It also is intimately connected with the monotonicity property.

Before getting to the result, let us pause to discuss what it means to say that a social choice function is not manipulable. There are many names for this property in the literature, including "truthfully implementable in dominant strategies," "dominant strategy incentive compatible," and "straightforward." We will use yet another name, probably the most popular in the literature.

Notation: we will often need to write a list of items, such as $(R^1, \ldots, R^i, \ldots, R^I)$, as it becomes after the substitution of the ith item by something else, for instance $(R^1, \ldots, \overline{R}^i, \ldots, R^I)$. To save space and mental energy, in such cases we will write $(\overline{R}^i, R^{-i})$ for $(R^1, \ldots, \overline{R}^i, \ldots, R^I)$. The symbol R^{-i} stands for the list of all the R^k items, for $k = 1$ to $k = I$, with R^i removed.

Axiom (Strategy-proofness). The social choice function $f : \mathcal{S} \to X$ is **strategy-proof** if for all i, all $\rho = (R^1, \ldots, R^i, \ldots, R^I) \in \mathcal{S}$, and all $\overline{R}^i \in \mathcal{R}$ such that $(\overline{R}^i, R^{-i})$ is in $\mathcal{S}$, $f(\rho) \, R^i \, f(\overline{R}^i, R^{-i})$.

In words, a social choice function is strategy-proof if each agent does himself no good by revealing a false preference ordering. This is required no matter what combination of preference orderings the other agents are reporting. So, if we asked everybody about their preferences in order to calculate and put in place the outcome $f(\rho)$ that corresponds to these preferences, no agent would find that misrepresenting his preferences results in something better for him. Naturally, the desirability of misrepresentation is evaluated according to the true preferences of each agent, as we assume that every agent always knows his true preferences.

The Gibbard-Satterthwaite Theorem requires one more condition on the social choice function. The condition can be called nonimposition.[6] It says that every social alternative has the opportunity to be chosen for at least one combination of individual preferences. No alternative is ruled out before agents have expressed their preferences.

Axiom (Nonimposition). The social choice function $f : \mathcal{S} \to X$ satisfies **nonimposition** if for each x in X there exists $\rho = (R^1, \ldots, R^I) \in \mathcal{S}$ such that $f(\rho) = x$.

We are now ready for the last important result of this section, given as formulated in Mas-Colell et al., 1995, page 874.

Theorem 1.3 (Gibbard-Satterthwaite Theorem). *Assume that the set of social alternatives X is finite and has at least three elements, that $\mathcal{S} = \mathcal{P}^I$, and that the social choice function $f : \mathcal{S} \to X$ satisfies nonimposition. Then f is strategy-proof if and only if it is dictatorial.*

The Arrow and Gibbard-Satterthwaite theorems were catalysts for a research agenda of what is possible in social choice and in mechanism design. The rest of the book is devoted to such results.

As we mentioned in the beginning, the purpose of institutions is to reconcile individual preferences into a social order, as opposed to anarchy. There are many ranges of alternatives that agents in a society care about: political leadership, consumption goods, road systems, environmental conditions and radio spectra, to name a few. In all these cases, agents' preferences over the relevant alternatives are aggregated via an institution into a choice of an alternative or a few alternatives for society. This is expressed in the theory of mechanisms by a social choice correspondence.

A social choice correspondence, a cousin of a social choice function, is a rule that takes an economy and chooses a set of allocations for it. You may also recall from your math courses that a correspondence associates each element of its domain to a set of elements of its range. A function, on the other hand, associates to each element of its domain exactly one element of its range. For a social choice correspondence, the domain is always some collection of economies, and the range is the set of all feasible allocations for these economies. In the literature, social choice correspondences are sometimes called solutions.

We turn now to some of the domains that we use in the study of social choice correspondences. We discuss in the next section the economist's workhorse domain, that of exchange economies. The appendix of the book contains an exposition of the public good domain.

---

[6]Sometimes it is called nondegeneracy.

1.7 Economic Domain

Social choice as we saw deals with social alternatives that we denoted by little letters such as x or y. Do not let this disguise the powerful generality of this way of looking at things. A social alternative in principle stands for all details of the state of society that agents care about. We often want a less general view of social alternatives, one that focuses on economic allocations. There are various ways of obtaining such a focus, and we explain now some of them, calling them economic domains. To keep this chapter from becoming too long, we have relegated further details on some domains, in particular those involving public goods, to the appendix of the book.

1.7.1 Exchange Economies

The most basic economic environment is the pure exchange economy. As before, there is a number I of agents, so the set of agents is $\mathcal{I} = \{1, 2, \ldots, I\}$. In our examples, we will usually have just two agents so we can illustrate concepts with the familiar Edgeworth Box (see section A.5. for a quick refresher on the Edgeworth Box). Each agent is exogenously endowed with a bundle of n distinct consumption goods. The agents are free to trade these endowments according to their individual preference orderings that rank the possible bundles of goods. In the most general case, these preferences are free to take any form and the consumption space is the n-dimensional non-negative orthant $\mathbb{R}_+^n$. In plain words, there are n goods and each can only be consumed in non-negative amounts. The open-faced bold $\mathbb{R}$ denotes the set of real numbers. We are assuming that the goods are continuously divisible, which makes the set of real numbers appropriate for their representation. The superscript n tells us there are n goods, and the subscript $+$ tells us that the amount of each good is to be allowed to take only non-negative values. Had we wanted only positive values, we would have used $++$; guess what we would use for non-positive and for negative values.

For each agent $i \in \mathcal{I}$, preferences are defined on the consumption space $\mathbb{R}_+^n$ and denoted by R^i. (We use the plain R for the same purpose as in the previous sections; do not confuse it with the $\mathbb{R}$ that we use for the set of real numbers. Note that even though the symbol is the same, a preference ordering R^i in this section is defined on a much larger space than in the previous section. There a preference ordering was defined on a finite set X while here it is defined on the uncountably infinite set $\mathbb{R}_+^n$.) A member of the consumption space x is called a **consumption bundle** or **consumption vector**. A consumption bundle for agent i is written as x_i, or, when we want the detailed amount of consumption of each good, as $x_i = (x_{i1}, \ldots, x_{in})$. The first subscript names the agent, and the second names the good. If x and y are two consumption bundles in the consumption set $\mathbb{R}_+^n$, then $x \, R^i \, y$ means "agent i considers bundle x at least as good as bundle y". Each agent also has an endowment vector of goods $\omega_i = (\omega_{i1}, \ldots, \omega_{in}) \in \mathbb{R}_+^n$.

We assume that each agent's preferences have the following properties. The first two we have seen in the social choice domain; the last one is new and appropriate for economic domains.

Completeness For each x, y in the consumption space, either $x\ R^i\ y$ or $y\ R^i\ x$.

Transitivity For each x, y, z in the consumption space, if $x\ R^i\ y$ and $y\ R^i\ z$, then $x\ R^i\ z$.

Continuity For each x in the consumption space, the set of points y in the consumption space such that $y\ R^i\ x$ is a closed set.

Continuity is not as obvious as completeness and transitivity. It says that the preference ordering of each agent is supposed to not be overly sensitive: if two bundles are near each other, they are ranked near each other as well. You do not need to worry about how it means this, unless you want to learn a little bit of elementary point-set topology, as you can find in Chapter 12 of Simon and Blume's textbook (Simon and Blume, 1994).

Under these assumptions, the preferences of each agent i in $\mathcal{I}$ can be represented numerically by a function $u_i : \mathbb{R}^n_+ \to \mathbb{R}$, which has the consumption space as its domain and takes real number values. This means that for all pairs x, y in the consumption space $\mathbb{R}^n_+$, $x\ R^i\ y$ is true if and only if $u_i(x) \geq u_i(y)$ is true. For this section, since we will consider environments in which preference orderings are representable by utility functions, we will usually define preferences directly via utility functions, since we expect that most readers are more comfortable with this notation.

The utility function of an agent can accommodate situations that involve risky choices.[7] Suppose that the objects of choice are probability distributions over a finite set of alternatives $X = \{x_1, \ldots, x_k\}$. We call such a probability distribution a **lottery** and it consists of k real numbers $q_i \in [0, 1]$, for $i = 1, \ldots, k$, such that $\sum_{i=1}^k q_i = 1$. We write the set of lotteries over the set X as $\Delta(X)$. Each member x_i of X corresponds to exactly one lottery in $\Delta(X)$, namely the lottery that has $q_i = 1$ and $q_j = 0$ for each $j \neq i$. In that sense, $\Delta(X)$ subsumes X and so is the proper domain of the utility function, as it contains all the certain outcomes, which are the members of X, as well as all the uncertain outcomes, which are the lotteries with the certain outcomes as prizes. A utility function $u : \Delta(X) \to \mathbb{R}$ has the **expected utility property** if for each lottery $\ell = (q_1, \ldots, q_k) \in \Delta(X)$, $u(\ell) = \sum_{i=1}^k q_i u(x_i)$. This says that the utility of a lottery is the expected value of the utilities received from each possible outcome of the lottery. There is an extensive literature that discusses axioms on a preference relation that imply that it can be represented by a utility function that has the expected utility property. We do not discuss these axioms in this book. The interested reader can refer to (Varian, 2006, Chapter 12) and (Mas-Colell et al., 1995, Chapter 6).

We summarize the characteristics of each agent by the pair (u_i, ω_i), the agent's utility function and endowment vector; if we assume that endowments are not privately owned, then u_i suffices. This is all the information that we will use to characterize an agent in

---

[7]We will consider such situations in later chapters.

an exchange economy. We also make the following assumptions on the utility function of each agent.

Monotonicity For each agent i and each x, y in the consumption space, if x is at least as large, coordinate by coordinate, as y, and strictly larger in one coordinate, then $u_i(x) > u_i(y)$. (This says that if you give an agent more of at least one good and no less of any other good, then the agent becomes better off.)

Convexity For each agent i, the utility function u_i is a quasi-concave function. (This says that, for each agent and consumption bundle, the set of consumption bundles that the agent considers as at least as good as it or better is a convex set. A convex set is one that has no holes, in the sense that the line connecting any two points in the set lies entirely in the set.)

Graphically, these two assumptions imply that each agent's indifference curves are all negatively sloped and convex as seen from the origin. These are standard assumptions on utility functions. They ensure that several desirable properties of the social choice correspondences we want to discuss hold.

For future reference, let us denote by $\mathcal{E}_{cee}$ the domain of exchange economies that satisfy the assumptions made in this section. The subscripted letters are to remind us that this is a domain of **c**lassical **e**xchange **e**conomies.

For each economy e from $\mathcal{E}_{cee}$, an **allocation** x is a list of consumption bundles $x = (x_1, x_2, \ldots, x_I)$ such that for each $i \in \mathcal{I}$, $x_i \in \mathbb{R}^n$. In words, an allocation lists the consumption bundle of each agent. As ω_{75} meant that agent 7 had ω_{75} units of good 5 in her initial endowment, x_{75} means that agent 7 has been allocated x_{75} units of good 5 to use as she sees fit (in an exchange economy, this means to consume it).

An allocation in e is **feasible for** e if (i) for each $i \in \mathcal{I}$, $x_i \in \mathbb{R}_+^n$, and (ii) $\sum_{i \in \mathcal{I}} x_i = \sum_{i \in \mathcal{I}} \omega_i$. In words, since we have assumed that the consumption set of each agent includes non-negative amounts of each good, the first requirement of feasibility is simply that no agent is given a negative amount of any good. The second requirement of feasibility can be seen more clearly if we write it component by component, instead of the vector form given above to be concise. In the more detailed form, it says that, for each good j from 1 to n, the sum of all consumed amounts of the good, $\sum_{i \in \mathcal{I}} x_{ij}$, equals the sum of the endowments of that good, $\sum_{i \in \mathcal{I}} \omega_{ij}$, i.e., the available amount of the good.

1.7.2 Social Choice Correspondences on the Exchange Economy Domain

Let us step back now to think about exchange economies without automatically presuming that we only want to study their competitive equilibria. In fact, there are several social choice correspondences that we can immediately, and profitably, study on the domain $\mathcal{E}_{cee}$. In this section we will look at the following social choice correspondences: the Pareto social choice correspondence, the Individually Rational social choice correspondence, the Core social choice correspondence, the No-Envy social choice correspondence, the Walrasian social choice correspondence (the familiar competitive equilibrium correspondence that we will formally define shortly), and combinations of these.

Studying correspondences rather than functions is useful because in most of the domains we will study, and certainly in the domain of exchange economies, insisting on single-valuedness of desired outcomes for each economy is counterproductive, as it will force us to ignore many interesting ways of reaching desired outcomes. Even the best-behaved exchange economy can have multiple Walrasian equilibria, for instance, and every exchange economy has an infinity of Pareto efficient allocations, as we will see in the next section.

The same multiplicity applies also to core allocations, envy-free allocations, and individually rational allocations, all of which will be defined shortly. In other words, many of the standard criteria of "goodness" for allocations do not narrow down the infinity of feasible allocations in an exchange economy to a single allocation.

1.7.3 The Pareto Social Choice Correspondence

The notion of a Pareto efficient allocation is standard; you likely learned about it in an undergraduate microeconomics course.

Definition 1.3 (Pareto Efficient Allocation). An allocation x is **Pareto efficient** for an exchange economy e in the domain $\mathcal{E}_{cee}$ if it is feasible for e and there is no other feasible allocation y such that for each agent i, $u_i(y_i) \geq u_i(x_i)$, with at least one of these inequalities strict.

This says that an allocation qualifies to be called Pareto efficient if it satisfies two criteria: first, it is a feasible allocation (why would we care about it otherwise?) and second, there is no other feasible allocation that can make one agent's utility higher without reducing the utility of any agent.

Note well that the definition of a Pareto efficient allocation makes no reference to the agents' endowments. It follows that Pareto efficiency makes no reference to any institutional structure that may be present in the economy. It may not have been obvious, but the mere definition of the endowment of each individual introduces the institution of private property into our economic domain. Pareto efficiency however is easily defined on a larger domain than $\mathcal{E}_{cee}$, namely, the domain that removes all reference of individual endowments from $\mathcal{E}_{cee}$ and introduces instead an aggregate endowment.

Definition 1.4 (Pareto Social Choice Correspondence). The **Pareto social choice correspondence** associates with each economy in the domain the set of Pareto efficient allocations in that economy.

Figure 1.2 illustrates the Pareto set (the set of Pareto efficient allocations) for an example exchange economy, using the familiar Edgeworth Box technique. The Pareto

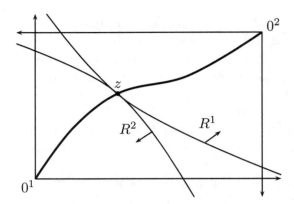

Figure 1.2: An Edgeworth box with the set of Pareto efficient allocations

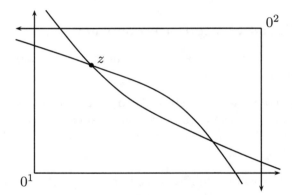

Figure 1.3: An Edgeworth box with a non-Pareto efficient allocation z

set is shown as the heavy curve from 0^1 to 0^2. The little arrows labeled by R^1 and R^2 show the direction of increasing preference of agents 1 and 2, respectively. One Pareto efficient allocation z is also shown, to illustrate the double tangency condition for Pareto efficient allocations in the interior of the Edgeworth box.

Suppose we are looking at an initial allocation. This can be the endowment, but it can also be any other feasible allocation. Naturally, if we started with a randomly chosen initial allocation z, we would be very surprised if it happened to be Pareto efficient. Figure 1.3 illustrates.

Since the indifference curves of the two agents that pass through the point z cross in our diagram, it is possible to increase the utility of one agent without decreasing the utility of the other by selecting any allocation within the lens that these two indifference curves create.

We have just examined the Pareto social choice correspondence. It is worth noting the existence of the slightly different Weak Pareto social choice correspondence. An allocation x is **Weakly Pareto Efficient** for an economy e in the domain $\mathcal{E}_{cee}$ if it is feasible for e and there is no other feasible allocation y such that for each agent i, $u_i(y_i) > u_i(x_i)$. The only difference from Pareto efficiency is that a feasible allocation is disqualified from being weakly Pareto efficient if there is another feasible allocation that yields higher utility to *all* agents, rather than higher utility to at least some agents and lower utility to no agent. On the domain we are discussing here, the two definitions of Pareto efficiency yield the same allocations for every economy.

1.7.4 The Individually Rational Social Choice Correspondence

For each economy, the Individually Rational social choice correspondence identifies the allocations that ensure the voluntary participation of all agents in the resource allocation mechanism. It is well to remember here that in many real-life situations, agents are free to not participate in a mechanism. You can think of mechanisms for such situations as two-stage processes: in the first stage the mechanism is proposed and agents decide to participate or not. In the second stage, the agents who decided to participate take part in the play of the game defined by the mechanism and the agents' characteristics.

Definition 1.5 (Individually Rational Social Choice Correspondence). An allocation x is **individually rational** for an economy e in the domain $\mathcal{E}_{cee}$ if it is feasible for e and leaves each agent i at least as well off as the agent's endowment, ω_i. The **Individually Rational social choice correspondence** associates with each economy in the domain the set of individually rational allocations in that economy.

Figure 1.4 illustrates the concept: the set of individually rational allocations for the economy in the figure is the lens-like area labeled "IR," which includes its boundary points.

1.7.5 The Core Social Choice Correspondence

Imagine that all agents receive a proposed allocation and then are free to discuss with each other, in groups of any size, whether this allocation is acceptable. If a group can do better for its members by ignoring the proposed allocation and redistributing the endowments of its members among themselves, then this group blocks this allocation. This idea captures an extreme form of cooperation among individuals in groups, and it requires neither market institutions nor a method for setting prices for goods. It requires instead that there is some way for agents to communicate with one another, and that someone proposes allocations to all.

Consider an allocation x and a coalition S, which is a subset of the set $\mathcal{I}$ of agents. An allocation for the coalition S is a vector of consumption vectors $x = (x_1, \ldots, x_{|S|})$, with

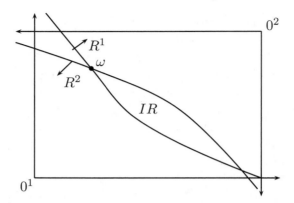

Figure 1.4: An Edgeworth box and the set of individually rational allocations

as many coordinates as there are members of S. (The number of members of any set S is denoted by $|S|$.) An allocation x is **feasible for** S if (i) for each $i \in S$, $x_i \in \mathbb{R}_+^n$ and (ii) $\sum_{i \in S} x_i = \sum_{i \in S} \omega_i$. As you can see, this would be the same as the definition of a feasible allocation that we gave in the section on the Pareto solution if the coalition S happened to be the set of all agents. Otherwise, it requires that the consumption bundles of the agents in S, $(x_1, \ldots, x_{|S|})$, use all of the endowments of those same agents. The coalition cannot receive resources from non-members and does not give resources to non-members.

Definition 1.6 (The Core). A coalition $S \subseteq \mathcal{I}$ **blocks** an allocation x if there is an allocation x' for the coalition S which is feasible for S and such that every agent in S is at least as well off under x' as under x and at least one agent in S is better off. The **core** of an economy e in the domain $\mathcal{E}_{cee}$ is the set of feasible allocations which are not blocked.

There is an alternative definition of the core that is sometimes used. In this definition, a coalition must make every member strictly better off in order to block. On our domain, these two definitions coincide, but on some other domains they do not. The difference between the two definitions is clearly similar to the difference between Pareto and weakly Pareto efficient allocations.

Classical general equilibrium theory has many results connecting the core and the set of Walrasian equilibria of an exchange economy. (Walrasian equilibria are described subsequently.) To summarize these results, the theory says that under general conditions, if an exchange economy has many individuals, then the set of all its core allocations is very close to the set of all its Walrasian allocations. This is a fundamental result, yet it is quite surprising. It connects the utmost competitive story, that of competitive markets achieving equilibrium, with a very cooperative story of individuals reaching an equilibrium by way of negotiations between and within coalitions.

The core also has some more properties that are easy to derive. Because the set of all agents counts as a coalition just as much as its proper subsets, the definition of the core implies that every allocation in the core must be Pareto efficient. Because sets with a single agent as a member are also coalitions, every allocation in the core must be individually rational. Hence the core of an exchange economy is a subset of its Pareto efficient individually rational allocations. If the economy has just two agents, in fact, the core and the set of Pareto efficient and individually rational allocations coincide, since there are no other coalitions but the ones containing a single member and the one containing both individuals.

1.7.6 The No-Envy Social Choice Correspondence

Fairness considerations are important for many individuals and are part of the formal study of welfare economics. One way to introduce fairness considerations in economic domains is to let the agents themselves decide if they are treated fairly. There are many approaches to this question; one of the earliest, and certainly a very simple and appealing one, involves the concept of no-envy.

Definition 1.7. An allocation x is called **envy-free** if for no pair of distinct agents i, j is it true that $u_i(x_j) > u_i(x_i)$. Otherwise, we could certainly say that i envies j's bundle of goods. The **No-Envy** social choice correspondence assigns to every economy in the domain $\mathcal{E}_{cee}$ the set of feasible allocations that are envy-free.

An advantage of the no-envy notion is that it requires no comparison of utility levels or units across individuals. Since each agent uses her own utility function to compare her consumption bundle with each other's consumption bundle, there is never the need to introduce interpersonal utility comparisons.

There is a neat graphical way of judging whether an allocation x is envy-free in the Edgeworth box. Draw the indifference curves for the two agents that pass through the allocation x. Find the allocation x' that is symmetric to x with the center of the box as the center of symmetry. This allocation, x', is the one that would emerge if the agents exchanged consumption bundles, as you can easily check geometrically. If x' does not lie above either agent's indifference curve through x, where "above" is taken to mean the agent's direction of increasing preference, then x is an envy-free allocation. Figure 1.5 shows an example where x is envy-free. In the figure, Ω stands for the aggregate endowment, so the center of the box is at $\Omega/2$.

1.7.7 Combinations of the Previous Social Choice Correspondences

Each one of the above social choice correspondences has its merits. We can combine solutions to get more desirable properties in one solution. For instance, we can study the

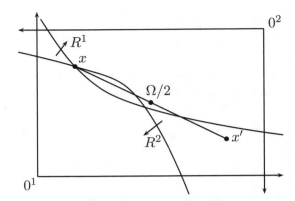

Figure 1.5: An envy-free allocation

Individually Rational Pareto Efficient solution, which selects for each economy in the domain the set of allocations that are both individually rational and Pareto efficient for that economy. Another solution that is often studied is the **Pareto Efficient No-Envy** solution, sometimes also called **fair**.

1.7.8 The Walrasian Social Choice Correspondence

We left for last the Walrasian social choice correspondence. It selects the set of competitive equilibrium allocations for each economy in the domain. By leaving it last we want to emphasize that it is not the only solution we can usefully study in the framework of mechanism design and implementation, not by a far cry. However, the Walrasian solution manages to be central in economic domains in ways that are deep and rather surprising. An example is in section 6.2.

The Walrasian social choice correspondence is named in honor of Léon Walras, who wrote an influential treatise Walras (1874), whose title translates to *Elements of Pure Economics,* on how to study supply and demand in many markets at once. This was his life's work. Economic theorists made a beautiful theory out of his framework, general equilibrium theory. The Walrasian solution is at the core of general equilibrium theory.

In our current context of an exchange economy, it is simple to define the Walrasian solution. First, we define the budget set of each individual. Following the spirit of "perfect competition," (nothing is really perfect, hence the quote marks) we assume that each agent is a price-taker. So we start with a price vector $p \in \mathbb{R}^n_+$, that gives every agent the necessary information on the prices of all the commodities. We are restricting these prices to not be negative, since we are thinking of the commodities as "goods" that agents would expect to pay to consume, rather than "bads" that agents would expect to pay to dispose of.

Given the price vector $p = (p_1, \ldots, p_n)$, the income of any agent i equals the value of i's endowment as evaluated at these prices. So agent i has income $p \cdot \omega_i$. We can just as well write this as $p_1\omega_{i1} + p_2\omega_{i2} + \cdots p_n\omega_{in}$, but $p \cdot \omega_i$ is briefer.

Note that when we write $p \cdot \omega_i$ for i's income, we are imagining that i brings her entire endowment vector to market and sells it there at the going prices, which are the ones in vector p. To square this with the idea that perhaps i will keep some of her endowment to consume at home, imagine that i sells this to herself.

Knowing the price vector tells us more than agents' incomes. It also allows us to calculate the cost of a desired consumption vector. Suppose i wants to consume the vector $x_i = (x_{i1}, x_{i2}, \ldots, x_{in}) \in \mathbb{R}_+^n$. Then i has to pay $p \cdot x_i = p_1 x_{i1} + p_2 x_{i2} + \cdots p_n x_{in}$ in the marketplace to achieve this consumption vector.

We are now ready for the budget of consumer i. A consumption vector x_i is affordable for agent i if $p \cdot x_i \leq p \cdot \omega_i$. In that case we say that x_i is in i's budget set for price vector p and endowment vector ω_i. More concisely, the budget set of agent i for price vector p and endowment vector ω_i is written as

$$B_W(p, \omega_i) \equiv \left\{ x_i \in \mathbb{R}_+^n \mid p \cdot x_i \leq p \cdot \omega_i \right\}. \tag{1.1}$$

Once the agent knows her constraint—the budget set for the current prices and her current endowment—she can maximize her utility over that budget set. This operation yields the demand that she will express for each good (or the demands, since it is possible for this problem to have multiple solutions). Properly speaking, it is the vector of quantities demanded by the agent for this specific price vector. In symbols, we write $x_i(p, \omega_i)$ for the set of vectors x_i that maximize $u_i(x_i)$ over the budget set $B_W(p, \omega_i)$.

We are finally ready to define Walrasian equilibrium.

Definition 1.8. A **Walrasian equilibrium** is a pair (x^*, p^*) of one allocation x^* and one price vector p^* such that (i) the allocation x^* is feasible and (ii) for every agent i, $x_i \in x_i(p, \omega_i)$. The **Walrasian social choice correspondence** associates to each economy e the set of Walrasian equilibrium allocations of e.

In words, a Walrasian equilibrium allocation always comes paired with a Walrasian equilibrium price vector; it must be feasible; and it must give each agent a consumption vector that maximizes the agent's utility over the agent's budget set for the Walrasian price vector.

1.8 Quasilinear Preferences and Their Uses

We have seen some wide-ranging impossibility results in social choice theory. One way to reach possibility results is to consider restricted domains of preferences. We just looked at the restriction to an economic domain. Another useful restriction is to the domain of quasilinear preferences. Here we briefly review quasilinear preferences and their properties.

Quasilinearity is a property of preferences and their corresponding utility functions. It is a very convenient property. If all preferences are quasilinear, finding a Pareto efficient allocation in an economy (with private goods only, or with private and public goods) becomes a simple matter of maximizing the sum of all agents' utilities. Also, quasilinear preferences can be used to focus on one good rather than continuing a full-blown general equilibrium analysis. In the context of Walrasian equilibrium, quasilinearity becomes a bridge between general equilibrium and partial equilibrium analysis. There are drawbacks, though. For instance, a consumer with quasilinear preferences who has an increase in income spends all the increase on only one good, hardly a property that's likely to be seen in reality. The presentation in this section owes much to Campbell (2006), where the interested reader can find more on this topic.

To define quasilinear preferences, start with a preference ordering over vectors x in some consumption set. (We will get more specific shortly.) To keep notation simple, we will work with the utility representation of the preference ordering, a function u. So the utility of x is $u(x)$. The crucial element of quasilinearity is that there is one coordinate of x, say x_1, and some function v that takes the remaining coordinates of x, $\hat{x}$, as an argument, so that

$$u(x) = x_1 + v(\hat{x}), \quad \forall x.$$

So, we are breaking up x into $x_1, \hat{x}$ and imagining that u depends linearly on x and possibly nonlinearly on $\hat{x}$. Almost always, when we make this assumption we also assume that the x_1 part of x is infinitely divisible. It is not necessary for the $\hat{x}$ part to be so.

Indeed, theorists often assume that x_1 stands for "money" or "all other goods." This is the connection to partial equilibrium: in partial equilibrium analysis, we focus on one commodity at a time (which would be $\hat{x}$) and treat the rest of the commodities as "all other goods." We then imagine that the consumer will not alter the proportion of her consumption levels of other goods when changing the consumption of $\hat{x}$, so it makes sense to consider "all other goods" as a monolithic quantity "money." Do not rush to compare this money with the money in macroeconomics; what we have here is not money, really, hence we have been using the quote marks so much.

In other analyses we can also have $\hat{x}$ stand for $x_2, \ldots, x_n$, the rest of the private goods that the agent consumes, or $y_1, \ldots, y_k$, the list of public goods available in the economy. We gain something by leaving the precise definition of $\hat{x}$ as general as we have. The result we are about to show will hold in all cases that can fit this framework, including private goods, public goods, and even the case that $\hat{x}$ is a discrete variable, as we will see in subsequent chapters.

Theorem 1.4 (Characterization of Pareto Efficiency under Quasilinearity). *Let an economy have I agents, each with a quasilinearity utility function u_i that takes the typical value $u_i(x_i) = u_i(x_{i1}, \hat{x}_i) = x_{i1} + v_i(\hat{x}_i)$. Assume that x_{i1} is a real number for all i. Finally, assume that the economy possesses at least one Pareto efficient allocation. Then, an allocation $z = (x_1, \ldots, x_i)$ is Pareto efficient if and only if z solves the problem of maximizing $\sum_i u_i(x_i)$ over the set of feasible allocations for the economy.*

The proof of this theorem is given in (Campbell, 2006, pages 104–105).

1.9 Appendix: Proofs

1.9.1 Arrow's Impossibility Theorem

Philip Reny wrote an elegant paper that presents proofs for slightly simplified versions of both the Arrow impossibility theorem and the Muller-Satterthwaite theorem, Reny (2001). We present here the first of those proofs with some extra commentary to make it more accessible, and we challenge you to do the other proof in the exercises. As with many social choice theory proofs, these proceed in many small steps and rely on strong logical thinking but not advanced mathematical techniques. Notably, there are many other proofs of these and related results in the literature, easily found by a little online scientific literature searching.

We start with the simplification of setting the domain of admissible individual preference profiles to $\mathcal{S} = \mathcal{P}^I$. Reminder: this says that agents can only express strict rankings of alternatives, in which no two alternatives are ranked as indifferent to each other. This simplification is only needed to make the proofs more easily accessible, by removing some extra notational burdens that would be required in order to build a more general proof. However, more general proofs exist, and so the domain of strict preference orderings is not necessary for the results.

With this out of our way, let us start with the proof of Arrow's impossibility theorem. For your convenience, here is its statement again, with the simplification we mentioned incorporated.

Theorem 1.5 (Arrow's Impossibility Theorem). *Assume that there are at least three alternatives and that the domain of admissible individual preference profiles, denoted $\mathcal{S}$, is $\mathcal{S} = \mathcal{P}^I$. Then every social welfare functional that satisfies the Pareto property and pairwise independence is dictatorial.*

Proof, (Reny, 2001). **Step 1.** Choose arbitrarily two distinct alternatives $a, b \in X$ and a profile of individual preference orderings ρ such that for every agent a is ranked highest and b is ranked lowest. The arbitrary choice of a, b is possible because we assume there are at least three alternatives. The arbitrary choice of the preference orderings is possible because by assumption the domain of the social welfare functional R contains all strict preference orderings and the ones we chose are strict.

Because of the Pareto property, a is strictly at the top of the social order $R(\rho)$. Indeed, consider any alternative x distinct from a. By the choice we have made of individual preference orderings in R, for each agent i it is true that $a \, P^i \, x$. The Pareto property then implies that $a \, P(\rho) \, x$ for every $x \in X$ such that $x \neq a$, proving that a is strictly at the top of the social ranking.

Now start amending the profile ρ by raising b in agent 1's ranking one position at a time. By Pairwise Independence, a remains at the top of the social ranking P as long as b is below a in agent 1's ranking. When b finally rises above a in agent 1's ranking, Pairwise Independence leaves two possibilities: either a is still at the top of society's ranking, or b is. If a remains at the top of society's ranking, then begin the same process of gradually lifting b upwards in the ranking of agent 2, and then agent 3, and so on, until the social ranking of b rises above that of a when b rises above a in the ranking of some agent n. This has to happen, for if it does not, then we will end up with everybody ranking b as their top choice, in which case by the Pareto property b must be now ranked top by society (and in this case, $n = I$). Diagram 1 shows the situation just before agent n's ranking of b rises above that of a, and in diagram 2 the situation just after this.

R^1	...	R^{n-1}	R^n	R^{n+1}	...	R^I		Social Order
b	...	b	a	a	...	a		a
a	...	a	b	.	...	.		.
.	...	.	.	.	...	.	$\longrightarrow$	.
.	...	.	.	.	...	.		b
.	...	.	.	.	...	.		.
.	...	.	.	b	...	b		.

Diagram 1

R^1	...	R^{n-1}	R^n	R^{n+1}	...	R^I		Social Order
b	...	b	b	a	...	a		b
a	...	a	a	.	...	.		a
.	...	.	.	.	...	.		.
.	...	.	.	.	...	.	$\longrightarrow$	.
.	...	.	.	.	...	.		.
.	...	.	.	b	...	b		.

Diagram 2

Step 2. Consider now diagrams $1'$ and $2'$ below. Diagram $1'$ is derived from diagram 1 and diagram $2'$ is derived from diagram 2 by dropping alternative a to the bottom of the ranking of every agent before n and to the second position from the bottom of the ranking of every agent after n. We will now show that these changes leave the top alternative of society unaffected, and that the social orderings are as shown in diagrams $1'$ and $2'$.

R^1	...	R^{n-1}	R^n	R^{n+1}	...	R^I		Social Order
b	...	b	a	$\cdot$	...	$\cdot$		a
$\cdot$	...	$\cdot$	b	$\cdot$	...	$\cdot$		b
$\cdot$	...	$\cdot$	$\cdot$	$\cdot$	...	$\cdot$	$\longrightarrow$	$\cdot$
$\cdot$	...	$\cdot$	$\cdot$	$\cdot$	...	$\cdot$		$\cdot$
$\cdot$	...	$\cdot$	$\cdot$	a	...	a		$\cdot$
a	...	a	$\cdot$	b	...	b		$\cdot$

Diagram $1'$

R^1	...	R^{n-1}	R^n	R^{n+1}	...	R^I		Social Order
b	...	b	b	$\cdot$	...	$\cdot$		b
$\cdot$	...	$\cdot$	a	$\cdot$	...	$\cdot$		$\cdot$
$\cdot$	...	$\cdot$	$\cdot$	$\cdot$	...	$\cdot$	$\longrightarrow$	$\cdot$
$\cdot$	...	$\cdot$	$\cdot$	$\cdot$	...	$\cdot$		a
$\cdot$	...	$\cdot$	$\cdot$	a	...	a		$\cdot$
a	...	a	$\cdot$	b	...	b		$\cdot$

Diagram $2'$

First, because b is top-ranked in the social order in diagram 2 and no agent ranking of b versus any other alternative changes from diagram 2 to $2'$, by Pairwise Independence b must be top-ranked in the social order in diagram $2'$.

Second, the profiles in diagrams $1'$ and $2'$ differ only in how agent n ranks a and b. By Pairwise Independence, in diagram $1'$ b must remain socially ranked above every alternative except possibly a. If b is ranked socially at least as high as a in diagram $1'$, then b would be socially ranked at least as high as a in diagram 1, by Pairwise Independence, which is a contradiction. We conclude that a is socially ranked first and b is socially ranked second in diagram $1'$.

Step 3. Consider an alternative $c \in X$ that is distinct from a and from b. Such an alternative exists because of the assumption that there are at least three alternatives. The profile of rankings in diagram 3 can be obtained from the profile in diagram $1'$

without changing the ranking of a versus any other alternative for any agent. Therefore, by Pairwise Independence, the top alternative in the social ranking in diagram 3 is a.

R^1	...	R^{n-1}	R^n	R^{n+1}	...	R^I		Social Order
.	...	.	a	.	...	.		a
.	...	.	c	.	...	.		.
.	...	.	b	.	...	.	$\longrightarrow$	.
c	...	c	.	c	...	c		.
b	...	b	.	a	...	a		.
a	...	a	.	b	...	b		.

Diagram 3

Step 4. Consider the profile of rankings in diagram 4, which is derived from diagram 3 by interchanging the ranking of a versus b for every agent to the right of agent n.

R^1	...	R^{n-1}	R^n	R^{n+1}	...	R^I		Social Order
.	...	.	a	.	...	.		a
.	...	.	c	.	...	.		.
.	...	.	b	.	...	.	$\longrightarrow$	c
c	...	c	.	c	...	c		.
b	...	b	.	b	...	b		b
a	...	a	.	a	...	a		.

Diagram 4

By Pairwise Independence, because a is socially top-ranked in diagram 3, the social ranking of a is above that of c and also above any other alternative except perhaps b in diagram 4. Because c is ranked above b in diagram 4 for every agent, c must rank socially above b by the Pareto property. We conclude that a ranks socially at the top and that c ranks above b in diagram 4.

Step 5. Consider an arbitrary profile of individual rankings with a ranked above b in agent n's ranking. If necessary, change this profile by moving c between a and b for agent n and to the top for everybody else. Pairwise Independence implies that this change does not alter the social ranking between a and b. Now the ranking of a versus c is as in diagram 4, by Pairwise Independence the social ranking of a is higher than that of c, which is ranked above b by the Pareto property.

By the transitivity of the social ordering, we conclude that if agent n ranks a above b, then so does society. Now recall that c was an arbitrarily chosen alternative, and repeat the argument with the roles of b and c reversed. This implies that if agent n ranks a above some other alternative, then so does the social ordering. We may conclude that agent n is a dictator for a. However, a was chosen arbitrarily. This implies that for every alternative $a \in X$ there is a dictator for a.

Finally, we claim that there cannot exist distinct dictators for distinct alternatives. Indeed, suppose that agent i were a dictator for alternative a and agent j were a dictator for alternative $b \neq a$, and suppose that i ranks a highest and j ranks b highest. Now the social ranking is not well-defined: which alternative should rank top? Since we have maintained the assumption that the social welfare functional is well-defined, this situation leads to a contradiction. Therefore a single agent is dictator for every alternative. We have concluded the proof of Arrow's impossibility theorem. QED

1.9.2 Gibbard-Satterthwaite Theorem

Given the fundamental importance of the Gibbard-Satterthwaite theorem for economic design, we will now guide you in working through a detailed proof of a variant of it for the case of two agents and three alternatives. This does not cover the fully general case for which the theorem holds, but it will give you a better feel for the logic of the result than a more general proof would. This proof is adapted from Austen-Smith and Banks (2005, pages 22–26). General proofs can be found in Gibbard (1973), Satterthwaite (1975), Campbell (2006, page 411), and Schmeidler and Sonnenschein (1978).

To do this proof, we will need a subsidiary axiom for social choice functions. This axiom follows from strategy-proofness, but we will not prove this here. Its proof is in Austen-Smith and Banks (2005, page 26).

Recall that the effective range of a function is the set of members of the range such that the function associates each one of these members with some element of the domain.

Axiom (Respect for Unanimity). A social choice function $f : \mathcal{R} \to X$ with effective range Π_f **respects unanimity** if and only if, for every profile $\rho = (R^1, \ldots, R^I)$ there exists a set $X_\rho^* \subseteq \Pi_f$ such that $(x, y) \in X_\rho^* \times \Pi_f \setminus X_\rho^*$ implies $x \, P^i \, y$ for all i, $f(\rho) \in X_\rho^*$.

This says that f respects unanimity if, whenever it is possible at some profile of preferences to split the range of f into two subsets such that every alternative in the first subset is preferred by every agent to every alternative in the second subset, then f chooses an alternative from the first subset. This is akin to the Pareto property we saw earlier, but not identical to it. Now we can start our proof of a variant of the Gibbard-Satterthwaite theorem, which we first restate for your convenience.

Theorem 1.6 (Gibbard-Satterthwaite Theorem). *Assume that the set of social alternatives X is finite and has at least three elements, that $\mathcal{S} = \mathcal{P}^I$, and that the social*

choice function $f : S \to X$ satisfies nonimposition. Then f is strategy-proof if and only if it is dictatorial.

Proof. We present the proof for the case where there are two agents and three alternatives, so $X = \{x, y, z\}$ and preference relations do not admit indifference. Each agent then has the following six possible preference orderings: $xyz, xzy, yxz, yzx, zxy, zyx$, where xyz stands for $x \, P^i \, y \, P^i \, z$, and so on, so the leftmost alternative is the one most preferred. This means that there are 36 possible lists of preference orderings, which can be summarized in a six-by-six table where agent 1's preference ordering is one of the rows, and 2's one of the columns.

	xyz	xzy	yxz	yzx	zxy	zyx
xyz		$f(\rho_{12})$				
xzy						
yxz						
yzx						
zxy						
zyx						

We have filled in one entry in the table to clarify notation. It shows that the entry in the first row and second column represents the value of the social choice function when the first agent's preference ordering is that of the first row and the second agent's that of the second row. We will proceed to fill in all of the entries methodically, using our axioms. When we can only tell that one of two alternatives can fill a table entry, we will write both with "or" in between. By the end, we will have the whole table filled and each entry will have one alternative in it.

Start by requiring that f respect unanimity. This makes the table look like the following.

	xyz	xzy	yxz	yzx	zxy	zyx
xyz	x	x	x or y			
xzy	x	x			x or z	
yxz	x or y		y	y		
yzx			y	y		y or z
zxy		x or z			z	z
zyx				y or z	z	z

Note the symmetry of the table (you may want to convince yourself it has to be symmetrical; it is an easy argument to make). To explain the entries, here is one example, that of entry 13. The preferences of the agents for that entry are xyz and yxz. Therefore we can split the set X into two subsets, $X^*_{\rho 13} = \{x, y\}$ and $X \setminus X^*_{\rho 13} = \{z\}$, according to the respect for unanimity axiom, so that every element of $X^*_{\rho 13}$ is preferred to every element of $X \setminus X^*_{\rho 13} = \{z\}$ by all agents. By the respect for unanimity axiom, the social choice function can take as a value only an element of $X^*_{\rho 13}$. A similar explanation applies to all the entries we have filled in.

Now we impose strategy-proofness on f and see what this implies for the entries of the table. Look first at the blank entry at location 23. We argue that only x or y can go there, otherwise strategy-proofness is violated. Indeed, suppose z went in entry 23. Agent 2 can now falsely report xzy, taking the report of xzy of agent 1 as given, and manipulate the social choice function into selecting x, which agent 2 prefers to z. By the strategy-proofness requirement, we cannot have this, so we exclude z from entry 23. With similar steps (left to you as an exercise), we now get the table into the following form.

	xyz	xzy	yxz	yzx	zxy	zyx
xyz	x	x	x or y	x or y	x or z	
xzy	x	x	x or y		x or z	x or z
yxz	x or y	x or y	y	y		y or z
yzx	x or y		y	y	y or z	y or z
zxy	x or z	x or z		y or z	z	z
zyx		x or z	y or z	y or z	z	z

At this point, we make an arbitrary choice for position 15: we choose z. We could have chosen x and obtained the same type of result. We now fill in the rest of the table as follows.

1. We must have $f(\rho_{16}) = z$. If not, 2 can manipulate the social choice function f at 16 by reporting zxy. It follows that for rows $i = 2, 3, 4, 5, 6$, we must have $f(\rho_{i6}) = z$, otherwise 1 can manipulate $f(\rho_{i6})$ by reporting any preference ordering of his that goes to the row that gets something else than z in column 6. Similarly, the whole fifth column must be filled with z.

2. It follows now that $f(\rho_{14}) = y$. If not, 2 can manipulate $f(\rho_{14}) = y$ by reporting zxy. Therefore, $f(\rho_{13}) = y$, otherwise 2 can manipulate $f(\rho_{13})$ by reporting yzx. Now it follows that $f(\rho_{23}) = y$, otherwise 1 can manipulate $f(\rho_{23})$ by reporting xzy. This now implies $f(\rho_{24}) = y$, so that 2 cannot manipulate $f(\rho_{24})$ by reporting yxz. But now we must fill the third and fourth columns for rows $3, 4, 5, 6$ with y, to avoid manipulations by 1 (exercise).

3. We must have $f(\rho_{32}) = x$, otherwise 2 can manipulate $f(\rho_{32})$ by reporting zxy, and from this it follows that $f(\rho_{31}) = x$, so that 2 cannot manipulate at 31 by reporting xzy. As an exercise, you can conclude that the rest of the first and second column must be filled with x.

But we now have the following table. Clearly, agent 2 is a dictator.

	xyz	xzy	yxz	yzx	zxy	zyx
xyz	x	x	y	y	z	z
xzy	x	x	y	y	z	z
yxz	x	x	y	y	z	z
yzx	x	x	y	y	z	z
zxy	x	x	y	y	z	z
zyx	x	x	y	y	z	z

QED

As an exercise, see what happens if at the point when we made the choice of z for entry 15, we chose instead x.

1.10 Exercises

Exercise 1: Completeness and Reflexivity (*Mas-Colell et al., Chapter 21, 1995*)

Prove that Completeness implies Reflexivity. (Hint: in the statement of Completeness, is it necessary that x must differ from y?)

Exercise 2: The Condorcet Paradox Again (*Jehle and Reny, Chapter 6, 2001*)

Consider the following social choice function for a society with only three individuals and three alternatives, $X = \{x, y, z\}$. The domain of the social choice function is all of $\mathcal{R}$. The social choice function is given in three rules. (1) If majority voting yields a transitive social peference ordering with a unique best alternative for each possible agenda, set $F(R^1, R^2, R^3)$ equal to this alternative. (2) If majority voting yields a transitive social preference ordering with no unique best alternative, then break the tie among all the alternatives that tie for best by the preset ranking "x is better than y which is better than z". (3) If majority voting fails to yield a transitive social preference ordering, set $F(R^1, R^2, R^3) = x$. Now consider the profile of preferences from the Condorcet Paradox example, $x\ P^1\ y\ P^1\ z$, $y\ P^2\ z\ P^2\ x$, and $z\ P^3\ x\ P^3\ y$.

1. Which alternative is selected by the social choice function F?

2. Does the social choice function F satisfy the Pareto axiom? Either prove that it does, or prove (by counterexample) that it does not.

3. Prove that the social choice function F is not dictatorial.

Exercise 3: Prove the Muller-Satterthwaite Theorem

Prove the Muller-Satterthwaite Theorem. As shown by Reny (2001), this requires only a minor adaptation of the proof we gave for Arrow's Impossibility Theorem. Try to write this proof without consulting Reny's paper.

Exercise 4: Strategy-proofness Implies Monotonicity

Prove that a strategy-proof social choice function satisfies the monotonicity axiom, if the domain of the social choice function is that of strict preference orderings, $\mathcal{P}^I$.

Exercise 5: Finding IR Allocations

Find the set of individually rational allocations for a classical exchange economy with two individuals and two goods, with $u_1(x_{11}, x_{12}) = x_{11}x_{12}$, $u_2(x_{21}, x_{22}) = x_{21}^{1/2}x_{22}^{1/4}$, $\omega_{11} = 1$, $\omega_{12} = 2$, $\omega_{21} = 2$, and $\omega_{22} = 1$.

Exercise 6: Finding PE-IR Allocations

Find the set of individually rational Pareto efficient allocations for the exchange economy of the preceding exercise.

Exercise 7: Finding PE, IR Allocations on the Boundary

Find the sets of Pareto efficient allocations, individually rational allocations, and their intersection, for the exchange economy with two goods and two individuals with $u_1(x_{11}, x_{12}) = x_{11} + x_{12}$, $u_2(x_{21}, x_{22}) = x_{22}$, $\omega_{11} = 10$, $\omega_{12} = 10$, $\omega_{21} = 5$, and $\omega_{22} = 20$. Hint: do not use calculus, instead proceed geometrically.

Exercise 8: Finding Walrasian Allocations

For the economy in exercise 5, find all Walrasian equilibria. Do the Walrasian equilibrium allocations you found belong to the Pareto and Individually Rational sets?

Exercise 9: Finding Walrasian Allocations on the Boundary

Repeat exercise 8 for the economy of exercise 7.

Exercise 10: Gibbard-Satterthwaite Proof Details

Find and fill in the gaps in the proof of the special case of the Gibbard-Satterthwaite theorem given in the appendix of this chapter. Explain exactly which variant of the Gibbard-Satterthwaite Theorem this proof establishes.

Chapter 2

Dominant Strategy Implementation: No Information Assumed

2.1 Definitions

We start with the domain of social choice, which we already have seen in chapter 1.[1] Recall that the society is represented by the set $\mathcal{I} = \{1, 2, \ldots, I\}$ of *agents*. This society must make a collective choice from the set X of possible *alternatives*. Each agent i has a *type* θ_i. The set of all possible types that agent i can have is denoted by Θ_i. Individual i's particular realized type θ_i is not publicly observable. We denote a profile of agents' types, also called an **environment**, by $\theta = (\theta_1, \ldots, \theta_I)$, where θ is drawn from $\Theta = \Theta_1 \times \cdots \times \Theta_I$. Unless we state otherwise, we mean θ_i to represent the ith agent's preference ordering over X, which we write as $R^i(\theta_i)$. In general, the type of an agent may include more information than the agent's preference ordering, so we make the notion of type visually distinct from the notion of preference relation. As in chapter 1, for each $i \in \mathcal{I}$ and each $x, y \in X$, $x \; R^i(\theta_i) \; y$ means "i, when of type θ_i, considers alternative x to be at least as good as alternative y."

The society has certain objectives to satisfy. Our job is to design a way to achieve these objectives. The social objectives are represented by a social choice function $f : \Theta \to X$ that maps each possible profile of agents' types $\theta = (\theta_1, \ldots, \theta_I)$ to a collective choice $f(\theta)$ in X. This is the problem of social choice theory. (We will also consider social choice correspondences in our general definitions, but we mostly focus on social choice functions in this chapter.)

We imagine a **central authority**, often called a planner, that is charged with achieving the objectives embodied in f. The central authority chooses a set of messages M_i for each agent $i \in \mathcal{I}$ and an outcome function $g : M_1 \times \cdots \times M_I \to X$ that assigns an alternative $g(m_1, \ldots, m_I)$ in X to every message profile $(m_1, \ldots, m_I) \in M_1 \times \cdots \times M_I$. The outcome function tells the agents exactly how the message each i chooses from his message set M_i will be used along with all the other agents' messages to determine an alternative. We write M as a shortcut for $M_1 \times \cdots \times M_I$ and we denote a mechanism by (M, g).

---

[1] This chapter has benefited from Jackson (2003) and Austen-Smith and Banks (2005).

Definition 2.1 (Mechanism and Strategy). For each message profile $m = (m_1, \ldots, m_I)$, where $m \in M = M_1 \times \cdots \times M_I$, we let $g : M \to X$ describe how agent messages get turned into a joint social choice. A pair (M, g) is called a **mechanism**. A **strategy** for player i is a function $m_i : \Theta_i \to M_i$ that assigns to each type $\theta_i \in \Theta_i$ of agent i a message $m_i(\theta_i) \in M_i$.

A strategy for an agent i is a plan that specifies, for every type θ_i that the agent can have, which message to send when i is participating in a mechanism (M, g).

Crucially, in this chapter we do not assume that any agent knows the other agents' characteristics. He *may* know them, but we want to find out what we can achieve by designing mechanisms that work well even if every agent only knows his own characteristic.

We have defined the notion of a strategy as a complete plan that an agent i makes before he knows his type θ_i. In chapter 4 we introduce the notion of Bayesian equilibrium of a game, and then this feature of a strategy will become more important than it is here. Here, each agent i does not have to plan ahead for what the other agents will do depending on which types they are; in a Bayesian equilibrium, each agent has to make plans that depend on his guess about the probabilities of the various type combinations of the other agents. In this chapter, no agent is assumed to have information about these probabilities.

When we put together a mechanism (M, g) with a profile of preference orderings, $R = (R^1(\theta_1), \ldots, R^I(\theta_I))$, we have a (noncooperative) game in normal form with the agents as players. The most convincing way to predict the behavior of players in such a game is to say that they will each play a strategy that is at least as good as any other available strategy *no matter which strategies all the remaining players are going to play.* Such a strategy is called a dominant strategy (a formal definition follows soon). Many games are such that no player has a dominant strategy, but if a player has a dominant strategy in a game, it is natural to assume that he will play this strategy. The possible nonexistence of dominant strategies does not have to be a problem for economic design, because here we have the freedom to *design* the mechanism, and therefore the game that the agents will play. Can we find mechanisms that get us the socially desired outcomes when every agent plays his dominant strategy?

Our task in mechanism design theory is to design such a mechanism (M, g), so that at the end, after agents have made their choices of strategies m^*, for every possible profile of types θ the equilibrium outcome $g(m^*(\theta))$ that arises from the interactions of agents coincides with the target social choice function $f(\theta)$. Naturally, we need a theory of how agents play the game (how they choose strategies). In this chapter, we assume that people will look for, and play, dominant strategies. So now we need to pin this concept down precisely.

Notation: recall that for any list of strategies $m = (m_1, \ldots, m_I)$, we write m_{-i} for the list that results from m after the removal of m_i. By a small abuse of notation, we also write m as (m_i, m_{-i}) whenever we want to emphasize that m contains the strategies of agent i, m_i, and of all the other agents, m_{-i}. Analogously, we write $m_{-i}(\theta_{-i})$ for the list that results from $(m_1(\theta_1), \ldots, m_I(\theta_I))$ after the removal of $m_i(\theta_i)$.

Definition 2.2 (Dominant Strategy Equilibrium). The strategy profile m^* is a **dominant strategy equilibrium** of mechanism (M, g) if, for each $\theta = (\theta_1, \ldots, \theta_I) \in (\Theta_1 \times \cdots, \Theta_I)$, each $i \in \mathcal{I}$, each $\widehat{m}_i \in M_i$, and each $m_{-i} : \Theta_{-i} \to M_{-i}$, we have

$$g(m_i^*(\theta_i), m_{-i}(\theta_{-i}))\ R^i(\theta_i)\ g(\widehat{m}_i, m_{-i}(\theta_{-i})). \tag{2.1}$$

In words, this definition says that for each agent i the strategy m_i^* is never strictly worse than any other strategy available to that agent, no matter what the types of the agents are and what strategies the other agents play. As we noted earlier, each agent can check whether a given strategy is dominant for him without knowing which type combination is the true one for the other agents. The definition of dominant strategy equilibrium ensures this by employing the quantifications "for each θ" (which implies *a fortiori* "for each θ_{-i}") and "for each m_{-i}." With these quantifications in force, the defining condition (2.1) tests the performance for agent i of the strategy m_i^* when i has each possible type θ_i against that of any other message $\widehat{m}_i$, for every possible combination of messages that all agents apart from agent i can send.

Definition 2.3 (Dominant Strategy Implementation). A social choice function f is **implemented in dominant strategies** by the mechanism (M, g) if (M, g) has at least one dominant strategy equilibrium and for each dominant strategy equilibrium $m^* = (m_1^*, \ldots, m_I^*)$ of (M, g) and for each $\theta \in \Theta$, $g(m^*(\theta)) = f(\theta)$.

This definition requires that the outcome of any dominant strategy equilibrium in some environment θ is equal to the desired social outcome, $f(\theta)$. For a social choice correspondence $F : \Theta \rightarrow\rightarrow X$, the same definition applies but with $g(m^*(\theta)) \in F(\theta)$ and the requirement that for each $x \in F(\theta)$, there exists a dominant strategy profile $m^{*\prime}$ such that $g(m^{*\prime}(\theta)) = x$.

The possibilities in designing different mechanisms are unlimited. As economic engineers we could be as creative as possible and design very sophisticated procedures depending on the targeted outcome. For one example, we can ask each agent to submit messages that contain his preference relation, a preferred alternative and an integer, and then use the integers to assign priority to agents according to who submitted the highest integer. As we will see later in our discussion of Nash implementation, this trick can be very effective in eliminating undesirable equilibria. For another example, we can ask each agent to submit a complete preference profile for the economy, assuming that agents know each other well. Then we could use the submitted profiles of the agents about each other to detect agents who disagree with all others about the profile of some agent. Depending on the situation, in fact, there is no limit to how imaginative we can be in designing mechanisms, but the simplest way to go about this is to just ask agents what are their preferences. That is to ask agents to reveal their types, collect the messages they send about their types $\widehat{\theta} = (\widehat{\theta}_1, \ldots, \widehat{\theta}_I)$, and then use the outcome function g to get outcomes $g(\widehat{\theta})$.

Definition 2.4 (Direct Mechanism). Let a social choice function $f : \Theta \to X$ be given. A **direct mechanism** is a mechanism (M, f) such that for each agent $M_i = \Theta_i$.

We now state the concept of truthful dominant strategy implementation, which is a mainstay of mechanism design theory.

Definition 2.5 (Truthful Dominant Strategy Implementation). A social choice function f is **truthfully implemented in dominant strategies** if there exists a direct mechanism (Θ, g) which has at least one dominant strategy equilibrium m^* such that for each $\theta \in \Theta$, $(m_1^*(\theta_1), \ldots, m_I^*(\theta_I)) = (\theta_1, \ldots, \theta_I)$ and $g(m^*(\theta)) = f(\theta)$. For a social choice correspondence F, the same definition applies but with $g(m^*(\theta)) \in F(\theta)$.

Thus in the case of a direct mechanism each agent, who already possesses certain type θ_i, sends a message to the planner that he is of type $\widehat{\theta}_i \in \Theta_i$, which may or may not be his true type and lets the planner choose the corresponding alternative based on the profile of messages provided. From the planner's point of view for the society's best interest it is desirable that agents reveal their true types, because a social choice function is designed to yield the best alternative for the society given that its arguments are the true types of agents in that society. To make agents tell the truth we must make truth-telling an optimal strategy for them or, in other words, employ a social choice function that is *incentive compatible* (or *truthfully implementable*).

Definition 2.6 (Dominant Strategy Incentive Compatibility). The social choice function f is **dominant strategy incentive compatible** if the direct mechanism (Θ, f) truthfully implements f in dominant strategies.

Thus if the social choice function is dominant strategy incentive compatible then each agent has a dominant strategy to tell the truth in the direct mechanism with f itself as the outcome function. You may want to check that a social choice function is dominant strategy incentive compatible if and only if it is strategy-proof, as defined in the previous chapter. In the literature, dominant strategy incentive compatible social choice functions are sometimes called truthfully implementable in dominant strategies, or, most often, strategy-proof.

2.2 Revelation Principle

Next comes a basic result of the theory of implementation in dominant strategies, first formulated in Gibbard (1973), as formulated in Austen-Smith and Banks (2005).

Theorem 2.1 (Revelation Principle for Dominant Strategies). *If the mechanism* (M, g) *implements the social choice correspondence* F *in dominant strategies, then there exists a social choice function* f' *that is dominant strategy incentive compatible.*

Proof. Let m^* be a dominant strategy equilibrium of the mechanism (M, g) such that for each $\theta \in \Theta$, $g(m^*(\theta)) \in F(\theta)$. Define a new mechanism (Θ, f') by setting for each $\theta \in \Theta$, $f'(\theta) = g(m^*(\theta))$. Because m^* is a dominant strategy equilibrium of the mechanism (M, g), it follows that for each $\theta \in \Theta$, each $\widehat{m}_i \in M_i$, and each $m^*_{-i} \in M_{-i}$,

$$g(m^*_i(\theta_i), m^*_{-i}(\theta_{-i})) \; R^i(\theta_i) \; g(\widehat{m}_i, m^*_{-i}(\theta_{-i})).$$

By the definition of f', this implies that for each $\theta \in \Theta$ and each $\widehat{\theta}_i \in \Theta_i$,

$$f'(\theta_i, \theta_{-i}) \; R^i(\theta_i) \; f'(\widehat{\theta}_i, \theta_{-i}).$$

This says that f' is dominant strategy incentive compatible.   QED

The logic of the proof is this. Suppose that the mechanism (M, g) implements the social choice correspondence F in dominant strategies, and that in this mechanism each agent i with type θ_i finds sending the message $m^*_i(\theta_i)$ better than sending any other of his messages regardless of other agents' strategies. Suppose now that we introduce a mediator who asks each agent to tell his type and if the reported type is θ_i, the mediator sends the message $m^*_i(\theta_i)$ for that reported type on behalf of the agent. Then each agent will find that revealing his true type is a dominant strategy. That is, if the social choice correspondence is implementable in dominant strategies, then it is truthfully implementable in dominant strategies by some direct mechanism (Θ, f'), which makes f' dominant strategy incentive compatible. (If F is a social choice function f, then $f = f'$.)

The first important implication of the revelation principle is that the search for a mechanism to implement a given social choice function f can be conducted at a first pass in the space of direct mechanisms. If it is possible to implement f in dominant strategies, then there must exist a direct mechanism that truthfully implements f in dominant strategies. This is a very useful conclusion, because it is much easier to search for direct mechanisms than to search the space of all mechanisms. Mechanism design theory uses this conclusion extensively.

The second important implication is that things look bleak for implementation in dominant strategies. The reason is the Gibbard-Satterthwaite theorem, theorem 1.3. When combined with the revelation principle, this theorem says that if there are at least three alternatives, the preferences of the agents are unrestricted, and we require that social choice functions satisfy nonimposition, we can only implement in dominant strategies dictatorial social choice functions. However, when we considered restricted domains of preferences, we find possibility results, as we see next.

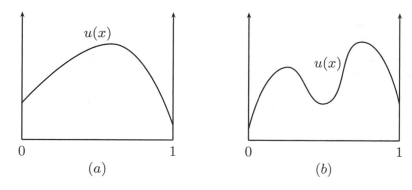

Figure 2.1: Single-Peakedness

2.3 Restricting Domains: Single-Peaked Preferences

Two fruitful domain restrictions are single-peaked and quasilinearity of preferences. We discuss single-peaked preferences here and quasilinear ones in the next section.

Single-peaked preferences are defined when X is single-dimensional, and are such that each agent has one alternative that is preferred over all other alternatives. Let this single preferred alternative, the **peak**, be x^*. Then if alternative x' is between alternatives x'' and x^*, then x' is preferred to x''. Intuitively, this says that x' is closer to the best alternative x^* than x'' and thus provides more satisfaction. Figure 2.1 uses a numerical representation of these preferences as utility functions to illustrate preferences which are single-peaked (panel a) and preferences which are not single-peaked (panel b). Several examples of single-peaked preferences exist, and we now list three.

Seating at a concert Ann goes to an open-seat rock concert. Ann's most preferred seating at the concert is in the tenth row. However, when Ann arrives at the concert the seats in the tenth row are taken, yet there are seats in both the twelfth and fifteenth row. In this situation, Ann would choose a seat in the twelfth row because it is closer to her ideal choice of the tenth row. If, on the other hand, the only open rows were the fifth and eighth rows, then Ann would choose a seat in the eighth row because again this row is closest to Ann's ideal choice.

Joint production (Sprumont, 1991) Abe, Bill, Cathie, Don, Ellen, and Fanny are working jointly on a project. They provide a homogeneous input, so each one's work input is interchangeable with the others', and the total amount of input required for the project is fixed. They have all agreed that each will be rewarded in proportion to the amount of work input supplied. Each person has preferences for bundles of work and pay and these preferences are monotonically increasing in pay, decreasing in effort, and exhibit increasing marginal disutility of work, which means that each person requires increasingly larger pay increments to provide the next small unit of work. If we represent the allotment of effort to each person as the share of the total work, then each person's preferences are naturally single-peaked.

Provision of an indivisible public good (Moulin, 1995, page 332) Amy, Bill, and Cory consider building a pool to which each of them will have free access. The pool can be of size $0, 1, 2,$ or 3. The preferences of each individual are expressed in terms of willingness to pay for pool size x, $u_i(x)$, minus the agent's cost share. All three have agreed to share the cost equally. For each agent i we have $u_i(0) = 0$, and also $u_A(1) = 10$, $u_A(2) = 13$, $u_A(3) = 16$, $u_B(1) = 11$, $u_B(2) = 21$, $u_B(3) = 22$, $u_C(1) = 9$, $u_C(2) = 17$, and $u_C(3) = 25$. The cost function is given by $c(0) = 0$, $c(1) = 9$, $c(2) = 21$, and $c(3) = 39$; note that it exhibits increasing marginal cost. Each person here has single-peaked preferences.

The idea of single-peaked preferences first found its application in political science. Imagine an election that all citizens would agree is to be determined by the policy positions of the candidate along a single, left-to-right, dimension. These policy positions are the social alternatives, and they may be about the size of government, the protection of privacy, the severity of the deterrent to crime, or any other relevant issue. Keep in mind that we are assuming all citizens to conceptualize the issue in the same way, so we rule out situations in which, for example, citizen Adam evaluates the candidates based on their positions on the level of taxes but citizen Eve does so based on their positions on abortion. Imagine also that each citizen i has a most preferred policy position x_i in the set of all possible positions X. An early result for this setup says that candidates will flock to the position of the median voter. (Recall that the median of a distribution is the point which leaves one-half to its left and one-half to its right. So the median voter's x_i is such that half the voters have a most preferred point less than x_i and half more than x_i. This setup was studied by Black (1958) who also proved the result about the median voter.) The single-peaked idea is also applicable to some economic domains such as the ones we presented as examples.

If the domain contains single-peaked preferences, there is a social choice function that is strategy-proof, anonymous and Pareto efficient, and in fact it is the only such social choice function, a remarkable result due to Sprumont (1991). We present it in the context of an example from Barberà et al. (1997); Sprumont (1991) has a formal definition. It is the *uniform rule*.

Consider a partnership of individuals who are to invest in a project; the benefits are to be shared in proportion to each partner's investment. (This is a variation of one of the examples in the beginning of this section.) Each partner has a peak amount she wants to invest, her ideal amount, and her preferences decline monotonically on either side of this amount. Because the sum of the peak amounts of all the partners may not equal the cost of the project, some partners may be forced to invest more or less than their ideal amounts. There are many social choice functions that can be used to decide how much each agent should invest in a domain made up of such partnership problems. One very simple social choice function sets all partner contributions equal to each other. While obviously egalitarian, it is not Pareto efficient, because it may happen that some partners want to invest more and some less than the equal share amount. In such a case, a Pareto improvement would be to allow some of the former to invest more and some of the latter less than the equal share.

The **uniform rule** social choice function is better than the egalitarian one. It allocates investment shares as follows, in the case that the sum of all peak investment amounts exceeds the project's cost (the other case is analogous). Start from the equal shares. If there are partners whose ideal shares are below the equal share, their shares are reset to equal their ideal shares. There is now a deficit that makes room for other partners to invest more than their equal shares. Divide the remaining total cost of the project equally among the remaining partners. If any of these partners have ideal shares less than this equal amount, set their shares equal to their ideal shares. Iterate this procedure until every remaining partner's ideal investment level is no less than the equal shares of the remaining total amount. Each one of these partners invests this equal share.

2.4 Restricted Domains: Quasilinear Domains and Groves Mechanisms

A fruitful and widely applicable domain for strategy-proof social choice functions is that of quasilinear preferences. On this domain there is defined a family of strategy-proof mechanisms known as the Groves mechanisms. (This section is based on Jackson, 2003.)

For our discussion of the Groves mechanisms we break down a typical social alternative x in two parts, $x = (d, t)$, where d is a social decision and $t = (t_1, \ldots, t_I)$ is a list of monetary transfers to the agents. This specialization of the set of social states is valid for any domain of social choice in which a money commodity is defined, as in the case of quasilinear utilities.

Once a decision d and the corresponding transfers t have been made, agent i receives utility

$$u_i(x, \theta_i) = u_i(d, t_i, \theta_i) = v_i(d, \theta_i) + t_i.$$

Note that we assume that each agent cares only for his or her own transfer t_i, not the entire transfer list t, even though the description of x includes the entire t. Also, the social planner knows everything in this specification, except for the θ_i values, which are private information of the agents.

Example 2.1. The decision d is whether to build a public project that costs c units of the money commodity. We have the set of possible decisions $D = \{0, 1\}$, so $d \in D$ means that d is either 0 or 1. Here, 0 stands for "do not build" and 1 stands for "build and share the cost equally among the agents."

The equal division of the cost of the project may create incentives that lead to not building it. To overcome this problem, we introduce transfer payments to the agents, t_i for each agent i. The amount t_i is to be paid to i if $t_i > 0$, otherwise it is to be paid by i. It is important that each t_i can be positive (a subsidy to i) or negative (a tax on i).

Utility for agent i is given by $u_i(d, t, \theta_i) = d\theta_i - \frac{dc}{I} + t_i$. This utility function is quasilinear. The $d\theta_i$ term captures the agent's net benefit from the project. If the project is built, $u_i(1, t, \theta_i) = \theta_i - \frac{c}{I} + t_i$ and if it is not built, $u_i(0, t, \theta_i) = t_i$.

As long as $\sum_{i=1}^{I} t_i \leq 0$, the central authority runs no deficit. This constraint accommodates unequal final shares of the cost of the project among the agents.   ◇

Example 2.2. This example extends the previous one by adding a choice of level for the public project. Instead of taking only two values, 0 and 1, now the public project can be built at any non-negative level y, which costs $c(y)$. At the same time, we extend the social decision to encompass not only the size y of the project but also the taxes $z_1, \ldots, z_I$ to be imposed on the agents. The set of social decisions is now

$$D \equiv \{(y, z_1, \ldots, z_I) \in \mathbb{R}_+ \times \mathbb{R}^I \mid \sum_{i=1}^{I} z_i = c(y)\}.$$

In words, D contains vectors of the form $(y, z_1, \ldots, z_I)$ where y is a non-negative real number and the z_i are all real numbers (negative, zero, or positive).   ◇

Example 2.3. This example concerns the allocation of an indivisible private good, and so it encompasses single-object auctions as a special case. Here, D contains vectors $(d_1, \ldots, d_I)$ where one of the d_i is 1 and the others are all 0. This can be written compactly as

$$D \equiv \{d \in \{0, 1\}^I \mid \sum_{i=1}^{I} d_i = 1\},$$

since the only way the sum of I numbers, that are either 0 or 1 individually, can equal 1 is if one and only one of the numbers equals 1.   ◇

In quasilinear domains, the social decision d made from the set D is separate from the choice of monetary transfers, t. Mathematically, this is because t_i enters additively in i's utility function and so it does not affect i's marginal willingness to pay to sway the decision d. Accordingly, we build social choice functions on this domain in two steps.

The first step concerns the choice of an element of D by society. A **decision rule** is a function $d : \Theta \to D$ that yields a decision $d(\theta)$ in D for every possible private information configuration $\theta = (\theta_1, \ldots, \theta_I)$.

A decision rule $d(\cdot)$ is **efficient** if for all θ in Θ and for all d' in D,

$$\sum_{i=1}^{I} v_i(d(\theta), \theta_i) \geq \sum_{i=1}^{I} v_i(d', \theta_i). \tag{2.2}$$

Note that this concept of efficiency as the maximization of total benefit corresponds with Pareto efficiency when utilities are quasilinear, as we are assuming in this section.

In the absence of monetary transfers, we would normally expect to have trouble getting agents to reveal truthfully their θ_i values. An example shows this possibility.

Example 2.4. The government of Brandywine Township must decide on whether to build a gazebo in the center of the township building lawn. Rich, Bob, and Lori, denoted R, B and L respectively, are the only citizens who will be affected and have a value distinct from zero. Rich and Bob are in favor of the project because they sit on the lawn during their breaks to relax. They would welcome the shaded seating the gazebo would provide. Lori, on the other hand, opposes the project because she believes that the gazebo would not make a nice addition to the landscaping of the township building. Suppose there is no cost to building the gazebo because of an endowment that a wealthy citizen left to the township to beautify their property.

First assume that each agent places a true value on the project of: $\theta_R = 5$, $\theta_B = 15$ and $\theta_L = -25$. The sum of these values is -5. Thus the efficient decision is not to build the gazebo. However, if the government were to just ask for the true values of these agents, then Rich and Bob would each have an incentive to exaggerate his, so that they could have the gazebo built. $\Diamond$

For this kind of manipulation to be avoided, the trick is to find the right pattern of transfers. This is the purpose of the transfers in our model.

A **transfer function** is a function $t : \Theta \to \mathbb{R}^I$, where $t_i(\theta)$ (as in $t(\theta) = (t_1(\theta), \dots, t_I(\theta))$) represents the payment i receives from the central authority (if $t_i(\theta) > 0$) or makes to the central authority (if $t_i(\theta) < 0$), based on the announcement of types $\theta = (\theta_1, \dots, \theta_I)$ by the agents.

A **social choice function** is in this domain a pair $(d(\cdot), t(\cdot))$ of a decision rule and a transfer function.

Suppose that $\hat{\theta}$ is the profile of types announced. Then, under a social choice function $(d(\cdot), t(\cdot))$, agent i receives utility

$$u_i(\hat{\theta}, \theta_i, d(\cdot), t(\cdot)) = v_i(d(\hat{\theta}), \theta_i) + t_i(\hat{\theta}).$$

A transfer function $t(\cdot)$ is **feasible** if $\sum_{i=1}^{I} t_i(\theta) \leq 0$ for all $\theta \in \Theta$. This says that the central authority does not run a deficit. If indeed it runs a surplus, feasibility implies that the surplus must be either given to an outsider or wasted. It cannot be returned to the agents in the economy without disturbing the incentives that the transfer scheme sets up. This implies that if $\sum_{i=1}^{I} t_i(\theta) < 0$ occurs, then the social choice function that the mechanism implements is not Pareto efficient, since it is Pareto dominated by an efficient social choice function that employs no transfers (but which may not have good incentive properties).

A transfer function $t(\cdot)$ is **balanced** if $\sum_{i=1}^{I} t_i(\theta) = 0$ for all $\theta \in \Theta$. This says that the central authority never runs a surplus or a deficit.

Recalling our earlier definition of a mechanism, we see that a decision rule and a transfer function constitute a mechanism, intended to implement the social choice function that the decision rule and transfer function also define. The fundamental result that ensures that this works is the following theorem. The first part of the theorem is due to Groves (1973) and the second is due to Green and Laffont (1977).

Theorem 2.2 (Groves and Green and Laffont).

1. *(Theodore Groves) If d is an efficient decision rule and for each i there exists a function $h_i : \times_{j \in \mathcal{I}, j \neq i} \times \Theta_j \to \mathbb{R}$ such that, for each $\theta \in \Theta$,*

$$t_i(\theta) = h_i(\theta_{-i}) + \sum_{j \neq i} v_j(d(\theta), \theta_j), \qquad (2.3)$$

   then (d, t) is dominant strategy incentive compatible (strategy-proof).

2. *(Jerry Green and Jean-Jacques Laffont) Conversely, if d is an efficient decision rule, (d, t) is strategy-proof, and the type spaces Θ_i are complete in the sense that $\{v_i(\cdot, \theta_i) \mid \theta_i \in \Theta_i\} = \{v : D \to \mathbb{R}\}$ for each i (that is, every possible function from D to $\mathbb{R}$ results from some $\theta_i \in \Theta_i$),[2] then for each i there exists a function $h_i : \times_{j \in \mathcal{I}, j \neq i} \Theta_j \to \mathbb{R}$ such that the transfer function t satisfies (2.3).*

Proof. To show part (1), suppose that contrary to the assertion of part (1), d is an efficient decision rule and suppose further that for every i there is a function $h_i : \times_{j \in \mathcal{I}, j \neq i} \Theta_j \to \mathbb{R}$ such that the transfer function satisfies (2.3) and at the same time (d, t) is not dominant strategy incentive compatible. We will now derive from this supposition a contradiction, to show that the supposition is incorrect. Our supposition implies that there is at least one i and at least a $\theta \in \Theta$ and a $\widehat{\theta}_i \in \Theta_i$ that satisfy

$$v_i(d(\theta_{-i}, \widehat{\theta}_i), \theta_i) + t_i(\theta_{-i}, \widehat{\theta}_i) > v_i(d(\theta), \theta_i) + t_i(\theta).$$

Using (2.3) along with this inequality, we find

$$v_i(d(\theta_{-i}, \widehat{\theta}_i), \theta_i) + h_i(\theta_{-i}) + \sum_{j \neq i} v_j(d(\theta_{-i}, \widehat{\theta}_i), \theta_j) > v_i(d(\theta), \theta_i) + h_i(\theta_{-i}) + \sum_{j \neq i} v_j(d(\theta), \theta_j).$$

---

[2] Note that the completeness assumption is strong: in particular, it requires that there is an uncountably infinite number of members of Θ_i for each i.

After we cancel out the term $h_i(\theta_{-i})$ from both sides and consolidate the resulting sums, this yields

$$\sum_{k=1}^{I} v_k(d(\theta_{-i}, \widehat{\theta}_i), \theta_k) > \sum_{k=1}^{I} v_k(d(\theta), \theta_k),$$

which contradicts (2.2). Therefore, d is not an efficient decision rule, and our supposition has led to a contradiction, thereby establishing part (1) of the theorem.

To show part (2), suppose that d is an efficient decision rule, (d, t) is dominant strategy incentive compatible, and that the type spaces are complete as defined in the statement of part (2). For each $\theta \in \Theta$, define $h_i(\theta) = t_i(\theta) - \sum_{j \neq i} v_j(d(\theta), \theta_j)$. This shows that there exists a function $h_i : \Theta \to \mathbb{R}$ such that for every $\theta \in \Theta$, we have

$$t_i(\theta) = h_i(\theta) + \sum_{j \neq i} v_j(d(\theta), \theta_j).$$

The domain of this function is $\Theta = \Theta_1 \times \Theta_2 \times \cdots \times \Theta_I$. It remains to show that this function is independent of θ_i, i.e., that its domain is effectively $\times_{j \in \mathcal{I}, j \neq i} \Theta_j = \Theta_1 \times \cdots \times \Theta_{i-1} \times \Theta_{i+1} \times \cdots \times \Theta_I$. So suppose to the contrary that there exist i, θ, and $\widehat{\theta}_i$ such that $h_i(\theta) > h_i(\theta_{-i}, \widehat{\theta}_i)$. Now set $\varepsilon = \frac{1}{2}[h_i(\theta) - h_i(\theta_{-i}, \widehat{\theta}_i)]$.

We claim that $d(\theta) \neq d(\theta_{-i}, \widehat{\theta}_i)$. If this were not true, we would have, from $h_i(\theta) > h_i(\theta_{-i}, \widehat{\theta}_i)$, that

$$t_i(\theta) - \sum_{j \neq i} v_j(d(\theta), \theta_j) > t_i(\theta_{-i}, \widehat{\theta}_i) - \sum_{j \neq i} v_j(d(\theta_{-i}, \widehat{\theta}_i), \theta_j) \implies t_i(\theta) > t_i(\theta_{-i}, \widehat{\theta}_i).$$

But this says that i strictly prefers $(d(\theta), t_i(\theta))$ to $(d(\theta_{-i}, \widehat{\theta}_i), t_i(\theta_{-i}, \widehat{\theta}_i))$, as the d part is the same in both cases but the transfer that i receives is larger under θ. Since we have assumed dominant strategy incentive compatibility, this cannot be true, as it would allow i to lie, when her type is $\widehat{\theta}_i$, by reporting θ_i and become better off. Hence $d(\theta) \neq d(\theta_{-i}, \widehat{\theta}_i)$ is indeed true.

By the completeness assumption, there exists some $\widetilde{\theta}_i \in \Theta_i$ such that

$$v_i(d(\theta_{-i}, \widehat{\theta}_i), \widetilde{\theta}_i) + \sum_{j \neq i} v_j(d(\theta_{-i}, \widehat{\theta}_i), \theta_j) = \varepsilon,$$

as well as, for all $\theta' \in \Theta$ such that $d(\theta') \neq d(\theta_{-i}, \widehat{\theta}_i)$,

$$v_i(d(\theta'), \widetilde{\theta}_i) + \sum_{j \neq i} v_j(d(\theta'), \theta_j) = 0.$$

These conditions, together with the assumed efficiency of the decision rule $d(\cdot)$, imply that $d(\theta_{-i}, \widetilde{\theta}_i) = d(\theta_{-i}, \widehat{\theta}_i)$. Indeed, by the efficiency of $d(\cdot)$, we have

$$v_i(d(\theta_{-i}, \widetilde{\theta}_i), \widetilde{\theta}_i) + \sum_{j \neq i} v_j(d(\theta_{-i}, \widetilde{\theta}_i), \theta_j) \geq v_i(d(\theta_{-i}, \widehat{\theta}_i), \widetilde{\theta}_i) + \sum_{j \neq i} v_j(d(\theta_{-i}, \widehat{\theta}_i), \theta_j).$$

But by the above construction of the function v_i, if $d(\theta_{-i}, \widetilde{\theta}_i) \neq d(\theta_{-i}, \widehat{\theta}_i)$, then the left hand side equals 0 while the right hand side equals $\varepsilon > 0$, which is impossible. Hence, $d(\theta_{-i}, \widetilde{\theta}_i) = d(\theta_{-i}, \widehat{\theta}_i)$ holds.

Applying dominant strategy incentive compatibility to $(\theta_{-i}, \widetilde{\theta}_i)$, we have

$$v_i(d(\theta_{-i}, \widetilde{\theta}_i), \widetilde{\theta}_i) + t_i(\theta_{-i}, \widetilde{\theta}_i) \geq v_i(d(\theta_{-i}, \widehat{\theta}_i), \widetilde{\theta}_i) + t_i(\theta_{-i}, \widehat{\theta}_i),$$

and

$$v_i(d(\theta_{-i}, \widehat{\theta}_i), \widehat{\theta}_i) + t_i(\theta_{-i}, \widehat{\theta}_i) \geq v_i(d(\theta_{-i}, \widetilde{\theta}_i), \widehat{\theta}_i) + t_i(\theta_{-i}, \widetilde{\theta}_i).$$

Because $d(\theta_{-i}, \widetilde{\theta}_i) = d(\theta_{-i}, \widehat{\theta}_i)$, these inequalities reduce to $t_i(\theta_{-i}, \widetilde{\theta}_i) \geq t_i(\theta_{-i}, \widehat{\theta}_i)$ and $t_i(\theta_{-i}, \widehat{\theta}_i) \geq t_i(\theta_{-i}, \widetilde{\theta}_i)$, therefore $t_i(\theta_{-i}, \widetilde{\theta}_i) = t_i(\theta_{-i}, \widehat{\theta}_i)$ holds.

But then the utility of i when truthfully announcing $\widetilde{\theta}_i$ when i's type is $\widetilde{\theta}_i$, equals

$$v_i(d(\theta_{-i}, \widetilde{\theta}_i), \widetilde{\theta}_i) + t_i(\theta_{-i}, \widetilde{\theta}_i) = v_i(d(\theta_{-i}, \widehat{\theta}_i), \widetilde{\theta}_i) + t_i(\theta_{-i}, \widehat{\theta}_i).$$

This in turn equals

$$v_i(d(\theta_{-i}, \widehat{\theta}_i), \widetilde{\theta}_i) + \sum_{j \neq i} v_j(d(\theta_{-i}, \widehat{\theta}_i), \theta_j) + h_i(\theta_{-i}, \widehat{\theta}_i) = \varepsilon + h_i(\theta_{-i}, \widehat{\theta}_i).$$

The utility of i at $\widetilde{\theta}_i$ by misreporting $\widehat{\theta}_i$ equals $h_i(\theta)$, by a similar argument. Recalling that $\varepsilon = \frac{1}{2}[h_i(\theta) - h_i(\theta_{-i}, \widehat{\theta}_i)] > 0$, we see that this misreporting results in a positive utility gain. In the case of $h_i(\theta) < h_i(\theta_{-i}, \widehat{\theta}_i)$, the proof would proceed in exactly the same fashion. Since the positive utility gain contradicts the assumed dominant strategy incentive compatibility of (d, t), we have completed the proof of part (2).   QED

The theorem identifies a class of transfer functions, called Groves schemes, which align the agents' incentives so as to ensure that the efficient decision arises when agents play dominant strategies. The best way to understand the structure of these transfer functions is to look first at a special case of a Groves scheme, the pivotal mechanism introduced by Clarke (1971).

The **pivotal mechanism** is built around the idea of making each agent internalize the effect his decision has on everybody else. To isolate this effect, we think of the possibility that i's report of θ_i might change the decision d that the rest of the society would have made had i not been a member of the society. If i's report does not change the decision, then i is not imposing a cost or bestowing a benefit to the rest of society by his report. We say that in that case i is not pivotal. If instead i's report leads to a change in the social decision from what it would have been in i's absence, then i is pivotal, and is required to reimburse the society for that change. The transfer scheme enforces this.

The transfer scheme that achieves this uses the function

$$t_i(\theta) = \sum_{j \in \mathcal{I}, j \neq i} v_j(d(\theta), \theta_j) - \max_{d \in D} \sum_{j \in \mathcal{I}, j \neq i} v_j(d, \theta_j). \tag{2.4}$$

This function has two parts. The first computes the benefits all agents apart from i receive from the decision $d(\theta)$ that results from everybody's report of their own θ_k coordinate, including the θ_i report. The second part, which is subtracted from the first, computes what would have been the maximum possible benefit for all agents apart from i if one only used their own reports of their θ_j to find the best d. If the first term is less than the second in absolute value, agent i is pivotal and his report has caused the others harm, so his transfer is negative, indicating i has to pay, and equal to the exact amount of this harm. The converse cannot arise: since the second term already is the maximum sum of benefits that the others can have, the only way the first term can differ from the second term is for the former to be less than the latter.

To understand this better we return to the example with Rich, Bob, and Lori.

Example 2.5. If the township government uses the Clarke mechanism, then Rich, Bob, and Lori will all report their true values. Neither Rich nor Bob is pivotal because the decision of not building the gazebo does not depend on them. That is, excluding either Rich or Bob's values in deciding whether to build the gazebo, the decision is still not to build. Thus, their transfers are equal to zero. However, Lori is pivotal. With just Rich and Bob the sum would be 20 and the gazebo would be built. However, when Lori is included the sum is -5 and the gazebo is not built. Thus, Lori is pivotal and must pay the government of Brandywine township 20, which is the sum of the benefits that Rich and Bob would have if the gazebo were built. Note that Lori still comes out ahead when the gazebo is not built because if it were built Lori would have benefit of -25, but instead she has -20.

Now assume that Lori does not place such a large negative value on the gazebo being built and the true values of the project are: $\theta_R = 5$, $\theta_B = 15$ and $\theta_L = -10$. The sum of the values is 10 and thus the gazebo is built. If the government of Brandywine township uses Clarke's mechanism, Bob is the pivotal agent. This is because if the government excluded Bob's value, then the sum of the values would be -5 and the gazebo would not be built. However, when Bob is included the sum is 10, thus, the gazebo is built. Here Bob is pivotal and must pay the government of Brandywine township 5. Note also that Bob still comes out ahead when the gazebo is built because if the gazebo were not built he would have payoff 0, but by building the gazebo, he has payoff $15 - 5 = 10$.   ◇

Clarke's idea of the pivotal mechanism is ingenious. Groves' idea led to a generalization. He noticed that the amount added to $\sum_{j \in \mathcal{I}, j \neq i} v_j(d(\theta), \theta_j)$ in the transfer calculation does not affect incentives as long as it does not depend on θ_i. If i cannot affect this amount, then adding it to $\sum_{j \in \mathcal{I}, j \neq i} v_j(d(\theta), \theta_j)$ cannot give i an incentive to lie. This is how we arrived at the $h_i(\theta_{-i})$ part of the transfer scheme in (2.3) in theorem 2.2. Another way to see this is to notice that for each i the motive to lie comes from the *difference* between the utility received from truthful revelation and that from a lie. The *level* of each of these utilities does not matter for this incentive.

Not everything is wonderful with the Groves mechanism family. Two main problems are (i) that a Groves mechanism may fail to achieve material balance and so it may lead to waste, and (ii) that it may make agents unwilling to participate.

2.4.1 Balance Problem

Recall that a transfer function is balanced if all the payments $t_i(\theta)$ to the agents sum to zero, for every θ. A simple example from Jackson (2003) shows the problem. Imagine a society of two agents who have to decide to provide or not a public project, in a special case of example 2.1. Each agent's value for the public project is a real number, positive or negative. Because of theorem 2.2, there exist functions h_1 and h_2 that satisfy (2.3). Suppose that the public project costs $3/2$ to provide.

Start with what feasibility of transfers implies. It says that, for every $\theta = (\theta_1, \theta_2)$ list, $0 \geq t_1(\theta) + t_2(\theta)$. Since the θs are any real numbers, they could in particular be $(\theta_1, \theta_2) = (1, 1)$. If so, then the efficient decision is to build the project, since the sum of the values $\theta_1 + \theta_2$ is 2, which exceeds the cost of the project. Hence for these θ_i values, $d = 1$ is chosen by the mechanism and feasibility implies

$$0 \geq t_1(1, 1) + t_2(1, 1).$$

From (2.3) and the above inequality then we get

$$0 \geq t_1(1, 1) + t_2(1, 1) = h_1(1) + h_2(1) + \left(1 - \frac{3}{4}\right) + \left(1 - \frac{3}{4}\right),$$

which yields

$$-\frac{1}{2} \geq h_1(1) + h_2(1). \tag{2.5}$$

But we can also imagine that θ might be given by $(\theta_1, \theta_2) = (0, 0)$. Now the efficient decision is not to build, $d = 0$. Following the reasoning we used for the $(\theta_1, \theta_2) = (1, 1)$ case, we get

$$0 \geq h_1(0) + h_2(0). \tag{2.6}$$

Hence either $-\frac{1}{4} \geq h_1(1) + h_2(0)$ or $-\frac{1}{4} \geq h_1(0) + h_2(1)$ is true, or both. To see this, negate both these inequalities and add them up side by side to immediately find a contradiction with (2.5) and (2.6) when summed together. Now, if $-\frac{1}{4} \geq h_1(1) + h_2(0)$ holds, then, noting that the efficient decision for $(\theta_1, \theta_2) = (1, 0)$ is $d = 0$, we have from (2.3) that

$$-\frac{1}{4} \geq t_1(1, 0) + t_2(1, 0).$$

Analogously, if it is $-\frac{1}{4} \geq h_1(0) + h_2(1)$ that holds, then we get $-\frac{1}{4} \geq t_1(0, 1) + t_2(0, 1)$. But this means that in at least one case among $(\theta_1, \theta_2) = (1, 0)$ and $(\theta_1, \theta_2) = (0, 1)$, the sum of the transfers is negative. We conclude that any Groves mechanism violates the balance condition in this public project example.

2.4.2 Voluntary Participation Problem

In our present setting, an agent i participates voluntarily if

$$v_i(d(\theta), \theta_i) + t_i(\theta_i) \geq 0, \tag{2.7}$$

where we assume that we have normalized the utility functions so that for any agent the utility of walking away from the mechanism is zero. **Voluntary participation** is said to occur when inequality (2.7) holds for all i and all θ.

But the example we just looked at to discuss the problem of the absence of balance tells us that either $-\frac{1}{4} \geq t_1(1, 0) + t_2(1, 0)$ or $-\frac{1}{4} \geq t_1(0, 1) + t_2(0, 1)$. In either case the project is not built. But then one agent must have a negative transfer, which means he has to pay, but he does not receive any benefit since the public project is not built. This agent would have been better off by refusing to participate and enjoying the zero utility that this would afford him.

2.5 The Vickrey Auction

Consider an auction for a single item, as briefly introduced in example 2.3. The relevant set of agents is the set of bidders in the auction. The seller, also a member of the society but not a player in the auction game, has zero valuation for the item. Agent i has the valuation $\theta_i \geq 0$ for the item on sale. The decision d can be written even more simply than in the example: let d be the label of the bidder who wins the item, or 0 in case there is no sale. So $d = 7$ would mean that bidder 7 won, for example.

The efficient decision in this case is the one that allocates the item to the bidder with the highest valuation, which we write as $d(\theta) = \arg \max_i \theta_i$. To see why, ask first what is the social value of giving the item to any particular bidder i. Since the seller has zero valuation, the total valuation of the society increases from 0 to θ_i. The payment that i may make to the seller does not alter this increase in social valuation: it simply redistributes it among the seller and bidder i. Hence in order to get to the highest social valuation, the bidder with the highest θ_i must receive the item.

How can we get the highest-valuation bidder to get the item? We can simply use the pivotal mechanism. The clever trick of the pivotal mechanism is to make each agent compensate the others when this agent is pivotal. In our context here, this means that the agent's report of her valuation makes her win, rather than anyone else's report. If agent i is the pivotal one, that means i wins the auction. In this case, the opportunity cost to society is the value of the item to the next-highest valuation bidder, $\max_{j \neq i} \theta_j$. This notation says to look among the θ_j valuations for everyone but $j = i$ and choose the largest one. According to the pivotal mechanism, we set $t_i(\theta) = -\max_{j \neq i} \theta_j$ if and only if agent i receives the item.

But have we not departed the world of auctions? As just described, how does the pivotal mechanism correspond to an auction? Simple. Imagine all agents submitting sealed bids. The rules of the auction specify that the winner is the submitter of the highest bid. They further specify that the winner has to pay the *second-highest* submitted bid. It is easy to check that this auction, called the *second-price auction* or *Vickrey auction* in honor of the first economist to analyze it formally, is equivalent to the pivotal mechanism of the previous paragraph. It immediately follows that *it is a dominant strategy for each bidder i to submit the true valuation θ_i as her bid.*

It is also equivalent, when the agents' valuations are independent of each other, to the traditional English auction in which the bidders are together in a room and the auctioneer cries out successively higher prices. Bidders indicate their willingness to pay the currently cried price by holding a hand or a sign up. When the price reaches a level such that only one bidder is actively bidding, this bidder is declared the winner and pays that price. Under these rules, it is a dominant strategy to bid your true valuation θ_i, and so to drop out when the price exceeds your θ_i. You can see that the price the winner has to pay is very close to the second-highest bidder valuation. How close depends on how big the increment is that the auctioneer employs to jump from price to price.

Let us now consider how the Vickrey auction might work when there are multiple items to be auctioned off. This will answer the inevitable question, "if the Vickrey auction is so good, why is it not used all the time?" To highlight the difficulties, we assume that the goods on sale are different, just like blocks of spectrum in an FCC auction are different. In this case, bidders vie for combinations of discrete items.

The first problem then is one of complexity.[3] On the face of it, nothing could be simpler than revealing your true θ_i. This is true only if you are bidding for one item. Imagine that the FCC has 20 blocks of electromagnetic spectrum on auction, and you are required

---

[3]On this issue, and on auctions in general, a good source is Milgrom (2004). The examples that follow are taken from this book and originate in Ausubel and Milgrom (2002).

to submit a bid on each one of the possible combinations of some blocks from these 20. The problem is that there is a large number of such combinations, over a million in fact. (There are $20!/(10!)^2 = 184756$ distinct ways to bundle 10 elements from a set of 20, and then one has to also count how many ways exist to bundle 9 elements, 11 elements, etc.) Allowing bids on all the possible packages of the items is too expensive for the bidders and the auctioneer.

The second problem arises when bidders face budget constraints. What if your true θ_i exceeds your ability to pay? Then you may not have a strategy that is always optimal, as you would in a Vickrey auction if you faced no budget constraint.

The third problem is more spectacular. Adding bidders to a Vickrey auction may reduce the revenue the auction raises! An example shows this. Suppose there are two spectrum licenses on auction. They are identical. There are two firms that will bid for them. Firm 1 has $\theta_1 = \$1$ billion for both of the licenses but does not value a single license at all, as it needs both to establish a viable business. Firm 2 has the same valuation pattern, but would pay up to \$900 million for both licenses. With these two bidders only, the auction effectively becomes a simpler one: an auction for the two licenses together, as a single item. As a result, bidder 1 wins the two licenses and pays \$900 million.

Now imagine that there are two more bidders, who are willing to pay up to \$1 billion for a single license each, but not willing to buy both licenses. Under the rules of the Vickrey auction, with all bidders playing their dominant strategies of truthful revelation, bidders 3 and 4 win the licenses. This is socially efficient, as it generates the highest value possible, \$2 billion. But the price paid now by the winners is *zero!* To see why this bizarre result is true, let's calculate the price for bidder 3 (it is the same story for bidder 4). According to the logic of the pivotal mechanism, which is the same as the Vickrey auction as we learned, the price that the winning bidder pays is the opportunity cost to the other bidders of the license it wins. In this case, this is the maximum bidder value of the two licenses together minus the maximum bidder value of one license alone, for bidders 1, 2, and 4. Since each of these maximum values are \$1 billion, their difference is zero.

The Vickrey auction has some more problems along these lines. We hope that we have whetted your appetite for the topic. We will have a little more to say about auctions in chapter 4. If you want to pursue the topic of auctions more systematically, you can read the aforementioned book, Milgrom (2004), as well as Krishna (2002) and Cramton et al. (2006).

2.6 Exercises

Exercise 11: Public Project Decision Rule

Describe the efficient decision rule in the 0–1 public project example.

Exercise 12: Truthful Incentive Compatibility and Strategy-proofness

Prove that a social choice function f is dominant strategy incentive compatible if and only if it is strategy-proof.

Exercise 13: Truthful Revelation of Preferences

Imagine a society that consists of a single married couple, Mario and Isabella. The couple is trying to decide whether to purchase a new Mercedes in black, white, or silver. Isabelle has only one type θ_I. Her most favorite choice is a white Mercedes, her intermediate choice is a silver Mercedes, and her least favorite choice is a black Mercedes. Mario, on the other hand, has two possible types: θ_M and $\bar{\theta}_M$. When Mario is type θ_M, his most favorite choice is a black Mercedes, his intermediate choice is a silver Mercedes, and his least favorite choice is a white Mercedes. However, when he is type $\bar{\theta}_M$, his most favorite choice is a silver Mercedes, his intermediate choice is a white Mercedes, and his least favorite choice is a black Mercedes. Suppose we wish to implement the following social choice function: $f(\theta_I, \theta_M) =$ silver and $f(\theta_I, \bar{\theta}_M) =$ white.
1. Will Mario choose to truthfully reveal his type?
2. Do you get the same answer when the desired social choice function is $f(\theta_I, \theta_M) =$ black and $f(\theta_I, \bar{\theta}_M) =$ white?
3. How about $f(\theta_I, \theta_M) =$ silver and $f(\theta_I, \bar{\theta}_M) =$ silver?

Exercise 14: Revelation Principle and Multiple Equilibria

Let $\mathcal{I} = \{1, 2\}$ and $X = \{a, b, c, d\}$. Each agent has two possible preference orderings, shown in decreasing order of preference, with indifferent alternatives on the same row:

R^1	$\tilde{R}^1$	R^2	$\tilde{R}^2$
b, d	d	c, d	d
a, c	c	a, b	b
	a		a
	b		c

Let the social choice function f be defined by: $f(R^1, R^2) = a$, $f(\tilde{R}^1, R^2) = c$, $f(R^1, \tilde{R}^2) = b$, $f(\tilde{R}^1, \tilde{R}^2) = d$. Let the mechanism (M, g) be such that for each i, $M_i = \{p_i, q_i, r_i\}$ and $g : M_1 \times M_2 \to X$ given by the following.

	p_2	q_2	r_2
p_1	a	b	b
q_1	c	d	c
r_1	c	b	a

Prove that the mechanism (M, g) implements f in dominant strategies. Consider now the direct mechanism $(\{R^1, \tilde{R}^1, \}, \{R^2, \tilde{R}^2\}, f)$. Prove that f is dominant strategy incentive compatible by showing that truthful revelation of preferences is a dominant strategy in the direct mechanism for each agent of each type. However, also prove that the direct mechanism does not implement f in dominant strategies, because when the preferences of each agent are R^i, sending the message $\tilde{R}^i$ is also a dominant strategy for each agent. Moreover, if the agents are of types R^1, R^2, then they prefer the outcome of this joint misrepresentation to the outcome of the truthful messages. (Hint: see Austen-Smith and Banks [2005, page 76], the source of this exercise.)

Exercise 15: Single-Peakedness Example

Verify the claim made on page 44 that each agent has single-peaked preferences over the provision of the pool.

Exercise 16: Dominant Strategy Property of the Vickrey Auction

Prove directly that it is a dominant strategy for each bidder i to bid the true valuation θ_i in the second-price auction. (Hint: consider overreporting and underreporting one's valuation and show that, no matter what the others report, it never improves a bidder's utility to overreport or underreport, and may occasionally reduce it.)

Exercise 17: Another Possible Equilibrium in the Vickrey Auction

Arrange the bidders in the second-price auction in order of valuation, and call the bidder with the highest valuation bidder 1. Now imagine that bidder 1 submits the bid θ_1, and all others submit the bid 0. Given everybody else's bids, would it make any bidder better off to submit a different bid? What does this mean for the significance of the Vickrey auction's dominant-strategy property? (See Osborne, 2004, page 83.)

Exercise 18: Dominant Strategy Incentive Compatibility

Assume we can guarantee that a social choice function $f : \Theta \to X$ is dominant strategy incentive compatible. Let there be another social choice function $\overline{f} : \overline{\Theta} \to X$, where $\overline{\Theta} \subset \Theta$, with a property that the outcome of the social choice function under type profile θ coincides with the outcome of the social choice function under type profile $\overline{\theta}$. Can we guarantee that the social choice function $\overline{f}$ is also dominant strategy incentive compatible?

Chapter 3

Implementation in Nash Equilibria: A Lot of Information Assumed

It would be nice to have strategies that are optimal no matter what others do, as the dominant strategies we considered in chapter 2 are. As we saw in that chapter, such strategies are not always available. Often the best strategy for an agent depends on the strategies of the others. In many applications of mechanism design the agents know each other well, so it makes sense to allow this dependency. Think of a choice over restaurants. You may prefer to eat Chinese food tonight but not wait in a long line. If everyone else decides to go to the Chinese restaurant, then it may be your best response to go to the Mexican restaurant where there is not a long line. Making decisions given what others do leads to an equilibrium concept formalized by John Nash. He recognized that a stable social outcome occurs when each agent does not want to unilaterally change her decision. That is, each agent chooses the best choice available to her given what everyone else chooses.

Each agent asks, "What should I do if I anticipate that everyone else is doing X?" When the action of each agent is the answer to this question, and each agent has anticipated all the other agents' actions correctly, the resulting decision profile is a Nash equilibrium.[1] The Nash equilibrium concept is central to game theory and deserves a few pages before we turn to using it for implementation.

3.1 A Quick Lesson on Nash Equilibrium

Game theory is a subject that studies individual behavior in terms of strategies available to the players. When each player chooses a strategy, some outcome arises, and this outcome results in a payoff for each player. For example, suppose there are two individuals, Amy and Bill, trying to decide on a restaurant. They each have two strategies, to either choose Mexican (M) or choose Chinese (C). The payoff, in terms of utility, that each

---

[1]The concept of equilibrium familiar from the study of mechanics in high school physics class is analogous to Nash equilibrium, in that an equilibrium is a state of rest that is stable unless some [outside] force acts upon it.

individual receives depends on his or her own strategy and the strategy of the other player. Although Amy prefers Mexican, if Bill also chooses Mexican, Amy will receive less utility than if she chooses Chinese when Bill chooses Mexican (she does not like Bill very much). Bill's preferences are similar, but he prefers eating Chinese by himself to eating Mexican by himself. The action taken by each individual, then, depends on the payoffs expected from each strategy combination. We say that a player is rational if she tries to maximize her payoff.

Game theorists describe such a situation as a normal form game.

Definition 3.1 (Normal Form Game). A **normal form game** is a collection of a set of players $\mathcal{I}$, a set of strategies S_i for each player $i \in \mathcal{I}$, and I outcome functions $u_i : S_1 \times \cdots \times S_I \to \mathbb{R}$, each of which shows the payoff associated with each strategy combination for the corresponding player i.

When there are two players and each has a finite number of strategies, it is convenient to represent a normal form game by a table (table 3.1). Consider the example shown below. Amy's (Player 1's) strategies are listed down the side, and Bill's (Player 2's) strategies are listed across the top. The payoff each receives is listed as a pair for each strategy combination. Amy's payoff is listed first and Bill's is second as follows:

Amy\ Bill	M	C
M	2,2	5,3
C	3,5	1,1

Table 3.1: Restaurant Game

Here, $u_A(M, M) = 2$, $u_A(M, C) = 5$, $u_B(M, M) = 2$, $u_B(M, C) = 3$, and so on, where A denotes Amy and B denotes Bill.

It is easy to change the example to reflect the case where Amy and Bill like each other.

In this simple game, we can ask several questions. The first is whether the players have dominant strategies. Neither player has a dominant strategy. If Amy goes to the Mexican restaurant it is best for Bill to go to the Chinese restaurant. Conversely, if Amy chooses the Chinese restaurant it is best for Bill to choose the Mexican restaurant. In general, it is unlikely that dominant strategies exist for a given randomly chosen game. In the absence of dominant strategies, the players must employ some other rationale for choosing strategies.

We will make some assumptions in order to predict what the outcome(s) of this game might be. First, we assume the individuals know the game and the payoffs. They must also know the payoffs to the other players for all possible strategy combinations.

Definition 3.2 (Common Knowledge). All players know the preference profile and the structure of the game, all know that all know it and so on ad infinitum.

A full characterization of common knowledge in the context of normal form games is beyond the scope of this book.

Common knowledge may seem like a strong assumption. However, social decisions are made daily within families, for instance, where family members probably know very well the preferences of the other members. Or consider an office environment where an employee chooses an effort level given the effort level of the other employees. The assumption that employees know fairly accurately the work ethic of co-workers (and all know that all know it and so on) probably holds.

Given this assumption, can we predict what outcome might constitute an equilibrium and thus what strategies (leading to this outcome) would be equilibrium strategies for Amy and Bill? This requires some definitions.

As in previous chapters, when discussing a mechanism we will denote a strategy for player i as m_i and a strategy for all other players except i as m_{-i}, where "m" reminds us of "message". All possible strategies for player i are in the set M_i and a strategy combination of all the players is denoted as m. For each possible m, an individual receives a payoff $u_i(m)$. Therefore if player i chooses strategy m_i and everyone else chooses m_{-i}^*, player i receives $u_i(m_i, m_{-i}^*)$.

Definition 3.3 (Best Response). A player i has a **best response strategy** m_i^* to m_{-i}^* if, for all $m_i \in M_i$, $u_i(m_i^*, m_{-i}^*) \geq u_i(m_i, m_{-i}^*)$.

The name "best response" makes the definition intuitive; at some *given* strategy profile of all the other players (m_{-i}^*), one player's best response is that strategy that yields her at least as much payoff as any of her other strategies.

Definition 3.4 (Nash Equilibrium Strategy). A strategy profile $(m_1^*, \ldots, m_I^*)$ is a **Nash equilibrium** if and only if m_i^* is a best response to m_{-i}^* for each i.

Using the Nash equilibrium concept, we can analyze the game of the example we just saw. If Amy chooses M, Bill's best response is C, since the payoffs for Bill are $u_B(C, M) = 3 > u_B(M, M) = 2$.

If C were not a best response for Bill, then there must have been some other strategy Bill would unilaterally want to choose. But if Amy chose M, the only other strategy Bill could choose is M and this outcome is worse for him as seen by the above inequality. Is the strategy profile $m = (M, C)$ a Nash equilibrium? Indeed it is, as Amy cannot change her strategy and achieve a higher payoff for herself and Bill cannot change his strategy and achieve a higher payoff for himself. Yet we can see, that by the same logic, the strategy combination (C, M) is also a Nash equilibrium. (Exercise: Verify that this is true.) Thus we see that this solution concept faces the difficulty of sometimes leading to multiple equilibria. Thinking about the topic of this chapter, then, we might wonder how this problem affects implementation in Nash equilibrium. This will be an issue the planner needs to address for Nash implementation.

Another problem a planner may face is the non-existence of a Nash equilibrium. That is, there exist games that have no pure strategy Nash equilibrium. We leave for an exercise an example of this phenomenon (see exercise 19).

3.1.1 Nash Equilibrium in Mixed Strategies

A nice feature of the Nash equilibrium concept is that every normal form game with a finite number of players and a finite number of strategies has at least one Nash equilibrium. However, there exist games in which the single Nash equilibrium employs mixed strategies, where players randomize over their pure strategies. Using our Restaurant Game example, a pure strategy for Amy or Bill is either Mexican or Chinese. A mixed strategy is using a randomizing device, such as the flip of a coin, to choose a pure strategy.

Definition 3.5 (Mixed Strategy). A **mixed strategy** of a player i in a normal form game is a probability distribution over the set of i's strategies, that is, an assignment of a non-negative real number $q_i(m_i) \geq 0$ to each pure strategy $m_i \in M_i$ such that $\sum_{m_i \in M_i} q_i(m_i) = 1$.

Example 3.1. [**Nash equilibrium in mixed strategies**] Suppose Amy and Bill each decide to randomize their choice of Mexican or Chinese. With probability p, Amy chooses Mexican and with probability $(1-p)$ she chooses Chinese. Similarly, Bill chooses Mexican with probability q and Chinese with probability $(1-q)$.

In order to find the Nash equilibria in mixed strategies, we must determine what probabilities Amy could use that would make Bill indifferent between his two pure strategies and simultaneously what probabilities Bill could use that would make Amy indifferent between her two pure strategies. As it turns out, this is equivalent to finding each player's mixed strategy best responses, a convenient fact that we will not prove here.

Letting u_i denote the utility (or payoff) associated with each strategy combination for player $i = \{\text{Amy}, \text{Bill}\}$, the expected utility[2] for player i is:

$$U_i(p,q) = pq u_i(M,M) + p(1-q) u_i(M,C) + (1-p)q u_i(C,M) + (1-p)(1-q) u_i(C,C)$$
$$(3.1)$$

At any mixed strategy Nash equilibrium, Bill would choose his pure strategies with a probability that makes Amy indifferent between choosing Mexican or choosing Chinese. Amy will be indifferent if:

$$U_{\text{Amy}}(M,q) = q(2) + (1-q)(5) = q(3) + (1-q)(1) = U_{\text{Amy}}(C,q).$$
$$(3.2)$$

---

[2]See page 19 for the definition of utility functions that have the expected utility property.

In words, Amy's expected payoff from choosing Mexican must equal her expected payoff from choosing Chinese. Setting the two expected payoffs equal to one another, we find that an equilibrium mixed strategy for Bill is to choose Mexican with a probability $q = 4/5$. Analogously, an equilibrium mixing strategy for Amy would satisfy:

$$U_{\text{Bill}}(p, M) = p(2) + (1 - p)(5) = p(3) + (1 - p)(1) = U_{\text{Bill}}(p, C). \tag{3.3}$$

In this case, Amy's strategy is also to choose Mexican with $p = 4/5$, as we see by solving this equation. $\Diamond$

Finding mixed strategy Nash equilibria in games with more than two players or more than two strategies is harder than in this example, although a similar procedure may be applied. A complicating factor is that each player who has more than two strategies can consider a probability distribution that assigns positive probability to any subset of his strategies. This increases the complexity of computation of mixed strategy Nash equilibria drastically, as the number of distinct subsets of a set with n elements increases exponentially when n increases.

A word of caution on mixed strategies and implementation. Because a game may have mixed strategy Nash equilibria, a planner seeking to achieve a social choice correspondence may have to take mixed strategy equilibria into account as well (especially if these strategies lead to undesired outcomes). Often, theorists restrict attention to pure strategy Nash equilibria.

3.2 Nash Equilibrium in Implementation

In order for us to implement a social choice correspondence in Nash equilibrium, we need a mechanism (M, g), defined as in the previous chapters. The difference here is that we will employ Nash equilibrium as the equilibrium concept for solving the game that a mechanism leads to in every environment, instead of dominant strategy equilibrium (chapter 2) or Bayesian equilibrium (chapter 4). Let us recall first the basic definition of a mechanism and strategies in a mechanism from section 2.1.

Definition 3.6 (Mechanism and Strategy). For each profile of messages m, where $m \in M = M_1 \times \cdots \times M_I$, we let $g : M \to X$ describe how agent strategies get turned into a joint social choice. A pair (M, g) is called a **mechanism**. A **strategy** for player i is a function $m_i : \Theta_i \to M_i$ that assigns to each type $\theta_i \in \Theta_i$ of agent i a message $m_i(\theta_i) \in M_i$.

Definition 3.7 (Nash Equilibrium of a Mechanism). Given a mechanism $\Gamma = (M, g)$, where $g : M \to X$, an environment $\theta = (\theta_1, \ldots, \theta_I) \in \Theta$, and a set of possible outcomes X, a profile $m(\theta) = (m_1(\theta_1), \ldots, m_I(\theta_I))$ is a **Nash Equilibrium**

of (M, g) **played in** θ if for each $i \in \mathcal{I}$ and each $\overline{m}_i \in M_i$, $g(m_i(\theta_i), m_{-i}(\theta_{-i}))$ $R^i(\theta_i)$ $g(\overline{m}_i, m_{-i}(\theta_{-i}))$. For every $\theta \in \Theta$, denote the set of **Nash equilibria of the mechanism** $\Gamma = (M, g)$ **in a environment** $\theta \in \Theta$ as $\mathcal{N}(\Gamma, \theta)$.

The definition says that a Nash equilibrium is a list of messages $m(\theta)$ sent by the agents such that for an individual i, given the messages everyone else sends, denoted as $m_{-i}(\theta_{-i})$, there is no other message $\overline{m}_i$ that individual i could choose that would lead to an outcome i prefers to $m_i(\theta_i)$, given the preference relation of the agent's type, θ_i.

Note that in environments with complete information, such as in this chapter, it is more intuitive to use the term strategy to denote the message $m_i(\theta_i)$ that agent i sends, rather than the entire function $m_i : \Theta_i \to M_i$. It is often presented in this way in the literature. This should not be confusing, as long as one keeps in mind that it simply shifts the perspective in time to the point where agent i is aware of θ_i and does not need to plan what message to send if i had some other type θ_i'. This terminological shift makes no difference for implementation theory, since the task of the mechanism designer remains to make the mechanism give the right incentives to agents for every type profile $\theta \in \Theta$ for the agents.

Compare this definition to the definition of a Nash equilibrium in the previous section. For a mechanism, the requirement that each agent plays a best response is extended to each type of each agent. In an one-off game such as that between Amy and Bill, each agent has only one type. This makes clear what a mechanism does: it creates a different game for each environment θ, since different environments correspond to different payoff functions. Extending the example of Amy and Bill to a case where they each have multiple types requires multiple payoff tables, one for each θ, to completely describe the mechanism in terms of its constituent normal form games.

The assumptions made in the previous section, that the environment is one of perfect information and that common knowledge prevails among the agents, are also made here. Although these assumptions may seem strong, think of constitution writers (mechanism designers) today writing a constitution (mechanism) that will be used by future generations. Each member of a future generation may have very good knowledge of the entire preference profile of that generation; but the constitution writers have no idea what preference profile may prevail in the future. They only know what goals they would like to achieve in each preference profile that may arise.

We turn now to the question of implementing a social choice correspondence in Nash equilibria. Recall that a social choice correspondence assigns to each environment a set of alternatives that society deems desirable. We write a social choice correspondence as $F : \Theta \rightrightarrows X$, where the double arrow indicates that it is a correspondence and not a function (appendix A contains the definition of correspondence on page 255).

Definition 3.8 (Nash Implementation). Let $F : \Theta \rightrightarrows X$ be a social choice correspondence. Then we say that F is **Nash implementable** if there exists a mechanism

(M, g) such that for all $\theta \in \Theta$ we have (a) $g(\mathcal{N}(\Gamma, \theta)) \subseteq F(\theta)$ and (b) $F(\theta) \subseteq g(\mathcal{N}(\Gamma, \theta))$. If such a mechanism (M, g) exists, we say that it **Nash implements** F.

The definition requires that, for each environment θ, the set of Nash equilibrium outcomes of the mechanism in that environment is equal to the set of alternatives selected by the social choice correspondence F for that environment, $F(\theta)$. Notably, *every* Nash equilibrium outcome for some environment θ is required to belong to $F(\theta)$.

There is also a weaker definition of Nash implementation sometimes employed in the mechanism design literature. This definition only requires that one Nash equilibrium outcome of the game induced by the mechanism for an environment θ belong to the $F(\theta)$, but does not require this of all Nash equilibria. This is important because as we showed by example in the previous section, normal form games can have multiple Nash equilibria. Therefore, if a social choice correspondence did not contain all of the Nash equilibrium outcomes of the mechanism for every environment, it would be very difficult to predict whether the socially desired goals would actually be achieved. Some Nash equilibrium might prevail that leads to an alternative not recommended by the social choice correspondence. As William Thomson has noted, this notion of Nash implementation fails to implement F even if no Nash equilibrium outcome is out of $F(\theta)$; instead, it implements some other social choice correspondence that selects for each θ some subset of $F(\theta)$. But since a social choice correspondence embodies desired properties of alternatives for society, the economic designer is not free to arbitrarily restrict F to a smaller social choice correspondence.[3] We avoid weaker definitions of Nash implementation.

Given the limitations of dominant strategy implementation, we might wonder how many social choice correspondences can be Nash implemented. To answer this question, we could take social choice correspondences one at a time and try to design a mechanism that Nash implements it. This is a research direction that has been and is being followed. Another direction leads to more general results. The general approach studies whether a social choice correspondence must exhibit certain properties in order to be Nash implementable. The results from this research are useful because, if all Nash implementable social choice correspondences exhibit the same characteristics, the cataloguing approach will go much quicker. Rather than trying to Nash implement a social choice correspondence to see if it is Nash implementable, one only need to check if it displays certain properties. For an analogy, think of a doctor trying to diagnose a patient. If the doctor had to find every bacterium that causes severe stomach pain and test whether it was killed by a certain medicine, the process would be quite time consuming. (And perhaps deadly for the waiting patient!) If instead, the doctor knew that all bacteria causing severe stomach pain and that are killed by this medicine have a characteristic DNA, then it is simply a

---

[3]For this point and additional discussion of notions of implementation, see Thomson (1996).

matter of checking whether the patient's bacteria have this DNA to know whether the medicine can be used.

To find characteristics of social choice correspondences that would make them Nash implementable, we go back to the definition of Nash Implementation which requires that the desired alternative must be a Nash equilibrium of some mechanism for every environment (preference profile). Therefore, think of an alternative that is a best response outcome under one society's preference profile and call that outcome a. Now consider a second preference profile. If in the second profile alternative a did not fall in anyone's ranking, it must still be a best response outcome and so a Nash equilibrium outcome. A Nash implementable social choice correspondence must also continue to select this alternative. Eric Maskin identified this condition in Maskin (1999), a paper originally circulated in 1977, where he proved that this condition is necessary for a social choice correspondence to be Nash implementable, and also provided a partial converse. The condition is now widely referred to as Maskin Monotonicity, although a better name for it might be Maskin invariance.

Definition 3.9 (Maskin Monotonicity). Let $F : \Theta \rightarrow\rightarrow X$ be a social choice correspondence. Then we say that F is **Maskin Monotonic** if for all $\theta = (\theta_1, \ldots, \theta_I) \in \Theta$, all $\tilde{\theta} = (\tilde{\theta}_1, \ldots, \tilde{\theta}_I) \in \Theta$, and all $a \in F(\theta)$ such that $a \notin F(\tilde{\theta})$, there exist an alternative $b \in X$ and an agent $i \in \mathcal{I}$ such that $a \, R^i(\theta_i) \, b$ and $b \, P^i(\tilde{\theta}_i) \, a$.

This says that if an alternative is socially desirable in one environment but not in another environment, then at least one person had a preference reversal between the environments. If society found an alternative desirable given everyone's preferences in one environment and in another environment no one ranks this alternative any lower, society as a whole should still find it desirable. This requirement carries some philosophical weight as an expression of the sovereignty of the agents who make up the society, because a social choice correspondence that violates Maskin Monotonicity relies on information extraneous to the preferences of the agents. But Maskin Monotonicity also ties directly to the logic of Nash equilibrium, as we stated before its definition.

Economics is the study of trade-offs in the presence of scarcity. Social choice, as a branch of economics, studies the way in which societies trade off individual preferences to achieve social objectives. Unless the social choice correspondence is dictatorial, this involves some compromises. Maskin monotonicity identifies a property of how a social choice correspondence must handle compromise if it is to be Nash implemented.

Maskin Monotonicity narrows the candidate social choice correspondences that can be Nash implemented considerably. The following example demonstrates how one can check a social choice correspondence for Maskin Monotonicity.

Example 3.2. [**Maskin Monotonic social choice correspondence**] Suppose there are three agents and two environments $\theta, \tilde{\theta}$ and the set of alternatives is $X = \{a, b, c, d\}$.

Agent 1's preferences change between the two profiles while the other two agents have the same preferences as follows, where alternatives are listed in descending order of preference and there are no two alternatives that some agent considers indifferent to each other.

$R^1(\theta_1)$	$R^1(\tilde{\theta}_1)$	$R^2(\theta_2) = R^2(\tilde{\theta}_2)$	$R^3(\theta_3) = R^3(\tilde{\theta}_3)$
b	c	d	a
a	a	a	c
c	d	b	b
d	b	c	d

Assume the social choice correspondence is the rule that says, "take the union of the sets of each agent's top two alternatives and remove any alternative that some agent ranks last". Then the social choice correspondence is given by $F(\theta) = \{a, b\}$ and $F(\tilde{\theta}) = \{a\}$. We can check that this is indeed Maskin Monotonic. Since $b \in F(\theta)$ but $b \notin F(\tilde{\theta})$ there must exist some other alternative x, such that $b\, R^i(\theta_i)\, x$ and $x\, P^i(\tilde{\theta}_i)\, b$. This is true for $i = 1$ and for $x = c$ or $x = a$ or $x = d$. $\Diamond$

Maskin Monotonicity may not seem particularly restrictive. It is somewhat surprising then, that many well-known social choice correspondences are not Maskin Monotonic and therefore are not Nash implementable. The following example shows that, in general, the Walrasian correspondence is not Maskin Monotonic. This example is originally due to Leonid Hurwicz and first appeared in a paper, to our knowledge, in Hurwicz et al. (1995), which was circulated as a working paper in the 1980s. See Jackson (2001, page 671) for a discussion and more examples.

Example 3.3. [**The Walrasian Social Choice Correspondence is not Maskin Monotonic.**] Consider the two-good exchange economy pictured in figure 3.1. Note that the preferences of the two agents are monotonically increasing and convex but the indifference curves of agent 2 are allowed to intersect the axes. The directions of increasing preference for the three indifference curves indicated are shown with little arrows. There are two agents and two possible environments $\theta, \tilde{\theta}$, and only agent 1's preferences are different between the two environments. Notice that point a is a Walrasian equilibrium allocation in environment θ but not in $\tilde{\theta}$. Therefore the Walrasian social choice correspondence does not select allocation a in the second environment. But a has not fallen in the ranking of feasible allocations by any agent in the change from environment θ to environment $\tilde{\theta}$, and Maskin monotonicity therefore implies that a should be a Walrasian equilibrium allocation in environment $\tilde{\theta}$. Since there is an allocation such as b which is within agent 1's budget set that passes through a, and hence affordable for agent 1, but preferred to a in environment $\tilde{\theta}$, it follows that a does not maximize the preferences of agent 1 in environment $\tilde{\theta}$ and so it is not a Walrasian equilibrium allocation in this environment.

The fundamental reason a is not a Walrasian equilibrium allocation in environment $\tilde{\theta}$ is that the definition of Walrasian equilibrium assigns each agent a budget set that extends beyond the boundaries of the Edgeworth box. This reflects the fact that in the standard Walrasian equilibrium story, agents have no way of knowing what the aggregate endowment of the economy is, and so do not know where the boundaries of the Edgeworth Box are. Hence an allocation such as b can disqualify an allocation such as a from being a Walrasian equilibrium allocation, even though b is infeasible for the economy as a whole. ◇

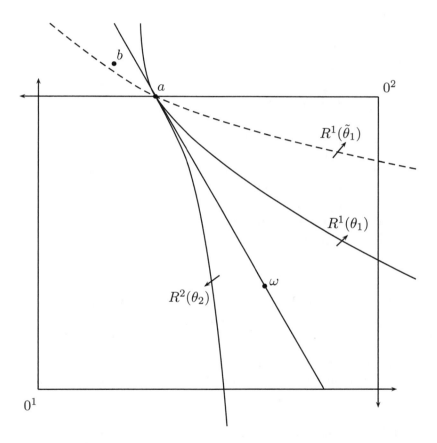

Figure 3.1: The Walrasian social choice correspondence is not Maskin Monotonic

A Maskin Monotonic variant of the Walrasian social choice correspondence does exist. It is defined in such a way as to make infeasible allocations irrelevant for the choice of each agent. In the standard Walrasian definition, the budget set of agent i is the set of consumption vectors that i can afford, given i's endowment and a price vector. Formally, as we saw in section 1.7.8 the budget set is defined by $B_W(p, \omega_i) \equiv \{x_i \in \mathbb{R}^n_+ \mid p \cdot x_i \leq p \cdot \omega_i\}$.

As shown in figure 3.1 for the budget set of agent 1, a budget set can include consumption vectors that are not part of any feasible allocation for the economy. This is because if a price of a good is small enough, the budget set allows the agent to purchase an amount of this good that exceeds the aggregate endowment of the good in the economy.

The budget set can be modified to avoid this possibility. For convenience, let $\Omega = \sum_{k \in \mathcal{I}} \omega_i$ stand for the aggregate endowment vector. The required modification for exchange economies is: $B_{CW}(p, \omega_i, \Omega) \equiv \left\{ x_i \in \mathbb{R}^n_+ \mid p \cdot x_i \leq p \cdot \omega_i \text{ and } x_i \leq \Omega \right\}$. The **Constrained Walrasian social choice correspondence** is defined in the same way as the Walrasian one, but it uses the budget set $B_{CW}(p, \omega_i, \Omega)$ for each agent i instead of the budget set $B_W(p, \omega_i)$.

The definition of the budget set $B_{CW}(p, \omega_i, \Omega)$ makes it depend on information that a single agent does not normally have. No agent can be expected to know the aggregate endowment of the economy. Since the Constrained Walrasian social choice correspondence is Maskin Monotonic, and satisfies the No Veto Power condition that we define next, it is Nash implementable. The question of whether it makes unreasonable informational assumptions on the agents can therefore be redirected from the correspondence to any mechanism that implements it.

We have seen that Maskin Monotonicity is necessary for Nash implementation, and if it were also sufficient for it, we would have a very neat characterization of Nash implementable social choice correspondences. But it is not quite sufficient. When there are at least three people another condition must be imposed to reach a sufficiency result. The condition used by Maskin and by most early theoretical work is No Veto Power. This requires that if everyone has the same top choice except at most one person, that choice will be in the set of social choices.

Definition 3.10 (No Veto Power). Let $F : \Theta \twoheadrightarrow X$ be a social choice correspondence. We say that F satisfies **No Veto Power** if, whenever some outcome $a \in X$ is top-ranked in X for at least $I - 1$ agents in some environment $\theta \in \Theta$, then $a \in F(\theta)$.

No Veto Power requires that if all but one agents agree on which alternative is best, then this alternative is selected by the social choice correspondence, irrespectively of the preferences of the remaining agent. On some domains, No Veto Power is not a demanding condition. For instance, on any domain of economies with at least one private good and at least three agents with preferences that are increasing in this good, there does not exist a combination of $I - 1$ agents and an allocation that all these agents rank the highest. The reason is that in any allocation of such an economy, every agent's top-ranked allocation gives all of the private good to herself. As a result, the premise of the No Veto Power condition is never satisfied, and therefore the condition holds vacuously. However, on a domain such as the one we just discussed but with only two agents, No Veto Power is so demanding that no social choice correspondence satisfies it. We return to this issue in section 3.3. On a social choice domain without a private good, No Veto

Power is demanding, because if there is a group of $I - 1$ agents who rank one alternative x the highest, then a social choice correspondence must completely ignore how bad this alternative may be for the remaining agent, and select it.

Although No Veto Power is not a necessary condition for Nash implementation, if the social choice correspondence is Maskin Monotonic and satisfies No Veto Power, then it is Nash implementable.

Theorem 3.1 (Maskin [1999]). *If $I \geq 3$ and a Social Choice Correspondence satisfies Maskin Monotonicity and No Veto Power, then it is Nash implementable.*

The proof of this result is constructive.[4] It employs what is known as the *canonical mechanism*. We present the proof here because it is so instructive for understanding the way Maskin Monotonicity and No Veto Power are utilized by a mechanism. Furthermore, understanding the canonical mechanism will help you understand better the refinements made in the literature in order to address some potentially undesirable features of the canonical mechanism.

Proof. **Step 1: The Canonical Mechanism.** Let a social choice correspondence $F : \Theta \rightarrow\rightarrow X$ satisfy Maskin Monotonicity and No Veto Power. Define a mechanism (M, g) as follows. The message space for individual $i \in \mathcal{I}$ is $M_i = X \times \Theta \times \mathbb{N}$, where $\mathbb{N}$ is the set of nonnegative integers with typical element n. So each individual's message consists of announcing an alternative, an environment (profile of types that specify the preferences of the agents) and a nonnegative integer.

The outcome function, $g : M \rightarrow X$, takes these announcements and prescribes the following.

Rule 1 If $m_1 = m_2 = \cdots = m_I = (a, \theta, n)$ and $a \in F(\theta)$, then $g(m) = a$.

Rule 2 If there exists an $i \in \mathcal{I}$ such that $m_j = (a, \theta, n)$ for all $j \neq i$, where $a \in F(\theta)$ and $m_i = (b, \cdot, \cdot)$ where $m_j \neq m_i$, then $g(m) = b$ if $a\, R^i(\theta_i)\, b$ and $g(m) = a$ if $b\, P^i(\theta_i)\, a$.

Rule 3 For any other m, use the labels $m_i = (a, \cdot, n_i)$ for the agent messages in m, let i^* be the lowest indexed i such that $n_i \geq n_j$ for all $j \neq i$, and then assign $g(m) = a_{i^*}$.

Step 2: Checking that the canonical mechanism implements F in Nash equilibria. For the following we write the true preference profile as θ and therefore any announcement θ' is a deviation or false announcement. The mechanism (M, g) induces a game (M, g, θ) in normal form. We will check whether the set of Nash equilibrium outcomes of this game coincides with $F(\theta)$.

Step 2a: Checking that each $a \in F(\theta)$ is a Nash equilibrium of the canonical mechanism. We verify that for any $a \in F(\theta)$, it is a Nash equilibrium for all agents to announce $m_i = (a, \theta, 0)$. Any unilateral deviation by an agent i would not be profitable as this

---

[4]The first correct proof of a similar theorem with additional assumptions was given by Williams (1986). The first complete proof of this theorem was given by Saijo (1988). The proof we give here is from Repullo (1987) and Moore and Repullo (1990). We adapted its presentation from Jackson (2001).

would fall under rule 2. Then since $a\ R^i(\theta)\ b$, the agent i does not gain by getting an outcome b and therefore does no better by the false announcement.

Step 2b: Checking that the canonical mechanism does not have a Nash equilibrium that leads to an outcome not in $F(\theta)$. We must also check that every Nash equilibrium outcome is in $F(\theta)$. Suppose m is a Nash equilibrium that falls under rule 3. Then for each individual i, $g(m)$ must be the most preferred outcome. Otherwise i could unilaterally deviate by announcing a higher integer and getting her most preferred outcome, which would contradict the assumption that m is a Nash equilibrium. By No Veto Power, since $g(m)$ is a most preferred outcome, it follows that $g(m) \in F(\theta)$.

If m is a Nash equilibrium that falls under rule 2, then any other agent $j \neq i$ (i is as defined by rule 2) could unilaterally deviate and induce rule 3. Then $j = i^*$ could get her most preferred outcome a_j. Thus for m to be a Nash equilibrium under rule 2, it must be the case that $g(m)$ is the most preferred outcome by all agents $j \neq i$. By No Veto Power, $g(m) \in F(\theta)$.

Lastly, suppose m is a Nash equilibrium under rule 1. In this case all agents are unanimous. So either they are all telling the truth or they are all lying. If they are all telling the truth, then by No Veto Power, $g(m) \in F(\theta)$. So suppose they all are lying by announcing $m = (a, \theta', n)$ and $a \in F(\theta')$ where $\theta \neq \theta'$. Then an agent i could deviate and cause the alternative $b \neq a$ such that $a\ R^i(\theta'_i)\ b$ to be selected, by announcing $m'_i = (b, \theta, n_i)$. This implies that (m'_i, m_{-i}) falls under rule 2. Therefore it must be that if $a\ R^i(\theta'_i)\ b$ then $a\ R^i(\theta_i)\ b$. Thus by monotonicity $a \in F(\theta)$.   QED

A description of the canonical mechanism in words is useful. The mechanism says that if the group unanimously agrees on a preference profile and an outcome the social choice correspondence would pick for that profile, they will get that outcome. If they all agree except one person, the mechanism checks to see if that person had something to gain by deviating and the mechanism questions her credibility. If she has nothing to gain, she may be blowing the proverbial whistle. How do we check? If her announcement makes her better off in the environment θ announced by the group (even though she claims it is not that environment) then we conclude she is not credible. If she would not be better off if she got her announcement and the environment were the one announced by the group, the outcome will be the one from her announcement. Lastly, if the above two cases do not hold, then the outcome will be the alternative that is part of the message of the agent who announced the highest integer.[5]

The canonical mechanism highlights some useful principles for implementing social goals. It is important to keep in mind that the Nash solution concept assumes an environment of complete information in which the equilibrium is defined at a particular preference profile which all agents know and we assume that rational behavior means for

---

[5] In case of a tie, assume every individual is numbered in an already chosen order $1, \ldots, I$. Then the lowest indexed person (of those who tied) is chosen to pick an alternative.

each to play her best response holding all other agents' strategies constant. Unanimous agreement would seem to imply that this outcome is truly desired given the characteristic profile of the group.

Unfortunately, self-interested behavior sometimes leads to tacit collusive agreements. Since the true environment may or may not be verifiable, what assurance do we have that all agents have not coordinated their announcements so that they all contain the same false environment? The second rule of the canonical mechanism is used to give incentives to whistle-blowers so that such strategy combinations are not Nash equilibria. If everyone is lying in the same way about the true environment, then someone could be better off by announcing some other environment given the true environment since the mechanism calls for a lone dissenter to be rewarded with her choice. The only caveat is that the dissenter must prove she is not lying and the true environment is the one announced by everyone else. In that case, the dissenter's announced outcome is really better for her in the environment announced by the others. (Otherwise by the monotonicity property of the social choice correspondence, the dissenter's choice would also be in the social choice correspondence and there would be no conflict.) Therefore, her credibility will be called into question and the group consensus will prevail. But if she is not lying, her desired outcome does not give her (strictly) higher payoff in the untrue environment announced by the others. Thus the dissenter has nothing to gain by untruthfully dissenting and is therefore a credible whistle-blower. This incentive only works if the social choice correspondence is Maskin Monotonic. However, given that the true environment may not be verifiable, it is important that the practitioner keep in mind that this mechanism does not guarantee that a group of agents will not conspire. Nash equilibrium does not rule out the possibility of deviations by coalitions of agents, and the canonical mechanism does not guard against collusion of groups smaller than the entire set of agents. Chapter 5 discusses double implementation, which addresses this problem.

The canonical mechanism is complicated and requires a great deal of individual reasoning power. Each agent's message must include a full preference profile, and so the calculations needed to find the best response are mind-boggling. This is the price we pay for the generality of the the canonical mechanism, which works for every possible Nash implementable social choice correspondence no matter on which domain it is defined. When dealing with a specific social choice correspondence, a simpler implementing mechanism may be found.[6] Nonetheless, it is interesting to test the canonical mechanism in experiments. We discuss such research in section 10.5.

There are two main criticisms associated with the canonical mechanism: (1) the size of the strategy space becomes excessively large and computationally costly as the number of individuals increases and/or the number of choices increases and (2) the integer game causes the mechanism's strategy space to become unbounded off the equilibrium path.

---

[6]We present such mechanisms in sections 6.3 and 6.4.

The next section describes an important contribution that deals with the first critique. The second critique is discussed in chapter 5.

3.2.1 Strategy Space Reduction

If a mechanism requires a large strategy space, the cost to individuals in terms of communication and computation is also large. For example, the canonical mechanism requires each agent to announce a type profile of all other agents (environment), an alternative that is socially optimal with respect to the announced type profile, and an integer. If we have a society with only a hundred members, the central authority's task of communicating and recording everyone's messages, and of computing the final outcome given all participants' reports is very complicated; doing this with millions of society members truly boggles the mind. If we could devise mechanisms with smaller strategy spaces, such that a message process that computes the objective contains all of the information about the economy in some much smaller language, we could improve upon the operational cost of those mechanisms.

Saijo (1988) shows a way to achieve a significant reduction in the size of the strategy space required to prove the necessary and sufficient conditions for Nash implementation. In this mechanism each participant is required to announce his own preferences, his neighbor's preferences, an alternative, and a nonnegative integer n that is between 0 and $I - 1$. We denote an element of M_i by $m_i = (\theta_i^i, \theta_i^{i+1}, a_i, n)$, where the announcement by participant i about participant $i + 1$'s type (which, we recall, determines $i + 1$'s preferences) is denoted by θ_i^{i+1}.

This mechanism uses the idea of cyclic announcement of messages proposed in Hurwicz (1979). To understand this idea assume that all participants are put in a circle, facing toward its center. Then, assuming that the agents are arranged clockwise, part of the strategy for participant i is to announce her own type, θ_i^i, and a type for the agent standing to her left, θ_i^{i+1}. The last agent, I, announces her own type and the first agent's, $(I+1) \bmod I = 1$, type. Figure 3.2 is the graphic representation of the arrangement of the agents. The symbol "mod" stands for the remainder in division: hence, $(I+1) \bmod I = 1$, and so on.

We are now ready to examine Saijo's mechanism, which has three rules analogous to those used in the canonical mechanism.

Rule I If $\theta_i^i = \theta_{i-1}^i$ and $a_i = a$ for all i, and $a \in F(\theta_1^1, \ldots, \theta_I^I)$, then $g(m) = a$.

Rule II If $\theta_i^i = \theta_{i-1}^i$ for all i except j or $j + 1$, $a_i = a$ for all i except j, and $a \in F(\theta_1^1, \ldots, \theta_{j-1}^{j-1}, \theta_{j-1}^j, \theta_j^{j+1}, \ldots, \theta_I^I)$, then $g(m_j, m_{-j}) = a_j$ if $a \, R(\theta_{j-1}^j) \, a_j$, otherwise $g(m_j, m_{-j}) = a$.

Rule III If neither one of Rules I and II is applicable, then $g(m_1, m_2, \ldots, m_I) = a_t$, where $t = (\sum_{k \in \mathcal{I}} n_k) \bmod I + 1$.

Rule I tells us that if all agents report a as an alternative, and if all agents' reported

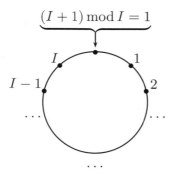

Figure 3.2: Cyclic arrangement of agents

types match, then the outcome of the mechanism is going to be a. Rule II covers the possibility that one or two agents will misreport types; Saijo calls these agents *deviators*. In this case, either agent j or agent $j - 1$, or both, are deviators.

Rule II determines if deviator j is blowing the whistle on all the other players who are lying or whether j is lying. It says, "Everyone except j announced the same preferences for each other and the same outcome a. Furthermore, when we remove the preference announcements of agent j and replace them with the announcements of her immediate neighbor $j - 1$ about her type, we find that outcome a is in the resulting $F(\theta_1^1, \ldots, \theta_{j-1}^{j-1}, \theta_{j-1}^j, \theta_{j+1}^{j+1}, \ldots, \theta_I^I)$. So if j is lying, then the outcome announced by j denoted as a_j will make j better off in environment $(\theta_1^1, \ldots, \theta_{j-1}^{j-1}, \theta_{j-1}^j, \theta_{j+1}^{j+1}, \ldots, \theta_I^I)$ than a (otherwise j would not have lied)." Therefore the mechanism checks to see whether a_j is indeed better for person j if her true type were the one announced for her by agent $j - 1$. If, instead, it is found that a_j is less preferred by person j than a, then the outcome is a_j. Therefore agent j is a credible deviator who is blowing the whistle on all the other agents.

Rule III is a type of integer game where the participants' integer announcements, n_i, are summed. This sum is divided by the number of participants and the individual designated by the remainder plus one chooses any alternative. For example, if there are three people and they choose the integers $2, 1, 2$, then the sum is 5. Divide 5 by 3 and the remainder is 2. Add 1 to get 3 and therefore individual 3 would be designated to choose the alternative. The purpose, as before, of this rule is to keep the strategies focused on an equilibrium. If Rule III is invoked and individual i is designated to choose, any individual $k \neq i$ could unilaterally deviate and choose, n_k, such that $k = \left(\sum_{k \in \mathcal{I}} n_k \right) \bmod I + 1$; hence the original strategy profile that invoked Rule III was not a Nash equilibrium.

The main difference between the canonical mechanism and Saijo's mechanism is Rule II. The reduction of the strategy space poses a minor challenge in identifying who exactly is deviating. If $\theta_i^i = \theta_{i-1}^i$ for all i, and $a_i = a$ for all i except person j, then the deviator is easily identified. In this case, Rule II is similar to Rule 2 of the canonical mechanism. Person j's announcement is implemented only if it is no better for this person than the choice picked by everyone else. The determination of whether it is no better for person j is evaluated at the preference profile announced by person $j - 1$ for person j. For example, assume m is a Nash equilibrium strategy profile. Then, by definition, no individual would receive a more preferred alternative by announcing $\overline{m}_i$ when everyone else announces m_{-i}. Suppose some individual j, did deviate by changing the alternative choice. Then Rule II applies. This tells the planner (or referee) to eliminate the preference profile announcements of person j and then check whether, given the profile announcements of everyone else, the alternative they chose is socially optimal according to the social choice correspondence. If so, then the planner is to only award agent j her announced alternative if this alternative is no better for her given the preferences announced for her. Therefore, this unilateral deviation does not give her an alternative that is any better from her original Nash equilibrium strategy.

If instead agents j and $j - 1$ disagree about j's preference profile, then one or both of them has deviated. In this case rule II provides a way to find a preference profile that is not affected by the announcements of potential deviators. Suppose again individual j and/or individual $j - 1$ decided to deviate from the Nash equilibrium strategy, m, such that $\theta_j^j \neq \theta_{j-1}^j$. Since it is unclear who deviated, Rule II says to check that the announced alternative is socially desirable first under the preference profile when person j's profile announcements are left out of all the announced profiles and then when person $j - 1$'s profile announcements are left out (but j's are back in). If the alternative announced is in the social choice correspondence under both truncated profiles then both are deviators. If the alternative announced is in the social choice correspondence under only one of the truncated profiles, the deviator is identified. Suppose this is agent j, then neither Rule I nor Rule III can be induced. Instead, the outcome will have to be restricted to the lower contour set $L(a, R(\theta_{j-1}^j))$ of alternatives that the preference $R(\theta_{j-1}^j)$ ranks as no better than a, as Rule II indicates. But agent j will not be happy with this outcome because the lower contour set is evaluated by agent $j - 1$'s announcement, θ_{j-1}^j. Therefore, this lower contour set is unaffected by agent j's strategies. The following theory summarizes the results of Saijo's analysis.

Theorem 3.2 (Saijo [1988]). *Suppose that the number of participants is at least three. If the social choice correspondence F satisfies the Maskin Monotonicity and No Veto Power conditions, then the mechanism (M, g), defined by Rules I, II and III and with strategy space M as defined in this section, implements F in Nash equilibria.*

3.3 Two Person Cases

So far we have discussed principles for Nash implementation when there are at least three individuals. Since Nash implementation assumes that agents have a great deal of knowledge about the environment, it seems natural that this concept would be especially appropriate in settings where there are only two individuals. Obviously the canonical mechanism would not be effective since dissenting merely makes the situation a "her word versus my word" dilemma. Also No Veto Power is much too strong a condition: only the alternatives that are best for each one person alone would be in the social choice correspondence if it had to satisfy No Veto Power. For example, in an exchange economy giving all of the goods to one agent is that individual's top choice, assuming that every agent has increasing preferences; but then the two agents' top choices are distinct and No Veto Power cannot be satisfied. So what kind of social choice correspondences are Nash implementable in two person domains?

Moore and Repullo (1990) introduced the condition Restricted Veto Power. This condition along with Maskin Monotonicity and the existence of an outcome that is considered bad by each agent are necessary and sufficient for a social choice correspondence to be Nash implemented when there are only two people. The **Restricted Veto Power** condition specifies that an individual cannot arbitrarily (or maliciously) veto another person's choice. That is, an agent does not have a right to veto an outcome unless it is strictly worse for him than any outcome in the range of F. A **bad outcome** z is such that under any preference profile the alternative z is worse for every agent to every alternative in the range of the social choice correspondence.

The existence of a bad outcome is an interesting condition. This property can provide the correct incentives if it is a credible threat that the bad outcome can be imposed. For example, if free disposal is available to the central authority, giving nothing to either party would be a bad outcome. Its use is as a stick to direct individuals towards the desired equilibrium. If the threat were actually carried out the mechanism would most likely violate voluntary participation. Furthermore, the option of giving everyone the zero allocation is undesirable and would likely lead to *ex post* renegotiation, subverting its power to influence incentives.

Another necessary and sufficient condition for a social choice correspondence to be Nash implemented when there are only two players is given in Dutta and Sen (1991). This condition is notationally cumbersome to describe, but is intuitive. It comes from the recognition that, with two agents, implementation requires a mechanism that can distinguish the true type profile if the two agents announce distinct messages. Thus, any implementable social choice correspondence needs to have a form of self-selection. In other words, if the two individuals announce differently, then the alternative the mechanism recommends from these divergent strategies must be a Nash equilibrium under the true profile. This presupposes the existence of a socially desirable alternative that is in the maximal set (defined below) of both individuals under a profile from the set of choice sets announced.

Some notation will make this clear. There are two agents, $1, 2$ in $\mathcal{I}$; when we want to indicate one of them but not necessarily 1, we will write i or j. As before, a preference ordering over the set of alternatives X for each agent is written as $R^i(\theta_i) \in \mathcal{R}$ for every type $\theta_i \in \Theta_i$. Define the asymmetric preferences as $a\ P^i(\theta_i)\ b$, meaning "a is strictly preferred to b". Then define the **lower contour set for agent** i **at alternative** a as $L_i(a, \theta) = \{c \in X \mid a\ R^i(\theta_i)\ c\}$ and the strict lower contour set as $SL_i(a, \theta) = \{c \in X \mid a\ P^i(\theta_i)\ c\}$. For any $i \in \mathcal{I}$, $\theta = (\theta_1, \theta_2) \in \mathcal{R}^2$ and set of alternatives $S \subseteq X$, define the **maximal set** in S for agent i in environment θ as $M_i(C, \theta) = \{a \in S \mid a\ R^i(\theta_i)\ c\ \forall c \in C\}$. We write Θ for $\Theta_1 \times \Theta_2$.

Dutta and Sen (1991) define condition β as follows.

Definition 3.11 (Condition β). A social choice correspondence $F : \Theta \rightarrow\rightarrow X$ satisfies **condition β** if there exists a set X^* which contains the range of F and for each $i \in \mathcal{I}$, $\theta \in \Theta$ and $a \in F(\theta)$, there exists a set $C_i(a, \theta) \subseteq X^*$, with $a \in C_i(a, \theta) \subseteq L_i(a, \theta)$ such that for all $\theta' \in \Theta$ we have:

1. (a) For all $b \in F(\theta')$, $C_1(a, \theta) \bigcap C_2(b, \theta') \neq \emptyset$.
   (b) There exists $x \in C_1(a, \theta) \bigcap C_2(b, \theta')$ such that if for some $\bar{\theta} \in \Theta$, $x \in M_1(C_1(a, \theta), \bar{\theta}) \bigcap M_2(C_2(b, \theta'), \bar{\theta})$, then $x \in F(\bar{\theta})$.
2. if $a \notin F(\theta')$, then there exists at least one $j \in \mathcal{I}$ and $b \in C_j(a, \theta)$ such that $b \notin L_j(a, \theta')$.
3. $[M_i(C(a, \theta), \theta') \backslash \{a\}] \bigcap M_j(X^*, \theta') \subseteq F(\theta')\ \forall i \in \mathcal{I}$ and $j \neq i$.
4. $M_1(X^*, \theta') \bigcap M_2(X^*, \theta') \subseteq F(\theta')$.

Part (2), (3), and (4) should look familiar (albeit in different notation than we used previously) as they are the conditions for Nash implementation when there are at least three individuals. Part (1) involves a little more explanation so we will leave it for last.

Part (2) is Maskin Monotonicity. If an alternative is to be excluded from the social choice correspondence under one environment, it must be the case that it has fallen in the ranking of one of the individuals.

Part (3) is a less restrictive form of No Veto Power. This property says that for any environment, alternative pair and a set of unilateral deviations from this pair, if another alternative under a different profile is maximal for an individual from this set then this alternative should be specified by the social choice correspondence under the latter environment as long as the second alternative is also maximal for the other agent over the whole range of F.

Part (4) is the unanimity condition. If there are some alternatives that are in both individuals' maximal sets, a social choice correspondence should select these alternatives.

It remains to explain (1), which is unique to two-person Nash implementation theory. Part 1(a) is a self-selection condition. It employs the sets $C_1(a, \theta)$ and $C_2(b, \theta')$. $C_1(a, \theta)$ is a set of alternatives that agent 1 considers no better than a in environment θ, and $C_2(b, \theta')$ is a set of alternatives that agent 2 considers no better than b in environment θ'. To really get an idea what these sets are, we look at an example, taken from (Dutta and Sen, 1991, page 123).

Let F be some social choice correspondence that is Nash implementable. We can represent any mechanism in a tabular form, since there are only two agents. We choose to represent a mechanism that Nash implements F. We let the rows correspond to the messages of agent 1, drawn from the set M_1, and the columns correspond to the messages of agent 2, from M_2. The cells of the table contain the outcomes of the mechanism. So in our example table below, $g(m_{11}, m_{21}) = a$ and $g(m_{12}, m_{22}) = b$. Cells with outcomes that we do not want to specify exactly, as we do not need them for our explanation, contain asterisks. The ellipses in the end of the top row and the first column are there to indicate that there are possibly many more messages available to the agents. Incomplete as it is, this table suffices for our purpose.

	m_{21}	m_{22}	$\cdots$
m_{11}	a	$*$	$*$
m_{12}	x	b	$*$
$\vdots$	$*$	$*$	$*$

Suppose we have chosen the order in which we wrote the messages in the table so that (m_{11}, m_{21}) is a Nash equilibrium of the mechanism for preference profile θ and (m_{12}, m_{22}) is a Nash equilibrium of the mechanism for preference profile θ'. Because F is implemented in Nash equilibrium by the mechanism, we must have $a \in F(\theta)$ and $b \in F(\theta')$. Let $C_1(a, \theta)$ be the set of alternatives that agent 1 can obtain by playing any of his messages when agent 2 plays m_{21}. Let $C_2(a, \theta)$ be the set of alternatives that agent 2 can obtain by playing any of her messages when agent 1 plays m_{11}. In the table, $C_1(a, \theta)$ is the set of outcomes in the m_{21} column and $C_2(a, \theta)$ is the set of outcomes in the m_{11} row.

Because (m_{11}, m_{21}) is a Nash equilibrium of the mechanism for preference profile θ, $C_1(a, \theta) \subseteq L_1(a, \theta)$ and $C_2(a, \theta) \subseteq L_2(a, \theta)$, otherwise at least one agent would have a profitable deviation from (m_{11}, m_{21}) in profile θ. Proceeding the same way for the m_{12} row and the m_{22} column, we must have $C_1(b, \theta') \subseteq L_1(b, \theta')$ and $C_2(b, \theta') \subseteq L_2(b, \theta')$. Now the outcome that corresponds to (m_{12}, m_{21}), shown as x in the m_{12} row and the m_{21} column, belongs to the intersection of $C_1(a, \theta)$ and $C_2(b, \theta')$, which therefore is not empty, as required by condition 1(a).

Now suppose that x is maximal for agent 1 in the set $C_1(a, \theta)$ and maximal for agent 2 in the set $C_2(b, \theta')$ for some third preference profile $\bar{\theta}$. Because of this double maximality, x must be a Nash equilibrium outcome of the mechanism in preference profile $\bar{\theta}$. By the Nash implementability of F, it follows that $x \in F(\bar{\theta})$, which shows the rationale for condition 1(b).

We now state the main result of Dutta and Sen (1991).

Theorem 3.3 (Dutta and Sen [1991]). *If there are two individuals, a social choice correspondence is implementable in Nash equilibrium if and only if it satisfies condition* β.

The proof of this theorem uses a form of the canonical mechanism. The main difference is that the message space for each agent is enlarged to include the option to raise a flag. Formally, the message space for individual i is $M_i = \{(a^i, \theta^i, k^i, r^i) \in \mathcal{A} \times \Theta \times \mathbb{N} \times \{F, NF\} | a^i \in F(\theta)\}$. The set $\{F, NF\}$ is a strategy choice for the individual to either raise a flag or no flag.

The mechanism takes these announcements and prescribes the following.

1. If $m_1 = m_2 = (a, \theta, k^i, NF)$ then the outcome is a.

2. If the agents announce different alternatives and profiles (and neither raises a flag), then the outcome will be that x as specified by condition (1b) of Condition β.

3. If the agents announce a different alternative and profile and one person raises a flag, the individual who raised the flag chooses an alternative to which he can unilaterally deviate given the other agent's message.

4. If the agents announce differently and raise a flag, then the agent who announced the highest integer chooses any alternative from the range of F with ties going to agent 1.

The complete proof follows along the same lines as the necessary and sufficient conditions for the many person case. It can be found in Dutta and Sen (1991).

Dutta and Sen (1991) noted in their footnote 3 that this mechanism was not completely specified. It leaves open the alternative that an individual chooses if Rule 3 or Rule 4 is invoked. Busetto and Codognato (2009) take up this issue and formulate a mechanism that has individuals specify an alternative selection rather than raising a flag. In the Busetto and Codognato (2009) mechanism, individuals effectively raise a flag by announcing an integer greater than 0. In this way, the strategy space remains a 4-tuple and is completely specified.

3.4 Exercises

Exercise 19: Mixed Strategy Nash Equilibria

Bill and Steve are deciding when to debut their companies' new high tech phones. Bill's costs are lower but Steve's phone has better quality. There are two main trade shows in which they can debut their new phones. The cost to debut at the first show is higher than the second. If one debuts first, he can capture more of the market. If both debut at the first show, their products get confused and they split market share such that they cannot recoup the higher cost of the first show. If Steve debuts first and Bill second, Bill's phone will be seen as an inferior copycat and he will not recoup his costs. If Bill debuts first he will capture market share before the better phone is introduced. If they both debut at the second show they will split market share, but they will also not incur the higher cost of the first show. Given the payoff structure below answer the following questions. (Steve's payoffs are listed first. Bill's payoffs are listed second in table 3.2.)

Steve\ Bill	Show 1	Show 2
Show 1	$-2,-1$	$+4,-2$
Show 2	$+2,+4$	$0,+6$

Table 3.2: Technology Debut Game

1. What is Steve's best response to each of Bill's strategies?
2. Does a Nash equilibrium exist in pure strategies?
3. What are the mixed strategy Nash equilibria?

Exercise 20: Pareto Correspondence

1. Assume that in an exchange economy there are two agents with strictly monotonic preferences. Prove that the Pareto correspondence is Maskin monotonic.
2. Now assume that agent one can have weakly monotonic preferences, such as $R^1(\tilde{\theta}_1)$ in figure 3.3, your diagrammatic hint. The preferences shown by $R^1(\theta_1)$ and $R^2(\theta_2)$ have parallel indifference curves and are strictly monotonic. The preferences corresponding to $R^1(\tilde{\theta}_1)$ also have parallel indifference curves; they express the fact that type $\tilde{\theta}_1$ of agent 1 does not care at all to consume the good measured vertically, but has monotonic preferences with respect to the other good. Prove that the Pareto correspondence is not Maskin Monotonic. You will need to consider whether a point such as z is Pareto efficient in environment (θ_1, θ_2) and in environment $(\tilde{\theta}_1, \theta_2)$, and you will need to combine your conclusion about this with the formal statement of Maskin Monotonicity. See Thomson (1999b) for more details and the answer. See figure 3.3 for a hint.

Exercise 21: Electoral Voting Rules

Many electoral voting rules are not Maskin Monotonic. Show by example that each of the following may not be Maskin Monotonic. See Austen-Smith and Banks (2005, page 84) for examples.

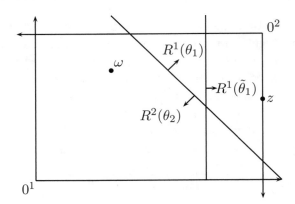

Figure 3.3: Hint for Exercise 20

1. The plurality rule: the alternative with the most votes wins.

2. The Borda count as described in chapter 1, example 1.1.

Exercise 22: Constrained Walrasian Social Choice Correspondence

Show that the Constrained Walrasian Social Choice Correspondence is Maskin monotonic. Note that according to the Constrained Walrasian Social Choice Correspondence, every agent maximizes with respect to both his budget constraint and the availability of resources.

Exercise 23: Walrasian Correspondence with Cobb-Douglas Preferences

Assume that only preferences representable by utility functions of the kind $u_i(x_1, x_2) = x_1^a x_2^b$, for some positive parameters a, b, are allowed. Show that the Walrasian social choice correspondence is Maskin Monotonic for exchange economies with this restriction on preferences. (See Thomson (1999b).)

Chapter 4

Bayesian Equilibrium and Mechanisms: Some Information Assumed

4.1 Preliminary: How to Represent Information

In chapter 2 we did not rely on agents knowing anything about the others' types, which were truly private information. The whole idea behind dominant strategies is that a player in a game can figure out her dominant strategies without the need to know anything about the other players. In chapter 3, on the other hand, we assumed that each agent knew the others' types, so the types of the agents were private information only with relation to the central authority, which did not know them. Here we will make the intermediate assumption that agents who participate in a mechanism know something about the others, but not everything.

We start with a standard information representation device. Let S be a set of states of nature. A **state of nature** describes exactly all payoff-relevant details of the world.

One mathematical definition is needed before we start. Given any set A, a **partition of** A is a collection of sets, called **cells of the partition,** $\{P_1, P_2, \ldots, P_k\}$ for some positive integer k such that for any i, $P_i \neq \emptyset$ and $P_i \subseteq A$, and for every $i \neq j$, $P_i \cap P_j = \emptyset$. In words, a partition chops up the set into non-overlapping pieces that, when taken all together, cover the whole set.

We represent an agent's information by a partition of the set of states, called an **information partition**. The agent has this partition in mind before the state is realized. When the state is realized, the agent learns which set in her partition contains the state. This is a flexible and powerful setup. It can handle situations from complete knowledge to complete ignorance, with many gradations in between.

Suppose the agent has exact knowledge of the state of the world. We represent this by the information partition $\{\{s_1\}, \{s_2\}, \ldots, \{s_n\}\}$, which is the finest information partition possible. For a partition made up of singleton cells (sets that have one member each), this simply says that for every state of nature the agent knows the state.

On the other hand, suppose the agent does not know anything about what state of nature is true; we represent this by the coarsest information partition possible—$\{S\}$. In this case, the only cell in the partition is the set of states itself, which means that the agent learns nothing new when informed which set of the partition contains the realized state.

Intermediate situations are possible and quite useful. An agent might have some information about the state of nature but not complete information. For example, suppose there are four states of nature: s_1 means "it is cold and raining outside," s_2 means "it is warm and raining outside," s_3 means "it is cold and dry outside," and s_4 means "it is warm and dry outside." An agent who is inside a building and can get information about the weather outside only by looking through a window has the information partition $\{\{s_1, s_2\}, \{s_3, s_4\}\}$. An agent who is inside a building without windows but with a digital readout of an outside thermometer has the information partition $\{\{s_1, s_3\}, \{s_2, s_4\}\}$.

In game theory, the state of nature describes the characteristics of the players and of the game. John Harsanyi showed in a monumental series of three articles (Harsanyi [1967; 1968a; 1968b]) that all the uncertainty about a game with incomplete information can be reduced to a construction in which we imagine that each player has a set of types. These types reflect the agent's characteristics, the agent's beliefs about the characteristics of the other agents, the agent's beliefs about the beliefs of the other agents, and so on. It can be shown, amazing as it is, that a finite (but probably quite huge) set of types suffices to approximate the original setup of states of nature and the cascade of beliefs about beliefs. However, having said this, we will from now on ignore this conceptual foundation of types and simply take the type sets of the agents as given. (For more on this topic, you can start by reading Bergemann and Morris [2005], Heifetz and Neeman [2006] and then following up on their citations.)

The next preliminary is Bayesian updating. Suppose that an agent has an information partition and has assigned probabilities to each state in the set of states of nature. This probability distribution is called the agent's **prior**. This agent is then able to express a probability for each event that is either a cell in her partition or a union of cells in her partition. Denote the prior by $q \colon S \to [0, 1]$. The interpretation of the prior is that for each state s from S, $q(s)$ is the probability that the agent thinks the state will occur before the agent learns which cell of her information partition contains the realized state.

Now imagine that the state of nature is realized and the agent receives a signal that tells her to which cell of her information partition the true state belongs; denote this cell by E, standing for "event", and note that, by definition of partition, $E \subseteq S$. The prior probability of an event E is $\sum_{t \in E} q(t)$. Now the agent knows more than before, so she can update her probability distribution to a new one that is called the **posterior**. Here is the definition of the posterior, for any $s \in E$:

$$q(s|E) = \frac{q(s)}{\sum_{t \in E} q(t)}. \tag{4.1}$$

For any $s \notin E$, we set $q(s|E) = 0$. (We are assuming that $q(t) > 0$ for some $t \in E$, so that the prior probability of the event E is positive.) This formula says that, once we know that a cell E in the information partition contains the realized state, then (i) for every state in E, its probability is now best estimated by the ratio of its prior probability to the prior probability of all the states in E, and (ii) for every state not in E, its probability is now best estimated as zero.

Example 4.1. Recall the weather example in which there are four states of nature: s_1 means "it is cold and raining outside," s_2 means "it is warm and raining outside," s_3 means "it is cold and dry outside," and s_4 means "it is warm and dry outside." Suppose that the information partition of the agent is the one from looking out of the window, $\{\{s_1, s_2\}, \{s_3, s_4\}\}$. Suppose that the prior is given by $q(s_1) = 0.1$, $q(s_2) = 0.3$, $q(s_3) = 0.05$, and $q(s_4) = 0.55$. If the agent learns that it is dry outside by looking out of the window, this means that the cell $\{s_3, s_4\}$ contains the true state and plays the role of E in our general notation above. Hence the agent's posterior is given by $q(s_1|E) = 0$, $q(s_2|E) = 0$, $q(s_3|E) = 0.05/(0.05 + 0.55) = 0.05/0.6 = 1/12$, and $q(s_4|E) = 0.55/0.6 = 11/12$. ◇

4.2 Bayesian Equilibrium

Harsanyi's contribution to the theory of games of incomplete information was deep. Its central insight was the transformation of a game with incomplete information into a game of imperfect information that can then be solved with the standard technique of Nash equilibrium, which we studied in chapter 3. For the resulting Bayesian equilibrium concept of Harsanyi, we need to define information sets for agents, the beliefs of each agent about his information and the actions he can take. Given all these, we can study the strategic behavior of the agents when they do not have perfect information.

Our job is going to require some notation to describe what agents know. As before, let the agents in the set $\mathcal{I} = \{1, 2, \ldots, I\}$ constitute the society under study. Each agent i among them has a set of possible types Θ_i, which we assume to be finite. We could think of these types as being the potential personalities of these agents, personalities which include the agents' preferences. The state in this society, in the sense of s in the previous section, is the profile $\theta = (\theta_1, \theta_2, \ldots, \theta_I)$ of the types of all agents. As before, it will be often handy to write θ as (θ_i, θ_{-i}), where θ_{-i} stands for the list of types of all agents except agent i. We will also write Θ for the Cartesian product $\Theta_1 \times \Theta_2 \times \cdots \times \Theta_I$, which has elements of the form $\theta = (\theta_1, \theta_2, \ldots, \theta_I)$.

We assume that there is a common prior q that every agent has. For every profile of types θ, the prior gives the probability $q(\theta)$ of this profile actually being the one in the population. We also assume that for every θ we have $q(\theta) > 0$; in words, every profile of types has a positive probability (possibly very small, but never zero) of occurring. By the time that any agent i comes to play the game, she knows her type θ_i but does not know the types of the others. It follows that agent i has an information partition containing one cell per possible type θ_i of the agent; every cell of this partition has the form $\{(\theta_i, \theta_{-i}), (\theta_i, \theta'_{-i}), (\theta_i, \theta''_{-i}), \ldots\}$, where we keep θ_i the same and vary θ_{-i} over all possibilities. Since θ_i uniquely determines the cell of i's partition that occurs, we can use θ_i also as a name for the cell of the partition, thereby avoiding the need to carry around E notation as in the previous section.

Given type θ_i that the agent knows about herself, she has posterior probability $q(\theta_{-i}|\theta_i) = q(\theta_i, \theta_{-i}) / [\sum_{\theta'_{-i}} q(\theta_i, \theta'_{-i})]$. The sum in the denominator ranges over all possible combinations of the agents other than agent i. This is once again simply the conditional probability of a particular combination of the others' types given one's own type.

Example 4.2. Andy and Bess are wondering how an arm-wrestling match between them will turn out. Each has two possible types, Strong and Weak, so θ_A and θ_B can each take the values S, W. The state space is $\{(S, S), (W, S), (S, W), (W, W)\}$ where we write types in the order (θ_A, θ_B). The common prior is $q(S, S) = 0.2$, $q(W, S) = 0.15$, $q(S, W) = 0.25$, $q(W, W) = 0.4$. Suppose that in fact Andy has type W and Bess has type S. Then their posteriors are as follows. For Andy, we have $q(\theta_B = S|\theta_A = W) = q(W, S)/[q(W, S) + q(W, W)] = 0.15/0.55 = 3/11$ and $q(\theta_B = W|\theta_A = W) = q(W, W)/[q(W, S) + q(W, W)] = 0.4/0.55 = 8/11$. For Bess, $q(\theta_A = S|\theta_B = S) = q(S, S)/[q(S, S) + q(W, S)] = 0.2/0.35 = 4/7$ and $q(\theta_A = W|\theta_B = S) = q(W, S)/[q(S, S) + q(W, S)] = 0.15/0.35 = 3/7$.   ◇

To complete the game description, denote by M_i each agent's set of actions and assume it is finite. A list of actions then takes the form $m = (m_1, m_2, \ldots, m_I)$, where m_1 is taken from M_1, m_2 from M_2, and so on. Agent i's payoff is measured by a utility function $u_i : M \times \Theta \to \mathbb{R}$ which has the expected utility property (see page 19) and takes the value $u_i(m, \theta)$ when the list of actions is $m = (m_1, m_2, \ldots, m_I)$ and the state is $\theta = (\theta_1, \theta_2, \ldots, \theta_I)$. Note the generality of this formulation: the agent's utility depends on the actions and the types of all agents. In many applications it is reasonable to restrict the utility to depend only on m and θ_i, in which case it is $u_i(m, \theta_i)$.

To describe the strategy of an agent in such a game, we imagine the agent thinking about how to play the game before she knows her type. In this situation, she has to make plans on what action to take for every possible type with which she may be "incarnated" into the game when agents learn their types. We define a **strategy** for player i as a function $\sigma_i : \Theta_i \to M_i$. The idea is that the agent makes a comprehensive plan of action that anticipates each possible type θ_i the agent can be and chooses an action $m_i = \sigma_i(\theta_i)$ to play if this type is realized. (It is possible to imagine the players planning to choose actions randomly, which is to say, to play mixed strategies. We will not investigate this possibility for Bayesian games here.)

How will the agents choose among the many strategies they have available? We model this choice by imagining that each agent takes the other agents' strategies as given and plays a strategy that will maximize her own conditionally expected utility for every possible type she can be. The **conditionally expected utility** for type θ_i is given by the expression

$$U_i(\sigma_i, \sigma_{-i}) \equiv \sum_{\theta_{-i} \in \Theta_{-i}} q(\theta_{-i}|\theta_i) u_i((\sigma_i(\theta_i), \sigma_{-i}(\theta_{-i})), \theta). \tag{4.2}$$

In this expression we have employed some shortcut notation: $\sigma_{-i}(\theta_{-i})$ stands for the list of all the actions played by the other agents according to their types, in other words, it stands for $(\sigma_1(\theta_1), \ldots, \sigma_{i-1}(\theta_{i-1}), \sigma_{i+1}(\theta_{i+1}), \ldots, \sigma_I(\theta_I))$. A similar shortcut is σ_{-i}, which stands for the list of strategies (the functions as opposed to their particular values depending on the types) $(\sigma_1, \ldots, \sigma_{i-1}, \sigma_{i+1}, \ldots, \sigma_I)$.

Example 4.3. Recall Andy and Bess. Assume each has two possible actions: C, for "challenge" and G, for "give in". Regarding utilities, assume that for each one of them (i either A or B), and writing i's variable always before that of $-i$'s, $u_i(C, C, (S, S)) = 1$, $u_i(C, G, (S, S)) = 3$, $u_i(G, C, (S, S)) = -1$, $u_i(G, G, (S, S)) = 1$, $u_i(C, C, (S, W)) = 4$, $u_i(C, G, (S, W)) = 2$, $u_i(G, C, (S, W)) = -3$, $u_i(G, G, (S, W)) = -1$, $u_i(C, C, (W, S)) = -2$, $u_i(C, G, (W, S)) = 5$, $u_i(G, C, (W, S)) = 2$, $u_i(G, G, (W, S)) = 0$, $u_i(C, C, (W, W)) = 0$, $u_i(C, G, (W, W)) = 4$, $u_i(G, C, (W, W)) = -2$, and finally $u_i(G, G, (W, W)) = 0$.
To interpret these numbers, take for instance $u_i(C, G, (S, W)) = 2$: it says that if a player plays C while the other plays G and the first player is a Strong type while the second is a Weak type, then the first player receives utility of 2. Note that we assumed that both Andy and Bess have the same utility functions; otherwise we would have had to specify twelve numbers for Andy and twelve for Bess. Assume that Andy's strategy is $\sigma_A(S) = C$ and $\sigma_A(W) = G$ and that Bess's strategy is $\sigma_B(S) = C$ and $\sigma_B(W) = C$. Now imagine that the state is realized as (W, S). Andy learns that he is a Weak type and Bess that she is a Strong type in this case. The conditionally expected utility for Andy is then

$$
\begin{aligned}
U_A(\sigma_A, \sigma_B) &= \sum_{\theta_B \in \Theta_B} q(\theta_B|\theta_A = W) u_A((\sigma_A(\theta_A = W), \sigma_B(\theta_B)), (\theta_A = W, \theta_B)) \\
&= q(S|W) u_A(\sigma_A(W), \sigma_B(S), (W, S)) + q(W|W) u_A(\sigma_A(W), \sigma_B(W), (W, W)) \\
&= \frac{3}{11} u_A(G, C, (W, S)) + \frac{8}{11} u_A(G, C, (W, W)) \\
&= \frac{3}{11} \times 2 + \frac{8}{11} \times (-2) = -\frac{10}{11}.
\end{aligned}
$$

Calculating Bess's conditionally expected utility is similarly tedious but straightforward. All possible combinations of types and strategies can be considered and the resulting expected utilities can be calculated in this fashion. ◇

With the above concepts in hand, we are ready to define Bayesian equilibrium. The basic idea behind this notion of equilibrium is that every agent has a complete plan for playing the game (a strategy), whichever type she will be when the game begins, and the plan is calculated to yield the highest possible conditionally expected utility, taking the strategies of all other agents as given.

Definition 4.1 (Bayesian Equilibrium). A **Bayesian equilibrium** of the game we have defined in this section is a list of strategies $\sigma = (\sigma_1, \sigma_2, \ldots, \sigma_I)$ such that for each agent i, each message m_i in M_i, and each type θ_i in Θ_i, we have

$$\sum_{\theta_{-i} \in \Theta_{-i}} q(\theta_{-i}|\theta_i) u_i((\sigma_i(\theta_i), \sigma_{-i}(\theta_{-i})), \theta) \geq \sum_{\theta_{-i} \in \Theta_{-i}} q(\theta_{-i}|\theta_i) u_i((m_i, \sigma_{-i}(\theta_{-i})), \theta).$$

In this definition, each type θ_i of each agent i calculates the expected utility, given her type and what the other players are playing, of following the recommendation of the strategy, which is to play $\sigma_i(\theta_i)$. She then compares it to the expected utility of playing any other action m_i. For $\sigma_i(\theta_i)$ to be the best thing to play, it has to yield the highest expected utility, which the definition ensures. You will get some practice in finding Bayesian equilibria in the exercises, where we will revisit the story of Andy and Bess.

4.3 The Bayesian Revelation Principle

We turn now to the revelation principle in the context of Bayesian equilibrium; this section and the next are based on Jackson (2003). We will also discuss a classic example of an incentive compatible mechanism that achieves budget balance, something that the Groves class of mechanisms we saw in section 2.4 fails to do. We assume in the rest of this chapter that the domain of social choice is split into two parts, as in our discussion of the Groves mechanisms. Recall that in this domain, a social choice function has two parts, d, t, where d is a collective choice item and t is a system of monetary transfers to the agents. Both are functions of the profile of types of the agents, θ.

Suppose that we endow each agent i with a message space M_i. In the previous subsection M_i was a set of unspecified actions. Here we interpret these actions as messages that the agents send to a central authority. Once everyone's message is received, resulting in a message list $m = (m_1, m_2, \ldots, m_I)$, then the central authority puts in place the choice $g(m) = (g_d(m), g_t(m))$, where the outcome function g is known to the agents in advance. Imagine that m is the list of messages sent. Each agent i evaluates the outcome by means of the quasilinear utility function $u_i(m, g_{t_i}(m), \theta_i) = v_i(g_d(m), \theta_i) + g_{t_i}(m)$. Note that we are assuming that each agent's utility depends on her own type θ_i but not on the others' types, and that utility functions are all quasilinear. These assumptions narrow down our domain significantly and produce many insights into mechanism design, some of which we present in the remainder of this chapter.

Earlier we looked for mechanisms in which each agent had a dominant strategy, so that the agent did not need to know anything about the other agents in order to play this strategy. Here we have set up a model of incomplete information and we assume that the agents will play strategies that constitute a Bayesian equilibrium.

When engaged in a mechanism (M, g), the agents' strategies are functions of their types; the definition of Bayesian equilibrium applies as before, except we now write the strategies as $m_i : \Theta_i \to M_i$ functions, to remind ourselves that they are choices of messages, and we write the utility functions in the quasilinear form.

Definition 4.2 (Bayesian Equilibrium of a Mechanism). A list of strategies $m = (m_1, m_2, \ldots, m_I)$ is a **Bayesian equilibrium** of the mechanism (M, g) if the following is true for each $i \in \mathcal{I}$, each $\theta_i \in \Theta_i$, and each $\widehat{m}_i \in M_i$:

$$\sum_{\theta_{-i} \in \Theta_{-i}} q(\theta_{-i}|\theta_i) \left[v_i(g_d(m_i(\theta_i), m_{-i}(\theta_{-i})), \theta_i) + g_{t_i}(m_i(\theta_i), m_{-i}(\theta_{-i})) \right] \geq$$

$$\sum_{\theta_{-i} \in \Theta_{-i}} q(\theta_{-i}|\theta_i) \left[v_i(g_d(\widehat{m}_i, m_{-i}(\theta_{-i})), \theta_i) + g_{t_i}(\widehat{m}_i, m_{-i}(\theta_{-i})) \right].$$

The left-hand side of this inequality is the conditionally expected utility of type θ_i of agent i from playing the message $m_i(\theta_i)$ recommended by the equilibrium strategy m_i. The right-hand side is the conditionally expected utility of type θ_i of agent i from playing some other message $\widehat{m}_i$ instead. The definition requires the former to never be less than the latter. Note that we have given the definition of Bayesian equilibrium for a mechanism only for the quasilinear case, but extending it to the general case, to match definition 4.1 is easy (try it).

The definition of a mechanism (M, g) allows a great variety of possible strategy spaces, and as in chapter 2 we could use a method of learning something useful for great batches of mechanisms at once. Fortunately, a version of the revelation principle also works with Bayesian equilibrium.

A direct mechanism sets the message space M_i for each agent equal to Θ_i, so that the agent can only send an announcement of her type, and sets g equal to a social choice function (d, t).

Definition 4.3 (Bayesian Incentive Compatible Mechanism). A direct mechanism $f = (d, t)$ is **Bayesian incentive compatible** if truthful submission of θ_i by each player is a Bayesian equilibrium. This can also be expressed as the requirement that for all $i \in \mathcal{I}$ and all $\theta_i, \theta_i' \in \Theta_i$, we have:

$$\sum_{\theta_{-i} \in \Theta_{-i}} q(\theta_{-i}|\theta_i) \left[v_i(d(\theta_i, \theta_{-i}), \theta_i) + t_i(\theta_i, \theta_{-i}) \right] \geq$$

$$\sum_{\theta_{-i} \in \Theta_{-i}} q(\theta_{-i}|\theta_i) \left[v_i(d(\theta_i', \theta_{-i}), \theta_i) + t_i(\theta_i', \theta_{-i}) \right].$$

Here we think of θ_i as the true type of agent i and θ_i' as an untruthful report of this type. The definition requires that each type of each agent cannot gain by lying about her type. The definition therefore ensures that truthful revelation is a Bayesian equilibrium of the direct mechanism. It does not ensure that other Bayesian equilibria of the same direct mechanism do not exist, but this is a topic we revisit later.

Definition 4.4. A mechanism (M, g) **realizes** a social choice function $f = (d, t)$ in Bayesian equilibrium if there is a Bayesian equilibrium μ of (M, g) such that, for all $\theta \in \Theta$, $g(\mu(\theta)) = f(\theta)$.

This says that *one* Bayesian equilibrium of the mechanism must exist that yields the outcome that fits with the social choice function, but other Bayesian equilibria might also exist, and they might yield different outcomes.

We are now ready for the Revelation Principle.

Theorem 4.1 (Revelation Principle for Bayesian Equilibrium). *Let a mechanism (M, g) realize a social choice function $f = (d, t)$ in Bayesian equilibrium. Then the direct mechanism f is Bayesian incentive compatible.*

Proving this is as easy as it was in chapter 2 for dominant strategies, except it requires a bit more notation, so the proof is left as an exercise.

The revelation principle tells us that every social choice function that is realized in Bayesian equilibrium is Bayesian incentive compatible. Therefore, a search for all social choice functions that can be realized in Bayesian equilibrium can be confined to the class of Bayesian incentive compatible social choice functions. This class of social choice functions is reasonably easy to analyze. In particular, it is not too hard to check if a given social choice function is Bayesian incentive compatible by going through the definition of Bayesian incentive compatibility for every agent and every type (although it can be tedious to do so).

4.4 The Mechanism of d'Aspremont and Gérard-Varet and of Arrow

Recall from chapter 2 that a decision rule d is efficient if for all $\theta \in \Theta$ and for all $d' \in D$,

$$\sum_{i=1}^{I} v_i(d(\theta), \theta_i) \geq \sum_{i=1}^{I} v_i(d', \theta_i).$$

This definition takes the *ex post* perspective, that is, it demands that the social surplus be maximized *after* the true type profile has been revealed. (Compare with *ex post voluntary participation* in subsection 4.4.1.) Efficient allocations are important because they leave no unexploited opportunities to improve welfare. Can we realize this decision rule in Bayesian equilibrium? We will need to be inventive in our choice of the transfer scheme t that accompanies d to complete the social choice function $f = (d, t)$, just as we needed to be inventive with the transfer schemes of the Groves mechanisms that we saw in section 2.4. Such inventiveness was demonstrated independently by d'Aspremont and Gérard-Varet (1979) and Arrow (1979).

To describe the transfer function briefly, we will use shorthand notation for the expectation conditional on θ_i. This notation uses $\mathbb{E}_{\overline{\theta}_{-i}}[h(\theta) \mid \theta_i]$ for the conditional expectation of any function h of the θ variables, given θ_i. For example, instead of

$$\sum_{\theta_{-i} \in \Theta_{-i}} q(\theta_{-i}|\theta_i) \left[v_i(d(\theta_i, \theta_{-i}), \theta_i) + t_i(\theta_i, \theta_{-i})\right], \quad \text{we write}$$

$$\mathbb{E}_{\overline{\theta}_{-i}}\left[v_i(d(\theta_i, \overline{\theta}_{-i}), \theta_i) + t_i(\theta_i, \overline{\theta}_{-i}) \mid \theta_i\right].$$

One new wrinkle is the bar over θ_{-i}. It is there to remind us that $\overline{\theta}_{-i}$ is the random variable vector of the types of all agents other than i, over which the expectation is being taken.

The transfer to agent i that was developed by d'Aspremont and Gérard-Varet (1979) and Arrow (1979) is the following.

$$t_i(\theta) = \mathbb{E}_{\overline{\theta}_{-i}}\left[\sum_{j \neq i} v_j(d(\overline{\theta}), \overline{\theta}_j) \mid \theta_i\right] - \frac{1}{I-1}\sum_{k \neq i} \mathbb{E}_{\overline{\theta}_{-i}}\left[\sum_{j \neq k} v_j(d(\overline{\theta}), \overline{\theta}_j) \mid \theta_k\right]. \quad (4.3)$$

The first sum is the total value of the social decision, as determined by all agents' types, for all agents except i. From this we subtract the average of the same sums for everybody else. So this formula says to pay agent i the expected value the other agents get, but then to have agent i pay back the average of the expected payments to all other agents based on the same idea.

As the next theorem shows, if the types of the agents are statistically independent of each other this transfer function achieves two things: (i) it ensures incentive compatibility and (ii) is balanced. Recall that a transfer system t is called balanced if for all θ the total payments are zero: $\sum_i t_i(\theta) = 0$.

Theorem 4.2. *If for each i the random variables $\overline{\theta}_i$ and $\overline{\theta}_{-i}$ are statistically independent, the decision rule d is efficient, and $t = (t_1, t_2, \ldots, t_I)$ is given by equation (4.3), then $f = (d, t)$ is Bayesian incentive compatible and t is balanced.*

Proof. First we prove that the transfer system is balanced. Adding up all $t_i(\theta)$ we find:

$$\sum_i t_i(\theta) = \sum_i \mathbb{E}_{\overline{\theta}_{-i}}\left[\sum_{j\neq i} v_j(d(\overline{\theta}),\overline{\theta}_j) \mid \theta_i\right] - \frac{1}{I-1}\sum_i \sum_{k\neq i} \mathbb{E}_{\overline{\theta}_{-i}}\left[\sum_{j\neq k} v_j(d(\overline{\theta}),\overline{\theta}_j) \mid \theta_k\right]$$

$$= \sum_i \mathbb{E}_{\overline{\theta}_{-i}}\left[\sum_{j\neq i} v_j(d(\overline{\theta}),\overline{\theta}_j) \mid \theta_i\right] - \frac{1}{I-1}\sum_i (I-1)\mathbb{E}_{\overline{\theta}_{-i}}\left[\sum_{j\neq i} v_j(d(\overline{\theta}),\overline{\theta}_j) \mid \theta_i\right]$$

$$= \sum_i \mathbb{E}_{\overline{\theta}_{-i}}\left[\sum_{j\neq i} v_j(d(\overline{\theta}),\overline{\theta}_j) \mid \theta_i\right] - \sum_i \mathbb{E}_{\overline{\theta}_{-i}}\left[\sum_{j\neq i} v_j(d(\overline{\theta}),\overline{\theta}_j) \mid \theta_i\right]$$

$$= 0.$$

The reason for the step to the second equation is that the sum being subtracted consists of the sum, done repeatedly for every agent i, $\mathbb{E}_{\overline{\theta}_{-i}}\left[\sum_{j\neq i} v_j(d(\overline{\theta}),\overline{\theta}_j) \mid \theta_i\right]$. Adding these sums for all agents, we see that every $\mathbb{E}_{\overline{\theta}_{-i}}\left[\sum_{j\neq i} v_j(d(\overline{\theta}),\overline{\theta}_j) \mid \theta_i\right]$ term appears $I-1$ times.

Now we prove that (d,t) is Bayesian incentive-compatible. For each agent i and each type θ_i of i, the conditionally expected utility from submitting some report θ_i' (true or not) is

$$\mathbb{E}_{\overline{\theta}_{-i}}\left[v_i(d(\theta_i',\overline{\theta}_{-i}),\theta_i) + t_i(\theta_i',\overline{\theta}_{-i}) \mid \theta_i\right] =$$

$$\mathbb{E}_{\overline{\theta}_{-i}}\left[v_i(d(\theta_i',\overline{\theta}_{-i}),\theta_i) \mid \theta_i\right] + \mathbb{E}_{\overline{\theta}_{-i}}\left[\sum_{j\neq i} v_j(d(\overline{\theta}),\overline{\theta}_j) \mid \theta_i'\right]$$

$$- \frac{1}{I-1}\sum_{k\neq i}\mathbb{E}_{\overline{\theta}_{-i}}\left[\mathbb{E}_{\overline{\theta}_{-i}}\left[\sum_{j\neq k} v_j(d(\overline{\theta}),\overline{\theta}_j) \mid \overline{\theta}_k\right] \mid \theta_i\right].$$

Because of the statistical independence assumption, the second term on the right might as well be conditioned on θ_i rather than θ_i', with a corresponding change from θ_i to θ_i' inside the v_j functions, and the double conditional expectation in the third term is redundant. Therefore the conditional expected utility of reporting θ_i' becomes

$$\mathbb{E}_{\overline{\theta}_{-i}}\left[v_i(d(\theta_i',\overline{\theta}_{-i}),\theta_i) + \sum_{j\neq i} v_j(d(\theta_i',\overline{\theta}_{-i}),\overline{\theta}_j) \mid \theta_i\right] - \frac{1}{I-1}\sum_{k\neq i}\mathbb{E}_{\overline{\theta}_{-i}}\left[\sum_{j\neq k} v_j(d(\overline{\theta}),\overline{\theta}_j)\right].$$

The second term of this expression is independent of θ_i' and therefore can be ignored, since the problem is to maximize this expression by choice of θ_i'. But the first term is maximized when $\theta_i' = \theta_i$, because this choice maximizes the expression

$$v_i(d(\theta_i', \theta_{-i}), \theta_i) + \sum_{j \neq i} v_j(d(\theta_i', \theta_{-i}), \theta_j) = \sum_{i=1}^{I} v_i(d(\theta_i', \theta_{-i}), \theta_i),$$

for every θ_i, θ_{-i}, since d is by assumption efficient.   QED

4.4.1 Voluntary Participation

A mechanism typically specifies penalties for some agents when certain strategy profiles are played. What makes agents want to participate? In the economics literature "individual rationality" means that each agent would rather participate in the play of the mechanism than take his endowment and leave the mechanism. As a term for this, individual rationality is not the best. A much better term is voluntary participation, which we already used in chapter 2 and continue to use here.

To investigate voluntary participation we need first to ask at which point in time agents declare their willingness to participate in the mechanism. Three points in time suggest themselves: (i) before the agents know anything about their types (*ex ante* point of view), (ii) after each agent learns his type but before the mechanism has been run, (*interim* point of view) and (iii) after each agent learns his type and the mechanism has been run (*ex post* point of view).

We have already encountered voluntary participation in chapter 2. We continue from there, recalling that we first normalize the utility functions of the agents so that not participating in the mechanism yields utility zero. In order to start with a familiar notion, we discuss ex post voluntary participation first.

Definition 4.5 (*Ex Post* Voluntary Participation). Ex post voluntary participation requires that after the agents have learned their private information and the mechanism has been run, no agent wishes to leave. In formal terms, for all $\theta = (\theta_1, \dots, \theta_I) \in \Theta$ and for all $i \in \mathcal{I}$, we must have

$$v_i(d(\theta), \theta_i) + t_i(\theta) \geq 0.$$

This definition does not mention the beliefs of the agents. Indeed, they are not needed *ex post*, as all relevant information has been revealed. As a result, *ex post* voluntary participation is exactly the notion of participation we saw in section 2.4, where we also saw that Groves mechanisms do not always satisfy it. It is in fact a very stringent requirement and one can argue that it is not particularly compelling for this very reason. It imposes an inequality for every θ and every agent i. If it turns out that a mechanism violates ex post voluntary participation for some value of the profile θ that was not realized, should we take this as a damning criticism of the mechanism?

It may be more reasonable, depending on the context, to assume that agents have the ability to walk away from the mechanism once they have learned their private θ_i, but before they have seen how the mechanism turns out. This leads to the notion of interim voluntary participation.

Definition 4.6 (*Interim* Voluntary Participation). **Interim voluntary participation** requires that for all $i \in \mathcal{I}$ and all $\theta_i \in \Theta_i$,

$$\mathbb{E}_{\overline{\theta}_{-i}} \left[v_i(d(\theta_i, \overline{\theta}_{-i}), \theta_i) + t_i(\theta_i, \overline{\theta}_{-i}) \mid \theta_i \right] \geq 0.$$

This notion envisions agents using their private information to find their conditionally expected utility of participation, and then comparing it to the zero utility of non-participation. Note that if a mechanism satisfies *ex post* voluntary participation, it must also satisfy *interim* voluntary participation. It is a simple exercise in logical thinking to prove this from the definitions. If a mechanism satisfies interim voluntary participation, however, it does not follow that it must satisfy ex post voluntary participation.

Finally, we can also have situations in which it makes sense to assume that agents must commit to the mechanism before they even know their private information, θ_i. For instance, firms participating in an auction for off-shore oil drilling rights may have to commit to participate before they conduct sufficient tests to nail down their value for the rights being auctioned. Such cases fit the notion of *ex ante* voluntary participation.

Definition 4.7 (*Ex Ante* Voluntary Participation). *Ex ante* **voluntary participation** requires that for all i,

$$\mathbb{E}_{\overline{\theta}} \left[v_i(d(\overline{\theta}_i, \overline{\theta}_{-i}), \overline{\theta}_i) + t_i(\overline{\theta}_i, \overline{\theta}_{-i}) \right] \geq 0.$$

Here agent i does not condition the expectation on θ_i, as she does not know θ_i. Ex ante voluntary participation is the easiest to satisfy of the three kinds of voluntary participation we have defined. Indeed, if a mechanism does not satisfy it, it is probably not worth considering at all. The reason is this. If a few agents are in expectation worse off by participating, then there must be others that are better off in expectation by participating. Then we can change the transfer scheme of the mechanism to get another mechanism that make the former agents willing to participate by transferring money to them from the others, and without making the others unwilling to participate. If there is no latitude to make such changes to the transfers, then the mechanism does not even achieve the property that the sum of everybody's expected utility from the mechanism is no less than the utility of non-participation. If so, then it is unclear why we should take such a mechanism seriously.

Note that if a mechanism satisfies interim voluntary participation, then it satisfies ex ante voluntary participation. Once again, the proof of this is an easy logical exercise. The converse does not hold.

We have seen that ex post voluntary participation is a severe requirement, and ex ante voluntary participion less so. How about interim voluntary participation? It turns out to be severe also. The following result is from Jackson (2003).

Theorem 4.3. *In the economic domain with one private and one public good, a mechanism cannot satisfy simultaneously all of the properties: (i) interim voluntary participation, (ii) Bayesian incentive compatibility, (iii) efficient decision making, and (iv) feasibility.*

Proof. We show an example economy where if a mechanism satisfies properties (i), (ii), and (iii), then it violates (iv). Consider the public project example economy from section 2.4.1, with a small modification. There are two agents, each Θ_i is $\{0, 1\}$, and the cost of the public project is $c = \frac{3}{4}$. For each agent, the two types are equally likely and statistically independently distributed from the types of the other agent. Efficiency requires that the project be built when one or both of the agents is of type $\theta_i = 1$. To specify the efficient decision we assume that if the agents both are of type 1, then they split the cost equally, but this is not a limitation of our proof, since the equal split is irrelevant as it can wash out in the transfer payments.

Because of interim voluntary participation, we have (when we take $\theta_1 = 0$ and $\theta_2 = 0$)

$$\frac{1}{2}\left(t_1(0, 1) + t_1(0, 0)\right) \geq 0 \quad \text{and} \quad \frac{1}{2}\left(t_2(1, 0) + t_2(0, 0)\right) \geq 0. \tag{4.4}$$

Applying the definition of Bayesian incentive compatibility in the case $\theta_1 = 1$ is the true value for agent 1, we get

$$\frac{1}{2}\left(1 - \frac{3}{8} + t_1(1, 1) + 1 - \frac{3}{4} + t_1(1, 0)\right) \geq \frac{1}{2}\left(1 + t_1(0, 1) + t_1(0, 0)\right). \tag{4.5}$$

Together, (4.4) and (4.5) yield

$$t_1(1, 1) + t_1(0, 1) > 0. \tag{4.6}$$

Doing the same thing but for agent 2, we get

$$t_2(1, 1) + t_2(1, 0) > 0. \tag{4.7}$$

Combining (4.4), (4.6), and (4.7), we find that the sum of all transfers to both agents for all states is positive: $\sum_{\theta_1 \in \{0,1\}, \theta_2 \in \{0,1\}} \left(t_1(\theta_1, \theta_2) + t_2(\theta_1, \theta_2)\right) > 0$. As this violates feasibility, our proof is complete.   QED

4.5 Optimal Auctions

We turn now to the use of the mechanism design approach to find the type of auction that maximizes the seller's revenue. This will show a tiny, but important, part of the theory of auctions. We do not cover auctions systematically in this book, as to do so requires an entire book, and such books already exist, as we mentioned at the end of section 2.5. In addition to those, Wolfstetter (1999, Chapter 8) has an introductory presentation that covers all the main points with a minimum of mathematical fuss; it is the basis of this section. The seminal work in the analysis of optimal auctions is Myerson (1981).

The auction setup we consider is simple and is described as the *symmetric independent private values auction model with risk-neutral agents*. The assumptions maintained in this model are:

Single Item The auction is for a single indivisible object, such as a painting.

Private Values Each bidder knows what her valuation is but not what the other bidders' valuations are.

Symmetry *Ex ante,* each bidder looks like every other bidder and has the same *ex ante* valuation distribution.

Independence The bidders' valuations are continuous random variables that are distributed independently of each other.

Risk Neutrality The seller and the bidders are risk-neutral.

We will show the general procedure for solving for a symmetric Bayesian equilibrium of an auction game that satisfies these five assumptions. Along the way, we will encounter the remarkable revenue equivalence theorem, which says that all auctions in a large class yield the same expected revenue for the seller and the same expected payment for each buyer. We will then show how the framework of mechanism design can be used to design an auction that is optimal in the sense of maximizing the seller's expected revenue.

We denote by $\overline{\theta}_i$ the random variable of bidder i's valuation for the object on sale and by θ_i its realization. This is consistent with our notation in chapter 2. We assume that every valuation is distributed according to the same distribution with cumulative distribution function $F : [0, \theta_H] \to [0, 1]$, which we assume to be strictly increasing everywhere in its domain and to be differentiable so that is has a density function f. This says that every valuation is at least 0 and at most θ_H, and all bidders have the same distribution. Because of the assumption that the valuations are independently distributed, it follows that the cumulative distribution function of the random variable that holds all bidder valuations is, for any list of numbers $(v_1, \ldots, v_I)$, each from the interval $[0, \theta_H]$,

$$F(v_1, v_2, \ldots, v_I) = F(v_1)F(v_2) \cdots F(v_I). \tag{4.8}$$

This is interpreted as the probability that the actual realization of bidder 1's valuation θ_1 is not larger than the number v_1, the same for bidder 2, and so on until the last bidder.

The cumulative distribution function F is assumed to be common knowledge among the seller and all the bidders. Therefore, when each bidder participates in the auction, she is playing a Bayesian game in which her type is her realized valuation, θ_i.

The strategies available to each bidder have two parts: whether to participate in the auction, and if one participates, how much to bid. Since the game that the auction defines is a Bayesian game, the strategies are functions of the types, which are the valuations. So a strategy of bidder i is a pair of functions $b_i : [0, \theta_H] \to \mathbb{R}_+$ and $P_i : [0, \theta_H] \to \{0, 1\}$. Note the different notations and what they mean. Even though both functions share the same domain $[0, \theta_H]$, which is the set of possible valuations, they take different values. The bidding function b_i gives, for every valuation θ_i in $[0, \theta_H]$, a nonnegative amount $b_i(\theta_i)$ of money that agent i, when she has this valuation θ_i, will bid. The participation function P_i can only take the values 0 and 1; 1 is interpreted as choosing to participate in the auction. We also assume that each bidder's participation function takes the form $P_i(\theta_i) = 1$ if and only if $\theta_i \geq v_0$ for some value $v_0 \in [0, \theta_H]$. So the problem of finding a bidder's optimal strategy is reduced to finding the bidding function and the threshold value v_0 of this bidder. Furthermore, as we will only look at symmetric Bayesian equilibria, all bidding functions and threshold values will be common among the bidders. This is important to realize, as it means that the auctions we are analyzing may have other Bayesian equilibria that we are not going to find with our present approach.

Any auction rules we can imagine can be written as an allocation rule d and a payment rule t. The allocation rule is again an incarnation of the social decision d of chapter 2. Here, $d = (d_1, d_2, \ldots, d_I)$ is a function with domain $[0, \theta_H]^I$ and range the probability distributions that determine who gets the item. In other words, $d_i(b_1, b_2, \ldots, b_I)$ takes the bids submitted by all bidders and tells us the probability that, under these particular bids, i gets the item. We require that $\sum_{i \in I} d_i(b_1, b_2, \ldots, b_I) \leq 1$ and that each $d_i(b_1, b_2, \ldots, b_I)$ is nonnegative. We do not insist that $\sum_{i \in I} d_i(b_1, b_2, \ldots, b_I)$ must equal 1, because we want to leave the possibility open that no bidder wins the item given certain bid lists. Similarly, $t = (t_1, t_2, \ldots, t_I)$ is the payment function that tells each bidder i the expected payment she has to make, $t_i(b_1, b_2, \ldots, b_I)$, when the submitted bid list is $(b_1, b_2, \ldots, b_I)$. We say "expected payment" because we do not want to rule out the possibility that the auction rules may include a lottery that determines payments.

Given a bid b_i, we denote the expected value that a bidder has for winning by $\widehat{d}_i(b)$. Similarly, we denote by $\widehat{t}_i(b_i)$ the bidder's expected payment. We have to use an expectation because bidder i does not know what the other bids are. To illustrate, suppose that each bidder uses the same equilibrium bidding function b^*. Consider bidder 1. We have

$$\widehat{d}_1(b_1) = \mathbb{E}_{\overline{\theta}_{-1}} \left[d_1(b_1, b_2^*(\overline{\theta}_2), \ldots, b_I^*(\overline{\theta}_I)) \right], \tag{4.9}$$

where the expectation is taken over the random variables $\overline{\theta}_2, \ldots, \overline{\theta}_I$. Since bidders are all symmetric, we can just as well write this as

$$\widehat{d}(b) = E\left[d(b, b^*(\overline{\theta}_2), \ldots, b^*(\overline{\theta}_I))\right].$$ (4.10)

Similarly,

$$\widehat{t}(b) = E\left[t(b, b^*(\overline{\theta}_2), \ldots, b^*(\overline{\theta}_I))\right].$$ (4.11)

Note that, because we have assumed the bidders' valuations to be independent, these functions do not depend on the individual bidder's valuation.

The mechanism of the auction has now been described. Since we have assumed the bidders to be risk neutral, their payoff functions are simple. They are even simpler when we assume that all play their equilibrium strategies. In this case, for each bidder i, the payoff of playing bid b and participation threshold v_0 is

$$U(b, \theta_i) = \widehat{d}(b)\theta_i - \widehat{t}(b).$$ (4.12)

With the setup behind us, we can now see that the strategy (b^*, v_0) is a symmetric Bayesian equilibrium of the auction game if, for all $\theta \geq v_0$, we have

$$U(b^*(\theta), \theta) \geq U(b, \theta) \quad \forall b,$$ (4.13)
$$U(b^*(v_0), v_0) = 0.$$ (4.14)

The first condition says that no type θ of any bidder can find a profitable deviation from the bid dictated by the optimal strategy, $b^*(\theta)$. The second says that the expected payoff of a bidder whose type equals the threshold v_0 is precisely zero: a bidder is teetering on the brink of not participating exactly when she expects zero utility from participating. We can now deduce two properties of the equilibrium bidding function.

Theorem 4.4 (Monotonically Increasing Bid Functions [Wolfstetter, 1999]).
In the symmetric independent private values auction model as set up in this section, if the probability of winning the auction is increasing in one's bid, then the bidding function b^* of the symmetric Bayesian equilibrium is monotonically increasing.

Proof. The indirect utility function of a bidder who has valuation θ and chooses the equilibrium bid b^* when every other bidder follows the equilibrium bid strategy b^* is

$$\widehat{U}(\theta) \equiv U(b^*(\theta), \theta) = \widehat{d}(b^*(\theta))\theta - \widehat{t}(b^*(\theta)).$$ (4.15)

This is the maximized value of the bidder's expected utility because by definition of the equilibrium, b^* yields the maximal possible expected utility when all others follow b^*. By the envelope theorem (see page 259 for a refresher), we have

$$D\widehat{U}(\theta) = D_\theta U(b^*(\theta), \theta) = D_\theta[\widehat{d}(b^*(\theta))\theta - \widehat{t}(b^*(\theta))] = \widehat{d}(b^*(\theta)).$$ (4.16)

We claim now that the function $\widehat{U}$ is convex. To show this, take any two members of its domain, θ, θ', take any real number λ from the interval $[0,1]$, and write $\theta'' = \lambda\theta + (1-\lambda)\theta'$. Because of the optimality of the function b^*, we have that $\widehat{d}(b^*(\theta))\theta - \widehat{t}(b^*(\theta)) \geq \widehat{d}(b^*(\theta''))\theta - \widehat{t}(b^*(\theta''))$ and $\widehat{d}(b^*(\theta'))\theta' - \widehat{t}(b^*(\theta')) \geq \widehat{d}(b^*(\theta''))\theta' - \widehat{t}(b^*(\theta''))$. Multiply the first inequality by λ and the second by $1-\lambda$ and note that because both of these multipliers are nonnegative, the inequality direction is preserved. Add the resulting inequalities, recall the definition of $\widehat{U}$, and you find

$$\lambda\widehat{U}(\theta) + (1-\lambda)\widehat{U}(\theta') \geq \widehat{d}(b^*(\theta''))[\lambda\theta + (1-\lambda)\theta'] - \widehat{t}(b^*(\theta'')) = \widehat{U}(\theta''),$$

which proves that $\widehat{U}$ is a convex function.

Because $\widehat{U}$ is a convex function, its derivative is a nondecreasing function. From (4.16) it then follows that $\widehat{d}(b^*(\theta))$ is a nondecreasing function of θ. Because $\widehat{d}$ itself is an increasing function by assumption, it follows that the equilibrium bid function is nondecreasing. But it must in fact be strictly increasing. If it were not so, it would be constant over some interval (θ_ℓ, θ_h). If so, a bidder whose valuation is in this interval would be able to earn a higher expected payoff by a slight increase of her bid, since there is a positive probability that the second highest bid will be in this interval, and then we would not be at a Bayesian equilibrium, a contradiction. QED

For the next result, we denote by $\theta^{\max}$ the highest realized valuation among the bidders.

Corollary 4.1. *The bidder with the highest valuation, $\theta^{\max}$, wins the auction if this valuation exceeds the threshold level v_0. In this case, the probability of winning in the symmetric Bayesian equilibrium equals the probability that all other bidders' valuations are below θ^{max}, which is $[F(\theta^{max})]^{I-1}$.*

Using these results, we can prove the following famous result.

Theorem 4.5 (Revenue Equivalence [Myerson, 1981; Riley and Samuelson, 1981]). *Let v_0 be a threshold value. All auctions such that (i) the highest bid wins, (ii) there is a symmetric Bayesian equilibrium, and (iii) the threshold value is v_0, generate the same expected revenue for the seller and the same expected payment for each bidder.*

The proof is included as an exercise at the end of the chapter. However, it is worth noting that the expected revenue of the seller is shown, as part of this proof, to equal the following.

$$\int_{v_0}^{\theta_H} \left(\theta - \frac{1 - F(\theta)}{f(\theta)} \right) \left(D_\theta[F(\theta)]^I \right) d\theta. \tag{4.17}$$

The first term in parentheses is a central feature of the optimal auction that we turn to now. In it, f is the probability density of F. We are assured that it is positive by the assumption we made earlier that F is strictly increasing from 0 to θ_H. We will give it an interpretation after we present how one finds the optimal auction.

In this context, "optimal auction" means "the auction that maximizes the seller's expected revenue." To look for such an auction, we employ the Bayesian revelation principle, which we presented earlier in this chapter. According to it, every Bayesian equilibrium in every auction we can imagine corresponds to the truthful equilibrium of a direct auction which yields the same probabilities of winning the auction and the same expected payments. It is left as an exercise to show how this statement follows from the version of the Bayesian revelation theorem presented earlier.

Let $\theta = (\theta_1, \theta_2, \ldots, \theta_I)$ be the valuation profile of the bidders and let $v = (v_1, v_2, \ldots, v_I)$ be the list of the reports the bidders submit in the direct auction about their valuations. We write $q_i(v)$ for the probability of winning for bidder i when the report list is v. We write $p_i(v)$ for the expected price of bidder i when the report list is v. A direct auction that results from a Bayesian equilibrium of another auction via the revelation principle must satisfy three constraints: the budget constraint, incentive compatibility, and voluntary participation.

We no longer need to assume that all agents have the same probability distribution. We denote by F_i the cumulative distribution function of bidder i, and we maintain the assumption that it is differentiable and strictly increasing.

The **budget constraint** of the auction is that, for all report lists v,

$$\sum_{i=1}^{I} q_i(v) \leq 1. \tag{4.18}$$

This says that the probability that the item is sold never exceeds one. It can be less than one if the bidders' threshold is not reached.

The **incentive compatibility constraint** is that, for each valuation profile θ, each bidder i, and each report $v_i \neq \theta_i$, the true report θ_i yields at least as much utility to i as the false one. To write this concisely, we employ the notation

$$U_i(v_i \mid \theta_i) \equiv \mathbb{E}_{\overline{\theta}_{-i}} \left[q_i(\overline{\theta}_1, \ldots, v_i, \ldots, \overline{\theta}_I)\theta_i \right] - \mathbb{E}_{\overline{\theta}_{-i}} \left[p_i(\overline{\theta}_1, \ldots, v_i, \ldots, \overline{\theta}_I) \right].$$

The incentive compatibility constraint then says that for all θ, all i, and all $v_i \in [0, \theta_H]$,

$$U_i(\theta_i \mid \theta_i) \geq U_i(v_i \mid \theta_i). \tag{4.19}$$

The **voluntary participation constraint** says that each bidder must be assured an expected utility for participating in the auction that is at least as much as her outside option, here normalized to yield zero expected utility. The constraint says that for all bidders i and all $\theta_i \in [0, \theta_H]$,

$$U_i(\theta_i \mid \theta_i) \geq 0. \tag{4.20}$$

The **problem of maximizing expected revenue for the seller** now becomes to choose the lists of functions of probabilities of winning, $q = (q_1, \ldots, q_I)$, and expected payment functions, $p = (p_1, \ldots, p_I)$, to maximize the expression

$$\sum_{i=1}^{I} E\left[p_i(\overline{\theta}_1, \ldots, \overline{\theta}_I)\right] - \sum_{i=1}^{I} E\left[q_i(\overline{\theta}_1, \ldots, \overline{\theta}_I)\right] c, \tag{4.21}$$

where c denotes the valuation of the seller for the item on auction, subject to the budget, incentive compatibility, and voluntary participation constraints.

The solution that Myerson derived is an ingenious modification of the Vickrey second-price auction. First, let us make the assumption that for every i, the expression

$$\gamma_i(\theta_i) \equiv \theta_i - \frac{1 - F_i(\theta_i)}{f_i(\theta_i)} \tag{4.22}$$

is strictly increasing. We call $\gamma_i(\theta_i)$ the *priority level* of bidder i when she has the valuation θ_i. It is well defined because for all $i \in \mathcal{I}$ and all θ_i, we have $f_i(\theta_i) > 0$ by assumption.

The optimal auction proceeds as follows. First, bidders report their valuations. The auctioneer calculates the priority levels associated with these valuations and ranks them from lowest to highest. Second, if the highest priority level is below the seller's valuation, c, the item is not sold. However, if the highest priority level exceeds c, the bidder with that priority level wins the item. Third, the winning bidder is the only one to make a payment, and the payment equals the lowest valuation that would still allow this bidder to have the highest priority level.

It is the third item, the payment rule, that reflects the second-price idea of Vickrey. The payment is calculated by setting the winning bidder's priority level equal to the second-highest priority level. This ensures that the optimal auction has very strong incentive properties: in addition to being incentive compatible (which we know it is because one of the constraints imposed on its calculation was incentive compatibility itself), it also ensures that it is a *dominant* strategy for each bidder to submit her true valuation.

The priority levels have a nice interpretation. Each priority level has two terms. The first is the valuation of the bidder and the second is a corrective term that is subtracted from the valuation. The corrective term, $(1 - F_i(\theta_i))/f_i(\theta_i)$, measures the information cost to the seller of the fact that bidders' true valuations are private information. Indeed, had the seller known all θ_i valuations, the seller would simply have offered the item for sale to the bidder with the highest θ_i for a price of a penny less than θ_i, and the bidder would have bought the item at that price. So we can view $(1 - F_i(\theta_i))/f_i(\theta_i)$ as the concession that has to be made to the bidder because of the bidder's private information. We could think of it as the value to the bidder of the fact that this information is private to the bidder.

In fact, there is a second nice interpretation of the priority levels. Imagine the auction situation treated as a standard monopoly problem where $c = 0$ so that revenue equals profit and there is only one bidder. But there is no bidding. Instead, the seller just names a price p and the buyer decides to buy or not at this price. The total (expected) revenue of the seller in this case equals $p(1-F(p))$. Hence the marginal revenue is $1-F(p)-pf(p) = 0$. Solving this equation for the monopolist's profit-maximizing price, p^*, we find that this price is found exactly when the equation $p - \frac{1-F(p)}{f(p)} = 0$ is satisfied. Remembering that we have $c = 0$ here, this equation can also be written as $\gamma(p) = p - \frac{1-F(p)}{f(p)} = c$. So in this way, a buyer with valuation θ gets the item if and only if $\gamma(\theta) > c$, i.e., if and only if this buyer would have gotten the item in the optimal auction. This demonstrates the role of the priority level as marginal revenue.

The optimal auction is a significant milestone in auction theory and mechanism theory, but it has some flaws. First, the seller needs to have precise knowledge of the distributions F_i of the private valuations of the bidders. It is hard to have this information in practice. Second, even under our assumption that priority levels are increasing in valuations, the optimal auction may result in an *ex post* Pareto inefficient outcome. This can happen in two sets of circumstances. For one, the bidder with the highest priority level does not necessarily win the object, because it is possible that a valuation results in a priority level that is less than the seller's cost, c. For another, it is possible that the bidder with the highest priority level is not the bidder with the highest valuation, when the distributions of the valuations are not equal across bidders. The failure of the optimal auction to be always Pareto efficient reinforces our caution from chapter 1 to always be mindful of the social choice correspondence that a mechanism attempts to implement. In the present case, the optimal auction is designed to maximize the expected revenue of the seller, so it should not be a big surprise that it does not achieve efficiency.

4.6 Bilateral Trading

In an auction we have one seller and multiple potential buyers, so an auction is a particular form of a monopolistic market. A different model considers the situation where the seller side and the buyer side have the same bargaining power. The simplest way to look at this is in a situation with one seller and one buyer, the old bilateral monopoly setup that microeconomics textbooks used to offer as an unsolved problem, but with the additional complication of asymmetric information.

We present a general theory of mechanisms in the case where agents' beliefs are independently distributed, the set of types of each agent is an interval of real numbers, and their utility functions are quasilinear. We apply this theory to bilateral trading, but the enterprising reader will have no problem applying it also to the discussion we gave earlier on optimal auctions. The formulation of the problem and the results we discuss here are due to Myerson (1981) and Myerson and Satterthwaite (1983). Our presentation follows the treatment of (Myerson, 1991, section 6.5) and offers additional details to make the material easier to absorb.

We start with a slight adaptation of our setup of this chapter. The I agents are as before. Each agent i has a set of types that is an interval $\Theta_i = [\theta_{iL}, \theta_{iH}]$, where $\theta_{iL} < \theta_{iH}$. Each agent i's utility function has the form $u_i(d, t) = d_i\theta_i + t_i$, where the pair (d, t) is a social decision in which $d = (d_1, \ldots, d_I)$ is a vector of net trades and $t = (t_1, \ldots, t_I)$ a vector of payments to the agents. Remember that we interpret t_i as the payment to agent i, so if we want to talk about a payment that i makes, then t_i will be negative. We appeal to the revelation principle which will allow us to consider only direct mechanisms in this section. Given a direct mechanism and reports $\theta = (\theta_1, \ldots, \theta_I)$ from the agents, each agent i performs the net trade $d_i(\theta)$ and pays $-t_i(\theta)$ for it.

Each agent i has a cumulative distribution function $F_i : [\theta_{iL}, \theta_{iH}] \to [0, 1]$ so that for every $v_i \in [\theta_{iL}, \theta_{iH}]$, $F_i(v_i)$ expresses the probability that i's type is no more than v_i. We assume that all the F_i are statistically independent, strictly increasing, and differentiable, so each F_i has a probability density function f_i which is strictly positive.

We will have many occasions to write the expected value of d_i given θ_i and the same for t_i, so we will use the following shorthand notations:

$$Q_i(\theta_i) = \int_{\theta_{-i} \in \Theta_{-i}} d_i(\theta_i, \theta_{-i}) \prod_{j \neq i} f_j(\theta_j)\, d\theta_{-i}, \quad T_i(\theta_i) = \int_{\theta_{-i} \in \Theta_{-i}} t_i(\theta_i, \theta_{-i}) \prod_{j \neq i} f_j(\theta_j)\, d\theta_{-i}.$$

We think of $Q_i(\theta_i)$ as the expected amount of the net trade of agent i in the direct mechanism, conditional on θ_i. We hope you will forgive us for changing to the Q notation to emphasize that these are expected quantities. Similarly, $T_i(\theta_i)$ is the expected payment to agent i in the direct mechanism, conditional on θ_i. We could have employed the notation $\mathbb{E}_{\bar{\theta}_{-i}}$ in place of the integrals on the right-hand-sides, but it is better to be explicit about the nature of these integrals; you will see why soon. The notation $\prod_{j \neq i} f_j(\theta_j)$ stands for the product $f_1(\theta_1) \cdots f_{i-1}(\theta_{i-1}) \cdot f_{i+1}(\theta_{i+1}) \cdots f_I(\theta_I)$, as you probably already figured out. This is the probability density of the type profile $\theta = (\theta_1, \ldots, \theta_I)$ conditional on θ_i. It has this product structure because of the assumption of statistical independence of the agents' type distributions.

When the type profile is $\theta = (\theta_1, \ldots, \theta_I)$ and all agents report their types truthfully, each agent i receives the following expected utility, conditional on its type θ_i:

$$U_i(\theta_i | \theta_i) = Q_i(\theta_i)\theta_i + T_i(\theta_i).$$

When all other agents $j \neq i$ report their types truthfully but i reports $\widehat{\theta}_i$ instead, i receives the following expected utility, conditional on θ_i:

$$U_i(\widehat{\theta}_i | \theta_i) = Q_i(\widehat{\theta}_i)\theta_i + T_i(\widehat{\theta}_i).$$

This means that the incentive compatibility constraints can be written as: for every agent $i \in \mathcal{I}$, for every type $\theta_i \in \Theta_i$, and for every type $\widehat{\theta}_i \in \Theta_i$, $U_i(\theta_i|\theta_i) \geq U_i(\widehat{\theta}_i|\theta_i)$, or written in more detail,

$$Q_i(\theta_i)\theta_i + T_i(\theta_i) \geq Q_i(\widehat{\theta}_i)\theta_i + T_i(\widehat{\theta}_i). \tag{4.23}$$

Since this true for all type profiles, it also holds when the true type of i is $\widehat{\theta}_i$, which yields

$$Q_i(\widehat{\theta}_i)\widehat{\theta}_i + T_i(\widehat{\theta}_i) \geq Q_i(\theta_i)\widehat{\theta}_i + T_i(\theta_i). \tag{4.24}$$

Adding these two inequalities side-by-side, canceling out the T_i terms from both sides, and rearranging, we get

$$Q_i(\theta_i)(\theta_i - \widehat{\theta}_i) \geq Q_i(\widehat{\theta}_i)(\theta_i - \widehat{\theta}_i). \tag{4.25}$$

Writing this as

$$\left[Q_i(\theta_i) - Q_i(\widehat{\theta}_i) \right] (\theta_i - \widehat{\theta}_i) \geq 0, \tag{4.26}$$

we see that it implies that the function Q_i is non-decreasing. Therefore, Q_i has a Riemann integral over its domain, $[\theta_{iL}, \theta_{iH}]$.

In fact, inequalities (4.23) and (4.24) also imply the inequalities

$$Q_i(\theta_i)(\theta_i - \widehat{\theta}_i) \geq U_i(\theta_i|\theta_i) - U_i(\widehat{\theta}_i|\widehat{\theta}_i) \geq Q_i(\widehat{\theta}_i)(\theta_i - \widehat{\theta}_i). \tag{4.27}$$

The steps required to show this are not too hard, but they have not been explained elsewhere as far as we know. Here is how they work.

Start with the difference $U_i(\theta_i|\theta_i) - U_i(\widehat{\theta}_i|\widehat{\theta}_i)$. By the definition of the U_i function,

$$U_i(\theta_i|\theta_i) - U_i(\widehat{\theta}_i|\widehat{\theta}_i) = Q_i(\theta_i)\theta_i + T_i(\theta_i) - Q_i(\widehat{\theta}_i)\widehat{\theta}_i - T_i(\widehat{\theta}_i).$$

By (4.23), therefore, we can replace the term $Q_i(\theta_i)\theta_i + T_i(\theta_i)$ on the right-hand side by $Q_i(\widehat{\theta}_i)\theta_i + T_i(\widehat{\theta}_i)$ and the expression cannot get larger, so that

$$U_i(\theta_i|\theta_i) - U_i(\widehat{\theta}_i|\widehat{\theta}_i) \geq Q_i(\widehat{\theta}_i)\theta_i + T_i(\widehat{\theta}_i) - Q_i(\widehat{\theta}_i)\widehat{\theta}_i - T_i(\widehat{\theta}_i) = Q_i(\widehat{\theta}_i)(\theta_i - \widehat{\theta}_i).$$

As you can see, this is the right-hand inequality in (4.27). To get the left-hand inequality, start again with

$$U_i(\theta_i|\theta_i) - U_i(\widehat{\theta}_i|\widehat{\theta}_i) = Q_i(\theta_i)\theta_i + T_i(\theta_i) - Q_i(\widehat{\theta}_i)\widehat{\theta}_i - T_i(\widehat{\theta}_i),$$

but now use (4.24), multiplied by -1, to replace the term $-Q_i(\widehat{\theta}_i)\widehat{\theta}_i - T_i(\widehat{\theta}_i)$ by $-Q_i(\theta_i)\widehat{\theta}_i - T_i(\theta_i)$. Because multiplying an inequality by -1 changes its direction, this substitution yields

$$U_i(\theta_i|\theta_i) - U_i(\widehat{\theta}_i|\widehat{\theta}_i) \leq Q_i(\theta_i)\theta_i + T_i(\theta_i) - Q_i(\theta_i)\widehat{\theta}_i - T_i(\theta_i) = Q_i(\theta_i)(\theta_i - \widehat{\theta}_i).$$

Having established (4.27), we now use it to show a neat trick: the function $Q_i(\theta_i)$ is the derivative of $U_i(\theta_i|\theta_i)$ with respect to θ_i almost everywhere on the interval $[\theta_{iL}, \theta_{iH}]$. Indeed, because Q_i is Riemann-integrable, it is bounded and continuous almost everywhere on the interval $[\theta_{iL}, \theta_{iH}]$ (see (Shilov and Gurevich, 1977, chapter 1, Theorem 4)). Now consider the inequalities (4.27) applied to a point θ_i at which Q_i is a continuous function. By our last assertion, this is true for all points in the interval $[\theta_{iL}, \theta_{iH}]$ except perhaps a finite or countably infinite number of points. Now divide the inequalities by $\theta_i - \widehat{\theta}_i$ if it is positive, or by its negative if it is negative, and take these inequalities as $\widehat{\theta}_i \to \theta_i$ from above or below. This process should convince you that at such a point θ_i, $D_{\theta_i} U_i(\theta_i|\theta_i) = Q_i(\theta_i)$. From this follows a famous and very useful result of Myerson. This says that for every $\theta_i, \widetilde{\theta}_i \in \Theta_i$,

$$U_i(\theta_i|\theta_i) = U_i(\widetilde{\theta}_i|\theta_i) + \int_{\widetilde{\theta}_i}^{\theta_i} Q_i(s_i)\, ds_i. \tag{4.28}$$

Before θ_i is revealed, the expected value of i's payment equals

$$-\int_{\theta_{iL}}^{\theta_{iH}} T_i(\theta_i) f_i(\theta_i)\, d\theta_i = \int_{\theta_{iL}}^{\theta_{iH}} [Q_i(\theta_i)\theta_i - U_i(\theta_i|\theta_i)]\, f_i(\theta_i)\, d\theta_i \tag{4.29}$$

$$= \int_{\theta_{iL}}^{\theta_{iH}} \left[Q_i(\theta_i)\theta_i - U_i(\widetilde{\theta}_i|\theta_i) - \int_{\widetilde{\theta}_i}^{\theta_i} Q_i(s_i)\, ds_i \right] f_i(\theta_i)\, d\theta_i. \tag{4.30}$$

Now we introduce a new function. It is left as an exercise for you to find out just how it relates to γ_i from section 4.5.

$$\psi_i(\theta_i, \widetilde{\theta}_i) = \begin{cases} \theta_i - \dfrac{\int_{\theta_i}^{\theta_{iH}} f_i(s_i)\, ds_i}{f_i(\theta_i)} & \text{if } \theta_i > \widetilde{\theta}_i, \\[3ex] \theta_i + \dfrac{\int_{\theta_{iL}}^{\theta_i} f_i(s_i)\, ds_i}{f_i(\theta_i)} & \text{if } \theta_i < \widetilde{\theta}_i. \end{cases} \tag{4.31}$$

Continuing from (4.30), we have

$$-\int_{\theta_{iL}}^{\theta_{iH}} T_i(\theta_i) f_i(\theta_i)\, d\theta_i = \int_{\theta_{iL}}^{\theta_{iH}} \left[Q_i(\theta_i)\theta_i - \int_{\widetilde{\theta}_i}^{\theta_i} Q_i(s_i)\, ds_i \right] f_i(\theta_i)\, d\theta_i - U_i(\widetilde{\theta}_i|\theta_i)$$

$$= \int_{\theta_{iL}}^{\theta_{iH}} Q_i(\theta_i)\theta_i f_i(\theta_i)\, d\theta_i - \int_{\theta_{iL}}^{\theta_{iH}} \int_{\widetilde{\theta}_i}^{\theta_i} Q_i(s_i)\, ds_i f_i(\theta_i)\, d\theta_i - U_i(\widetilde{\theta}_i|\theta_i)$$

$$= \int_{\theta_{iL}}^{\theta_{iH}} Q_i(\theta_i)\psi_i(\theta_i, \widetilde{\theta}_i) f_i(\theta_i)\, d\theta_i - U_i(\widetilde{\theta}_i|\theta_i)$$

$$= \int_{\theta_{1L}}^{\theta_{1H}} \cdots \int_{\theta_{iL}}^{\theta_{iH}} \cdots \int_{\theta_{IL}}^{\theta_{IH}} q_i(\theta)\psi_i(\theta_i, \widetilde{\theta}_i) f_1(\theta_1) \cdots f_i(\theta_i) \cdots f_I(\theta_I)\, d\theta_1 \ldots d\theta_i \ldots d\theta_I. \tag{4.32}$$

We can now apply the last equation we derived (4.32) in conjunction with (4.28) to the trading problem between a seller and a buyer.

In this trading problem, there is an indivisible object that the seller wants to sell and the buyer wants to buy. Let the seller be agent 1 and the buyer be agent 2. Let θ_1 denote the value of the object to the seller and θ_2 the value of the object to the buyer. As usual, θ stands for the type profile (θ_1, θ_2). By feasibility, for every θ we have $q_2(\theta) = -q_1(\theta)$, which says that, whatever the values of the seller and buyer, any purchase q_2 must match an equal sale q_1. For the same reason, for every θ we have $-t_2(\theta) = t_1(\theta)$. In our notation, $t_1(\theta)$ is the price that the mechanism makes 1 receive when the type profile is θ and $-t_2(\theta)$ the price it makes the buyer pay under the same type profile.

The type of the seller that is least willing to trade is the one with the highest possible valuation for the object, θ_{1H}; the type of the buyer that is least willing to trade is θ_{2L}. Putting $\widetilde{\theta}_1 = \theta_{1H}$ and $\widetilde{\theta}_2 = \theta_{2L}$ in (4.32), and remembering that $T_1(\theta) + T_2(\theta) = 0$, which follows immediately from feasibility which implies $-t_2(\theta) = t_1(\theta)$, we have the following.

$$0 = -\int_{\theta_{2L}}^{\theta_{2H}} \int_{\theta_{1L}}^{\theta_{1H}} (t_1(\theta_1) + t_2(\theta_2)) f_1(\theta_1) f_2(\theta_2) \, d\theta_1 d\theta_2 \tag{4.33}$$

$$= -\int_{\theta_{2L}}^{\theta_{2H}} T_2(\theta_2) f_2(\theta_2) \, d\theta_2 - \int_{\theta_{1L}}^{\theta_{1H}} T_1(\theta_1) f_1(\theta_1) \, d\theta_1$$

(using (4.32))

$$= \int_{\theta_{2L}}^{\theta_{2H}} \int_{\theta_{1L}}^{\theta_{1H}} [Q_2(\theta)\psi_2(\theta_2, \theta_{2L}) + Q_1(\theta)\psi_1(\theta_1, \theta_{1H})] f_1(\theta_1) f_2(\theta_2) \, d\theta_1 d\theta_2$$

$$- U_1(\theta_{1H}|\theta_1) - U_2(\theta_{2L}|\theta_2)$$

$$= \int_{\theta_{2L}}^{\theta_{2H}} \int_{\theta_{1L}}^{\theta_{1H}} Q_2(\theta) [\psi_2(\theta_2, \theta_{2L}) - \psi_1(\theta_1, \theta_{1H})] f_1(\theta_1) f_2(\theta_2) \, d\theta_1 d\theta_2$$

$$- U_1(\theta_{1H}|\theta_1) - U_2(\theta_{2L}|\theta_2). \tag{4.34}$$

The last step follows from $Q_2(\theta) = -Q_1(\theta)$, which follows from $q_2(\theta) = -q_1(\theta)$ from feasibility and the definition of Q_1, Q_2.

Let us look at a specific example now to make the result evident. Suppose that $\theta_{1L} = \theta_{2L} = 0$, $\theta_{1H} = \theta_{2H} = 1$, and both f_1 and f_2 are the probability density function of the uniform distribution over $[0, 1]$, $f_i(\theta_i) = 1$ for all $\theta_i \in [0, 1]$. Straightforward calculations show that

$$\psi_1(\theta_1, \theta_{1H}) = \psi_1(\theta_1, 1) = 2\theta_1, \qquad \psi_2(\theta_2, \theta_{2L}) = \psi_2(\theta_2, 0) = 2\theta_2 - 1.$$

Putting these in (4.34), we get

$$\int_0^1 \int_0^1 2\left(\theta_2 - \theta_1 - \frac{1}{2}\right) d\theta_1 d\theta_2 = U_1(1|\theta_1) + U_2(0|\theta_2) \geq 0. \tag{4.35}$$

This says that, conditionally on the occurrence of trade, the expected difference between the buyer's valuation for the object, θ_2, and the seller's valuation, θ_1, must be at least $1/2$. The inequality follows from interim individual rationality, as you can show easily. The reason for the discrepancy is the temptation for the buyer and seller to play hard to get, which in this model translates to pretending to be the type least willing to trade.

But there is the following mathematical fact, ready to trip up the bilateral trading mechanism:

$$\int_0^1 \int_0^{\theta_2} \left(\theta_2 - \theta_1 - \frac{1}{3} \right) d\theta_1 d\theta_2 = 0.$$

It can be shown that this contradicts (4.35), hence there is no Pareto efficient, incentive compatible trading mechanism that ensures interim voluntary participation in this example. (Incidentally, this is a blow to the so-called Coase theorem, on which we have more to say in section 8.1.)

4.7 Exercises

Exercise 24: Posteriors

Amanda and Braden both opened businesses in the same town selling the same product. The product may be made using either old technology O or new technology N. Let Amanda's type be θ_A and Braden's type be θ_B. Their types can take the values O or N, reflecting the technology each uses. The state space is $\{(O,O),(O,N),(N,O),(N,N)\}$ where the types are written in the order (θ_A, θ_B). The common prior is $q(O,O) = 0.1$, $q(O,N) = 0.25$, $q(N,O) = 0.2$, $q(N,N) = 0.45$. Calculate the posteriors for Amanda and Braden for each combination of types.

Exercise 25: Conditionally Expected Utility

Using the information in examples 4.2 and 4.3, calculate Bess's conditionally expected utility when the realized state is (W, S).

Exercise 26: Bayesian Equilibria 1

Continuing with the example of Andy and Bess from examples 4.2 and 4.3, calculate the Bayesian equilibria.

Exercise 27: Bayesian Equilibria 2

Continuing from exercise 24, assume that both Amanda and Braden have two possible actions when selling the product: price low L and price high H. Additionally for each one of them (i either A or B), and writing i's variable always before that of $-i$'s, the utilities are as follows: $u_i(L, L, (O, O)) = 2$, $u_i(L, H, (O, O)) = 5$, $u_i(H, L, (O, O)) = -5$, $u_i(H, H, (O, O)) = 0$, $u_i(L, L, (O, N)) = -2$, $u_i(L, H, (O, N)) = 1$, $u_i(H, L, (O, N)) = -10$, $u_i(H, H, (O, N)) = -5$, $u_i(L, L, (N, O)) = 2$, $u_i(L, H, (N, O)) = 10$, $u_i(H, L, (N, O)) = 2$, $u_i(H, H, (N, O)) = 5$, $u_i(L, L, (N, N)) = 2$, $u_i(L, H, (N, N)) = 5$, $u_i(H, L, (N, N)) = -5$, and finally $u_i(H, H, (N, N)) = 0$. Calculate the Bayesian equilibria.

Exercise 28: The Revelation Principle

Prove the Revelation Principle for Bayesian Equilibrium.

Exercise 29: Revenue Equivalence

Prove the revenue equivalence theorem. Hint: See Wolfstetter (1999), Chapter 8.

Exercise 30: Revelation Principle for Auctions

Show how the revelation principle we discussed for auctions is a consequence of the more general revelation principle we presented in section 4.3.

Exercise 31: Optimal Auction with Identical Bidders

Suppose that $I = 2$ in the symmetric private information auction model. Suppose also that $\theta_H = 1$ and each bidder's valuation is distributed according to the uniform probability distribution on $[0, 1]$. Find the priority levels. Show that the item is sold only if the highest valuation is higher than $\frac{1}{2} + \frac{c}{2}$. Show that this implies that the optimal auction is not efficient. Hint: See Wolfstetter (1999, chapter 8).

Exercise 32: Functions ψ_i and γ_i

Show how the function ψ_i defined in equation (4.31) relates to the function γ_i of section 4.5.

Exercise 33: Bilateral Trading with Discrete Types

Consider the bilateral trading model of section 4.6 but now assume that each trader only has two possible types, θ_{iL} and θ_{iH}, instead of the entire interval of types as in that section. Assume that $\theta_{2H} > \theta_{1H} > \theta_{2L} > \theta_{1L}$. Explain how this assumption makes this set-up most interesting for the bilateral trading problem. Write β for the probability that the buyer, trader 2, has the high valuation θ_{2H}, and γ for the probability that the seller, trader 1, has the low valuation, θ_{1L}. Set up the incentive compatibility and participation constraints and prove that interim voluntary participation is incompatible with efficiency. Hint: See Bolton and Dewatripont (2005, pages 243–250).

Chapter 5

Refined Nash Implementation

Implementation in a refinement of Nash equilibrium is implementation that uses a sharper equilibrium concept than Nash equilibrium. A **Nash equilibrium refinement** selects, for each game of complete information, a subset, possibly a proper one, of the set of Nash equilibria of the game. Each refinement seeks to augment the best-response logic of Nash equilibrium to come closer to a comprehensive theory of what rational behavior in a game may be. The use of refinements in implementation helps to eliminate the undesirable equilibria of a mechanism while maintaining the desirable equilibria. The chapter considers three refinements of Nash equilibrium: subgame perfect equilibrium, undominated Nash equilibrium, and strong Nash equilibrium.

We also use the term "refined Nash implementation" to refer to a variant of what one means by implementation in Nash equilibrium. In the last section of this chapter we present one prominent such variant, virtual implementation.

We represent the characteristics of agents by type profiles $\theta \in \Theta$, as in chapter 2. The use of types rather than preference profiles is a matter of taste, as long as one is careful as to what types denote. In this chapter, as before, they denote preference relations. We retain the assumption that each agent knows the information of each other and that the game structure is common knowledge. When less information can be assumed for the agents, we will state that explicitly.

5.1 Implementation in Subgame Perfect Equilibrium

An important refinement of Nash equilibrium is subgame perfect equilibrium. To introduce the concept we need first to consider extensive form games. We do so very briefly, as a careful formal exposition needs extensive notational set-up. For more details, (Osborne, 2004, Chapter 5) and (Mas-Colell et al., 1995, Chapter 9) are excellent sources.

In an **extensive form game,** players take actions at different points of time. An extensive game has **perfect information** if every time a player has to take an action, the player knows the entire sequence of actions that have been taken before in the game. A simple example of an extensive form game of perfect information is shown in figure 5.1. A **strategy** for a player in an extensive form game is a complete plan of action that specifies which action the player is planning to take in every possible contingency in the game in which this player may have to take an action. The strategies each player adopts determine whether a particular subgame is ever reached and the actions taken in the subgame. Given this definition, a **Nash equilibrium** is defined as a profile of strategies, one per player, such that each strategy is a best response for its player to the strategies of the other players.

A **subgame** of an extensive form game with perfect information is a subset of the game that starts at an action node of some player and terminates when there are no more actions to be taken by any player. It is an extensive form game with perfect information itself. A **proper subgame** of an extensive form game with perfect information is a subgame that does not equal the game. In an extensive form game with perfect information, each player has complete information about all choices in the game that lead to any particular subgame. A strategy profile for the entire game **induces** a strategy profile for a subgame which is the strategy profile of the smaller game that results from following the strategy recommendations of each player in the entire game. A Nash equilibrium of an extensive form game with perfect information is a **subgame perfect** equilibrium of the game when it induces a Nash equilibrium in every subgame of the game.

We illustrate subgame perfect equilibrium with a simple, classical example, before turning to its use in implementation. Consider a market dominated by an incumbent firm, player I. Another firm is considering entry into this market; call it E. The tree shown in figure 5.1 shows the possible actions of each player in this two-player game.

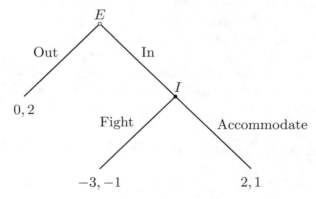

Figure 5.1: The Entrant-Incumbent Game

The game tree shows that E plays first and chooses between staying out of the market or going in. If E stays out, then I remains the incumbent monopolist and makes a positive profit, while E makes no profit; the game then is over. This is shown by the $0, 2$ payoff pair shown after "Out"; we write the payoff to the first player, E, first. If E chooses to enter, however, then I must choose to Accommodate the entry by not pricing its product very aggressively, or to Fight by engaging in a price war. In each case, the game ends after the payoffs that ensue from these choices are realized. The exact numbers we have chosen for the payoffs matter less than the size relationship between the three payoffs for each player.

The best way to solve this kind of game is to start from the end. This is called **backward induction** and also, in more general cases of games, **sequential rationality**. The last player who gets to play is I and its choice at that point in the game is pretty obvious: it will choose to Accommodate, to get the payoff of 1 rather than -1 that would come from the choice to Fight. The part of the game that starts where I gets to play is a proper subgame of the whole game. It is a game on its own, and yet it is a proper subset of the whole game.

Having concluded that if I gets the chance to play, it will choose Accommodate, we can now simplify the problem that E faces at the very beginning of the game. It can anticipate, just like us, the game theorists, the action of I and conclude that, should E enter, I will not put up a fight. Hence, E compares the payoff of 0 from staying out and the payoff of 2 from entering and having I accommodate the entry, and chooses to enter. We have now found the unique subgame perfect equilibrium of this game: it is the pair of strategies (In, Accommodate if In) for the two players. We have pieced it together by solving each subgame of the game separately, starting from the end of the game. This simplified our work, since the last subgame, the one where I has to play, is a one-player game and therefore trivial to solve for a Nash equilibrium, which for a one-player subgame simply means the strategy that yields the highest payoff to the player.

When we use the concept of subgame perfect equilibrium, we can implement more social choice correspondences than with Nash equilibrium. Moore and Repullo (1988) and Abreu and Sen (1990) find that when using the idea of sequential rationality certain undesirable equilibria can be eliminated. Sequential rationality is a less stringent requirement than Maskin Monotonicity. It leads to the necessary condition for subgame perfect Nash implementation known as indirect monotonicity.

Moore and Repullo (1988) introduced the concept of indirect monotonicity. Parts 1 and 2 of the following definition come from their paper. We also include the modifications introduced by Abreu and Sen (1990).

Definition 5.1 (Indirect Monotonicity). A social choice correspondence $F : \Theta \rightarrow\rightarrow X$ satisfies **indirect monotonicity** if there exists $B \subseteq X$ such that $F(\theta) \subseteq B$, for every profile $\theta \in \Theta, \phi \in \Theta$, and for every outcome $a \in X$ such that $a \in F(\theta)$, and $a \notin F(\phi)$, there exists $L < \infty$, and there exists a sequence of agents $j(0), \ldots, j(L)$ and a sequence of outcomes $a_0 = a$, $a_1, \ldots, a_L, a_{L+1}$ belonging to B such that:

1. $a_k \, R^{j(k)}(\theta) \, a_{k+1}, \ k = 0, 1, \ldots, L;$
2. $a_{L+1} \, P^{j(L)}(\phi) \, a_L;$

3. a_k is not ϕ-maximal for $j(k)$ in B; $k = 0, 1, \ldots, L$; and

4. if a_{L+1} is ϕ-maximal in B for every agent except $j(L)$
   $$\implies [L = 0 \text{ or } j(L-1) \neq j(L)].$$

Here $j(k)$ is the individual who moves at the kth stage of the game.

The first condition in definition 5.1 states that in each stage of the game, the particular individual that moves ranks the alternative at the current stage to be at least as good as the alternative in the next stage. The second condition states that the individual that moves in this last stage has a second profile in which the individual's preferences strictly change. Condition three states that at each stage of the game, the alternative in that stage is not optimal in the second profile for the individual whose turn it is to move. Finally, condition four states that if in the last stage of the game, every individual but the last to move in the game finds the last alternative to be at least as good in the second profile as every alternative in B, then either there is only one stage in the game or the individual at the last stage of the game is a different individual than the one at the second to the last stage of the game.

The difference between definition 5.1 and Maskin Monotonicity is that indirect monotonicity requires a reversal of preferences between two alternatives to take place but not necessarily involving the alternative a. However, there must be an appropriate "connection" with a as described in definition 5.1. In addition, when $L = 0$, that is, there is only one stage in the game, Maskin Monotonicity is satisfied.

Abreu and Sen (1990) formulated both necessity and sufficiency results for implementation via subgame perfect equilibrium. The necessity result states that indirect monotonicity is a necessary condition for a social choice correspondence to be implementable via subgame perfect equilibrium. The sufficiency result states that when there are at least three individuals, a social choice correspondence that satisfies both No Veto Power (as it is defined in chapter 3) and indirect monotonicity can be implemented via subgame perfect equilibrium. Both of these results are now stated formally.

Theorem 5.1 (Necessity [Abreu and Sen, 1990]). *If F is subgame perfect implementable, then F satisfies indirect monotonicity with respect to some $B \subseteq X$.*

Theorem 5.2 (Sufficiency [Abreu and Sen, 1990]). *Let $I \geq 3$. If F satisfies indirect monotonicity and No Veto Power with respect to some $B \subseteq X$, then F is subgame perfect implementable.*

Two examples follow, which are based on the examples in Abreu and Sen (1990). The first example demonstrates a social choice correspondence which is subgame perfect implementable but not Nash implementable. The second example is a social choice correspondence which is not subgame perfect implementable.

Example 5.1. Majority Rule (Abreu and Sen, 1990, page 295)

Amanda, Brittany, and Emma, denoted A, B, E respectively, have two preference profiles, one for the morning, θ, and one for the afternoon, ϕ, over a set of alternatives, X. The set X contains three alternatives where the girls choose between apples, bananas or cantaloupe denoted by a, b, c respectively. The following table describes their preferences:

$R^A(\theta) = R^A(\phi)$	$R^B(\theta) = R^B(\phi)$	$R^E(\theta)$	$R^E(\phi)$
a	c	b	c
b	a	c	b
c	b	a	a

Here Amanda and Brittany have no change in preferences between the two states. However, Emma reverses her first two preferences between the two states. That is, in the morning, Emma prefers bananas to cantaloupe, but in the afternoon she prefers cantaloupe to bananas.

The correspondence chooses the majority winner, which in this case is such that the outcome is the alternative that wins in a pairwise vote, as long as one exists. If a majority winner does not exist then the correspondence chooses the set X. Thus, $F(\theta) = \{a, b, c\}$ and $F(\phi) = \{c\}$.

We can easily see that this result is not Nash implementable. According to Maskin Monotonicity, a must be an element of $F(\phi)$ because for no individual does there exist (1) an alternative such that a is at least preferred to the alternative in the morning, and (2) the alternative is strictly preferred to a in the afternoon. However, a is not an element of $F(\phi)$.

On the other hand, we will see that since the correspondence does satisfy indirect monotonicity with respect to the set of alternatives X, this result is subgame perfect implementable.

In the case of $a \in F(\theta)$, $a \notin F(\phi)$, the sequences that satisfy the four parts of definition 5.1 are $a_0 = a$, $a_1 = b$, $a_2 = c$ and $j(0) = B$, $j(1) = E$. Here $L = 1$ such that Brittany moves first in the game and Emma moves second. Then, according to part 1 of the definition, $a_0 \ R^{j(0)}(\theta) \ a_1$ and $a_1 \ R^{j(1)}(\theta) \ a_2$. Thus, part 1 is satisfied because $a \ R^B(\theta) \ b$ and $b \ R^E(\theta) \ c$. According to part 2 of the definition, $a_2 \ P^{j(1)}(\phi) \ a_1$. Thus, part 2 is satisfied because $c \ P^E(\phi) \ b$. Part 3 is satisfied because neither $a_0 = a$ nor $a_1 = b$ is ϕ-maximal for either $j(0) = B$ or $j(1) = E$, respectively. Finally, part 4 is satisfied because the first part of the if statement is false. We can see that $a_2 = c$ is not ϕ-maximal for every agent except $j(1)$. In fact, it is ϕ-maximal for $j(1) = E$.

In the case of $b \in F(\theta)$, $b \notin F(\phi)$, the sequences that satisfy the four parts of definition 5.1 are $a_0 = b$, $a_1 = c$ and $j(0) = E$. Here $L = 0$ and Emma makes her move in the first stage of the game, choosing between bananas and cantaloupe. Part 1 of the definition, $a_0 \ R^{j(0)}(\theta) \ a_1$, is satisfied because $b \ R^E(\theta) \ c$. Part 2, $a_1 \ P^{j(0)}(\phi) \ a_0$, is satisfied because $c \ P^E(\phi) \ b$. Part 3 is satisfied because $a_0 = b$ is not ϕ-maximal for $j(0) = E$. Finally, part 4 is satisfied because again the first part of the if statement is false. Here $a_1 = c$ is not ϕ-maximal for every agent except $j(1)$. In fact, it is not ϕ-maximal for A, and it is ϕ-maximal for $j(1) = E$.

Finally, according to the sufficiency result, theorem 5.2, F is subgame perfect implementable because there are at least three individuals and both No Veto Power and indirect monotonicity conditions are satisfied.   ◇

Example 5.2. Plurality Rule (Abreu and Sen, 1990, page 296)

Again, Amanda, Brittany, and Emma, denoted A, B, E respectively, have two preference profiles, the morning, θ, and the afternoon, ϕ, over a set of alternatives, X. The set X contains three alternatives where the girls choose between apples, bananas or cantaloupe denoted by a, b, c respectively. The following table describes their preferences:

$R^A(\theta) = R^A(\phi)$	$R^B(\theta) = R^B(\phi)$	$R^E(\theta)$	$R^E(\phi)$
a	b	c	b
b	c	b	c
c	a	a	a

The correspondence in this example chooses the outcome that is ranked the highest by the largest number of individuals. In the event of a tie, the entire set of alternatives is chosen. Thus, $F(\theta) = \{a, b, c\}$ and $F(\phi) = \{b\}$.

In the case of $a \in F(\theta)$ and $a \notin F(\phi)$, the sequence of outcomes must be $a_0 = a$, $a_1 = c$, and $a_2 = b$. We see then that to satisfy part 1 of definition 5.1, only individual A can be $j(0)$. This states that Amanda must move in the first stage of the game, because a is ranked last by all other individuals in profile θ. Parts 1 and 2 would then be satisfied as in example 1 with $j(1) = E$. However, part 3 of the definition is violated because a is ϕ-maximal for A; that is, Amanda's maximum outcome is apples. Part 4 is satisfied because $a_2 = b$ is not ϕ-maximal for every agent except $j(1)$. In fact, it is not ϕ-maximal for A, and it is ϕ-maximal for $j(1) = E$. Therefore, since part 3 of indirect monotonicity is not satisfied, according to the necessity result, theorem 5.1, F is not implementable in subgame perfect equilibrium.   ◇

5.1.1 Subgame Perfect Implementation in Quasilinear Environments

The general idea of how subgame perfect implementation works can be seen by a simplified mechanism that Moore and Repullo introduced in (Moore and Repullo, 1988, Section 5). The general mechanism they use to cover any environment is based on this simplified mechanism. The environment is like the quasilinear environment of Section 2.4, with two agents and the special convention that t_1 represents a payment by agent 1, while t_2 represents a payment to agent 2. Formally, there is a nonempty set of possible public good choices, D, and two finite type sets Θ_1 and Θ_2 for the agents. A social alternative has three parts: $d \in D$ which is a choice of public good level, $t_1 \in \mathbb{R}$ which is a payment by agent 1 to the central authority, and $t_2 \in \mathbb{R}$ which is a payment to agent 2 by the central authority. Each t_i can be negative. The agents have quasilinear utility functions and evaluate a social alternative (d, t_1, t_2) as follows:

$$u_1(d, t_1, t_2, \theta_1) = v_1(d, \theta_1) - t_1,$$
$$u_2(d, t_1, t_2, \theta_2) = v_2(d, \theta_2) + t_2.$$

A social choice function f takes an argument (θ_1, θ_2) and returns a social alternative $f(\theta_1, \theta_2) = (d(\theta_1, \theta_2), t_1(\theta_1, \theta_2), t_2(\theta_1, \theta_2))$. Consider a particular such function f. It may or may not be Maskin Monotonic; we will show how to implement it in subgame perfect equilibrium nevertheless.

Let Δt stand for a large positive number; precisely, a number that exceeds any utility level that can be achieved by the agents for any outcome in the range of the social choice function f. For any $\theta_1 \in \Theta_1$ and any $\phi_1 \in \Theta_1$ with $\theta_1 \neq \phi_1$ (these will be specified in the mechanism below), let $x \in D, y \in D, t_x \in \mathbb{R}, t_y \in \mathbb{R}$ be such that x and y are chosen by the social choice function f for some combination of types and

$$v_1(x, \theta_1) - t_x > v_1(y, \theta_1) - t_y \text{ and}$$
$$v_1(x, \phi_1) - t_x < v_1(y, \phi_1) - t_y.$$

A quadruplet (x, y, t_x, t_y) with this property is always possible to find in this environment.

We can now describe the mechanism, which proceeds in stages. Stage 1 is designed to give the incentive to agent 1 to reveal θ_1 truthfully, and stage 2 to do the same for agent 2.

Stage 1

Stage 1.1: Agent 1 announces a type $\theta_1 \in \Theta_1$, and play moves on to stage 1.2.

Stage 1.2: Agent 2 chooses whether to:

Agree and play moves on to stage 2; or

Challenge by announcing $\phi_1 \neq \theta_1$ and play moves on to stage 1.3.

Stage 1.3: Agent 1 chooses between the alternatives $(x, t_x + \Delta t, t_x - \Delta t)$ and $(y, t_y + \Delta t, t_y + \Delta t)$. If agent 1 chooses $(x, t_x + \Delta t, t_x - \Delta t)$, it is put in place, which means that x is produced, agent 1 pays to the central authority $t_x + \Delta t$, and agent 2 receives from the central authority $t_x - \Delta t$, so the central authority accumulates a surplus of $2\Delta t$. The game then ends. If agent 1 chooses $(y, t_y + \Delta t, t_y + \Delta t)$, it is put in place, which means that y is produced, agent 1 pays to the central authority $t_y + \Delta t$, and agent 2 receives from the central authority $t_y + \Delta t$, so the central authority breaks even. The game then ends.

Stage 2 Same as in Stage 1, but with the roles of agents 1 and 2 interchanged. If at Stage 2.1 agent 2 has announced $\theta_2 \in \Theta_2$ and at Stage 2.2 agent 1 has agreed, then the social alternative $(d(\theta_1, \theta_2), t_1(\theta_1, \theta_2), t_2(\theta_1, \theta_2))$ is put in place and the game ends.

Theorem 5.3 (Moore and Repullo, 1988). *For every true type profile $(\theta_1, \theta_2) \in \Theta_1 \times \Theta_2$, the unique subgame perfect equilibrium of the above mechanism has the outcome $f(\theta_1, \theta_2) = (d(\theta_1, \theta_2), t_1(\theta_1, \theta_2), t_2(\theta_1, \theta_2))$, thus the mechanism implements the social choice function f in subgame perfect equilibrium.*

Proof. Consider stage 1. If agent 1 lies and reports ϕ_1, then it is best for agent 2 to challenge agent 1 with the truth, θ_1. Indeed, after such a challenge, the play of the game moves to stage 1.3, where agent 1 chooses $(y, t_y + \Delta t, t_y + \Delta t)$ (recall the properties of the quadruplet (x, y, t_x, t_y)). The reason this is best for agent 2 is that she receives the large transfer of money Δt for challenging 1. Because Δt is large enough, agent 1 is worse off than having told the truth at stage 1.1, so he will not choose to lie then.

If agent 1 tells the truth in stage 1.1, then agent 2 will find it best not to challenge him falsely in stage 1.2. Indeed, if agent 2 were to challenge θ_1 via ϕ_1, then in stage 1.3 agent 1 would choose $(x, t_x + \Delta t, t_x - \Delta t)$, which penalizes agent 2 by the large amount Δt. Once again, because Δt has been chosen to be larger than any utility level that any agent can achieve in any outcome in the range of the social choice function f, agent 2 certainly prefers not to have to pay Δt.   QED

Two properties of this mechanism are worth discussing. First, when the agents play their subgame equilibrium strategies, then the mechanism balances, meaning that the central authority realizes neither surplus nor deficit. Out of equilibrium the central authority may realize a large surplus, if stage 1.3 or 2.3 has been reached. This is a questionable feature of the mechanism in practice, as, if it were invoked, there would be strong pressure on the central authority not to impose the large penalties on the two agents. However, if there are three or more agents, the mechanism can easily be adapted to have the penalty imposed on any two players be paid to a third one, and not to the central authority. This would make the central authority's budget balance in and out of equilibrium. It would be just as likely to be strongly protested by the penalized agents, of course, as in the case of just two agents.

The second important feature of this mechanism is its parsimony in the information level it demands of the agents. Even though we are generally assuming complete information in this chapter, as in chapter 3, for this mechanism to work it is enough that each agent i know only one other agent j's preference parameter θ_j. This feature is similar to the informational structure assumed by Saijo in the mechanism we examined in section 3.2.1.

5.2 Implementation Using Undominated Strategies

A weakly dominated strategy for a player is a strategy such that there exists another strategy for the player that yields the player at least as much payoff no matter what strategies the others play. Let $\Gamma = (M, g)$ be a mechanism. A strategy[1] $m_i \in M_i$ is **weakly dominated** for i by $\widehat{m}_i \in M_i$ at environment $\theta \in \Theta$ if $g(\widehat{m}_i, m_{-i}) \, R^i(\theta) \, g(m_i, m_{-i})$ for all $m_{-i} \in M_{-i}$ and $g(\widehat{m}_i, m_{-i}) \, P^i(\theta) \, g(m_i, m_{-i})$ for some $m_{-i} \in M_{-i}$. We call a strategy profile $m \in M$ **undominated** if it is not weakly dominated for any $i \in \mathcal{I}$ and any $\theta \in \Theta$. Let the set of undominated strategies of a mechanism at θ be $\mathcal{U}(\Gamma, \theta)$.[2]

An **undominated Nash equilibrium** of a mechanism (M, g) at an environment θ is a strategy profile $m \in M$ which is a Nash equilibrium of (M, g) in θ and such that the strategy m_i of each agent is not weakly dominated at environment θ by any other strategy of that agent. Recall that $\mathcal{N}(\Gamma, \theta)$ denotes the set of Nash equilibria of Γ played at environment θ. The set of undominated Nash equilibria of Γ played at θ is $\mathcal{UN}(\Gamma, \theta) = \mathcal{U}(\Gamma, \theta) \cap \mathcal{N}(\Gamma, \theta)$, the intersection of the sets of undominated strategies and the set of Nash equilibrium strategies. The corresponding set of undominated Nash equilibrium outcomes of the mechanism (M, g) is $g(\mathcal{UN}(\Gamma, \theta))$.

Undominated Nash implementation of a social choice correspondence $F : \Theta \to\to X$ occurs when for each $\theta \in \Theta$, $F(\theta) = g(\mathcal{UN}(\Gamma, \theta))$. We say then that F is **implemented in undominated Nash equilibria.**

A social choice correspondence $F : \Theta \to\to X$ is **implemented in undominated strategies** if for each $\theta \in \Theta$, $F(\theta) = g(\mathcal{U}(\Gamma, \theta))$.

Bounded and unbounded mechanisms are used to implement undominated Nash equilibria, and as we will see, the difference of what the two kinds of mechanisms can achieve is significant.

Definition 5.2 (Bounded Mechanism). A mechanism is **bounded** if for any weakly dominated message $m_i \in M_i$ at some $\theta \in \Theta$, there exists a message $\widehat{m}_i \in M_i$ which weakly dominates m_i and is undominated at θ.

Before we can move forward to the results, we make the following assumption, as stated in Jackson (2001) and first formulated by Palfrey and Srivastava (1989).

Definition 5.3. The social choice problem with type set Θ satisfies **strict value distinction** if for every $\theta \in \Theta$ and every $\phi \in \Theta$ such that $\theta \neq \phi$:
  1. For all i, there exists $a \in X$ and $b \in X$ such that $a \, P^i(\theta) \, b$,
  2. For all i, if $R^i(\theta) \neq R^i(\phi)$ there exists $a \in X$ and $b \in X$ such that $a \, P^i(\theta) \, b$ and $b \, P^i(\phi) \, a$.

---

[1] We adopt here the terminology that m_i is the strategy of agent i at environment θ; see the discussion of this issue right after the definition of Nash equilibrium for a mechanism on page 63.

[2] The presentation in this section benefited from the exposition in Jackson (2001).

The first part of definition 5.3 does not allow any agent type to be completely indifferent between all alternatives. The second part requires that any change in preferences does not result in indifference between any alternatives. Thus, strict value distinction requires indifference curves to cross at some point if there is a change in preferences. The assumption of strict value distinction is satisfied in most areas of application of implementation in economics and political science.

Jackson (1992) investigated implementation in undominated strategies, without requiring Nash equilibrium, and also implementation in undominated Nash equilibrium.

Theorem 5.4 (Jackson, 1992). *If each agent's preferences satisfy the condition of strict value distinction, then any social choice correspondence can be implemented in undominated strategies.*

This theorem shows that if we expect each agent to play an undominated strategy, without paying attention to whether it is a best response to the other agents' strategies, then, when strict value distinction is satisfied, every social choice correspondence, even if it does not satisfy Maskin Monotonicity, is implementable! This result is surprising because the solution concept of undominated strategies does not require much information or computational ability on the part of the agents. An agent does not need to know the other agents' types or even to have common knowledge of the game with them, in order to find and play his undominated strategies. He simply has to eliminate any weakly dominated strategies he may have and play one of the remaining strategies. The reason undominated strategy implementation works so well is that it allows the construction of games with infinite strategy spaces, in which for each agent i there are cascades of strategies such that strategy m_i is weakly dominated by strategy m_i', which in turn is weakly dominated by strategy m_i'', and so on without end. The use of a mechanism that has this property in every environment gives the designer the ability to eliminate undesirable strategies by building such endless cascades to make them weakly dominated. Mechanisms that do this tend to be very complicated, which is why we do not present them here; Jackson (1992) and Palfrey and Srivastava (1991) are the best sources for such mechanisms.

We illustrate the cascades of weakly dominated strategies in the following example. It demonstrates clearly how the use of undominated strategies with unbounded mechanisms may result in an unreasonable solution to the implementation problem.

Example 5.3. An unbounded mechanism that implements in undominated strategies a strange social choice correspondence (Jackson, 1992, page 761). Let $\mathcal{I} = \{1, 2\}$, $X = \{a, b\}$, $\Theta = \{(\theta_1, \theta_2), (\theta_1', \theta_2)\}$ and $a\, P^1(\theta_1)\, b$, $b\, P^1(\theta_1')\, a$, $a\, P^2(\theta_2)\, b$. Let the social choice function F be defined by $F(\theta_1, \theta_2) = b$ and $F(\theta_1', \theta_2) = a$. This F is strange indeed. It goes directly against the preferences of agent 1, the only one whose preferences change from (θ_1, θ_2) to (θ_1', θ_2), and therefore it does not select Pareto efficient alternatives and is not Maskin Monotonic. It even rejects the alternative a which is unanimously rated best in environment (θ_1, θ_2).

		m_2	m_2'	m_2''							
	M_2										
	m_1	b	a	a	a	$\ldots$	a	a	a	a	$\ldots$
		b	a	a	a	$\ldots$	b	b	b	b	$\ldots$
		b	b	a	a	$\ldots$	b	b	b	b	$\ldots$
		b	b	b	a	$\ldots$	b	b	b	b	$\ldots$
M_1		$\vdots$	$\vdots$	$\vdots$	$\vdots$		$\vdots$	$\vdots$	$\vdots$	$\vdots$	
	m_1'	a	b	b	b	$\ldots$	b	b	b	b	$\ldots$
		a	a	a	a	$\ldots$	a	b	b	b	$\ldots$
		a	a	a	a	$\ldots$	a	a	b	b	$\ldots$
		a	a	a	a	$\ldots$	a	a	a	b	$\ldots$
		$\vdots$	$\vdots$	$\vdots$	$\vdots$		$\vdots$	$\vdots$	$\vdots$	$\vdots$	

This table represents the alternatives selected by the outcome function g of a mechanism $\Gamma = (M_1 \times M_2, g)$. The messages in message space M_1 are shown as labels of the rows, and the messages in message space M_1 are shown as labels of the columns. Each horizontal or vertical ellipsis represents a countably infinite number of rows or columns, respectively.

At type θ_2, her only type, agent 2 has only one undominated strategy, to send message m_2. At type θ_1, agent 1 has only one undominated strategy, to send message m_1. Finally, at type θ_1', agent 1 has only one undominated strategy, to send message m_1'. Therefore, this mechanism implements F in undominated strategies.

To see this, note that for agent 2, m_2 is undominated because it is the only strategy for 2 that, if agent 1 plays m_1', results in a (check this claim, and all subsequent claims, in detail, using the definition of weakly dominated strategy). Any strategy for 2 in the right half of the table is weakly dominated by m_2'. But m_2' is weakly dominated for agent 2 by m_2'', m_2'' is weakly dominated for agent 2 by the strategy to its immediate right, and so on without end. As a result, the only undominated strategy of agent 2 is m_2. Similarly, the only undominated strategy for agent 1 at θ_1 is m_1 and the only undominated strategy for agent 1 at θ_1' is m_1'. It follows that when the environment is (θ_1, θ_2), the only undominated strategy outcome of the mechanism Γ is b, and when the environment is (θ_1', θ_2), the only undominated strategy outcome of the mechanism Γ is a. Therefore, Γ implements F in undominated strategies.

The elimination of weakly dominated strategies in this mechanism is not a very convincing way of solving the mechanism in either one of the possible environments (θ_1, θ_2) or (θ_1', θ_2). Strategy m_2 survived the elimination of weakly dominated strategies and every strategy in the sequence $m_2', m_2'', \ldots$ was eliminated as it was weakly dominated by the strategy to its right. In this infinite string of strategies, there is no undominated strategy. So we eliminated all of these strategies and we predicted that agent 2 will play m_2. Yet, the payoff for agent 2 from playing m_2 is worse, depending on the strategy that agent 1 plays, than the payoff for agent 2 of playing any one of the eliminated strategies. This infinite chain of eliminating strategies is similar to the use of an integer game in the canonical mechanism from chapter 3, which is also considered an undesirable feature of a mechanism.   ◇

The use of unbounded mechanisms, which allows the cascades of weakly dominated strategies we just discussed, is undesirable. Unfortunately, if we insist that only bounded mechanisms be used, the set of social choice correspondences that can be implemented in undominated strategies shrinks drastically.

Definition 5.4 (Strategy Resistance). A social choice correspondence $F : \Theta \rightarrow\rightarrow X$ is **strategy resistant** if for each $\theta \in \Theta$ each $(\theta_i', \theta_{-i}) \in \Theta$ with $\theta_i \neq \theta_i'$, and each $y \in F(\theta_i', \theta_{-i})$, there exists $x \in F(\theta)$ such that $x \, R^i(\theta_i) \, y$.

To understand this condition, interpret θ as the true environment, θ_i' as a misrepresentation of i's type in the environment, and y as an alternative that F selects when i sends the misrepresentation. The condition then demands that there is some alternative x that can be obtained when i sends the true θ_i that i considers at least as good as y.

The strategy resistance property is very similar to strategy-proofness. The disappointment that the next theorem brings should therefore not be too surprising. Recall the Gibbard-Satterthwaite theorem, theorem 1.3., as an example of the restrictive nature of strategy-proofness.

Theorem 5.5 (Jackson, 1992). *A social choice correspondence which can be implemented in undominated strategies by a bounded mechanism is strategy resistant. A social choice function which can be implemented in undominated strategies by a bounded mechanism is strategy-proof.*

Palfrey and Srivastava (1991) introduced a weaker condition, called "Property Q," or value distinction, which allows for more indifference than strict value distinction. However, the agents must not be indifferent between all alternatives when preferences change in the second state. They then formulated the following results, which are true for unbounded mechanisms. Please refer to Palfrey and Srivastava (1991) for details.

Theorem 5.6 (Palfrey and Srivastava, 1991). *If F is undominated Nash implementable, then F satisfies Property Q.*

Theorem 5.7 (Palfrey and Srivastava, 1991). *Let $I \geq 3$. If F satisfies Property Q and No Veto Power, then F is implementable in undominated Nash equilibrium.*

For implementation in undominated Nash equilibrium when property Q is satisfied, Maskin Monotonicity is not needed. According to these results, most voting rules, which are not Nash implementable, are implementable in undominated Nash equilibrium.

Finally, Jackson et al. (1994) introduce the following definition.

Definition 5.5 (Chaining). The social choice correspondence F is **chained** at $x \in X$, $\theta \in \Theta$, $\phi \in \Theta$ if there exists an individual, $i \in \mathcal{I}$, and alternatives, $y_1, y_2 \in X$, such that $y_1 \ P^i(\theta) \ y_2$ and $y_2 \ P^i(\phi) \ y_1$ where either:

1. $y_1 = x$ or
2. There exists an individual $j \neq i$, and alternatives z_1 and $z_2 \notin \{x, z_1\}$ such that:
   - $z_2 \ P^j(\phi) \ x$, $z_2 \ P^i(\phi) \ z_1$
   - $z_1 = x$ or $x \ P^j(\theta) \ z_1$

In definition 5.5 there is at least one individual who switches preferences between the two states. The first part of this definition states that if x is an outcome of the social choice correspondence F under state θ and not an outcome of the social choice correspondence F under state ϕ, then the social choice correspondence F satisfies the standard monotonicity condition. The second part of the definition states that if monotonicity is not satisfied, then there is another individual j who is linked to individual i. They are linked as follows: there are two alternatives z_1 and z_2, such that under state ϕ, individual j strictly prefers z_2 to x and individual i strictly prefers z_2 to z_1 when z_1 is equal to x or individual j strictly prefers x to z_1 under state θ. This ensures that there is an individual for whom it is not a best response to play the same strategy under both states.

In addition, the results by Jackson et al. (1994) depend on the mechanism satisfying the best response property, which is defined as follows.

Definition 5.6 (Best Response Property). A mechanism (M, g) has the **best response property** if for all $i \in \mathcal{I}$, all $\theta \in \Theta$, and all $m_{-i} \in M_i$, there exists an $m_i \in M_i$ such that $g(m_i, m_{-i}) \ R^i(\theta) \ g(\hat{m}_i, m_{-i})$ for all $\hat{m}_i \in M_i$.

Theorem 5.8 (Jackson et al., 1994). *If $I \geq 3$, A is finite, F satisfies No Veto Power and is chained, then F is undominated Nash implementable by a bounded mechanism satisfying the best response property.*

Here we present two examples. The first example shows an unbounded mechanism that is implemented in undominated Nash equilibrium. The second example shows a correspondence that can be implemented in undominated Nash equilibrium via a bounded mechanism.

Example 5.4. Unbounded Mechanism (Jackson, 1992, page 765)

Assume there are five individuals, Dave, Helen, Keith, Mel, and Tara, denoted by D, H, K, M, and T, respectively. They must choose between two alternatives; going to the movies, a, and going to the park, b. Finally there are two preference profiles: one for Saturday, θ, and one for Sunday, ϕ, with their preferences described in the table below.

$R^D(\theta) = R^D(\phi)$	$R^H(\theta) = R^H(\phi)$	$R^K(\theta) = R^K(\phi)$
a	a	b
b	b	a
$R^M(\theta) = R^M(\phi)$	$R^T(\theta)$	$R^T(\phi)$
b	b	a
a	a	b

These preferences satisfy the strict value distinction condition because each individual strictly prefers one alternative to the other on Saturday, and the only individual to change preferences between the two states, Tara, does not become indifferent between the two alternatives on Sunday. Tara still has strict preferences between the two alternatives on Sunday.

The correspondence is such that $F(\theta) = a$ and $F(\phi) = b$. Although this seems to be an unreasonable solution, this correspondence can be implemented in undominated Nash equilibrium because $I \geq 3$, preferences satisfy the strict value distinction condition and the correspondence satisfies the No Veto Power condition.

However, as Jackson (1992) shows, this correspondence can only be implemented by an unbounded mechanism and not by a bounded mechanism. This is because it is not guaranteed that Tara will not play a dominated strategy. Each strategy that provides her prefered outcome on Sunday, ϕ, of going to the movies, a, is dominated by an infinite cascade of strategies.

$\Diamond$

Example 5.5. Bounded Mechanism

Here we will show that example 5.2, which was not implementable in subgame Nash equilibrium is implementable via a bounded mechanism in undominated Nash equilibrium.

Recall the three individuals, Amanda, A, Brittany, B, and Emma, E, have the following preferences over alternatives apples, a, bananas, b, and cantaloupe, c, in the morning, θ, and in the afternoon, ϕ.

$R^A(\theta) = R^A(\phi)$	$R^B(\theta) = R^B(\phi)$	$R^E(\theta)$	$R^E(\phi)$
a	b	c	b
b	c	b	c
c	a	a	a

The correspondence chooses the outcomes as follows: $F(\theta) = \{a, b, c\}$ and $F(\phi) = \{b\}$.

Here the chained condition is satisfied as follows.

In the case of $a \in F(\theta)$ and $a \notin F(\phi)$, let $x = a$, $y_1 = c$, $y_2 = b$, $z_1 = a$ and $z_2 = c$. Individual i is Emma; that is, she has a change in preferences between y_1 and y_2 from the morning, θ, to the afternoon, ϕ. That is, $c \, P^E(\theta) \, b$ and $b \, P^E(\phi) \, c$. Then individual j is Brittany, where both Brittany and Emma have an alternative z_2 that they strictly prefer to the alternative $x = z_1$ in the afternoon, ϕ. That is, $c \, P^B(\phi) \, a$ and $c \, P^E(\phi) \, a$.

In the case of $c \in F(\theta)$ and $c \notin F(\phi)$, the standard monotonicity definition, part 1 of the chained condition, is satisfied because c drops ranking for Emma from one state to the other.

Thus, since the social choice correspondence F satisfies both the chained condition and No Veto Power, there are three individuals and the set of alternatives is finite, F can be implemented by a bounded mechanism in undominated Nash equilibrium. Jackson et al. (1994) show the more general result that with three or more individuals, the plurality social choice correspondence is chained.   ◊

5.3 Double Implementation

Double implementation occurs when a social choice correspondence is implemented in two different equilibria.

Here we will discuss double implementation in both Nash equilibria and strong Nash equilibria. We restrict ourselves to environments with a private and public goods for simplicity and because this kind of environment has wide applicability. Finding a mechanism that double implements a social choice correspondence in both Nash and strong Nash equilibria is important when the designer does not know whether the members of the economy can form coalitions and cooperate. The Nash equilibrium concept rules out unilateral strategy deviations by players. The strong Nash equilibrium concept rules out in addition coordinated strategy deviations by any group of players acting in concert via a coalition.

5.3.1 Definitions

We consider a domain of general equilibrium economies with one private and k public goods. The definitions of an allocation and a feasible allocations are as in section A.6, but with $n = 1$ as here we have only one private good.

Each agent $i \in \mathcal{I}$ has a positive endowment $\omega_i > 0$ of the private good and a utility function $u_i : \mathbb{R}_+^{1+k} \to \mathbb{R}$ with $u_i(x_i, y)$ expressing the utility i derives from consuming the amount x_i of the private good and the non-negative k-dimensional vector y of the amounts of the public goods.

Each public good j is produced by a bureau also labeled by j. The production technology for public good j is given by a cost function $c_j : \mathbb{R}_+ \to \mathbb{R}_+$ and $c_j(y_j)$ denotes the amount of the private good needed to produce the level y_j of the public good j. We assume that for each j the cost function c_j is continuous, strictly increasing, and satisfies $c_j(0) = 0$. This means that there are no sudden jumps in the cost of production, producing more costs more, and producing no output costs nothing.

Denote by $F(e)$ the set of feasible allocations of the economy e. In our present setting, this means that $\sum_{i=1}^{I} x_i + \sum_{j=1}^{k} c_j(y_j) \leq \sum_{i=1}^{k} \omega_i$.

Definition 5.7 (Foley-Core). Let $S \subseteq \mathcal{I}$ be a coalition. The allocation $z = (x, y) \in F(e)$ can be **improved upon by** S if there exists a vector of private good levels for the members of S, $(x_i')_{i \in S}$, and a $y' \in \mathbb{R}_+^k$ such that

1. $\sum_{i \in S} x_i' + \sum_j c_j(y_j') \leq \sum_{i \in S} \omega_i$, and
2. for each $i \in S$, $u_i(x_i', y') \geq u_i(x_i, y)$, with strict inequality for some i.

An allocation $z \in F(e)$ is in the **Foley-core of** e if there does not exist a coalition $S \subseteq \mathcal{I}$ that can improve upon z.

The Foley-core is similar to the concept of the core in the classical exchange economy. The core was discussed in detail when the core social choice correspondence was introduced in section 1.7.5.

We employ a slightly different notion of a mechanism in this section. The strategy sets $M_1, \ldots, M_I$ are as before, as is the shorthand notation M for the Cartesian product $M_1 \times \cdots \times M_I$. However, the outcome function g now has the domain $M \times \mathcal{E}$ and assigns to each member (m, e) of the domain, which consists of a strategy profile m and an economy e an allocation for the economy e. $\mathcal{E}$ stands for a suitably restricted class of public good economies; we define it further below.

Given a mechanism (M, g), and economy $e \in \mathcal{E}$, and a strategy profile $m \in M$, we denote by $v_i(m) = u_i(g(m, e))$ the utility of individual i when m is played in the mechanism in the environment of the economy e. To make it easy to keep track of coordinated deviations from a strategy profile m by coalitions, we introduce the notation m_S for the sub-profile of m made up by the strategies of the members of a coalition S. Analogously, m_{-s} denotes the sub-profile of m made up by the strategies of the agents who are not members of the coalition S.

A mechanism $\Gamma = (M, g)$ is a **feasible mechanism** if for all economies e, and for all strategy profiles $m \in M$, we have $g(m, e) \in F(e)$.

Next, we formally define both Nash and strong Nash equilibrium. The definition of Nash equilibrium is as before, but we repeat it in this context to make the comparison with strong Nash equilibrium easier.

Definition 5.8. Given an economy $e = (u, \omega, c)$, and a mechanism $\Gamma = (M, g)$, a strategy profile $m \in M$ is a **Nash equilibrium** of Γ played in e if for all $i \in \mathcal{I}$, and for all $m_i' \in M_i$,

$$u_i(g(m, e)) \geq u_i(g(m_i', m_{-i}, e)).$$

This is the typical definition of Nash equilibrium where an agent plays his best response to the strategy profile of all the others. No individual agent wishes to deviate from a Nash equilibrium strategy profile. Let $N(\Gamma, e)$ denote the set of Nash equilibria of the mechanism Γ played in the economy e. Denote the set of **Nash equilibrium allocations played at** e by $NA(\Gamma, e)$.

Definition 5.9. Given an economy $e = (u, \omega, c)$, and a mechanism $\Gamma = (M, g)$, a strategy profile $m \in M$ is a **strong Nash equilibrium** of Γ played in e if there does not exist a coalition $S \subseteq \mathcal{I}$ and a sub-profile of strategies $(m'_i)_{i \in S}$, such that for all $i \in S$,

$$u_i(g(m'_S, m_{-S}, e)) \geq u_i(g(m, e)),$$

with strict inequality for some $i \in S$.

A strong Nash equilibrium is a strategy profile m such that there is no coalition of individuals that can form and employ strategies that result in an outcome that is at least as good as $g(m, e)$ for every member of the coalition and strictly preferable for at least one member of the coalition. Let $S(\Gamma, e)$ denote the set of strong Nash equilibria of the mechanism Γ played in the economy e, and let $SA(\Gamma, e)$ denote the set of strong Nash equilibrium allocations.

The domain of **classical economies**, $\mathcal{E}_c$, is such that every utility function u_i is quasi-concave and each cost function is convex. This says that each agent's preferences have diminishing marginal rate of substitution and each public good's production function has increasing marginal cost.

The **boundary** of the set $\mathbb{R}_+^{k+1}$ contains each vector in $\mathbb{R}_+^{k+1}$ that has at least one coordinate equal to zero. The **interior** of the set $\mathbb{R}_+^{k+1}$ is the set of strictly positive vectors $\mathbb{R}_{++}^{k+1}$. An economy e is **essential** if for each $i \in I$, if (x_i, y) is in the boundary of $\mathbb{R}_+^{k+1}$ and (x'_i, y') is in the interior of $\mathbb{R}_+^{k+1}$, then $u_i(x_i, y) < u_i(x'_i, y')$. The domain of **essential economies,** is a subset of $\mathcal{E}_c$ in which every economy is essential. It is denoted by $\mathcal{E}_{ce}$. In each essential economy, each agent prefers to have a consumption vector with a strictly positive amount of every good, both public and private, to any consumption vector that has zero amount of some good, no matter how large the amounts of the other goods might be in the second vector.

5.3.2 Ratio Correspondence

Corchón and Wilkie (1996) define mechanisms which double implement the ratio social choice correspondence. They seek to implement social choice correspondences which select allocations that are both efficient and individually rational. The requirements of this double implementation as stated by Corchón and Wilkie (1996) are to

(1) not limit technology to constant returns to scale;

(2) allow for coalitions of individuals who conspire to manipulate the outcome; and

(3) create a mechanism that is similar to market operations.

These requirements are satisfied by the ratio correspondence. Lindahl correspondences, which are described in the appendix, are unable to satisfy the first condition because constant returns to scale are needed to find efficient and individually rational outcomes.

The ratio r_{ik} is the portion of the cost of the public good k that individual i is required to contribute. The following two definitions are from Corchón and Wilkie (1996).

Definition 5.10. A pair (r, z) where $r = (r_1, \ldots, r_I)$, for each agent $r_i \in \mathbb{R}^k_+$, and for each public good k, $\sum_{\mathcal{I}} r_{ik} = 1$, and $z = (x, y) \in \mathbb{R}^{I+k}_+$ is a **ratio equilibrium**, and z is a **ratio allocation** for $e = (u, \omega, c)$ if

1. for each $i \in \mathcal{I}$, $x_i + r_i \cdot c(y) \leq \omega_i$, and
2. if $x'_i + r_i \cdot c(y') \leq \omega_i$ then $u_i(x_i, y) \geq u_i(x'_i, y')$.

The first part of definition 5.10 requires for each agent that the amount of the private good he consumes plus the fraction of the cost of the public good to the agent multiplied by the total amount of the cost is no greater than the agent's endowment of the private good. The second part ensures that the ratio allocation z yields each agent the largest level of utility given the affordability constraint of the first part. We let $RE(e)$ denote the set of ratio equilibria of the economy e.

Definition 5.11. The **ratio correspondence**, R, selects for each economy $e \in \mathcal{E}_{ce}$ the set of ratio allocations $RE(e)$.

Corchón and Wilkie (1996) define the cost share game as follows.

Definition 5.12. The **Cost Share Game** $\Gamma_1 = (M, g)$ is specified by the following components:

1. For all $i \in \mathcal{I}$, $M_i = [0, 1]^k \times \mathbb{R}^k$ with generic element $m_i = (r_i, y_i)$.
2. $g : M \times \mathcal{E}_{ce} \to \mathbb{R}^{I+k}$ where

$$g(m, e) = (g_x(m, e), g_y(m, e)) = \left(\omega_1 - r_1 \cdot c(\sum y_i), \ldots, \omega_I - r_I \cdot c(\sum y_i); \sum y_i \right)$$

if for each $j = 1, \ldots, k$, $\sum_i r_{il} \geq 1$ and $\sum y_i \geq 0$, and $g(m, e) = (\omega_1, \ldots, \omega_I; 0)$ otherwise.

The first part of definition 5.12. states that a strategy of each agent has two parts: the fraction (ratio) vector $r_i = (r_{i1}, \ldots, r_{ik})$ and a proposed incremental public goods vector $y_i = (y_{i1}, \ldots, y_{ik})$. The second part of the definition defines the outcome function. The outcome function assigns each agent an amount of the private good equal to the agent's endowment minus the agent's share of the cost of providing the public good times the level of the public good produced. The level of each public good is equal to the sum of all agents' contributions to the public good, which is why we called the y_i vectors incremental. This outcome occurs only when the sum of the share of the costs of each individual to produce a positive level of the public good is at least one. Otherwise, each individual keeps his endowment and the level of the public good is zero.

Corchón and Wilkie (1996) find the following two results for the cost share game Γ_1.

Theorem 5.9 (Corchón and Wilkie, 1996). *Any ratio equilibrium allocation for e is a Nash equilibrium outcome of Γ_1 played in e: $R(e) \subseteq NA(\Gamma_1, e)$.*

Theorem 5.10 (Corchón and Wilkie, 1996). *Any Nash equilibrium allocation of Γ_1, such that the level of at least one public good is positive, is a ratio equilibrium allocation for e: $NA(\Gamma_1, e) \cap \{z \in F(e) \mid y \neq 0\} \subseteq R(e)$.*

The cost share game is constructed in such a way that each agent is forced to take ratios as given. Nevertheless, it may happen that there is no production of any public good in an equilibrium of the cost share game. This necessitates the additional condition imposed at the end of theorem 5.10. However, by restricting at least one public good to be an essential good for one individual, we can ensure that at least one public good is provided at a positive level.

Corollary 5.1 (Corchón and Wilkie, 1996). *In the essential goods domain, $e \in \mathcal{E}_{ce}$, any Nash equilibrium allocation of the game Γ_1 played in e is a ratio equilibrium allocation for e: $NA(\Gamma_1, e) \subseteq R(e)$.*

Corchón and Wilkie (1996) also find that the set of ratio equilibrium allocations for e is equivalent to the set of strong Nash equilibrium outcomes of the game.

Theorem 5.11 (Corchón and Wilkie, 1996). *Any ratio equilibrium allocation for e is a strong Nash equilibrium outcome of Γ_1 played in e: $R(e) \subseteq SA(\Gamma_1, e)$.*

Theorem 5.12 (Corchón and Wilkie, 1996). *Any strong Nash equilibrium allocation for e is a ratio equilibrium allocation for e: $SA(\Gamma_1, e) \subseteq R(e)$.*

The cost share game Γ_1 does not always result in an outcome that is feasible for each agent. An agent may be asked to make a contribution of his private good to the production of the public good that is greater than his endowment. The outcome function is also discontinuous. It may happen that as an agent reduces his y_i incremental contributions by a small amount, the outcome changes by a large amount to the outcome with no production of the public goods. A modified version of the game corrects these problems on the domain of the essential economies $\mathcal{E}_{ce}$.

The modified market game defined by Corchón and Wilkie (1996) is as follows.

Definition 5.13. Let $\Delta^{(I-1)}$ denote the set of I-dimensional non-negative vectors each of whose coordinates sum to one. The **Modified Cost Share Game** $\Gamma_2 = (M, g)$ is specified by the following components:

1. For all $i \in \mathcal{I}$, $M_i = [0,1]^k \times \mathbb{R}^k$ with generic element $m_i = (r_i, y_i)$. Given $r \in \triangle^{(I-1)k}$ let

$$r'_{ij} = \begin{cases} r_{ij} & \text{if } \sum_{i \in \mathcal{I}} r_{ij} \geq 1, \\ 1 - \sum_{h \neq i} r_{hj} + \dfrac{|1 - \sum_{i \in \mathcal{I}} r_{ij}|}{I} & \text{otherwise,} \end{cases}$$

and $y(m)$ be a continuous function of $s \in M$ such that; for all i, $r'_i \cdot c(y(m)) \leq \omega_i$, and when for all i, $r'_i \cdot \sum y_i \leq \omega_i$, then $y(m) = \sum y_i$.

2. $g : M \times \mathcal{E}_{ce} \to \mathbb{R}^{I+k}$ where, $g(m, e) = (\omega_1 - r'_1 \cdot c(y(m)), \ldots, \omega_I - r'_I \cdot c(y(m)); y(m))$.

The first part of the modified definition 5.13 defines each agent's share of the cost of providing the public good so that the sum of all the agent's costs is at least one. Thus, if the sum of the shares of the cost to each agent to produce the public good j do not sum to at least one, then the share of the cost to each agent is one minus the sum of the shares of the cost to all other agents plus the average of the absolute value of one minus the sum of the shares of the cost to all agents. The second part of the definition defines the outcome function in this cost share game. The outcome function assigns each agent an amount of the private good equal to the agent's endowment minus the agent's share of the cost of providing the public good times the level of the public good produced, and the level of the public good is equal to the sum of each agent's contribution to the public good. Here the amount of the public good produced depends on the strategy profile of the agents.

In addition, the necessary condition of Maskin Monotonicity is required for the double implementation results. However, Maskin Monotonicity is satisfied by the ratio correspondence on the essential economies domain. The feasible implementation result was summarized by Corchón and Wilkie (1996) as follows.

Theorem 5.13 (Corchón and Wilkie, 1996). *The feasible and continuous game Γ_2 double implements the ratio correspondence on the domain $\mathcal{E}_{ce}$: $NA(\Gamma_2, e) = SA(\Gamma_2, e) = R(e)$.*

For more discussion of the ratio social choice correspondence, please refer to subsection A.6.6 on page 270 in the appendix.

5.4 Virtual Nash Implementation

Maskin Monotonicity is a demanding condition; not all social choice correspondences of interest satisfy it. For instance, we saw in chapter 3 that the Walrasian social choice correspondence is not Maskin Monotonic. In this case, the closely related constrained

Walrasian correspondence is Maskin Monotonic. In other cases, the failure to satisfy Maskin Monotonicity means that certain social choice correspondences of interest simply are not Nash implementable. Virtual Nash implementation shifts attention from a social choice correspondence that selects sets of outcomes for each preference profile, to one that selects sets of lotteries over outcomes, that is, a stochastic social choice correspondence.

The approach of virtual implementation concludes that things are not quite so bleak. If we scale down our ambition to the approximate rather than the exact implementation of a social choice correspondence, we can do better than with Nash implementation. The approximation means that with a probability very close to one the target social choice correspondence is implemented, but with the remaining probability some other correspondence is implemented.

Virtual Nash implementation was independently proposed by Matsushima (1988) and Abreu and Sen (1991). The name could be better, as approximate, rather than virtual, implementation is a better description of the concept. However, the term "virtual" has been established in the literature and we will keep it here as well. In chapter 7 we discuss virtual implementation in Bayesian equilibrium. Now we proceed to virtual Nash implementation, and we base our presentation on Serrano (2004).

Let $X = \{x_1, \ldots, x_k\}$ be a finite set of social alternatives. To approximate social choice correspondences, we will use lotteries, which are simply probability distributions over the set X. Let $\Delta(X)$ stand for the set of all such lotteries. Let $\Delta_+(X)$ stand for the set of lotteries in which every social alternative receives positive probability (however small it may be). In virtual implementation theory, a social choice correspondence is a non-empty valued correspondence that associates to every type profile $\theta \in \Theta$ a non-empty subset of the set of all lotteries, $\Delta(X)$. A mechanism $\Gamma = (M, g)$ is as before, but with the difference that g maps into $\Delta(X)$, so that for each message profile $m \in M$, $g(m)$ is a lottery over X. By contrast, in Nash implementation theory, a social choice correspondence associates to each type profile a set of social alternatives, not a set of lotteries over social alternatives as here. The case of Nash implementation is a special case of the present one, as we can always represent the choice of a particular social alternative for certain by a lottery that assigns that alternative probability equal to one.

In order to discuss approximation of social choice correspondences, we first need to define what we mean by two lotteries being close to each other. We do this in the most standard way. For any two lotteries $\ell = (\ell_1, \ldots, \ell_k) \in \Delta(X)$, $\ell' = (\ell'_1, \ldots, \ell'_k) \in \Delta(X)$, let the distance $d(\ell, \ell')$ be equal to the Euclidean distance of ℓ and ℓ', defined by

$$d(\ell, \ell') = \left[\sum_{i=1}^{k} (\ell_i - \ell'_i)^2 \right]^{1/2} .$$

We measure the distance of two sets of social alternatives by the largest distance of any two lotteries, the first taken from the one set and the second from the other set. Formally, let θ be a type profile and $F(\theta)$, $H(\theta)$ the sets of alternatives selected by two social choice correspondences F and H for that profile. We define the distance between $F(\theta)$ and $H(\theta)$ if there is a one-to-one and onto (see section A.1) function $\pi : F(\theta) \to H(\theta)$ between the sets $F(\theta)$ and $H(\theta)$; then our definition of the distance is

$$d(F(\theta), H(\theta)) = \sup_{\ell \in F(\theta)} d(\ell, \pi(\ell)).$$

The symbol *sup* stands for the **supremum** of a set of numbers, which is the smallest number that is still larger than any number in that set. This is also known as the least upper bound.[3] The reason for requiring the existence of a one-to-one and onto function π that relates the sets $F(\theta)$ and $H(\theta)$ is technical. We require it to avoid mathematical difficulties that arise when one or both of these sets are strange in a certain mathematical sense. While we have imposed the requirement to make our definition of distance complete, the mechanism designer can in practice safely assume that the social choice correspondence she is trying to implement is not strange in this mathematical sense.

We denote by $\mathcal{N}(\Gamma, \theta)$ the set of Nash equilibria of mechanism Γ played in the type profile θ, and by $g(\mathcal{N}(\Gamma, \theta))$ the set of Nash equilibrium outcomes of a mechanism Γ played in type profile θ.

Definition 5.14 (Virtual Nash Implementation). A social choice correspondence $F : \Theta \longrightarrow \longrightarrow \Delta(X)$ is **virtually Nash implementable** if for every $\epsilon > 0$ there exists a mechanism $\Gamma = (M, g)$ such that for every type profile $\theta \in \Theta$, $d(F(\theta), g(\mathcal{N}(\Gamma, \theta))) < \epsilon$.

This definition says that a social choice correspondence F is virtually Nash implementable if there is a mechanism (M, g) whose Nash equilibrium lottery at type profile θ is at most an ϵ away from $F(\theta)$. So the mechanism does not Nash implement F, but it Nash implements a social choice correspondence that is close to F, in the sense of the distance function d. Since we can take ϵ to be as small a number as we wish, we can have these two lotteries be quite close to each other. Exact Nash implementability corresponds to this definition when $\epsilon = 0$.

Before we discuss the theorem that characterizes which social choice correspondences are virtually Nash implementable, we define a condition on social choice correspondences that will play the central role in that result.

Definition 5.15 (Ordinality). A social choice correspondence F is **ordinal** if $F(\theta) \neq F(\theta')$ implies that there exists an agent i and two lotteries $p, p' \in \Delta(X)$ such that $u_i(p, \theta) \geq u_i(p', \theta)$ and $u_i(p', \theta') > u_i(p, \theta')$.

---

[3]In most cases, the supremum is just the maximum, but the supremum is a more general concept: for instance, the open interval $(0, 1)$ has no maximum, but its supremum is 1. The one-to-one function π serves the purpose of ensuring that the sets $F(\theta)$ and $H(\theta)$ are structurally similar.

This says that in order for the correspondence F to change its choice of outcomes from one type profile to another there must be at least one agent whose ranking of some lotteries changes due to that change of type profile. In this section we represent preferences by expected utility functions, in order to be able to handle preferences over lotteries. An expected utility function that represents an agent's preference relation depends to an extent on the intensity of the agent's likes or dislikes. If we transform an expected utility function by, say, raising it to the power of the square, it no longer represents the agent's attitude towards risk, although it is still a faithful representation of the agent's rankings among pairs of lotteries. This kind of transformation of an expected utility function may turn an expected utility function that exhibits the attitude of risk aversion into one that exhibits the attitude of risk loving. The ordinality condition asserts that the intensity of the agents' preferences over lotteries should not matter for the selection of outcomes by a social choice correspondence. Only how an agent ranks lotteries should matter. Ordinality rules out social choice correspondences inspired by utilitarian philosophy, since in order to maximize the sum (weighted or not) of utilities of the agents, as utilitarianism requires, one must take account of preference intensities.

Finally, we need a condition on our preference domain that asserts that no admissible preference ordering regards all alternatives as indifferent to each other.

Definition 5.16 (No Total Indifference). The domain satisfies **No Total Indifference** if for each agent i and each type profile θ there exist alternatives $x, x' \in X$ such that $u_i(x, \theta) > u_i(x', \theta)$.

Theorem 5.14 (Matsushima, 1988; Abreu and Sen, 1991). *If the domain satisfies No Total Indifference and there are at least three agents, then any ordinal social choice correspondence $F : \Theta \longrightarrow\longrightarrow \Delta(X)$ is virtually Nash implementable.*

Proof. Start by assuming that F always picks sets of lotteries with all probabilities positive, that is, $F(\theta) \subseteq \Delta_+(X)$ for all θ. We first prove that F is Maskin Monotonic. Let θ and θ' be two preference profiles, and let $\ell \in \Delta$ be a lottery such that $\ell \in F(\theta)$ and $\ell \notin F(\theta')$. According to the definition of Maskin Monotonicity, definition 3.9, what remains to be shown to establish Maskin Monotonicity is that there is some agent $i \in \mathcal{I}$ and some lottery $\widehat{\ell} \in \Delta$ such that $u_i(\widehat{\ell}, \theta) \leq u_i(\ell, \theta)$ and $u_i(\widehat{\ell}, \theta') > u_i(\ell, \theta')$.

As F is ordinal, there exists an agent $i \in \mathcal{I}$ and two lotteries $\ell', \ell'' \in \Delta$ such that $u_i(\ell', \theta) \geq u_i(\ell'', \theta)$ and $u_i(\ell'', \theta') > u_i(\ell', \theta')$. As a result of the expected utility property of the u_i functions, these two inequalities are equivalent to the following two:

$$\sum_{j=1}^{k} \ell'_j u_i(x_j, \theta) \geq \sum_{j=1}^{k} \ell''_j u_i(x_j, \theta)$$

and

$$\sum_{j=1}^{k} \ell''_j u_i(x_j, \theta') > \sum_{j=1}^{k} \ell'_j u_i(x_j, \theta').$$

These can be rewritten equivalently as

$$\sum_{j=1}^{k} (\ell''_j - \ell'_j) u_i(x_j, \theta) \leq 0 \tag{5.1}$$

and

$$\sum_{j=1}^{k} (\ell''_j - \ell'_j) u_i(x_j, \theta') > 0. \tag{5.2}$$

Now consider the potential lottery $\widehat{\ell}$ that is defined as $\widehat{\ell}_j = \ell_j + \lambda \ell''_j - \lambda \ell'_j$ for all $j = 1, \ldots, k$, for some positive real number λ. To verify that $\widehat{\ell}$ is a legitimate lottery, we need to check that $\sum_{j=1}^{k} \widehat{\ell}_j = 1$ and that for every $j = 1, \ldots, k$ we have $\widehat{\ell}_j \geq 0$. The first is easy to check:

$$\sum_{j=1}^{k} \widehat{\ell}_j = \sum_{j=1}^{k} [\ell_j + \lambda \ell''_j - \lambda \ell'_j] = 1 + \lambda - \lambda = 1,$$

since $\sum_{j=1}^{k} \ell_j = 1$, $\sum_{j=1}^{k} \ell'_j = 1$ and $\sum_{j=1}^{k} \ell''_j = 1$ because ℓ, ℓ', ℓ'' are lotteries. To ensure the non-negativity of each $\widehat{\ell}_j$, we note that $\ell_j > 0$ because $\ell \in \Delta_+(X)$ by assumption. Thus, even if for some j the amount $(\ell''_j - \ell'_j)$ is negative, we can always choose $\lambda > 0$ to be small enough so that $\ell_j > -\lambda(\ell''_j - \ell'_j)$, so that $\widehat{\ell}_j = \ell_j + \lambda \ell''_j - \lambda \ell'_j > 0$.

By adding side-by-side to the inequality (5.1) multiplied by λ the equality $\sum_{j=1}^{k} \ell_j u_i(x_j, \theta) = u_i(\ell, \theta)$ and to the inequality (5.2) multiplied by λ the equality $\sum_{j=1}^{k} \ell_j u_i(x_j, \theta') = u_i(\ell, \theta')$, we obtain

$$u_i(\widehat{\ell}, \theta) \leq u_i(\ell, \theta) \quad \text{and} \quad u_i(\widehat{\ell}, \theta) > u_i(\ell, \theta').$$

This establishes that F is Maskin Monotonic.

Because F always selects interior lotteries and because of the No Total Indifference assumption, the No Veto Power assumption is satisfied, by the fact that no agent has a most preferred lottery in $\Delta_+(X)$. So F is Maskin Monotonic and satisfies No Veto Power. Since there are also at least three agents, by theorem 3.1., F is Nash implementable.

Finally, we deal with the case of a social choice correspondence F that has range $\Delta(X)$, not $\Delta_+(X)$. If this is the case, then there is a social choice correspondence F_ϵ, for every

$\epsilon > 0$, such that $d(F(\theta), F_\epsilon(\theta)) < \epsilon$ and the range of F_ϵ is contained in $\Delta_+(X)$.[4] Therefore, there exists a Nash implementable social choice correspondence F_ϵ that is as near to F in terms of the distance function d as desired, concluding the proof.   QED

This is a remarkable result. It shows that many social choice correspondences that are not Nash implementable because they are not Maskin Monotonic (as we have seen in the exercises of chapter 3) are nevertheless virtually Nash implementable. But it does not deliver us to implementation paradise. Virtual implementation allows us to sidestep this problem by working with a nearby lottery F_ϵ that *is* Maskin Monotonic when F is not.

As Jackson (2001) remarks, there are two serious problems with virtual Nash implementation. First, it is in some sense a surrender: instead of implementing F, the society settles for implementing some other F_ϵ near F. Even though the outcomes of these social choice correspondences, in the lottery space, are arbitrarily near each other, it is still possible, with small probability, that the actual outcome chosen is far away from what F would have yielded, especially if it is an outcome that receives zero probability in $F(\theta)$ for some preference profile θ. For the proof of the theorem, we assumed that the agents take these small probability events seriously and believe that, should they arise, they will be enforced by the central authority. However, this is a questionable assumption if such an outcome involves a large amount of inefficiency; the agents may reasonably expect to be able to renegotiate away from such an outcome.

Second, virtual Nash implementation depends crucially on the expected utility assumption on preferences. While we cannot devote the large space necessary to discuss this issue in appropriate detail, we note that many recent innovations in economic theory have been prompted by empirical findings that agents violate expected utility in predictable ways. A theory that is sensitive to the removal of the expected utility assumption is not likely to survive in the future when implementation theory is less likely to employ expected utility theory.

Finally, in a point related to the first one raised by Jackson, allowing the approximation of a social choice correspondence by a nearby random one highlights the need of implementation theory to assume that the agents have absolute trust in the entity that runs the mechanism. It would be easy for this entity to cheat and claim that the random allowance for error happened, then choose an allocation that departs drastically from the social choice correspondence that it was supposed to implement.

---

[4]You can see it in your mind's eye as a "shaving" by an amount less than ϵ of the parts of any $F(\theta)$ that touch the boundary of $\Delta(X)$.

Chapter 6

Applications of the Economic Design Approach

This chapter demonstrates some of the ways economic design theory has been and can be applied to problems of online reputation systems, market competition, allocation of public goods and public bads, allocating goods in ways that are envy-free, insurance, and providing national security.

6.1 Manipulation-Resistant Online Reputation Systems

We are familiar with Web sites that allow trading over the Internet, such as eBay or Amazon.com. Anyone trading this way faces the possibility of being defrauded, for instance by being sent substandard goods. Because of this, reputation systems have been developed to infuse more trust in online transactions. These systems generally consider a history of an entity's interaction with other entities and compute from it an index of trustworthiness for each entity. Note that we say "entity" for a participant in such online interactions, as such a participant may be an individual, an organization, or even a fake individual or organization created in order to manipulate some other entity's reputation.[1]

Online reputation systems face various threats that emanate from the strategic behavior of participating entities. At least three such threats have been studied:

1. As entities operate under pseudonyms, any entity with a bad reputation can get a new pseudonym and start afresh with an untainted reputation (*whitewashing*).
2. Entities that report feedback may do so incompletely or falsely (*incorrect feedback*).
3. Finally, an entity may report feedback on transactions that never happened, and can do so by creating pseudonyms for entities that do not exist (*phantom feedback*).

To save space, we consider here only the case of reputation systems based on the notion of **transitive trust,** which means that the credibility of each entity's feedback depends on the credibility of its other actions. This will become clear as we develop the necessary concepts and notation.

---

[1]This section is based on Friedman et al. (2007), which we recommend highly to readers who want to pursue this subject in more detail.

For simplicity, we ignore the time element in the feedback about entities, and we consider everything that follows as happening at a single point in time. Then the feedback can be written as a trust graph. First of all, a **weighted directed graph** (V, E, t) has three parts: a set of vertices, V, a set of directed edges which are connections among vertices, E, and a function $t : E \to \mathbb{R}$ that assigns to each edge in the graph a weight. The term "directed edge" signifies a connection (i, j) of a vertex i with some vertex j that goes from i to j.

Now we can have a **trust graph** to express the kind of reputation system we study. In such a graph, V is the set of agents, which represent entities, E is the set of directed edges among the agents, and $t : E \to \mathbb{R}_{++}$ is the weight function, which is not allowed to give negative or zero weights to edges. For any edge (i, j), we interpret $t(i, j)$ as the trust level that i reports about j, which is based on the interactions that i and j have had before.

We represent a reputation aggregation mechanism as a function F that is defined on the set of all weighted directed graphs and assigns to each such graph $G = (V, E, t)$ a vector of real values $F(G) = (F_1(G), \ldots, F_{|V|}(G))$, where $|V|$ denotes the number of the members of the set V and $F_v(G)$ stands for the reputation value of vertex $v \in G$ in graph G. Once we have these reputation values, we can determine a ranking of all vertices (agents). Of course, we rule out consideration of the trivial reputation aggregation mechanisms, which are those that assign the same value to all vertices of a graph.

In case this seems too abstract, note that it captures the reputation systems that people have proposed and used. For example, a special case of an F is Google's famous PageRank algorithm for ranking Web sites. Here, a vertex represents a Web site, and the existence of edge (v, w) signifies that Web site v has a link to Web site w. For any $v \in V$, let $\mathrm{Out}(v)$ stand for the number of edges emanating from v; this is called the *outdegree* of v. For any edge $(v, w) \in E$, set $t(v, w) = 1/\mathrm{Out}(v)$. (This is well defined as $\mathrm{Out}(v)$ must be at least 1, since there is at least the edge (v, w) emanating from v.) We can now see a simple version of PageRank, where the ranking function is

$$F_v(G) = \epsilon + (1 - \epsilon) \sum_{v' : (v', v) \in E} F_{v'}(G) t(v', v). \tag{6.1}$$

This ranking function gives each Web site v a small value ϵ and adds to it the product of $(1 - \epsilon)$ with the sum of the values that the site earns from all other sites that link to it, where each linking site v' gives site v a worth equal to the product of its own worth, $F_{v'}(G)$, and $t(v', v)$. Since $t(v', v)$ is just the inverse of how many outgoing links v' has, it dilutes the force of the recommendation of v from v' that is implicit in the existence of the link (v', v). For example, if a Web site with high PageRank, such as www.nytimes.com, adds a link to my personal Web site, I should be glad that a web site with a high $F_{v'}(G)$ is linking to mine, but since there are very many outgoing links from www.nytimes.com, the benefit my Web site receives to its PageRank value is small.

Another example is the PathRank reputation system, in which $F_v(G)$ is the inverse of the length of the shortest path from some arbitrarily chosen starting vertex v_0 to v.

A reputation system may have a number of desirable properties. A reputation system is *symmetric* if the reputations it assigns to vertices depend only on the structure of the graph, and not on the labels of the vertices. A reputation system is *monotonic* if adding an incoming link to a vertex v does not reduce the rank of v relative to any other vertex w. The simple version of PageRank we just defined is symmetric and monotonic. Examples of non-symmetric reputation systems are easily found in the literature; the PathRank system is one, since in it the start vertex v_0 has a position of privilege.

In a transitive trust model, an entity only receives indirect rewards and penalties via the ratings of it that other entities provide. So there is no incentive to provide correct feedback, and, depending on F, there may be an incentive to provide incorrect feedback in order to boost one's own ranking. These notions lead us directly to the concept of rank-strategyproofness.

Definition 6.1. A reputation system is **rank-strategyproof** if, for every $G = (V, E, t)$ and every $v \in V$, v cannot increase its rank by the way it rates other vertices.

Satisfying rank-strategy-proofness is difficult. For instance, a reputation system cannot be at the same time nontrivial, monotonic, symmetric, and rank-strategyproof. However, the PathRank system is nontrivial, monotonic, and rank-strategyproof; as we know, it is not symmetric. More results like these can be found in Altman and Tennenholtz (2007).

We turn now to **sybil attacks** on reputation systems, which are attacks in which a single entity makes multiple online identities (pseudonyms) in an attempt to increase the reputation of its primary identity.[2] Assume that any vertex can create any number of sybil vertices with any set of ratings between these vertices. Also, assume that any vertex v can divide its incoming rating (trust) edges among the sybils in any way such that the total trust amount $\sum_{v':(v',v)\in E} t(v', v)$ remains constant and that v can manipulate its outgoing links in any way it wants. Note that the assumption that v can divide incoming trust edges at will is strong; if we think of a Web site spawning new ones, there is no obvious way that this division can be done unless somehow all other Web sites that linked to the original one cooperate.

Definition 6.2. Let $G = (V, E, t)$ be a graph and $v \in V$ a vertex of G that corresponds to an entity. We say that a graph $G' = (V', E', t')$ and a subset $U' \subseteq V'$ are a **sybil strategy** for entity v in the graph $G = (V, E, t)$ if $v \in U'$ and when we collapse U' into the single vertex with label v in G' we get the graph G. We refer to U' as the **sybils** of v. We denote a sybil strategy by (G', U').

---

[2]Wikipedia, accessed on September 6, 2008, says this about "sybil": "In antiquity, the oracular seeresses of the Ancient Near East and the Mediterranean were referred to by the Greek term 'sibyls.' In modern times, when 'Sibyl' is adopted for a woman's name, the conventional spelling is 'Sybil'."

The set of vertices U' represents v and all its pseudonyms.

There are (at least) two interesting ways to define sybilproofness.

Definition 6.3. A reputation function F is **value-sybilproof** if for every graph $G = (V, E, t)$ and every vertex $v \in V$, there is no sybil strategy (G', U') for v, with $G' = (V', E', t')$ such that for some $u \in U'$, $F_u(G') > F_v(G)$.

Value-sybilproofness requires that no entity can create pseudonyms in such a way as to achieve a higher reputation value for one of these pseudonyms than its original pseudonym (v) had.

Definition 6.4. A reputation function F is **rank-sybilproof** if for every graph $G = (V, E, t)$ and every vertex $v \in V$, there is no sybil strategy (G', U') for v, with $G' = (V', E', t')$ such that for some $u \in U'$ and $w \in V \setminus \{v\}$, $F_u(G') \geq F_w(G')$ and $F_v(G) < F_w(G)$.

Rank-sybilproofness requires that no entity v can create pseudonyms in such a way as to have one of these pseudonyms rank higher than some other vertex w that originally ranked higher than v. Note the similarity with the preference reversal in the definition of Nash monotonicity.

Theorem 6.1 (Cheng and Friedman, 2005). *There does not exist a nontrivial, symmetric, rank-sybilproof reputation function.*

Proof. Let $G = (V, E, t)$ be a trust graph and F a reputation function. Since F is nontrivial, there exist $v, w \in V$ such that $F_w(G) > F_v(G)$. Construct a new graph G' as two disjoint copies of G and consider the sybil strategy (G', U') of vertex v where U' is the second copy of G combined with v. Symmetry implies that there exists a vertex $u \in U'$ such that $F_u(G') = F_w(G')$. Therefore F is not rank-sybilproof.   QED

You may wonder about the implicit assumption that the creation of sybils is completely costless. In practice it carries a small cost. In an attempt to model this cost, we consider now a modification of rank-sybilproofness that restricts the number of sybils an entity can create.

Definition 6.5. Let K be a positive integer. A reputation function F is **K-rank-sybilproof** if it is rank-sybilproof for all possible sybil strategies (G', U') with $|U'| \leq K + 1$.

Unfortunately, this restriction does not bring us a better result.

Theorem 6.2 (Cheng and Friedman, 2005). *There is no nontrivial, symmetric, K-rank-sybilproof reputation function for $K > 0$.*

The proof of this is an extension of the proof of the previous theorem.

Lest you lose heart, not all results in this area are negative.

Theorem 6.3 (Friedman et al., 2007). *The PathRank reputation function is value-sybilproof and rank-sybilproof.*

Proof. Let $G = (V, E, t)$ be a trust graph and v_0 the privileged vertex for the PathRank function. Recall that for any vertex $v \in V$, $F_v(G)$ is the inverse of the length of the shortest path from v_0 to v. Since the creation of sybils by v cannot decrease the length of the shortest path from v_0 to v, the PathRank reputation function is value-sybilproof. Rank-sybilproofness follows because the only case in which a vertex v can affect the value of another vertex w is when v is on the shortest path from v_0 to w. In this case, by the definition of the PathRank reputation function, we have $F_v(G) > F_w(G)$, so the conclusion of the definition of rank-sybilproofness is satisfied vacuously.   QED

This section has only scratched the surface of this interesting topic. For more information, consult our main source, Friedman et al. (2007), and the book in which it appears for a large number of additional results about mechanisms when computers are involved.

6.2 Walrasian Implementation via Market Games

We turn now to the market mechanism. Markets are studied extensively within the framework of neoclassical general equilibrium theory. Implementation theory gives us a new and deep perspective on the incentives involved in the market mechanism.

Beviá et al. (2003) study a class of mechanisms they call **market games** and investigate whether these mechanisms can implement the Walrasian social choice correspondence in the absence of the auctioneer of neoclassical general equilibrium theory. For more on market-like mechanisms in a public goods context, see section 5.3.2.

In this section there are $n + 1$ goods where n is a natural number. Good 0 is a divisible private good that we think of as money. Goods $1, \ldots, n$ are private goods that can be divisible or indivisible. Because here we allow for indivisible private goods, we have a domain that is more general than the domain of the exchange economies we saw earlier. In a market mechanism a **strategy** m_i for each agent, i, has two parts: a **price offer vector**, $\pi_i \in \mathbb{R}^n$, and a **quantity vector**, $q_i \in \mathbb{R}^n$. We write (π, q) for a strategy profile m, where $\pi = (\pi_1, \ldots, \pi_I)$ and $q = (q_1, \ldots, q_I)$. Think of π_{ig} as the price bid made by i for good g. If for any good g, $q_{ig} > 0$, agent i is a **buyer** of good g and if $q_{jg} < 0$ for $i \neq j$, agent j is a **seller** of good g. An **allocation** is a vector $(x, t) \in \mathbb{R}^{(n+1)I}$ such that $x \in \mathbb{R}^{nI}$ is the vector of net trades of the agents and $t \in \mathbb{R}^n$ the vector of monetary payments to the agents. For each agent i, t_i is the net payment to i; when $t_i > 0$, i receives the amount t_i, and when $t_i < 0$, i pays the amount $-t_i$.

An allocation (x,t) is **balanced** if for each good g, $\sum_i x_{ig} \leq 0$ and $\sum_i t_i \leq 0$. This means that there is no excess purchases of any good, and no money is coming to the agents from outside the economy. An allocation (x,t) satisfies agent i's **budget constraint** at price vector p if $p \cdot x_i + t_i \leq 0$.

For each agent i, $x_{ig}(m)$ denotes the net trade of good g, for $g = 1, \ldots, n$, and $x_i(m)$ denotes the vector $x_i(m) = (x_{i1}(m), \ldots, x_{in}(m))$. In terms of the exchange economies we saw earlier, a net trade here corresponds to the difference between the endowment of the good g by agent i and the consumption level of good g by agent i.

The outcome function of the market mechanism takes a strategy profile m of all agents and assigns a price vector $p(m) \in \mathbb{R}^n_+$ and the set of balanced allocations $x(m) = (x_1(m), \ldots, x_I(m), t(m)) \in \mathbb{R}^{(n+1)I}$ that satisfy each agent's budget constraint at price vector $p(m)$ with equality, so for each i, $t_i(m), p(m)$ and $x_i(m)$ are related by $t_i(m) = -p(m)x_i(m)$.

The authors first propose two axioms to characterize a market game. These axioms express properties of the traditional neoclassical concept of a competitive market.

Axiom (U). The **Unanimity** axiom requires that, for each strategy profile $m = (\pi, q)$, if all buyers and sellers announce the same price offer vector π then this common offer vector also equals the trade price vector $p(m)$. Furthermore, if for each good g we have $\sum_i q_{ig} = 0$, then $x(m) = q$.

The first part of Unanimity ensures that when all agents agree in their announcements π_i, then this common announcement becomes the price vector. The second part ensures that if all markets clear, then trade occurs. To see how this relates to the general theory of implementation, compare Unanimity to Rule 1 of the canonical mechanism in chapter 3.

Axiom (VT). The **Voluntary Trade** axiom requires for each good $g = 1, \ldots, n$, each agent i, and each message m, $x_{ig}(m) > 0$ implies that $p_g(m) \leq \pi_{ig}$ and $x_{ig}(m) < 0$ implies that $p_g(m) \geq \pi_{ig}$.

The second axiom requires that if an agent is a net demander of a good, the trade price will be less than or equal to that agent's offer price and if the agent is a net supplier of a good the trade price will be greater than or equal to that agent's offer price.

Beviá et al. (2003) show that if a market mechanism satisfies the axioms **U** and **VT**, then there is a strategy profile that is both a Nash equilibrium and a strong Nash equilibrium for this mechanism, and which results in the Walrasian equilibrium outcome. An equilibrium strategy for each agent in the market for good g is to announce the same offer price for good g. The proof shows how the structure of a market game mechanism that satisfies **U** and **VT** effectively induces each agent to act as a price-taker. Recall that, as we saw in section 5.3 in the context of a public goods economy, in a Strong Nash equilibrium, no coalition can benefit by unilaterally deviating.

We state the last two axioms we need informally to save on notation; please refer to Beviá et al. (2003) for the formal presentation.

Axiom (R). The **Reactiveness** axiom requires that the pricing function p allow room for a seller to increase his price offer and the buyer to reduce his price offer whenever the price offer of the seller is below that of the buyer. Furthermore this can be done without affecting the allocation or the prices of the other goods.

The name of this axiom indicates the natural reactions of agents to bidding discrepancies as described. A buyer naturally would tend to reduce his bid, and a seller to increase his when the seller's bid is less than that of the buyer. Notice how this axiom parallels the process of groping for the equilibrium price that Walras termed "tâtonnement".

Axiom (SBC). The **Strong Bertrand Competition** axiom requires that a seller who drops his price offer for a good can sell as much as he wants, and a buyer who increases his price offer can buy as much as he wants. Furthermore, an agent can also have no trades, by matching the price bids of all other agents.

In the standard Bertrand duopoly model, a seller who drops the asking price gets the entire demand in the market. The SBC axioms requires only that he gets as much demand as he wants, and makes the same requirement on the buyer side.

Definition 6.6. We say that a Nash equilibrium strategy profile m^N is an **active Nash equilibrium** if for each good g there exists at least one agent j with $x_{jg}(m^N) > 0$.

This property means that each good is being bought in a positive amount by at least one buyer.

The main result of Beviá et al. (2003) is the following theorem:

Theorem 6.4 (Beviá et al., 2003). *In any market game that satisfies **U**, **VT**, **R**, and **SBC**, the Walrasian social choice correspondence is implemented both in active Nash equilibrium and in active strong Nash equilibrium.*

This result shows a way in which Walrasian equilibrium can be achieved without the services of the fictitious auctioneer that Walras postulated. Instead, in any market game that satisfies the four axioms, if the agents can reach an active Nash and strong Nash equilibrium, it results in a Walrasian equilibrium, and each Walrasian equilibrium corresponds to an active Nash and active Strong equilibrium. Therefore we can say that the auctioneer is not needed to reach Walrasian equilibria in market games that satisfy these four axioms.

6.3 Implementing the Lindahl Social Choice Correspondence

Since the suggestion by Erik Lindahl (1967) of a market-based method for financing public goods, much research has been devoted to the actual implementation of such a scheme. Traditional economic tools show how agents have an incentive to free ride on the provision of a public good by others, which poses problems for the achievement of Lindahl allocations. Walker (1981) Nash implements the constrained Lindahl social choice correspondence. For a full discussion of this correspondence, see section A.6.5. Walker's mechanism is one of the earliest ones proposed for this purpose. It has a relatively small message space and it neatly demonstrates that the Lindahl approach to providing and financing public goods can be made compatible with individuals' incentives.

Consider an economy with one private good and one public good. Write x_i for the amount of the private good consumed by agent i and write y for the amount of the public good consumed equally by all agents. For each agent i, q_i denotes a personalized price for the public good, expressed in terms of the private good.[3]

Each agent has the endowment level ω_i of the private good and a preference relation defined on $\mathbb{R}^2_+$ represented numerically by a utility function $u_i : \mathbb{R}^2_+ \to \mathbb{R}$. For a consumption bundle (x_i, y), $u_i(x_i, y)$ measures the agent's utility level. We assume that for each agent i, u_i is a strictly increasing and strictly quasi-concave function. This means that the indifference curves have everywhere negative slope and exhibit strictly decreasing marginal rate of substitution.

The public good can be produced from the private good by means of a production function that exhibits constant returns to scale. For simplicity, we let the marginal cost of production be equal to 1. This can be done by choosing the units of measurement of the two goods appropriately, because the technology has constant returns to scale.

An **allocation** is a list $z = (x_1, \ldots, x_I, y) \in \mathbb{R}^{I+1}_+$. Under an allocation z, each agent i consumes the amounts x_i and y of the private and public good, respectively. An allocation is **feasible** if $\sum_i x_i + y = \Omega$. This says that the aggregate endowment of the private good, Ω, is exactly used up to provide the aggregate private good consumption level $\sum_i x_i$ and the public good level y.

For each agent i, let $q_i \in \mathbb{R}_+$ be the **personalized price** of the public good. The **budget set** of each agent is: $B_L(\omega_i, q_i) \equiv \{(x_i, y) \mid x_i + q_i y \leq \omega_i\}$. For the constrained Lindahl equilibrium the budget set is: $B_{CL}(\Omega, q_i) \subseteq B_L(\omega_i, q_i)$. Each element of $B_{CL}(\Omega, q_i)$ satisfies the same budget constraint as in the description of $B_L(\omega_i, q_i)$ and is in addition required to be part of a feasible allocation. (Recall our discussion of the constrained Walrasian social choice correspondence in chapter 3 and refer to section A.6.5.) In this

---

[3]In section A.6.5 you can see how the Lindahl equilibrium definition can be extended to cover the case of multiple private and multiple public goods, as well as examples of its calculation.

section we only consider economies in which every Lindahl equilibrium assigns a positive amount of each good to each agent, for simplicity. This implies that constrained Lindahl equilibrium coincides with Lindahl equilibrium. We recall now the definitions of these concepts, which take a simpler form than in section A.6.5 because of the presence of only one private good, which means that we do not need to introduce a price vector for the private goods. Also, because of the assumption of constant returns in the production of the public good, there will be no profits from this production in Lindahl equilibrium, which simplifies the definitions that follow even further.

Definition 6.7 (Lindahl Equilibrium). A **Lindahl equilibrium** is a pair of a vector of personalized prices for the public goods, $(q_1, \ldots, q_I)$ and an allocation, $(x_1, \ldots, x_n, y)$, such that: (i) each individual i consumes the vector (x_i, y_i) that is rated highest according to i's preferences from i's Lindahl budget set $B_L(\omega_i, q_i)$; (ii) there is a common level y of the public good so that for each i, $y_i = y$; and (iii) the allocation $(x_1, \ldots, x_I, y)$ is feasible. A **Lindahl equilibrium allocation** is an allocation z that is part of some Lindahl equilibrium.

Definition 6.8 (Constrained Lindahl Equilibrium). A **constrained Lindahl equilibrium** is a pair of a vector of personalized prices for the public goods, $(q_1, \ldots, q_I)$ and an allocation, $(x_1, \ldots, x_n, y)$, such that: (i) each individual i consumes the vector (x_i, y_i) that is rated highest according to i's preferences from i's constrained Lindahl budget set $B_{CL}(\Omega, q_i)$; (ii) there is a common level y of the public good so that for each i, $y_i = y$; and (iii) the allocation $(x_1, \ldots, x_I, y)$ is feasible.

We assume that every Lindahl equilibrium allocation is strictly positive, which makes the constrained and unconstrained Lindahl equilibrium sets coincide.

A Lindahl equilibrium for each economy is specified by a list of personalized prices, $(q_1, \ldots, q_I)$, and an allocation, $(x_1, \ldots, x_n, y)$. The personalized price q_i in a Lindahl equilibrium is equal to agent i's marginal willingness to pay for the public good.

The mechanism of Walker (1981) specifies a set of strategies $M_i \subseteq \mathbb{R}$ for each agent $i \in I$ along with a two-part outcome function g_y, t such that $g_y : M \to \mathbb{R}_+$ and $t : M \to \mathbb{R}^I$. The outcome function takes a strategy profile m and returns a level $g_y(m)$ of the public good and a vector of taxes for the agents $(t_1(m), \ldots, t_I(m))$, expressed in units of the private good. Thus the outcome of a particular profile of messages $m = (m_1, \ldots, m_I)$ is an $(I+1)$-tuple $(g_y(m), t_1(m), \ldots, t_I(m)) \in \mathbb{R}_+ \times \mathbb{R}^I$. Negative taxes are allowed.

The outcome functions are defined as follows.

W1 $g_y(m) = \sum_{i \in \mathcal{I}} m_i$,
W2 For each $i \in \mathcal{I}$, $t_i(m) = (\frac{1}{I} + m_{i+2} - m_{i+1})g_y(m)$.

To see what is happening here, recall the cyclical arrangement of agents in figure 3.2. In that case one immediate neighbor to the right of each agent i submitted a message report on the agent's type. Here, the messages of the two agents immediately to the left of agent i are used in calculating an adjustment to i's tax rate away from the equal rate of $1/I$.

Thus each agent can choose to increase or decrease the level of the public good by his choice of m_i, by **W1**, but for each increase in m_i he pays a cost share of $q_i(m) = (1/I) + m_{i+2} - m_{i+1}$ by **W2**.[4] Agent i's payoff when the message profile is m is given by $u_i(\omega_i - q_i(m)g_y(m), g_y(m))$.

As discussed in chapter 3, the mechanism aligns individual incentives by having an agent take his price as given. We formalize this statement as the next theorem. We have adapted the first part of the proof from Vega-Redondo (2003, pages 88–89).

Theorem 6.5 (Lindahl Nash Implementation with Walker's Mechanism). *Given the assumptions made in this section, Walker's mechanism implements the Lindahl social choice correspondence in Nash equilibrium.*

Proof. We show first that if m^* is a Nash equilibrium of Walker's mechanism, then the allocation $(\omega_1 - q_1(m^*)g_y(m^*), \ldots, \omega_I - q_I(m^*)g_y(m^*), g_y(m^*))$ is a Lindahl equilibrium allocation with associated personalized prices $q_i(m^*) = t_i(m^*)$ for each agent.

Suppose that $(\omega_1 - q_1(m^*)g_y(m^*), \ldots, \omega_I - q_I(m^*)g_y(m^*), g_y(m^*))$ is not a Lindahl equilibrium allocation. Then there exists a public good level $\widetilde{y} \neq g_y(m^*)$ and an agent i who can achieve such that $u_i(\omega_i - q_i(m^*)\widetilde{y}, \widetilde{y}) > u_i(\omega_i - q_i(m^*)g_y(m^*), g_y(m^*))$. Note that by the definition of Walker's mechanism, each agent can achieve any level of the public good by submitting the appropriate message, taking the other agents' messages as given. The message that achieves $\widetilde{y}$ is $\widetilde{m}_i = \widetilde{y} - \sum_{j \neq i} m_j^*$. Then $u_i(\omega_i - q_i(m^*)\widetilde{y}, \widetilde{y}) > u_i(\omega_i - q_i(m^*)g_y(m^*), g_y(m^*))$ implies that m^* is not a Nash equilibrium strategy profile, a contradiction.

We now show that if $((q_i, \ldots, q_I), (x_1, \ldots, x_I, y))$ is a Lindahl equilibrium, then the allocation $(x_1, \ldots, x_I, y)$ is a Nash equilibrium outcome of Walker's mechanism. Define the strategy vector $(m_1^*, \ldots, m_I^*)$ as the solution of the system of I linear equations in the I unknowns $(m_1, \ldots, m_I)$ given as follows.

$$m_1 + m_2 + \ldots + m_I = y,$$

$$m_2 - m_1 = q_I - \frac{1}{I},$$

$$m_3 - m_2 = q_1 - \frac{1}{I},$$

$$\vdots$$

$$m_I - m_{I-1} = q_{I-2} - \frac{1}{I}.$$

---

[4]This mechanism does not guarantee individual feasibility, as it allows the tax imposed on an agent to exceed his endowment. This can only happen for non-equilibrium messages, however. Many mechanisms were proposed after Walker's that remedy this problem, but Walker's mechanism still remains one of the simplest to use for illuminating the essence of the problem of Nash implementing the Lindahl social choice correspondence.

The determinant of the coefficient matrix of this system equals $I > 0$ and therefore there is a unique solution to this system. Checking that the vector m^* found as the solution of this system is a Nash equilibrium of Walker's mechanism is a straightforward application of the mechanism's definition and the fact that $((q_i, \ldots, q_I), (x_1, \ldots, x_I, y))$ is a Lindahl equilibrium.   QED

Walker (1981) shows how this mechanism can easily be extended to many private and public goods as well as a continuum of individuals.

6.4 Implementing Fair Allocations

There are various notions of fairness of economic allocations. We have already defined envy-free allocations and the associated no-envy social choice correspondence in section 1.7.6. Recall that an envy-free allocation x in an exchange economy is such that, for every pair of agents i and j, we have $u_i(x_i) \geq u_i(x_j)$. This says that no agent would rather have another agent's consumption vector from this allocation. This is equivalent to the definition given previously in Section 1.7.6. We consider in this section the Nash implementation of envy-free allocations.

Thomson (2005) has proposed a simple and elegant way to implement envy-free allocations in Nash equilibria, and has shown how variations of this method can implement several other social choice correspondences beyond the no-envy one. This section is based on Thomson's paper. We consider here a class of exchange economies with n commodities in which the preference profile of an economy is $\rho = (R^1, \ldots, R^I)$ and the aggregate endowment is represented by a positive vector $\Omega \in \mathbb{R}^n_{++}$. The idea is that the agents in the economy jointly own Ω and the job of a social choice correspondence is to decide on how they should divide it among themselves. Since these economies are defined so as to focus on the distribution of the aggregate endowment Ω, they are given the name *distribution economies*.

We assume that each agent's preference R^i is represented by utility function $u_i : \mathbb{R}_+ \to \mathbb{R}$, but we will represent an economy by its preference profile ρ to emphasize that the fundamental defining feature is the list of preferences. We write X for the set of all feasible allocations of an economy, defined by $X = \left\{ x \in \mathbb{R}^{nI}_+ \mid \sum_{i \in \mathcal{I}} x_i = \Omega \right\}$. For future reference we also define a version of the feasible set expressed for a single agent, that shows the resources the agent could receive without exceeding the aggregate endowment: $X_0 = \left\{ x_0 \in \mathbb{R}^n_+ \mid x_0 \leq \Omega \right\}$.

For any distribution economy ρ in the class $\mathcal{E}_{cee}$, we write $EF(\rho)$ for the set of envy-free allocations x of the economy ρ and we recall that we have named this the **no-envy** social choice correspondence. You can easily check that EF is a Maskin-monotonic social choice correspondence.

A mechanism for achieving envy-free allocations when there are only two agents has been known for a long time: the divide-and-choose procedure. In this procedure, one agent divides Ω in two parts, and the other agent chooses the part he prefers. The divide-and-permute method expands this idea to accommodate any finite number of agents, not just two. In this case, the two first agents (in some arbitrary fixed ordering of the agents) are dividers, and every agent, including the dividers, is a chooser.

We now present the formal definition of the mechanism that embodies the divide-and-permute procedure. As a preliminary notational step, recall from your math classes that a **permutation** of an ordered list $x_1, \ldots, x_n$ is a rearrangement of the members of the list into a new ordering, so that each member appears exactly once in the new ordered list. Let the set $\mathcal{I}$ of agents have an arbitrary order, which we will keep constant throughout this section. Let $\Pi^{\mathcal{I}}$ stand for the class of all permutations of the set $\mathcal{I}$ of agents, and let π_0 stand for the identity permutation, which is such that $\pi_0(i) = i$, for every $i \in \mathcal{I}$. Finally, suppose that $f : X \to Y$ and $g : Y \to Z$ are two functions. The **composition** of f and g is the function $[\, g \circ f \,] : X \to Z$ defined by the rule $[\, g \circ f \,](x) = g(f(x))$ for every $x \in X$. This function takes an x from the domain of f, gets its image $f(x)$ by applying function f to x and then applies the function g to $f(x)$. We refer to the composition function as $g \circ f$ for brevity.

Definition 6.9 (Divide-and-Permute Mechanism). Let the message spaces M_1 and M_2 be defined by $M_1 = M_2 = X \times \Pi^I$ and let $M_3 = \cdots = M_I = \Pi^I$. Given a message list $m = ((x^1, \pi_1), (x^2, \pi_2), \pi_3, \ldots, \pi_I) \in M = M_1 \times \cdots \times M_I$, the outcome function $g : M \to X$ is defined by

$$
g(m) \;=\; \begin{cases} (0, 0, \ldots, 0) & \text{if } x^1 \neq x^2, \\ \pi_I \circ \pi_{I-1} \circ \cdots \circ \pi_1(x) & \text{if } x^1 = x^2 = x. \end{cases}
$$

The mechanism has the first two agents propose allocations x^1 and x^2 (we use superscripts to make clear these are entire allocations). If these allocations differ, then the entire endowment is taken from the agents, and every one consumes the zero bundle. If they are the same, then each agent i, including the first two, can influence which bundle among all the I bundles that the allocation x specifies, this agent can get, by its choice of permutation π_i. When agent i takes all the other agents' permutation choices π_j as given, as in a Nash equilibrium, then i can get any one of the bundles of the allocation x, that is, any one of the bundles $x_1, \ldots, x_I$, for herself by the appropriate choice of π_i. We leave the verification of this statement as an exercise.

Before proceeding to the first result on this mechanism, we note that the divide-and-choose mechanism, of which it is the successor, has a venerable history in the economics of justice (see Kolm, 1972 and Crawford, 1977). It also has a drawback compared to divide-and-permute: divide-and-choose implements one envy-free allocation, while divide-and-permute, as we will see, implements the entire set of envy-free allocations for every distribution economy. Of course, that also means that the divide-and-permute mechanism has many Nash equilibria in each distribution economy. This raises the standard criticism that agents would have a very hard time coordinating to any single Nash equilibrium of the mechanism, as they have to correctly anticipate exactly which Nash equilibrium every agent is thinking is being played.

We now turn to some results. For any message profile m, write $\mathrm{att}_i(m)$ for the set of consumption bundles that agent i can attain for herself, given that all others play according to m_{-i}. (This set only depends on m_{-i}, not all of the list m, but we write it as $\mathrm{att}_i(m)$ to simplify notation.)

Theorem 6.6 (Thomson 2005). *The divide-and-permute mechanism implements the no-envy social choice correspondence in Nash equilibria.*

Proof. We show first that if x is a Nash equilibrium of the divide-and-permute mechanism played in some distribution economy ρ, then x is an envy-free allocation for the distribution economy ρ.

Assume that x is a Nash equilibrium of the divide-and-permute mechanism played in some distribution economy ρ. Let $m = ((x^1, \pi_1), (x^2, \pi_2), \pi_3, \ldots, \pi_I)$ be an equilibrium such that $x = x^1 = x^2$. Concerning agent 1, we have that $\mathrm{att}_1(m) = \{0, x_1^2, x_2^2, \ldots, x_I^2\}$; the first of these bundles results if agent 1 plays any $x^1 \neq x^2$ and the others if agent 1 plays $x^1 = x^2$ and the appropriate permutation, in which case agent 1 receives one of the consumption bundles that agent 2 has proposed for some agent. Because $x^2 \in X$, at least one of the consumption bundles $x_1^2, x_2^2, \ldots, x_I^2$ has at least one positive coordinate. Therefore, (x^1, π) can be a best response to m_{-1} only if $x^1 = x^2$; otherwise, 1 is strictly worse off by receiving the zero consumption bundle. It follows that $x = \pi_I \circ \pi_{I-1} \circ \cdots \circ \pi_2 \circ \pi_1(x^1)$. The same argument applies to $\mathrm{att}_2(m)$. For any agent $i \in \{3, \ldots, I\}$, $\mathrm{att}_i(m) = \{x_1, x_2, \ldots, x_I\}$. So at a Nash equilibrium every agent has chosen the bundle that maximizes this agent's utility out of all the bundles that are available for the agents, hence the corresponding Nash equilibrium allocation is envy-free.

We show now that if x is an envy-free allocation for a distribution economy ρ, then it is an allocation that arises from a Nash equilibrium for the distribution economy ρ of the divide-and-permute game played in this economy.

Assume that x is an envy-free allocation for a distribution economy ρ. Let the message list m be set as $m = ((x, \pi_0), (x, \pi_0), \pi_0, \ldots, \pi_0)$. By the definition of the divide-and-permute mechanism, for this m we have $g(m) = x$. For agent 1 we have $\mathrm{att}_1(m) = \{0, x_1, x_2, \ldots, x_I\}$. Since x is an envy-free allocation, it follows that $u_1(x_1) \geq u_1(x_i)$ for every $i \neq 1$, and by strict monotonicity of preferences, $u_1(x_1) \geq 0$. Therefore m_1 is a best response for agent 1 to m_{-1}. The same argument applies to agent 2. For every other agent j, the envy-freedom of x similarly implies that m_j is a best response to m_{-j}. Hence m is a Nash equilibrium of divide-and-permute played in the distribution economy ρ.   QED

The basic idea of the proof is that the divide-and-permute mechanism forces the two dividers, agents 1 and 2, to propose a common allocation $x = (x_1, \ldots, x_I)$ for the entire economy. After that, because every agent can grab any one of the bundles in the allocation $(x_1, \ldots, x_I)$, but no other bundle, each agent ends up with a bundle that she does not think is inferior to any other agent's bundle. If she thought it was inferior, she could have taken the superior bundle by varying her permutation.

A number of nice properties of the divide-and-permute mechanism are worth mentioning explicitly. First, it does not really need every agent to announce a permutation; it can do just as well by requiring each agent i to announce a **transposition,** which is a permutation that exchanges exactly two components of the allocation, x_i and x_j, where x_j is the most preferred bundle in the allocation by agent i. Second, the mechanism implements the no-envy social choice correspondence even with just two agents in the economy, which is often more difficult than with three or more agents in the general theory of Nash implementation, as we have seen. Third, it is not necessary that the punishment for a disagreement among the allocations proposed by agents 1 and 2 be the destruction of the endowment Ω; it is enough to redistribute Ω in a preselected, arbitrary fashion, among all agents except agents 1 and 2.

The set of envy-free allocations of a distribution economy captures a prominent notion of what is an equitable allocation of resources. However, it has no connection with Pareto efficiency. In a typical exchange or distribution economy with the usual assumptions of monotonicity and convexity of preferences, there are an uncountable infinity of envy-free allocations, some of them Pareto efficient and most of them not so. This raises the natural question: can we implement the envy free and efficient social choice correspondence? Thomson's paper mixes the divide-and-permute mechanism with another one that Thomson developed to implement a very close cousin of the Pareto efficient correspondence and provides an affirmative answer. The mechanism that does the trick follows, but we need a bit of notational refreshment before we get to it.

Let Δ^{n-1} stand for the unit simplex in the n-dimensional space $\mathbb{R}^n$; this means that every element of Δ^{n-1} is a vector $x \in \mathbb{R}^n$ such that for each k we have $x_k \geq 0$ and also $\sum_{k=1}^n x_k = 1$ holds. The restriction to price vectors that they must belong to the unit simplex is a common method employed in general equilibrium theory to deal with the fact that when we have n goods, we only, in essence, have $n - 1$ relative prices to describe their relative scarcities in the marketplace.

Let $D = \{(x, p) \in X \times \Delta^{n-1} \mid \forall i, \ p \cdot x_i > 0\}$ and, for any given $(x_i, p) \in \mathbb{R}^n_+ \times \Delta^{n-1}$, let $B(x_i, p) = \{x_i' \in X_0 \mid p \cdot x_i' \leq p \cdot z_i\}$; this is the same definition as the one we gave for the budget set that an agent who has individual endowment vector x_i faces in section 1.7.8. Recall that $X_0 = \{x_0 \in \mathbb{R}^n_+ \mid x_0 \leq \Omega\}$. Recalling our definition of the Walrasian social choice correspondence in section 1.7.8, we say that a price vector $p \in \Delta^{n-1}$ supports a Pareto efficient allocation $x \in X$ in a distribution economy ρ if it makes x a

Walrasian equilibrium of the exchange economy specified by the preference profile ρ and the individual endowment vectors set to equal x_i for every $i \in \mathcal{I}$.

Definition 6.10 (Strong Pareto Social Choice Correspondence). The **strong Pareto social choice correspondence** selects, for each distribution or exchange economy ρ, every allocation $x \in X$ that is Pareto efficient for ρ and has a supporting price vector $p \in \Delta^{n-1}$ such that $p \cdot x_i > 0$ for each agent i.

This definition is almost identical to that of Pareto efficiency; it only adds the requirement that there is a price vector that supports the efficient allocation such that no agent's consumption bundle is valued at zero. In an exchange economy with monotonic preferences, as in this section, it selects all of the Pareto efficient allocations except the ones that assign the zero vector to some agents. In the Edgeworth box, this can be seen as the Pareto set with the origins of the two axis systems removed.

We are now ready to describe the mechanism that implements the intersection of the no-envy and the strong Pareto social choice correspondences.

Definition 6.11. Let the message spaces be $M_1 = M_2 = D \times \mathbb{N} \times X_0 \times \Pi^{\mathcal{I}}$ and $M_3 = \cdots = M_I = \mathbb{N} \times X_0 \times \Pi^{\mathcal{I}}$. Given a message profile $m = \left((x^1, p_1, t_1, x_1, \pi_1), (x^2, p_2, t_2, x_2, \pi_2), (t_3, x_3, \pi_3), \ldots, (t_I, x_I, \pi_I)\right) \in M$, let $i(m) = \sum_i t_i \pmod{I}$ and

$$
g(m) = \begin{cases}
(0, 0, \ldots, 0) & \text{if } \begin{cases} (x^1, p_1) \neq (x^2, p_2); \\ \text{or} \\ (x^1, p_1) = (x^2, p_2) \text{ and } x_{i(m)} \notin B(x^1_{i(m)}, p_1); \end{cases} \\
(0, \ldots, x_{i(m)}, \ldots, 0) & \text{if } \begin{cases} (x^1, p_1) = (x^2, p_2), \ x_{i(m)} \in B(x^1_{i(m)}, p_1) \\ \text{and } x_{i(m)} \neq x^1_{i(m)}; \end{cases} \\
x^1 & \text{if } (x^1, p_1) = (x^2, p_2) \text{ and } x_{i(m)} = x^1_{i(m)}.
\end{cases}
$$

Notational clarification: a superscript on a vector, such as x^1, denotes an entire $n \times I$-dimensional allocation vector, but a subscript as in x_1 denotes a consumption bundle for one agent, which is n-dimensional.

In this mechanism, the first two agents are again special in that they have more dimensions to their message spaces. Each one of these two agents, $i = 1, 2$, is to submit an entire allocation x^i, a proposed price vector p_i, a positive integer t_i, a consumption bundle x_i, and a permutation π_i. Each one of the remaining agents, $i = 3, \ldots, I$, is to submit a positive integer t_i, a consumption bundle x_i, and a permutation π_i.

The mechanism is inspired by the second fundamental theorem of welfare economics. The idea it encodes is this. The two first agents, the dividers, announce a pair of an allocation and a price vector each. The allocations are intended for the entire distribution economy. The prices are intended to serve as supporting prices. The outcome function pushes agents 1 and 2 to agree in their announcements of allocation vectors and price vectors. Furthermore, each agent announces an integer, t_i, which determines who can object to the recommendation of the dividers. Finally, each agent announces a consumption bundle x_i that she feels she should receive and a permutation. But an objection x_i is only taken seriously if, when evaluated at the common price vector announced by the dividers, it does not give i a higher amount than the bundle that the dividers have intended for i, x_i^1. Thomson (2005) proves the following.

Theorem 6.7 (Thomson, 2005). *The mechanism $\Gamma^{F \cap P}$ Nash implements the no-envy and strongly Pareto efficient social choice correspondence.*

We see that the mechanism $\Gamma^{F \cap P}$ yields all allocations that are both envy-free and strongly Pareto efficient when played in any distribution economy. In Thomson (2005) several variations are considered, that implement variants of the idea of no-envy. One such variant is one in which each agent i compares her bundle x_i not to every other agent's bundle, but to the average bundle of all other agents. For details on this and other variants of interest from the point of view of economic justice theory, we refer you to Thomson's paper.

6.5 Application to Negative Externality Problems: Pollution Abatement

A negative externality occurs when the actions of an agent make other agents worse off by affecting some variable that affects the other agents' welfare. A prominent example of a negative externality is environmental pollution. The emissions from a factory pollute the atmosphere and reduce the level of the public good "clean air" for every agent, but the firm that operates the factory is the sole decision-maker regarding the factory's emissions. The fundamental problem for society is that each polluter faces only a fraction of the cost of the pollution his emissions create, so his single-agent profit maximization problem inevitably results in a level of emissions that is too high relative to the Pareto efficient level. Thus unfettered free markets fail to bring about a Pareto efficient allocation when there are negative externalities, even under the assumption that all markets are perfectly competitive. The same kind of market failure happens for positive externalities, such as the positive spillovers created by basic scientific research, which tends to be provided at a level below the efficient level under free market conditions. This is the reason that we concentrated on implementing the Lindahl social choice correspondence rather than the Walrasian one on the domain of economies with public goods.

Since the time of Pigou (1920), a standard recommendation for bringing about the efficient level of pollution is to tax each emitter so that he faces the entire cost of his emissions that otherwise would fall on others who have no say on his emission decision. However, determining the efficient level of pollution and the tax levels to levy on polluters in order to achieve the efficient level requires information that the environmental agencies of governments do not possess, such as the benefits each polluter receives from his polluting emissions, the cost he faces for reducing his emissions, and the costs that pollution imposes on each agent. This information is dispersed in the population of agents. The approach of economic design is clearly the right tool to address this problem. It suggests to set up a mechanism to decentralize the emission decisions to the agents who have the appropriate information, while not allowing these agents to "game the system," as the colloquial expression goes.

An alternative approach is to allocate property rights as clearly as possible and to rely on the spontaneous bargaining among polluters and the other agents to achieve an efficient outcome, in the spirit of the Coase "theorem." See section 8.1 for a criticism of this approach, and Baliga and Maskin (2003), who give an example of why decentralized Coasian bargaining often breaks down. The incentive to free ride on other agents' abatement efforts often overwhelms pollution abatement agreements.

Duggan and Roberts (2002) apply to the problem of allocating pollution rights among firms a mechanism similar to the Walker (1981) mechanism that we saw in section 6.3. This mechanism assumes that a regulator can observe pollution emissions and the social cost of pollution but does not know the relevant characteristics of the firms. Previous studies have assumed implicitly or explicitly that the regulator knows the efficient level of pollution. Duggan and Roberts (2002) instead propose a mechanism where the unique Nash equilibrium strategies of the firms lead to the efficient level of total pollution outcome endogenously. The central authority, which is the environmental regulator, need not know what is the efficient level of pollution in order to employ this mechanism.

The mechanism operates on a domain of economies that have the following structure. There are at least two agents, the **firms,** that are indexed by $i \in \mathcal{I}$. Each firm has a set of types Θ_i. Let i's quantity of pollution generation be denoted by $y_i \in \mathbb{R}_+$. Let the monetary benefit firm i receives from emitting this pollution be a function given by $B_i : \mathbb{R}_+ \times \Theta_i \to \mathbb{R}_+$. For each level of pollution generated, $y_i \in \mathbb{R}_+$, and each type $\theta_i \in \Theta_i$, $B_i(y_i, \theta_i)$ is the indirect **benefit** a firm gets from its profit when operating its production plants, the operation of which causes the level of emissions y_i. We assume that B_i is a concave and differentiable function of y_i. We also assume that each firm's type is common knowledge among firms but is not known by the regulator. We assume that the **social monetary cost** of the firms' pollution emissions is a continuously differentiable function of all emissions, $C : \mathbb{R}_+^I \to \mathbb{R}_+$, which assigns to any non-negative vector of pollution generation levels $(y_1, \ldots, y_I)$ the non-negative cost level $C(y_1, \ldots, y_I)$. The firms and the regulator know the cost function. Finally assume that for each $\theta \in \Theta$, $\sum_{i \in \mathcal{I}} B_i(y_i, \theta_i) - C(y_1, \ldots, y_I)$ is a strictly concave function of $(y_1, \ldots, y_I)$, and that for each $i \in \mathcal{I}$ the limit of $D_{y_i} B_i(y_i, \theta_i) - D_{y_i} C(y_1, \ldots, y_I)$ as y_i approaches zero is infinity.

(Recall that for a function f with multiple arguments, $D_{y_i} f$ denotes the partial derivative of f with respect to argument y_i. See page 257 for the definition in equation [A.1].)

The efficient allocation of pollution is the vector $y^* = (y_1^*, \ldots, y_I^*)$ that maximizes $\sum_{i \in \mathcal{I}} B_i(y_i, \theta_i) - C(y_1, \ldots, y_I)$. Given the assumptions we have made, such a solution exists, is a strictly positive vector, and is unique. The solution of this maximization problem equates each firm's marginal private benefit at y_i^* with the marginal social cost of y_i^*. As Duggan and Roberts (2002) point out, if a regulator were to know the efficient level of pollution, the regulator could charge each firm a price equal to the marginal social cost that firm imposes on society, given the optimal level of all other firms. This level is the optimal Pigou tax for the firm. The mechanism they propose achieves the efficient level of pollution without assuming that the regulator has this knowledge.

The mechanism proposed by the Duggan and Roberts is as follows. Let $K > 0$ be an arbitrarily chosen large level of pollution generation.

- Each firm i has the strategy set $M_i \in [0, K] \times [0, K]$. A strategy $m_i = (\hat{y}_i, \bar{y}_{i-1})$ from this set has two parts: a pollution permit purchase, $\hat{y}_i$, and a quantity, $\bar{y}_{i-1}$, for the pollution level of firm $i - 1$.
- Given the strategy vector $m = (m_i, \ldots, m_I) \in \prod_{i \in \mathcal{I}} M_i$, the outcome function $g : \prod_{i \in \mathcal{I}} M_i \to R_+^I$ specifies a payment for each firm as:
$$g(m)_i = \hat{y}_i D_{\hat{y}_i} C(\hat{y}_1, \ldots, \hat{y}_{i-1}, \bar{y}_i, \hat{y}_{i+1}, \ldots \hat{y}_I) + |\bar{y}_{i-1} - \hat{y}_{i-1}|.$$

This mechanism uses the circular arrangement of agents that we have seen in sections 3.2.1 and 6.3. Each firm pays a personalized price of $q_i = D_{\hat{y}_i} C(\hat{y}_1, \ldots, \hat{y}_{i-1}, \bar{y}_i, \hat{y}_{i+1}, \ldots \hat{y}_I)$ which does not depend on its own strategy. The second term in the definition of $g(m)$ imposes a penalty on firm i for misreporting the demand of its neighbor; the penalty equals the absolute value of the difference of i's report about y_{i-1} and $i - 1$'s purchase $\hat{y}_{i-1}$.

One can see how the mechanism gives incentives to demand the efficient quantity and for firms to monitor one another through the payment penalty. A firm's personal price, q_i, is the marginal cost of i's demand at the level reported by firm $i + 1$. Therefore if firm i deviates by underreporting its demand, this lowers the firm's overall payment but also lowers its benefit from emitting the level efficient for its technology, because the firm must operate less efficiently. Given firm i's type, θ_i, underreporting is not more profitable than reporting the true amount of pollution that would maximize the firm's net benefit. Furthermore, its neighbor $i + 1$ has a best response of reporting i's demand accurately since it knows that it is a best response for i to report truthfully. If $i + 1$ underreports or over-reports i's demand it will pay a penalty.

As stated, this mechanism may be prone to manipulation through collusive behavior among firms. Duggan and Roberts (2002) offer such a modification of the mechanism that achieves implementation in Nash equilibrium that is immune to collusion by any pair of firms. They do not solve the problem of avoiding collusion by larger coalitions. In a working paper version of Duggan and Roberts (2002), the authors also discuss the implementation of efficient pollution levels in Bayesian equilibrium. Finally, the problem of pollution is dynamic: greenhouse gases accumulate over time. The mechanism we just described is static, but it may be the basis for a more sophisticated mechanism that works well on a domain of dynamic economies.

After looking at some theoretical applications of implementation, we now turn to two examples of how we can use the theory to do case studies. This gives insight into real-life institutions.

6.6 A Nearly Efficient Mutual Insurance Mechanism

For over a century, the tiny country of Andorra, located in the Pyrenees between France and Spain, has had a mutual fire insurance system. Cabrales et al. (2003) analyze this in the framework of mechanism design to gain insight into this system's efficiency and incentive properties. Therefore in the following, the mutual insurance system called *La Crema*[5] will be characterized as a mechanism and the language of implementation theory will be applied accordingly.

La Crema is an insurance cooperative. It is designed to provide fire insurance to property owners in the region. Initially it provided fire insurance for homes and barns but later households[6] could insure other property (e.g., woodsheds, mills, etc.). Each household in the economy has a value $\theta_i \in \mathbb{R}_+$ that describes the subjective value of their property to the household, in contrast to a value determined by a market. Each household knows its own value but does not know the values of others. If household i has a fire then that household will most likely lose the value θ_i since the mountainous nature of Andorra slows down the response of fire fighters. Given the value of his property and a belief about the probability of the burning of its property, each household forms an expectation of its wealth. There are $S = 2^I$ possible states in which some combination of farms burn. Let $s \in S$ be a list of farms that burned. For example, $s = \{2, 5, 7\}$ means that farms $2, 5$ and 7 burned. Denote by $S_i^{|s|}$ the set of states in which household i's farm burns along with $|s| - 1$ other farms. Basic insurance economics teaches us that a risk-averse household insures its property in order to increase its expected utility by equalizing his consumption levels over the possible states of nature as much as the available insurance policies allow.

La Crema provides a form of mutual insurance by giving a strategy set for each household, $M_i = [0, C]$ where C is an arbitrary maximum value, set at twice the highest

---

[5] According to the *Oxford Dictionary*, *Crema* is literally translated "cremation" and thus it seems to be an appropriate name for the provision of fire insurance.
[6] We treat households as the agents in this section. Each household is represented by its head, both in the functioning of the insurance system and in terms of the expected utility function of the household.

possible property value. A **strategy** for household i is an announcement $m_i \in M_i$ that expresses the value of its property. Each year each household submits a strategy, m_i, at the general assembly meeting, *consell de La Crema*. This strategy is recorded. Denote by $M' = \sum_{i \in \mathcal{I}} m_i$ the sum of all value announcements. For each state $s \in S$, let $M'_s = \sum_{i \in I \setminus s} m_i$. M'_s is the sum of all the values announced by those households whose farms did not burn.

The **outcome function** is as follows, and applies each year, using the recorded m_i announcements at the previous *consell de la Crema*. For each state s, each household $i \in s$, whose farm burned, is paid the amount $m_i(M'_s/M')$. Each household $j \notin s$, whose farm did not burn, pays the amount $m_j(M' - M'_s)/M'$, which is proportional to its announcement m_j.

Theorem 6.8 (Cabrales et al., 2003). *If all wealth levels are the same, truth-telling is a Nash equilibrium strategy.*

This can be seen by the two competing incentives a household faces when deciding on its best response strategy. For a household whose true value of wealth is θ_i, deviating from the strategy $m_i = \theta_i$ by announcing $\bar{m}_i = \theta_i + \epsilon$ increases household i's payment in every state $s \in S_i^{|s|}$ by $\epsilon M'_s/M'$ but also increases what it must pay in every state $s' \in S_j^{|s|} \neq \emptyset$ for any $j \neq i$ by $\epsilon(M' - M'_{s'})/M'$.

Cabrales et al. (2003) explain that these deviations result in households transferring wealth from states where their barn does not burn to states where it does burn, and vice versa for underreporting. This can be seen by a numerical example. Suppose your property is worth \$100 to you and the total wealth insured is \$500. Then by announcing your true wealth your fraction of total wealth is $\frac{1}{5}$ (recall that we have assumed equal wealth levels). If only your barn burns, you will receive $\frac{1}{5}\$400 = \$80$. If your barn does not burn, but someone else's does, you must pay $\frac{1}{5}\$100 = \$20$ leaving you with a net wealth of \$80. However if instead you over-report your wealth by \$5, you will receive $\frac{105}{505}(\$400) \approx \$83$ if your barn burns but will have to pay $\frac{105}{505}(\$405) \approx \$22$ which leaves you with a net wealth of \$78.

As we mentioned, the expected utility of a risk-averse agent is maximized by smoothing wealth across states. If all households have the same wealth the truthful announcement results in equal consumption across each state for each household. Therefore the truthful announcement is a Nash equilibrium of the *La Crema* mechanism.

The assumption of equal wealth is a highly implausible assumption in general and so the authors investigate what happens if households have different property values. In this case, truthful reporting is not a Nash equilibrium. If some households are fairly sure they have the top or bottom property value, those with property values below the average have an incentive to underreport their values and households with above average property values have an incentive to over-state their property values.

The authors found a similarly negative result when they examined the efficiency of equilibrium outcomes obtained by some characteristic societies (e.g., those with households characterized by various wealth and risk aversions). They present the following result as remark 3 (Cabrales et al., 2003, page 438).

Theorem 6.9 (Cabrales et al., 2003). *Assume there are at least three households, one of whom has a risk neutral expected utility function and the others have (possibly heterogenous) constant relative risk averse expected utility functions, and at least two households have different property values. Then there is no Pareto efficient allocation that is obtainable through the* La Crema *game.*

This negative finding is puzzling in view of the longevity of *La Crema,* which lends empirical support for the efficiency of the mechanism. Also, interviews with participants indicate that truth-telling is indeed an equilibrium strategy. This led Cabrales et al. (2003) to investigate the properties of the mechanism under the assumption that participant population is large.

They found that as the number of participants increase, truthful reporting approaches an ϵ-Nash equilibrium, which is an equilibrium in which each agent's strategy is within ϵ payoff units of being the best response to the other agents' strategies. As the number of participants increases, any one household's announcement has a smaller effect on the total insured wealth M and therefore the household's cost share becomes decreasingly dependent on one's own announcement, effectively making the household a price-taker. This results in the trade-off between states for which one's property burns and does not burn when one under- or over-reports that is roughly similar to the case of equal wealth given above.

In larger societies, the outcome of the mechanism also can achieve approximate efficiency. Rather than showing additional details of the findings, we refer the reader to Cabrales et al. (2003) for further analysis of the equilibrium and efficiency results as well as the formal proofs. The paper also discusses many fascinating historical details that may be of interest to the reader. The remainder of this section discusses the features of the mechanism in light of the theories presented in this book.

Although the mechanism is not costless to operate, is does minimize costs in two ways. First, property values are not formally verified, for instance by an outside appraiser. The only verification that is done is that a farm did indeed burn. This decentralization is achievable partly because individuals only pay when a barn burns. This is in contrast to other types of insurance systems where individuals pay a premium whether there is claim or not and therefore build up reserves in times when no claims are filed. The transfer of wealth between states balances the incentives of households to report truthfully. It also gives them an incentive to self-monitor their neighbors' behavior to ensure non-negligence. The information the insurance council needs to know concerning individual characteristics is quite minimal. Contrast this, for example, with some large premium-based insurance policies where the administrators often collect databases of statistical information concerning the characteristics of the participants in order to mitigate moral hazard concerns.

The second cost saving is in terms of the message space. Households need only report one number per property they want insured. Recall the criticism by many of theoretical mechanisms used in implementation theory, that they are much more complicated than necessary for specific applications. Mechanisms used for general proofs are necessarily complicated to achieve general applicability. Here we see explicitly how a mechanism intended for a specific application can have a small message space and a simple outcome function. In the *La Crema* mechanism, households need not report the wealth of everyone in the community, report the wealth of a neighbor, report an integer, or raise a flag.

Another important implementation question is whether agents choose to participate in a mechanism. *La Crema* satisfies the voluntary participation constraint because (1) in states where no farm burns no transfers are made; also no other taxation or fees are assigned based on the value announced (e.g., a property tax); and (2) as long as there is a positive probability of an household's farm burning and households are risk-averse, they can achieve higher expected utility by participating in the mechanism which smooths their consumption across states.

Notice the reappearance of the theme that an agent's payment not depend on one's own strategy. In large societies, since each household's wealth announcement makes up a smaller fraction of the total, increasing or decreasing one's announcement has only a small, and increasingly negligible as the society becomes larger, effect on the household's actual payment or reimbursement.

This case study demonstrates the application of economic design theory and its usefulness for gaining insight into the incentives institutions create and their effectiveness at achieving their purpose. It also points the way towards a large and open research area. Many institutions operate around the globe. Studying these using the tool of implementation and mechanism design will aid in discovering optimal ways of allocating resources in efficient ways that are voluntary (respect individual freedom) and incentive compatible (encourage honest rather than deceptive behavior). Furthermore, if an institution is not achieving its goals, this theoretical framework can help discover the nature of the incentives and why an undesirable equilibrium may be reached.

6.7 Financing the Athenian Fleet

The ancient Athenians used a mechanism that required neither direct taxation nor government procurement to finance their impressive fleet, as we have seen in the very beginning of this book. Kaiser (2007), on which this section is based, studied this historical example as a classic use of mechanism design, thousands of years before game theory or mechanism design became study fields. After placing the antidosis game in the mechanism design framework, he performed an econometric estimation of the probability that trierarchs would resort to the antidosis challenge and compared his results to the historical record.

As described at the beginning of this book, during the Classical period the Athenians instituted a liturgical system for the provision of public goods by private citizens. There were a few different public goods allocated through this system. The "command, outfitting and maintenance" of a trireme, an ancient war ship, for one year was known as a trierarchy (Kaiser, 2007). We discuss in this section the private provision of defense via the maintenance of a fleet by wealthy Athenian citizens via the trierarchy system. By analyzing this system in terms of mechanism design theory Kaiser (2007) demonstrates that the theory is not only of interest to economists, but also historians. Gaining a better understanding of the incentives institutions create helps predict individual behavior and can be used to fill in missing details of the historical record.

The implementation problem for the Athenian society was to provide naval defense at a given level, measured by the number of triremes. The level of the public good provided should maximize the net value received by society from the public good. The fleet required financing. Instead of direct taxation, the financing came from, in modern terms, outsourcing the provision of the fleet to private citizens. In what follows we bring the mindset of implementation theory to the study of the trierarchy system. We study only the element of the system that was intended to allocate the provision of the navel ships to wealthy citizens in a way that avoided free-riding. We do not model the overarching question of how the desired size of the trireme fleet was determined.

As usual the economy consists of I agents, the wealthy citizens, each with a type $\theta_i \in \Theta_i$. Here the type of an agent is a measure of one's true wealth. Let θ_i^* be the amount of i's **visible wealth** and $\widehat{\theta}_i$ be an individual's **self-reported wealth,** the amount the community can easily inspect or verify. Visible wealth included items such as land holdings, slaves, ownership of a workshop and mine contracts. Hidden wealth could be in the form of money lent out to bankers or others. Concealing wealth via dealings with bankers was costly because these transactions were not witnessed by third parties nor were they well documented (in order to keep them concealed). Dealing with a banker could just as easily lead to losing one's wealth as to successfully concealing it.

The social choice correspondence in this case was one that assigned a predetermined number of trierarchies to the same number of the wealthiest citizens. Since wealthy individuals had the most to lose from an invasion, they were likely the ones to benefit the most from having naval protection. As with any public good, though, once the fleet was provided all citizens benefited from it. A wealthy citizen would prefer to have an extra trireme protecting the city, but would prefer more to have someone else pay for the trireme. Hence there was an incentive to conceal one's true wealth since payment was based on one's wealth, and we saw that wealth concealment was possible. The implementation problem was how to extract the information on true wealth levels so as have the desired number of triremes provided.

The mechanism, that we examine as an embodiment of the antidosis procedure that underlies the trierarchy system, has multiple stages, as shown in figure 6.1. The game was initiated by the *demes*. The *demes* were small communities similar in size to villages; there were 139 of them, organized into 10 tribes. Each deme had its own government, and this body ranked the members of deme according to their visible wealth. This was reported to the *strategoi* (generals, a high rank in the Athenian polis), who assigned trierarchies to those citizens with the highest visible wealth. A citizen who was assigned a trierarchy is player 1 in our game. He could pay the amount T_1 that the trierarchy costs him, or challenge another individual, player 2. We assume that $\theta_1^* > \theta_2^*$: 1's visible wealth is higher than 2's. We analyze now the interaction of these two citizens subject to the antidosis procedure.

The first player to play is citizen 1. If citizen 1 accepts the trierarchy, then the game ends with the payoffs $\theta_1 - T_1$ for player 1 and θ_2 for player 2. We are measuring payoffs simply by the net wealth levels of the citizens, which amounts to assuming that they are risk neutral. If citizen 1 chooses to challenge citizen 2, the latter can either pay the trierarchy cost T_2 or offer to trade his visible wealth plus some amount x of his private wealth for the self-reported wealth of citizen 1. Citizen 1 now can either accept the trade of his self-proclaimed wealth $\widehat{\theta}_1$ and also pay the trierarchy cost T_1 or reject the trade. If the trade is rejected the outcome is decided by the court in a *diadikasia* proceeding. With probability P_1 the court rules that citizen 2 is responsible for the trierarchy (citizen 1 wins) and with probability $1 - P_1$ the court rules that individual 1 is responsible. In practice, this probability was a function of the proclaimed and visible wealths of the players, but here we are treating it as an exogenous constant. In court, each opponent would try to prove the liability of the other by trying to uncover the other's private wealth. We represent the decision of the court as a choice by nature, N, in the game tree of figure 6.1, which also shows the payoffs of the players from each history of actions that leads to the termination of the game. You may find it instructive to compare this game with the example of section 5.1.1.

The game is solved by backward induction. Citizen 1 is the last one to make a choice, if citizen 2 has offered a trade x (the choice of nature is mechanical and thus not amenable to strategic analysis). If 1 accepts the trade, he gets expected payoff $\theta_1 - \widehat{\theta}_1 + \theta_2^* + x - T_1$ and if he rejects the trade he gets expected payoff $P_1\theta_1 + (1 - P_1)(\theta_1 - T_1)$. Write θ_1^ε for the difference $\theta_1^* - \widehat{\theta}_1$. It follows, after a little algebra, that 1 will accept the trade if and only if $x \geq \theta_1^* - \theta_2^* - \theta_1^\varepsilon + P_1 T_1$.

If citizen 1 is to accept the trade, then citizen 2, when it is time for him to choose between taking the trierarchy or proposing a trade x, will propose at most $x = \theta_1^* - \theta_2^* - \theta_1^\varepsilon + P_1 T_2$. If

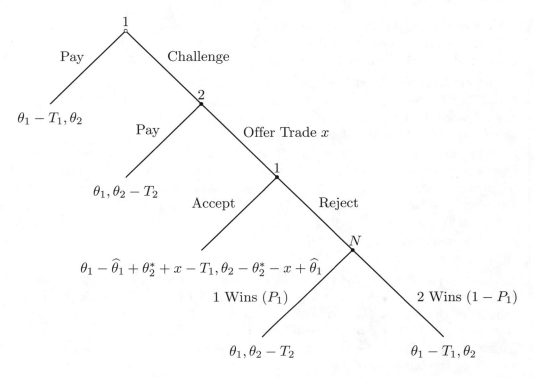

Figure 6.1: The Antidosis Game

it happens that $T = T_1 = T_2$, then the last two conclusions imply that $x = \theta_1^* - \theta_2^* - \theta_1^\varepsilon + P_1 T$ is the unique acceptable trade proposal. Finally, it follows that citizen 1 does not accept the trierarchy without a challenge unless $T_1 \leq 0$ or $P_1 = 0$, that is, unless the trierarchy costs him nothing or he has no hope of winning in court.

We refer the reader to the Kaiser (2007) paper for more detailed analysis as well as many interesting historical details. Kaiser reports that the trierarchy system lasted for about a century and a half, although the details were reformed a number of times, with the impetus for reform coming from wars. A minority of the known trierarchy assignments went to court, according to surviving historical evidence. A more comprehensive model of the trierarchy system as a mechanism may provide explanations for these facts, but it has not been developed yet.

A notable fact is that Athenian citizens were motivated not only by considerations of wealth but also by considerations of their honor and reputation. The game we presented here abstracts away from such issues. More generally, most of the mechanism and implementation literature keeps to classical assumptions of self-interest in modeling agents' preferences. The framework of the theory does not require such a narrow view of human motivations, and we hope that the theory will be enriched significantly in this direction soon. A nice example of just such enrichment is Ellingsen and Johannesson (2008).

Chapter 7

Bayesian Implementation

In chapter 4 we discussed the Bayesian equilibrium concept and the Bayesian revelation principle. We also examined in detail the mechanism of d'Aspremont-Gérard Varet and Arrow and applications of the Bayesian revelation principle to domains of auctions and bilateral trading with quasilinear preferences. In this chapter we turn to a problem of the approach that relies on the Bayesian revelation principle, that of multiple Bayesian equilibria of a mechanism. After we state the problem via an example, we develop the Bayesian Monotonicity condition, a condition similar to Maskin Monotonicity, and general results on Bayesian implementation. We conclude with a discussion of virtual Bayesian implementation.

7.1 Example of Multiple Bayesian Equilibria

We introduced the problem of multiple equilibria for the Nash equilibrium solution concept in section 3.1. Many mechanisms that use Bayesian equilibrium as the solution concept are susceptible to the multiplicity of equilibria problem. As an illustration, we present an example adapted from (Palfrey and Srivastava, 1989, page 674). In addition, we show a remedy that solves the problem of multiple equilibria for the example.

Consider a pure exchange economy with two agents, Mike and Dan, and two goods. Mike has two possible types, $\Theta_m = \{\theta_m, \theta_m^*\}$, and each type is equally likely. Dan has only one possible type, $\Theta_d = \{\theta_d\}$. We write the two possible type profiles for this economy as $\theta = (\theta_m, \theta_d)$ and $\theta^* = (\theta_m^*, \theta_d)$. The easiest way to represent Mike and Dan's preferences is to use the Edgeworth box, where Mike is agent 1 and Dan is agent 2. We show one indifference curve for Mike that corresponds to θ_m and one that corresponds to θ_m^*; for Dan we show two indifference curves that correspond to the one and only type of Dan, θ_d. We use figure 7.1 to depict each agent's preferences. The social choice correspondence specifies that if both agents are type θ, the outcome is $x(\theta)$, but if Mike is type θ_m^*, then the outcome is $x(\theta^*)$.

We find two Bayesian equilibria in this example. The first is the truth-telling equilibrium, and it is intuitive. Both Mike and Dan report their types truthfully, and as a result,

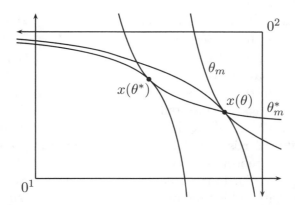

Figure 7.1: Preferences and Allocations for Example 7.1

the equilibrium occurs at the point where their indifference curves are tangent to each other.

However, there is another equilibrium, which occurs when Mike reports type θ_m irrespective of his true type. Note that Mike is indifferent between reporting θ_m and θ_m^* when he has type θ_m^*, as they put him on the same indifference curve.

But these two equilibria are not equally desirable. Although Mike is indifferent between the two outcomes, Dan prefers one to the other. If Mike turns out to be type θ_m^*, but he is reporting type θ_m, then this makes Dan worse off because it puts Dan on a lower indifference curve at point $x(\theta)$ instead of $x(\theta^*)$.

This example illustrates that some mechanisms have multiple equilibria, and that some of the equilibria may not be desirable. The important question is if there is anything we can do to eliminate these undesirable outcomes. In order to implement the desired social choice function, we must design a mechanism that not only generates an equilibrium that produces the desirable outcome, but also restricts other undesirable outcomes from arising as equilibria. We discuss how to do this in generality in the next section.

Here is a mechanism that works for the example. Add a strategy N to Dan's list of possible strategies. Dan can now play either θ_d or N. If Dan plays N when Mike plays θ_m, the outcome is $x(\theta^*)$. If Dan plays N when Mike plays θ_m^*, the outcome is $x(\theta)$. The outcome function of this mechanism is summarized in table 7.1.

Mike \Dan	θ_d	N
θ_m	$x(\theta)$	$x(\theta^*)$
θ_m^*	$x(\theta^*)$	$x(\theta)$

Table 7.1: Elimination of multiple Bayesian Equilibria

Adding a strategy to Dan's list of possible strategies helps us eliminate the undesirable outcome, and leaves us with two equilibria where both Mike and Dan truthfully report their types. To see this, suppose that Mike always plays strategy θ_m, whichever is his true type. Dan should then play strategy N because this puts him on a higher indifference curve, and the outcome in this case is $x(\theta^*)$. But if Dan plays strategy N, Mike should play θ_m^* when he is type θ_m because only then will he be able to induce the desired outcome, namely, $x(\theta)$. Therefore, we have eliminated the undesirable equilibrium.

Two Bayesian equilibria exist for this modified mechanism. One equilibrium occurs when both Mike and Dan report their types truthfully, so that the outcome at θ is $x(\theta)$, and the outcome at θ^* is $x(\theta^*)$. In the other equilibrium, Dan plays strategy N, and Mike plays the strategy opposite of his type in order to induce the desired outcome. Here is a summary of these equilibrium strategies.

Equilibrium 1: $\sigma_m(\theta_m) = \theta_m$, $\quad \sigma_m(\theta_m^*) = \theta_m^*$, $\quad \sigma_d(\theta_d) = \theta_d$.
Equilibrium 2: $\sigma_m(\theta_m) = \theta_m^*$, $\quad \sigma_m(\theta_m^*) = \theta_m$, $\quad \sigma_d(\theta_d) = N$.

This example illustrates how we can implement the desired social outcomes by modifying direct mechanisms to indirect mechanisms. We now turn to a general view of Bayesian implementation. To see what can be done by combining Bayesian equilibrium and undominated strategies, refer to Palfrey and Srivastava (1989) and Mookherjee and Reichelstein (1992).

7.2 Bayesian Implementation and Bayesian Monotonicity

We assume that the set that contains every possible environment $\theta = (\theta_1, \ldots, \theta_I)$ is common knowledge among the I agents, but which of these environments actually has been realized is not common knowledge. Reminder: a piece of information is common knowledge if every agent knows that every agents knows ... that every agent knows it, *ad infinitum*. Let Θ be the set of environments that is common knowledge. The case of full information occurs when Θ is a singleton. An environment, as before, designates a profile of types $\theta = (\theta_1, \ldots, \theta_I)$ of the agents.[1]

Set $\Theta = \Theta_1 \times \cdots \times \Theta_I$. The types are separable across agents. Each agent receives a signal on her type, but that does not imply that she necessarily knows the types of the others upon receipt of the signal, although this may be the case.

Each agent i has a prior belief, which is a probability distribution, $q_i \colon \Theta \to [0,1]$. We assume **non-redundant types:** for every i and every $\theta_i \in \Theta_i$, there exists $\theta_{-i} \in \Theta_{-i}$ such that $q_i(\theta) > 0$. The justification for this assumption is natural, as long as we model agents as maximizers of subjective expected utility. For such agents, situations that arise with zero probability are irrelevant.

---

[1]This section is based on Serrano (2004).

We do not require that all agents share the same prior, contrary to the long-standing argument by John C. Harsanyi, in order to maintain generality of the model. Harsanyi's common priors assumption is controversial. It is based on the premise that fundamentally all agents are the same in the beginning, that is, *ex ante*. An agent i becomes a distinct person when she receives her type, θ_i, which happens in the interim stage of our timeline. If we take this view, then there is no reason to assume that different agents should have different priors, since an agent's prior is attached to the agent *ex ante* in our models. A thorough discussion of the common priors assumption is beyond the scope of this book. It is enough to remember that we do not make the assumption in this section. We want to see some of the basic results on Bayesian implementation that do not depend on the common priors assumption.

Let Θ^* stand for the set of environments that happen with positive probability, that is, for all i, $q_i(\theta) = 0$ if and only if $\theta \notin \Theta^*$. Obviously, Θ^* is a subset of Θ, possibly a proper subset. Note that we have assumed that all agents agree on which environments cannot happen with positive probability.

Denote the conditional probability of agent i, to be called the **posterior belief,** by $q_i(\theta_{-i}|\theta_i)$. Let X be the finite set of alternatives and $\Delta(X)$ the set of all lotteries over X.

Agent i's utility function over lotteries is $u_i \colon \Delta(X) \times \Theta \to \mathbb{R}$, with typical element $u_i(\ell, \theta)$ that denotes the utility that i receives from outcome lottery ℓ when the state is of type θ. When we want the utility of an alternative $x \in X$, we use the lottery that gives that outcome probability 1.

Definition 7.1. Let a social choice function $f \colon \Theta \to X$ be given. The **interim expected utility** of agent i is

$$U_i(f|\theta_i) \equiv \sum_{\theta'_{-i} \in \Theta_{-i}} q_i(\theta'_{-i}|\theta_i) u_i(f(\theta_i, \theta'_{-i}), (\theta_i, \theta'_{-i})). \tag{7.1}$$

The interim expected utility expresses the average utility the agent i expects to get, when i uses the knowledge of his type to arrive at posterior/conditional probabilities of all type combinations of the other agents. Therefore the lottery that enters the interim expected utility has the alternatives $f(\theta_i, \theta'_{-i})$, for $\theta'_{-i} \in \Theta_{-i}$ and it assigns each such alternative the posterior probability $q_i(\theta'_{-i}|\theta_i)$.

The term "interim" comes from the implicit time line in this model, which we now make explicit. We imagine that at some point in time each agent i is assigned a type θ_i. If we want to model the choices of agents as happening based on the information they have at this stage, we need to talk about their *ex ante* expected utility, which takes the expectation of u_i for a given lottery over all combinations of θ, reflecting the fact that the agent does not even know its own θ_i. The interim stage comes after the *ex ante* stage. At this stage, we imagine that each agent i has learned his own type θ_i but not the others' types. This is the stage in which most analysts set their models, as it reflects most closely the majority of intended applications, and it is the stage at which we have chosen to defined expected utility, in equation (7.1). Finally, there is the *ex post* stage. At this stage, we imagine that every agent knows the complete list θ.

Note how flexible this specification is regarding information. The entire list of types is an argument in u_i and so in U_i; therefore we are allowing the information of any agent to affect the payoff of any other. Any kind of informational asymmetry can be accommodated this way. For instance, a used-car salesman's type would include information on the quality of the car he is selling to the current buyer, which affects the buyer's utility. The buyer can only have an average idea of this utility by receiving her type information, since presumably her type is uncorrelated with the salesman's and so tells her nothing about the salesman's type (which will be the θ_{-i} if we denote the buyer by i).

An **incomplete information problem** is a collection $E = (\mathcal{I}, X, (u_i, \Theta_i, q_i)_{i \in \mathcal{I}})$. We can, if desired, specialize our discussion to a particular economic problem. All it would take would be to consider a collection of incomplete information problems that share the same set of alternatives X. For example, X might be the possible outcomes of an auction, or the feasible allocations in an exchange economy, or the feasible allocations in an economy with private and public goods.

Each agent knows his type when he comes to participate in the mechanism. This is the agents' only informational advantage over the central authority, which does not know the types of the agents but knows the structure of the incomplete information problem just as well as they do.

We consider only social choice functions, not correspondences, as the notation required for correspondences would overburden an already busy notational system, and the main points can be made in our setup. For the appropriate analog to a social choice correspondence, the social choice set, see Palfrey (2002) or Jackson (1991).

Any two social choice functions f and h are **equivalent** if for every $\theta \in \Theta^*$ we have $f(\theta) = h(\theta)$. We denote equivalence of social choice functions by $f \approx h$. The notion of equivalence focuses on the set of environments Θ^*. We have assumed that for each environment θ in Θ^* there is at least one agent who believes that θ has a positive probability of happening. So two social choice functions are declared equivalent when they differ in their selection of alternatives only on environments that arise with zero probability in the opinion of every agent.

An incomplete information problem is **economic** if a part of each social alternative is an allocation of a private good such that each agent has strictly increasing utility of her own component of the allocation of that good. This definition can be generalized enough to encompass exchange and production economies but also economies with externalities and with public goods.

A mechanism is defined as in section 2.1. Consider a mechanism $\Gamma = (M, g)$ on an incomplete information problem E. In an incomplete information problem, a mechanism induces a game of incomplete information. If $f : \Theta \to X$ is a social choice function, the

direct mechanism of f has $M_i = \Theta_i$ for all i and $g = f$.

Definition 7.2 (Bayesian Equilibrium). A **Bayesian equilibrium** of a mechanism (M, g) is a profile of strategies $m^* = (m_1^*, \ldots, m_I^*)$ with $m_i^* : \Theta_i \to M_i$ for each $i \in \mathcal{I}$, such that, for each $i \in \mathcal{I}$, each $\theta_i \in \Theta_i$, and each $m_i' : \Theta_i \to M_i$,

$$U_i(g(m^*)|\theta_i) \geq U_i(g(m_i', m_{-i}^*)|\theta_i).$$

Denote by $\mathcal{B}(\Gamma)$ the set of Bayesian equilibria of the mechanism Γ and by $g(\mathcal{B}(\Gamma))$ the set of Bayesian equilibrium outcomes.

A Bayesian equilibrium is a Nash equilibrium of an incomplete information game that we view as being played by the types of each agent, rather than the agents. Each type of an agent acts separately, which shows up in that m_i^* is a function of the type θ_i. But every type of the same agent evaluates the expected utility of an outcome by the same expected utility function u_i. We could say that each type of an agent acts separately but shares its "parent" agent's utility function.

You may want to return to sections 4.1. and 4.2. to refresh your memory about Bayesian equilibrium by reviewing our introductory treatment of it. You should also convince yourself that the definition of Bayesian equilibrium of a mechanism that we gave in section 4.2 is the same as the one we just gave in this chapter. The only difference between the two is the more compact notation we have adopted in this chapter, in order to economize on notational complexity.

Definition 7.3. A social choice function $f : \Theta \to X$ is **Bayesian implementable** if there exists a mechanism $\Gamma = (M, g)$ such that $g(\mathcal{B}(\Gamma)) \approx f$.

This definition requires that the set of outcomes of the mechanism that arise from Bayesian equilibria of the mechanism must coincide with the set of outcomes of the social choice function. For a social choice function, the latter set is a singleton, of course. But we left the definition and the previous sentence more generally phrased on purpose, as they are readily applicable once you take the step onto the study of the Bayesian implementation of social choice correspondences.

Definition 7.4. A social choice function f is **Bayesian incentive compatible** (or **truthfully implementable in Bayesian equilibrium**) if for every $i \in \mathcal{I}$ and for every $\theta_i \in \Theta_i$ and every $\theta_i' \in \Theta_i$,

$$\sum_{\theta_{-i} \in \Theta_{-i}} q_i(\theta_{-i}|\theta_i) u_i(f(\theta_i, \theta_{-i}), (\theta_i, \theta_{-i})) \geq \sum_{\theta_{-i} \in \Theta_{-i}} q_i(\theta_{-i}|\theta_i) u_i(f(\theta_i', \theta_{-i}), (\theta_i, \theta_{-i})).$$

The revelation principle holds for Bayesian implementation. It says that every Bayesian equilibrium of a game of incomplete information induced by a mechanism has outcomes that are equivalent to the truth-telling equilibrium of a properly defined direct mechanism. Serrano (2004) gives a simple variation that makes it clear why Bayesian incentive compatibility is inevitably connected with Bayesian implementability of a social choice function. We presented a more restricted version of the Bayesian revelation principle in section 4.3.; there we only considered the case where the beliefs of each agent i came as the conditional probabilities $q(\theta_{-i}|\theta_i)$ of a prior probability distribution q, common to all agents, and furthermore we only looked at quasilinear utility functions. Serrano's version follows.

Theorem 7.1. *If f is a Bayesian implementable social choice function, then there exists a social choice function $\widehat{f}$ with $\widehat{f} \approx f$, such that $\widehat{f}$ is Bayesian incentive compatible.*

Proof. Because f is Bayesian implementable, there exists a mechanism $\Gamma = (M, g)$ and a Bayesian Nash equilibrium $m : \Theta \to M$ of Γ such that $g(m) \approx f$. Therefore, for any $m_i' : \Theta_i \to M_i$ and every $\theta_i \in \Theta_i$,

$$U_i(g(m)|\theta_i) \geq U_i(g(m'(\theta_i), m_{-i}(\theta_{-i}))|\theta_i).$$

Write, for every $\theta \in \Theta$, $\widehat{f}(\theta)$ for $g(m(\theta))$. The above inequality then implies that for every $\theta_i, \theta_i' \in \Theta_i$,

$$U_i(\widehat{f}(\theta_i, \theta_{-i})|\theta_i) \geq U_i(\widehat{f}(\theta_i', \theta_{-i})|\theta_i),$$

since the statement "for any $m_i' : \Theta_i \to M_i$" above implies "for $m_i : \Theta_i \to M_i$" in particular. By the definition of Bayesian incentive compatibility, this means that $\widehat{f}$ is Bayesian incentive compatible. Since we already have $g(m) = \widehat{f} \approx f$, we are done.   QED

Note that if $\Theta^* = \Theta$, then $\widehat{f} = f$.

The Bayesian revelation principle ties together Bayesian implementation and Bayesian incentive compatibility. The latter condition was developed originally in the analysis of what can be achieved when we only require that there is one Bayesian equilibrium of the mechanism that yields the same outcome as that selected by the social choice function. We can rephrase the Bayesian revelation principle to make clear this connection. It states that, if the central authority is able to design a mechanism so that the outcome of every Bayesian equilibrium of the mechanism is equivalent to the outcome selected by the social choice function, then there is at least one Bayesian equilibrium of the mechanism that is equivalent to the outcome selected by the social choice function. Viewed this way, the theorem makes perfect sense. From yet another perspective, it says that if a social choice function is not incentive compatible, then there is an agent who prefers to lie when all other agents tell the truth. It is not possible for such a social choice function to be Bayesian implementable. So incentive compatibility is a necessary condition for Bayesian implementability.

There are other necessary conditions for Bayesian implementation in addition to incentive compatibility. The multiple equilibrium problem that affects direct revelation mechanisms guarantees this. We need some more notation to state the next necessary condition for Bayesian implementability.

Consider a direct mechanism, an agent i, and a strategy of i, say $\alpha_i : \Theta_i \to \Theta_i$. (Remember, in a direct mechanism, $M_i = \Theta_i$ for all i.) The agent tells the truth if α_i is the identity mapping, that is, the mapping $\iota : \Theta_i \to \Theta_i$ such that for all $\theta_i \in \Theta_i$, $\iota(\theta_i) = \theta_i$. A **deception** is a collection $\alpha = (\alpha_i)_{i \in \mathcal{I}}$ of such mappings such that at least one of them is not the identity mapping.

Now consider a social choice function f and a deception α. Imagine that the planner tries to implement f but the agents employ the deception α. In this case, the composition $f \circ \alpha$ is what would really get implemented, where the function $f \circ \alpha : \Theta \to X$ is defined by, for every $\theta \in \Theta$, $f \circ \alpha(\theta) \equiv f(\alpha(\theta))$. In words, α hijacks the influence of the type profile θ before it has a chance to determine which alternative f picks.

We also need notation for a deception by a single type of a single player. Let an agent $i \in \mathcal{I}$, a type for this agent $\theta_i \in \Theta_i$, a social choice function $f : \Theta \to X$, and a deception $\alpha : \Theta \to \Theta$ be given. For every $\theta' \in \Theta$, define $f_{\alpha_i(\theta_i)}(\theta') \equiv f(\alpha_i(\theta_i), \theta'_{-i})$. This shows a hijacking of the type profile by a misreport by agent i of type θ_i only.

Definition 7.5. A social choice function $f : \Theta \to X$ is **Bayesian monotonic** if for every deception $\alpha : \Theta \to \Theta$, whenever $f \circ \alpha \not\approx f$, there exist $i \in \mathcal{I}$, $\theta_i \in \Theta_i$, and a social choice function $y : \Theta \to A$ such that

$$U_i(y \circ \alpha | \theta_i) > U_i(f \circ \alpha | \theta_i) \text{ and } U_i(f | \theta'_i) \geq U_i(y_{\alpha_i(\theta_i)} | \theta'_i) \text{ for all } \theta'_i \in \Theta_i. \tag{7.2}$$

The idea behind Bayesian monotonicity is similar to the preference reversal interpretation of Maskin Monotonicity discussed in Jackson (2001) and in chapter 3. The last part of the Bayesian monotonicity condition can also be interpreted as ruling out the incentive for a single agent to falsely claim that the others are misreporting when in fact they are being truthful.

The following result, in the formulation from Serrano (2004), shows that Bayesian monotonicity is inescapable in the discussion of Bayesian implementation. Careful study of the simple proof will show you that Bayesian monotonicity is entailed in the very logic of Bayesian equilibrium, just as Maskin Monotonicity is entailed in the logic of Nash equilibrium as we saw in chapter 3. As you study the proof, note that it is done from the point of view of a type of an agent who might deviate, and remember that Bayesian equilibrium is essentially a Nash equilibrium where the types of every one of the agents are viewed as independent actors with the same utility function.

Theorem 7.2. *If $f : \Theta \to X$ is a Bayesian implementable social choice function, then there exists a social choice function $\widehat{f}$ with $\widehat{f} \approx f$ such that $\widehat{f}$ is Bayesian monotonic.*

Proof. Since it does not matter for the proof what happens at type profiles $\theta \notin \Theta^*$, we will consider only the case $\widehat{f} = f$. By the definition of Bayesian implementability, there exists a mechanism $\Gamma = (M, g)$ and a Bayesian equilibrium m of the mechanism Γ such that $g(m) = f$ (which means that for all $\theta \in \Theta$, $g(m(\theta)) = f(\theta)$).

Since m is a Bayesian equilibrium of the mechanism Γ, no unilateral deviation by a type of some agent from the strategy profile m can yield the deviating agent type a higher interim expected utility. To see this formally, write Φ_i for the set of all social choice functions y such that, for all $\theta_i \in \Theta_i$ and for all $\beta_i : \Theta_i \to \Theta_i$, $U_i(f|\theta_i) \geq U_i(y_{\beta_i(\theta_i)}|\theta_i)$. Then, for every $i \in \mathcal{I}$ and for every $\theta_i \in \Theta_i$, the set of outcomes achievable by sending any message m_i' when the others follow the m strategy profile, $\{g(m_i', m_{-i}(\theta_{-i}))\}_{m_i' \in M_i}$, must be a subset of the set Φ_i.

Consider a deception α such that $f \circ \alpha \neq f$. Because f is Bayesian implementable, the strategy profile $\sigma \circ \alpha$, in which every type θ_i of every agent i plays $m(\theta_i)$, cannot be a Bayesian equilibrium of the mechanism Γ. Therefore, there exists a type θ_i who can force an outcome $y \circ \alpha$ that θ_i prefers to $f \circ \alpha$, by a unilateral deviation from $m \circ \alpha$. But then y can be induced by a unilateral deviation from m, and so it must belong to Φ_i. This shows the preference reversal that appears in the definition of Bayesian monotonicity.   QED

The final result in this section is a sufficiency theorem that gives conditions that ensure that a social choice function is Bayesian implementable. This is due to Jackson (1991). We present a version of the theorem from Serrano (2004) for exchange economies.

Theorem 7.3. *Let the incomplete information problem be that of an exchange economy. Let f be a social choice function that does not assign the zero consumption bundle to any agent. If there exists $\widehat{f}$ with $\widehat{f} \approx f$ such that $\widehat{f}$ is Bayesian monotonic and Bayesian incentive compatible, then f is Bayesian implementable.*

As Serrano points out, the requirement that the social choice function does not give any agent the zero bundle is not needed, and indeed it is not used by Jackson (1991); a more complicated proof is required if this assumption is removed. However, it is a fairly reasonable requirement. Also, Jackson (1991) provides a characterization of social choice sets, not just functions, that are Bayesian implementable.

7.2.1 Restrictiveness of Bayesian Monotonicity

Bayesian monotonicity is a necessary condition for Bayesian implementation, as we just saw. This is bad news for Bayesian implementation. In the general case of the social choice incomplete information problem, there is very limited scope for Bayesian Nash implementation, because too many interesting social choice functions are not Bayesian monotonic. We illustrate this here by going in detail over an example given by Serrano

(2004, page 405). This also gives a better feeling for what the Bayesian monotonicity condition means; admittedly, it is not the most obvious of mathematical conditions.

For the example, consider a tremendously simplified exchange economy in which there is only one commodity, money. At first sight, this does not seem to make sense: why would anyone trade with anyone else if the only thing to trade is money? And why would we care to study an economy in which there is no potential for any trades to be made?

There is a good answer to these questions. The type profiles of the agents stand for states of nature, in the sense of the word in insurance economics. As Debreu (1959) pointed out in his foundational book of modern general equilibrium analysis, we can think of the same good, when available at different times and/or different states of the world, as different commodities. One does not buy an umbrella; one buys an umbrella at a given location in a given state of nature (often a state that specifies that it is raining at the time and place of the umbrella purchase). When couched in these terms, an exchange economy takes the flavor of a mutual insurance situation, in which case trading money across states of nature is perfectly reasonable.

So here is our little example economy. There are four agents and the single commodity money, which the agents can consume in non-negative amounts. Money can be disposed of at no cost. It does not matter for our purpose here whether the money is infinitely divisible or indivisible with some smallest unit, such as the penny. Agents 1 and 2 have similar sets of types: $\Theta_1 = \{\theta_1, \theta_1', \theta_1''\}$ and $\Theta_2 = \{\theta_2, \theta_2', \theta_2''\}$. Agents 3 and 4 also have similar sets of types: $\Theta_3 = \{\theta_3, \theta_3'\}$ and $\Theta_4 = \{\theta_4, \theta_4'\}$. If all type profiles that can be generated from these type sets occurred with positive probability, we would have to consider $3 \times 3 \times 2 \times 2 = 36$ type profiles. But we assume that only three of these type profiles arise with positive probability, so that $\Theta^* = \{\theta = (\theta_1, \theta_2, \theta_3, \theta_4), \theta' = (\theta_1', \theta_2', \theta_3', \theta_4'), \theta'' = (\theta_1'', \theta_2'', \theta_3', \theta_4')\}$.

Agents 1 and 2 have complete information, so their posterior beliefs are given by $q_1(\theta|\theta_1) = q_1(\theta'|\theta_1') = q_1(\theta''|\theta_1'') = 1$ and $q_2(\theta|\theta_2) = q_2(\theta'|\theta_2') = q_2(\theta''|\theta_2'') = 1$. Agents 3 and 4 are fully informed when they are of the unaccented type, in other words, $q_3(\theta|\theta_3) = 1$ and $q_4(\theta|\theta_4) = 1$. However, when they are of the accented type, agents 3 and 4 are not completely informed. In such cases, their posterior beliefs are given as follows:

$$q_3(\theta'|\theta_3') = 0.25, \qquad q_3(\theta''|\theta_3') = 0.75,$$
$$q_4(\theta'|\theta_4') = 0.75, \qquad q_4(\theta''|\theta_4') = 0.25.$$

Each agent i has a utility function of the form $u_i(x, \phi) = x_i^{\lambda_i(\phi)}$ for every $\phi \in \Theta$, where $\lambda_i(\phi) \in (0, 1)$, so that $u_i(x, \phi)$ is an increasing and strictly concave function of x_i.[2] This assumption means that each agent type is risk-averse at a distinct rate. Indeed, the degree of absolute risk aversion for such a utility function is $(1 - \lambda_i(\phi))/x_i$, for $x_i > 0$,

---

[2] We could have used θ here for a generic element of Θ, but we have already used θ to designate a specific element of Θ^* and so of Θ.

and the degree of relative risk aversion is $1 - \lambda_i(\phi)$. All agents have the same endowment of one unit of money in each type profile.

We have seen that Bayesian incentive compatibility and Bayesian monotonicity are necessary conditions for Bayesian implementability of a social choice function. In this example, Bayesian incentive compatibility has no teeth. One can always design the social choice function in such a way as to exploit the full information that the first two agents enjoy. All that is needed for this is to punish any unilateral deviation from truth-telling by giving every agent zero money (which is why we assumed that money is freely disposable, an assumption often made in exchange economy models). We have two fully informed agents, so a unilateral deviation from the truth is detectable; and since our main concern is with Bayesian equilibrium, unilateral deviations are all the deviations we need to consider. So Bayesian incentive compatibility does not really restrict the class of Bayesian implementable social choice functions in this example.

The story is very different with Bayesian monotonicity. In fact, it only allows social choice functions that are constant over the set of type profiles that happen with positive probability! To see this, suppose that f is a social choice function such that for some type profile $\phi \in \Theta^*$ with $\phi \neq \theta$, $f(\phi) \neq f(\theta)$. We claim that f is not Bayesian monotonic.

To understand why, let α be a deception such that all types of each agent i report θ_i. This means $\alpha_1(\theta_1) = \alpha_1(\theta_1') = \alpha_1(\theta_1'') = \theta_1$, and similarly for agents $2, 3$, and 4. We have $f \circ \alpha \neq f$, as f when combined with this deception α, $f \circ \alpha$, always results in the outcome $f \circ \alpha(s) = f(\theta)$, for every type profile $s \in \Theta$ and so is constant over Θ^*, but we have assumed that f is not constant over Θ^*. Bayesian monotonicity now implies the preference reversal of (7.2), for some type s_i and some social choice function y. Because $f \circ \alpha(s) = f(\theta)$ for every type profile $s \in \Theta$, then for every agent i and type profile $s \in \Theta$, we have

$$U_i(f \circ \alpha | s_i) = \sum_{s_{-i}' \in \Theta_{-i}} q_i(s_{-i}' | s_i) u_i(f(\theta), (s_i, s_{-i}')).$$

Meanwhile,

$$U_i(f | \alpha_i(s_i)) = U_i(f | \theta_i) = \sum_{s_{-i}' \in \Theta_{-i}} q_i(s_{-i}' | \theta_i) u_i(f(\theta), (\theta_i, s_{-i}')).$$

Because of the one-dimensionality of the commodity space and because the utility functions are increasing, every utility function $u_i(x, s)$ ranks any two amounts of money the same no matter what s is. Given this and the above formulas for $U_i(f \circ \alpha | s_i)$ and $U_i(f | \alpha_i(s_i))$, for all i and all $s \in \Theta$ we have that $U_i(f | \alpha_i(s_i)) \geq U_i(y | \alpha_i(s_i))$ whenever $U_i(f \circ \alpha | s_i) \geq U_i(y \circ \alpha | s_i)$. But this means that a preference reversal of the kind required by (7.2) cannot be found.

We have now proved by contradiction the following.

Theorem 7.4. *There exists an incomplete information problem in which a social choice function f can only be Bayesian monotonic if it is constant on Θ^*.*

If we want agents to be as well off as they could be without engaging in the mechanism's game, which is the requirement of voluntary participation, we must ensure in this example that they each receive an expected utility of at least 1, which is the interim expected utility of their endowments. If we want our social choice function to select only efficient outcomes, then it should allow types θ_3' and θ_4' to exchange money across type profiles θ' and θ''. It follows that a social choice function that achieves voluntary participation and efficiency cannot be Bayesian monotonic, and hence cannot be Bayesian implementable.[3] In other words, any mechanism we come up with that has a Bayesian Nash equilibrium that achieves the desired non-constant social choice function will also have a Bayesian Nash equilibrium in which every type of every agent reports its part of the type profile θ, not matter whether this it true or not. The problem of multiple equilibria is indeed very difficult to solve.

7.3 Virtual Bayesian Implementation

As in chapter 5, we conclude with a look at an approximate version of implementation, in this case virtual Bayesian implementation. The main idea is the same as with virtual Nash implementation: instead of implementing a social choice correspondence F in Bayesian equilibrium, we seek to implement a different social choice correspondence that closely approximates F. The seminal references for this material are Abreu and Matsushima (1992b), Duggan (1997), Serrano and Vohra (2001) and Serrano and Vohra (2005). Our presentation is mostly based on Serrano (2004).

Recall the setup from section 5.4. $\Delta(X)$ is the set of lotteries over the finite set of alternatives X. A social choice function $F : \Theta \to \Delta(X)$ associates with each type profile $\theta \in \Theta$ a lottery over the alternatives. A mechanism $\Gamma = (M, g)$ has the usual message space M_i for each agent i and an outcome function $g : M \to \Delta(X)$ that associates with each message profile a lottery over the alternatives.

Let f, h be two social choice functions. We define their distance as follows:

$$d(f, h) = \sup\{|f(x|\theta) - h(x|\theta)| \,|\, \theta \in \Theta^*, x \in X\}.$$

This distance function takes two social choice functions f and h as its arguments and looks for the alternative x and the type profile θ that jointly make the difference between

---

[3]This is true whether we are talking about ex ante, interim, or ex post efficiency, as Palfrey and Srivastava (1987) demonstrate via examples, one of which is very similar to the example we are studying here.

the probabilities $f(x|\theta)$ and $h(x|\theta)$ as large as possible. Having found this difference, it proclaims it the distance between f and h.

Note that we do not require any condition similar to the one involving a one-to-one function in section 5.4. This is because in the present chapter we are only looking at social choice functions, and therefore their values are always single points, making the requirement of the existence of the one-to-one function trivially satisfied.

Definition 7.6 (Virtual Bayesian Implementation). A social choice function f is **virtually Bayesian implementable** if for every $\epsilon > 0$ there exists a social choice function f_e such that $d(f, f_e) < \epsilon$ and f_e is Bayesian implementable.

A version of the revelation principle holds for this implementation concept, so incentive compatibility is a necessary condition for virtual Bayesian implementation.

There is a condition that Serrano and Vohra (2005) dubbed virtual monotonicity, which is weaker than Bayesian monotonicity and characterizes virtual Bayesian implementation, along with incentive compatibility. However, it is more interesting, and more indicative of the permissive nature of virtual implementation, to see at what can be virtually Bayesian implemented with a mild condition on incomplete information problems, so we turn to this result next.

Definition 7.7 (Type Diversity). An incomplete information problem satisfies *type diversity* if there do not exist $i \in \mathcal{I}$, $\theta_i, \theta_i' \in \Theta_i$ with $\theta_i \neq \theta_i'$, $\beta \in \mathbb{R}_{++}$, and $\gamma \in \mathbb{R}$ such that

$$\text{for each } x \in X, \ U_i(x|\theta_i) = \beta U_i(x|\theta_i') + \gamma.$$

Type diversity means that the expected utility functions of two distinct types of an agent never rank every two alternatives the same way. The result of Serrano and Vohra (2005) about environments that satisfy type diversity follows, as stated in Serrano (2004).

Theorem 7.5 (Serrano and Vohra, 2005). *In economic environments that satisfy type diversity, a social choice function f is virtually Bayesian implementable if and only if there exists an equivalent social choice function $\hat{f}$ which is incentive compatible.*

This says that in an economic environment in which types are diverse, incentive compatibility is all one needs to virtually Bayesian implement a social choice function. The virtual Bayesian implementation approach works for more social choice functions than the Bayesian implementation approach, reminding us of the same comparison between virtual Nash implementation and Nash implementation. In view of the disappointing result in subsection 7.2.1, this is good news for a designer who would like to be able to implement, in an economic problem, some social choice function that is minimally interesting. We learned from theorem 7.4 that for some environments a social choice function is Bayesian monotonic only if it is constant on the set of environments Θ^*. Since Bayesian monotonicity is a necessary condition for Bayesian implementation, this essentially means that only constant social choice functions are Bayesian implementable. A constant social choice function selects the same outcome for every environment. It is hardly what we can call an interesting social choice function, as it totally ignores the types of the agents in making its selection. It is in this light that theorem 7.5 is so encouraging. It says that if the assumption of type diversity is appropriate for the problem at hand, the mechanism designer can implement any Bayesian incentive compatible social choice function in the approximate sense of virtual Bayesian implementation.

Our enthusiasm over theorem 7.5 must be tempered by the limitations of the virtual approach to implementation. These are the same for virtual Bayesian implementation as for virtual Nash implementation, and we refer you to page 131 for a discussion.

Chapter 8

Further Topics in Mechanism Design

This chapter presents some recent results in the mechanism design literature. Section 8.1. examines a unique class of mechanisms known as endogenous mechanisms. In an endogenous mechanism, agents are allowed to make side contracts with each other. The section explores the importance of allowing the agents to make side contracts with each other and its consequences for the efficiency of the mechanism. We discuss the scope of improving mechanism design by linking multiple mechanisms together in section 8.2. Section 8.3. examines mechanisms that are less sensitive to the assumed structure of the given environment, an approach known as robust implementation. In many instances, *ex post* implementation may be desirable due to its robustness properties. Nonetheless, section 8.4. shows that there exist significant limitations to *ex post* implementation. We conclude the chapter with exercises.

8.1 Endogenous Mechanisms

Thus far in the book we have explored mechanisms that do not allow the agents to make side contracts with each other. Jackson and Wilkie (2005), on which this section is based, allows for side contracting in their mechanisms to study whether side contracting lets the designer overcome externalities and minimize inefficiencies. In this section, we present the main results of their work, which the interested reader should consult for the proofs of the theorems we will discuss.

In the early contracting and bargaining literature a result known as the Coase Theorem[1] suggested that externalities could be overcome and efficiency achieved in many cases if agents are allowed to side contract with each other. This result requires an environment with no transactions costs, complete information, and enforceable binding contracts. But, as we show below, an economy may still fail to reach efficiency in such an environment.

To examine the properties of the Coasian contracting result, Jackson and Wilkie (2005) design *endogenous games and mechanisms*. Endogenous games contain smaller games

---

[1]Coase never formally proved such a theorem. You can judge how much support the results in this section give to the Coase "Theorem."

Amy\Bill	M	C
M	$2,2$	$-1,4$
C	$4,-1$	$0,0$

Table 8.1: Example 8.1

Amy\Bill	M	C
M	$2,2$	$-1+2,4-2$
C	$4-2,-1+2$	$0,0$

which equals

Amy\Bill	M	C
M	$2,2$	$1,2$
C	$2,1$	$0,0$

Table 8.2: Example 8.1 continued

in which agents may enter side contracts before playing the main game. If the agents decide to side contract with each other in the early stages, then their payoff functions are rewritten to reflect this side contracting. In the final stage, the agents play the new, altered game. The following example illustrates the idea of an endogenous game.

Example 8.1. (Jackson and Wilkie, 2005) Consider the prisoner's dilemma game of table 8.1. The game represents the payoffs Amy (the row player) and Bill (the column player) would receive if they were not allowed to side contract with each other. Playing C is the strictly dominant strategy for each player. Therefore, (C, C) is the unique Nash equilibrium of this game. As with any prisoner's dilemma game, there is a more efficient outcome, (M, M). The prisoner's dilemma can be thought of as the ultimate example of a negative externality: an agent's utility-maximizing choice reduces the utility of another.

Let us now allow the players to engage in side contracting before they play the game in order to examine whether and under what circumstances (M, M) could become an equilibrium outcome. After all, as Coase argued, side contracting might allow the designer to create incentives such that the players' actions will result in the most efficient outcome.

Start with the outcome (M, M). Bill could gain 2 by deviating and playing C instead of M, in which case the outcome would be (M, C). This would hurt Amy, since she would be worse off due to a loss of 3. Therefore, Amy is able to create the right incentive for Bill to play M by offering to give Bill a transfer of 2 contingent upon Bill playing M. Considering this transfer, Bill's weakly dominant strategy would be to play M instead of C. The same argument works if we start with Amy deviating. As a result, the original game is altered so that each player's weakly dominant strategy is M. Therefore, the equilibrium of the altered game is (M, M). Table 8.2 shows the new altered game after the agents are allowed to engage in side contracting. You can easily verify that the new equilibrium is (M, M) as we have argued.

This wonderful result holds up only when both Amy and Bill agree to make the exact reciprocal efficient transfers. But are these particular reciprocal transfers always part of

Amy\Bill	M	C
M	$2-(1+\epsilon)+(1-\epsilon), 2+(1+\epsilon)-(1-\epsilon)$	$-1+(1-\epsilon), 4-(1-\epsilon)$
C	$4-(1+\epsilon), -1+(1+\epsilon)$	$0,0$

or

Amy\Bill	M	C
M	$2-2\epsilon, 2+2\epsilon$	$-\epsilon, 3+\epsilon$
C	$3-\epsilon, \epsilon$	$0,0$

Table 8.3: Example 8.1 continued further

equilibrium play? The answer is unfortunately not affirmative. Imagine that, conditional on Bill playing M, Amy offers to make a transfer to Bill in the amount of $(1+\epsilon)$, where $\epsilon > 0$. Also, imagine that Bill does not reciprocate Amy's offer and instead offers Amy a transfer of $(1-\epsilon)$ conditional on Amy playing M. The new game is shown in table 8.3.

This new game has one unique Nash equilibrium, (C, M), which is inefficient. When the agents are allowed to make these specific side contracting offers, Bill will choose to play M, but it will be in Amy's best interest to play C. Therefore, the players do not find it in their best interest to make efficient transfer offers that would lead to the efficient equilibrium. As a matter of fact, as Jackson and Wilkie (2005) prove, there is no equilibrium with non-reciprocal transfers that results in the efficient play.   ◇

Notice that in the examples we have used there are only two players. As it turns out different, mostly positive, results are obtained in endogenous games with three or more players. In the rest of this section we present the main results that Jackson and Wilkie (2005) obtain for endogenous games with only two players. Then we compare these results with the results obtained for endogenous games with three or more players.

8.1.1 Notation and Definitions

Let $M = M_1 \times \cdots \times M_I$ be a finite pure strategy space in the endogenous game, which consists of two stages and $I \geq 2$ players. In the first stage of the game the players make simultaneous announcements regarding a profile of transfer functions. In other words, player i announces $t_i = (t_{i1}, ..., t_{iI})$ with $t_{ij} : M \to \mathbb{R}_+$. These announcements determine the promised payments that players make to each other as a function of all the players' actions chosen in the second stage of the game. Therefore, if the strategy profile m is played in the second stage of the game, player i's promised transfer to player j is $t_{ij}(m)$. We let t_i^0 denote the degenerate transfer function such that $t_{ij}^0(m) = 0$ for all $m \in M$, and let $t^0 = (t_1^0, ..., t_I^0)$.

In the second stage of the game the players choose their actions. The payoff that agent i receives is

- his second-stage payoff, plus

- all the transfers that were promised to player i contingent upon the actions played in the game, minus

- the transfers that player i promised to pay to other players contingent upon the actions played in the game.

Given a profile of transfer functions t and a strategy profile m played in the second stage of the game, the payoff to player i is defined as follows: $U_i(m,t) = v_i(m) + \sum_{j \neq i}(t_{ji}(m) - t_{ij}(m))$, where $v_i : M \to \mathbb{R}$ is player i's expected utility function that determines the payoffs in the second stage of the game. In other words, $v_i(m)$ are the payoffs that player i would get if there were no side contracting among the players. Let $NE(t)$ be the set of Nash equilibria of the second stage game with payoffs $U(m,t)$.

We also make the following assumptions:

- The transfer function that each player announces is binding.

- Players can refuse to accept a transfer from another player by announcing a transfer that returns the other player's transfer. (This is implicit in the definition of t_{ij}.)

Note that the second assumption implicitly views the players as being able to correctly guess what the others are planning to do, since all the transfer announcements are made simultaneously. This is an integral part of using Nash equilibrium as our solution concept, as this kind of mutual guessing is conceptually at the heart of Nash equilibrium.

Definition 8.1. A pure strategy profile $m \in M$ of the second stage of the game together with a vector of payoffs $\overline{u} \in \mathbb{R}^I$ such that $\sum_i \overline{u}_i = \sum_i v_i(m)$ is **supportable** if there exists a subgame perfect equilibrium (SPE) of the two-stage game, with t played in the first stage and m played on the equilibrium path in the second stage of the game, and $U_i(m,t) = \overline{u}_i$.

Supportability means that the pair of strategy profile m and utility level profile u emerge out of a subgame perfect equilibrium of the two-stage game (the endogenous game) that also involves some transfer vector t.

Definition 8.2. Consider a pure strategy profile $m \in M$ of the second stage of the game that is an equilibrium of the second stage when no transfers are possible such that $m \in NE(t^0)$. Such an equilibrium **survives** if there exists a SPE of the two-stage game, with t played in the first stage and m played on the equilibrium path in the second stage of the game, such that the net payoffs amount to $U_i(m,t) = v_i(m)$.

Amy\Bill	M	C
M	$2,2$	$-1,4$
C	$4,-1$	$0,0$

Table 8.4: Solo payoffs in example 8.1

Amy\Bill	M	C
M	$1-\epsilon, 3+\epsilon$	$-1,4$
C	$3-\epsilon, \epsilon$	$0,0$

Table 8.5: Solo payoffs 8.1

While supportability refers to a pair of a strategy profile m and utility vector $\overline{u}$, survivability is a property of a strategy profile m alone. Further, an m that is part of a supportable pair need not be an equilibrium of the underlying game. However, an m is said to survive if it is an equilibrium of the underlying game and also is part of a SPE of the two-stage full game with transfers.

Definition 8.3. Let $u_i^s = \sup_{t_i}[\min_{m \in NE(t_{-i}^0, t_i)} U_i(m, t_{-i}^0, t_i)]$ be player i's **solo payoff**. A solo payoff for player i is the payoff that i gets when he is allowed to announce any transfer function he wishes and other players cannot make any transfers.

The following illustration will help you understand the definition of solo payoffs. Refer to example 8.1, reproduced again in table 8.4. Assume that Amy is the only player that can make transfer offers. Specifically, Amy offers Bill a transfer of $(1 + \epsilon)$ conditional on Bill playing M. The new game is shown in table 8.5. This game has a unique Nash equilibrium (C, M). The solo payoff that Amy receives is 3, since we take the supremum of $(3 - \epsilon)$ over all $\epsilon > 0$.

The solo payoffs are important because they help us characterize the set of Nash equilibria of the non-endogenous underlying game that would survive and still be the subgame perfect equilibria of the endogenous game. The following theorem specifies which Nash equilibria of the original game will survive after the transfers are introduced and after the game is altered to an endogenous game when there are only two players.

Theorem 8.1 (Jackson and Wilkie, 2005). *If there are only two players, then a Nash equilibrium m of the underlying game survives if and only if $v_i(m) \geq u_i^s$ for both i. Moreover, if m survives then there is an equilibrium in the overall process where no transfers are made in the first stage of the game and m is played in the second stage of the game.*

Theorem 8.1 tells us that all the equilibria of the underlying game will survive to be equilibria in the endogenous game if and only if the payoff that each agent gets in the

Amy\Bill	M	C
M	2, 2	0, 0
C	0, 0	1, 1

Table 8.6: Efficient equilibrium survives

Amy\Bill	M	C
M	2, 2	0, 0
C	−2, 2	1, 1

Table 8.7: Efficient equilibrium survives

underlying game is at least as large as the payoff that each agent would get in an altered game that allows solo transfers. The following example from Jackson and Wilkie (2005) illustrates this.

Consider a simple game with two players, shown in table 8.6. This game has two Nash equilibria: (M, M) and (C, C). First, let's explore each player's solo payoffs if they were allowed to side contract with each other. Amy would want to give the right incentive to Bill to play M. If Amy offers Bill a transfer of 2 contingent upon (C, M), the resulting game would look like the game presented in table 8.7.[2] Hence Amy's solo payoff is 2. By the symmetry of the game, the same holds for Bill.

According to theorem 8.1. this game shall have only one equilibrium, namely (M, M). Since the solo payoff for each player in the endogenous game is $u_i^s = 2$, and each player receives a payoff that is at least as large as 2 when both play (M, M), then the only surviving equilibrium is (M, M). Notice that in this example only the efficient equilibrium survives. However, as we have previously said, this is rarely the case. We cannot rely on solo transfers to achieve efficiency, as the example of table 8.8 illustrates.

Amy\Bill	R	S	T
R	2, 2	0, 0	0, 0
S	0, 0	3, 0	0, 0
T	0, 0	0, 0	0, 3

Table 8.8: Efficient equilibrium does not survive

You can easily verify that the game in table 8.8 has three Nash equilibria: (R, R), (S, S), and (T, T). Now, consider what happens to this game when we allow a player to

---

[2]The analysis works the same way if Bill is the one making solo transfers.

Amy\Bill	R	S	T
R	$-\epsilon, 4+\epsilon$	$-2-\epsilon, 2+\epsilon$	$-2-\epsilon, 2+\epsilon$
S	$0, 0$	$3-\epsilon, \epsilon$	$0, 0$
T	$-\epsilon, \epsilon$	$-\epsilon, \epsilon$	$-\epsilon, \epsilon$

Table 8.9: Efficient equilibrium does not survive

make solo transfer offers. More specifically, we allow Amy to make the following offers. Conditional on Amy playing R she will make a transfer to Bill in the amount of $(2+\epsilon)$, and conditional on Amy playing T she will make a transfer to Bill in the amount of ϵ. Lastly, conditional on the play being (S, S) Amy promises a transfer of ϵ to Bill. Taking these solo transfers into consideration, what will the new game look like? Let's see table 8.9; as it makes clear, these solo transfers are a way for Amy to commit to play S.[3]

Indeed, by allowing Amy to make these specific solo transfers we are able to construct a dominant strategy for Amy; namely, strategy S. If Amy's dominant strategy is S, Bill will then find it in his best interest to play S as well. Since the original game is symmetric from Bill's point of view, we can allow Bill to make similar solo transfers such that (T, T) is the only equilibrium to survive. Therefore, the solo payoff for each player in the game is 3. We conclude that neither the efficient equilibrium nor the equilibrium in pure strategies survives when we allow Amy and Bill to make solo transfers. Different results may be obtained if we allow agents to play mixed strategies. Refer to Jackson and Wilkie (2005) for a discussion of mixed strategies.

These results tell us that side payments may not create incentives for agents to play efficient strategies. Further, the efficient equilibria that occur in the game without side contracting may not survive when side contracting is introduced. All this suggests that there might not exist strong incentives to alter the underlying game in pursuit of efficiency.

The following theorem provides a necessary condition for supportability and survivorship. It shows that in order to support a pair $(m, \overline{u})$, with two players, then the payoff levels in u must be at least as high as the solo payoffs of the players.

Theorem 8.2 (Jackson and Wilkie, 2005). *If there are only two players, then $(m, \overline{u})$ is supportable only if $\overline{u} \geq u_i^s$ for both i.*

We now turn to an illustration of how this theorem may be used in an example of voluntary contributions to a public good from Jackson and Wilkie (2005).

---

[3]A different table would be needed to study the case where Bill makes solo offers.

8.1.2 An Application: Public Goods

Suppose Amy and Bill engage in a game of voluntary contributions toward a public good. An example of a public good could be a park bench, located near Amy and Bill's houses, which they could occasionally use when they take walks around the park. Amy and Bill each must decide how much they are willing to contribute to have the park bench installed. Let their contributions be represented by $m_i \in \mathbb{R}_+$ for $i = A, B$. Let each player's utility be represented by $v_i(m_A, m_B) = 2\theta_i\sqrt{m_A + m_B} - m_i$ for $i = A, B$. Assume that if the bench is provided, it will be located closer to Amy's house than Bill's house. In other words, if Amy is player A and Bill is player B, the bench has more value to Amy than to Bill or $\theta_A > \theta_B > 0$. We normalize $\sum \theta_i = 1$ to ensure the existence of a unique Nash equilibrium.

The unique Nash equilibrium of this game can easily be calculated. It occurs at $m_A^N = \theta_A^2$ and $m_B^N = 0$, where N stands for "Nash equilibrium." We obtain this result by setting up a maximization problem for each player where each player is choosing to contribute an amount that will maximize his or her own utility given the contribution amount submitted by the other player. Let us start with Amy's utility function. Her objective is to maximize $v_A(m_A, m_B) = 2\theta_A\sqrt{m_A + m_B} - m_A$ by taking the amount of Bill's contribution as given and choosing her own contribution. This calculation leads to the result $m_A^N = \theta_A^2 - m_B$. Given the above assumptions, Bill's best response to Amy's contribution is $m_B^N = 0$. Therefore, $m_A^N = \theta_A^2$.[4] What can we say about the efficiency of the outcome in this game? Efficiency requires that the sum of Amy and Bill's contributions be $m_A + m_B = 1$. We obtain this result by looking for the combination of Amy and Bill's contributions $m_A + m_B$ that will maximize $v_A(m_A, m_B) + v_B(m_A, m_B)$. This maximization problem yields the following result: $(\theta_A + \theta_B)(\frac{1}{\sqrt{m_A + m_B}}) = 1$. Since we assumed that $\sum \theta_i = 1$ then it must be that $\sum m_i = 1$. Given this result then it must be that the total net utility $v_A(m_A, m_B) + v_B(m_A, m_B)$ at the efficient allocation must be 1.[5]

According to theorem 8.2., if a pair $(m, \overline{u})$ is to be supportable at some efficient m then the condition $\overline{u} \geq u_i^s$, or $\sum \overline{u}_i \geq \sum u_i^s$, has to be satisfied for each i. Since in this example we have $\sum \overline{u}_i = 1$, then in order for the condition in theorem 8.2. to be satisfied, we have to prove that $\sum u_i^s \leq 1$. We now show that this condition will not be satisfied, and therefore, efficiency will not be achievable in an endogenous game with transfers. This requires that we first calculate each player i's solo payoff u_i^s.

Consider Amy's transfer function $t_A(m) = \theta_A m_B$. In other words, Amy offers to transfer the amount $t_A(m)$ to Bill for any vector of contributions m. What would be the optimal contribution of each player given this offer by Amy? To answer this question, first rewrite each player's payoff function by including the transfer offer. Amy's new altered payoff

---

[4]Notice that this is a typical result in the public goods provision literature; since Amy places more value on the good than Bill, Bill will free-ride on Amy's contribution.

[5]Since $v_A(m_A, m_B) + v_B(m_A, m_B) = 2\theta_A - m_A + 2\theta_B - m_B = 2(\theta_A + \theta_B) - (m_A + m_B) = 2 - 1 = 1$.

function becomes $v_A(m) = 2\theta_A\sqrt{m_A + m_B} - m_A - \theta_A m_B$. Bill's new altered payoff function becomes $v_B(m) = 2\theta_B\sqrt{m_A + m_B} - m_B + \theta_A m_B$. The solution to this problem is a corner solution with $m_A = 0$ and $m_B = 1$; Amy contributes 0 and Bill contributes 1.[6] Therefore, Amy's transfer offer provides the right incentive for Bill to make a positive contribution. Even more, the incentive is large enough so that Bill ends up being the sole contributor. It follows that Amy's solo payoff is $u_A^s = v_A(0,1) = 2\theta_A\sqrt{0+1} - 0 - \theta_A = \theta_A$.

Now consider Bill's transfer function $t_B(m_A = 1, m_B) = \theta_A^2 - (2\theta_A - 1)$. In other words, Bill offers to make transfer $t_B(m)$ to Amy contingent upon Amy playing $m_A = 1$. Otherwise, Bill will not make any transfer to Amy. Given this offer by Bill, what is the equilibrium of the altered second stage game? Intuition tells us that Amy will choose to contribute $m_A = 1$, which is the same amount that she contributes when there are no solo transfers, for the following reason. Notice that Amy is already choosing to contribute $m_A = 1$ before the transfers are introduced. Amy will then continue to play the same strategy $m_A = 1$, when Bill's offer results in either the same or possibly a larger payoff for Amy. If Amy continued to play the same strategy $m_A = 1$, then given the specified transfer function $t_B(m_A = 1, m_B) = \theta_A^2 - (2\theta_A - 1)$, Amy will be at least as well off as she would be if there were no transfers. Therefore, the optimal play for her, when transfers are introduced, is to continue playing the same strategy $m_A = 1$, which is her optimal play in the original game without transfers.

We confirm this by showing that the following inequality is satisfied, $2\theta_A\sqrt{m_A + m_B} - m_A + \theta_A^2 - (2\theta_A - 1) \geq 2\theta_A\sqrt{m_A + m_B} - m_A$. The left-hand side is the payoff Amy would get when Bill offers a transfer, and the right-hand side is the payoff Amy would get in the underlying game without transfers. Rearranging this inequality and canceling some terms we get, $\theta_A^2 - (2\theta_A - 1) \geq 0$. Notice that the left-hand side of this inequality is a quadratic with a positive double root, namely, $\theta_A = 1$. Therefore, the inequality is satisfied. Even more, since we have assumed that θ's must be strictly greater than 0, this inequality has to hold strictly. You can now verify that Bill's optimal play is $m_B = 0$. Then, given Amy and Bill's optimal strategies, we calculate Bill's solo payoff, $u_B^s = v_B(1,0) = 2\theta_B\sqrt{1+0} - 1 - \left[\theta_A^2 - 2\theta_A + 1\right]$. This reduces to $u_B^s = 1 - \theta_A^2$.[7]

Recall that, in order to achieve efficiency in this endogenous game with transfers, we had to prove that $\sum u_i^s \leq 1$. In other words, the sum of Amy and Bill's solo payoffs should be no larger than 1 if we wish to achieve efficiency. In this example, we have $\sum u_i^s \geq \theta_A + 1 - \theta_A^2$, where the right-hand side of the inequality is always strictly greater than 1. Therefore, the requirement that $\sum u_i^s$ be less or equal to 1, (or $\sum \overline{u}_i \geq \sum u_i^s$,) is violated. We conclude that efficiency is not achievable in this endogenous game with transfers.

---

[6]The detailed calculation is left as an exercise at the end of the chapter.

[7]$u_B^s = 2\theta_B - (\theta_A^2 - 2\theta_A + 1) = 2(1 - \theta_A) - \theta_A^2 + 2\theta_A - 1 = 1 - \theta_A^2$.

	C	D
A	$0,0,3,0$	$0,0,0,2$
B	$0,0,0,2$	$0,0,2,0$

Table 8.10: The underlying game with four players

8.1.3 Positive Results for Endogenous Games with 3 or More Players

Contrary to the results obtained for the games played between only two agents, when additional players are introduced we are able to achieve positive results. The first of these results is stated in the following theorem.

Theorem 8.3 (Jackson and Wilkie, 2005). *When $I \geq 3$, then every pure strategy Nash equilibrium of the underlying game survives.*

Notice that this theorem is very different from theorem 8.1. It is a much more positive result, which ensures that an efficient outcome achieved in the underlying game will still be achievable in the game when side contracting is introduced. However, it also suggests that simply introducing side contracting might not allow us to eliminate undesirable equilibria that occur in the underlying game.

The next theorem provides an even stronger result than theorem 8.3. It suggests that not only Nash equilibrium outcomes in the underlying game are supportable in the endogenous game with side payments, but also any outcomes that give each agent a payoff larger than or equal to some Nash equilibrium payoff are supportable.

Theorem 8.4 (Jackson and Wilkie, 2005). *When $I \geq 3$ and m is a strategy profile, and there exists a Nash equilibrium $\hat{m}$ such that $v_i(m) \geq v_i(\hat{m})$ for all i, then $(m, v(m))$ is supportable.*

The following example (table 8.10) illustrates these two theorems. Consider a game with four players. The row player, player 1, can play either A or B, and the column player, player 2, can play either C or D. These two players are the only strategic players in the game. The other two players do not take action, but they derive some utility from the strategies chosen by the row and the column players. One may think of this as a principal-agent game in which the row and column players are agents acting on behalf of principals. Notice that in this game there are four Nash equilibria among which the strategic players are indifferent. However, the non-strategic players have conflicting preferences. Player 3 would prefer outcome (A, C) to any other outcome, while player 4 would prefer either (B, C) or (A, D) (he is indifferent between the two).

Assume that our objective is to design contracts that would support the efficient outcome. The efficient outcome in this game is (A, C) with payoffs $(0, 0, 3, 0)$. According to theorem 8.4., we should easily be able to find transfer functions that will allow us to

	C	D
A	$0,0,3,0$	$T,-3T,T,2+T$
B	$-3T,T,T,2+T$	$-2T,-2T,2+2T,2T$

Table 8.11: The endogenous game with four players

achieve this objective. If there is a Nash equilibrium and a second outcome that provides at least as much net utility as the Nash equilibrium, the second outcome will be supportable in an endogenous game with transfers. In addition, theorem 8.3. suggests that since the outcome (A, C) is a Nash equilibrium of the underlying game it should still be an equilibrium in an endogenous game with transfers.

Since there are only two strategic players in this game, we will look for two transfer functions for them that will give us the desired result. Let the column player commit not to play D by offering a transfer in the amount of $T > 3$ to each player in the game in case he does choose to play D. Also, let the row player commit not to play B by offering a transfer in the amount of $T > 3$ to each player in the game in case he chooses to play B. The new altered game is then as shown in Table 8.11.

This new game has only one Nash equilibrium. You can easily verify that this equilibrium is (A, C) with the payoffs $(0, 0, 3, 0)$. Therefore, we have achieved our objective of finding appropriate transfers that allowed us to make the desired outcome of the underlying game supportable.

Why are we able to achieve this positive result in the case of three or more players and not in the case of only two players? When the row player offers to make a transfer to all three players in case he plays B, he commits to a loss of $-3T$ if he chooses to play B. The column player cannot refuse the row player's promised transfer unless he is willing to return the amount higher than the amount received from the row player, that is, $3T$ instead of T. Doing that would make the column player worse off, so he would choose not to return the row player's transfer. The same goes if the row player were to refuse the column player's transfer. In a sense, the role of the principals in this game is to hold a bond against the agents, which commits the agents to play (or not play) certain strategies. The agents are not able to manipulate the game in their favor as easily as when there are only two players since the principals play the role of bond-holders in the game. There are a number of transfer functions that would have led to the same result.

We conclude this section by pointing out that the possibility of side contracting between agents may significantly alter the results of a mechanism that a designer wishes to implement. The theory on side contracting developed in this section (specifically, the theory regarding survivable equilibria) tells us that if there is a designer who wishes to implement a certain outcome (most likely an efficient outcome) via a mechanism where no side contracting between agents is allowed, then the designer has to be able to prevent the agents from side contracting. The agents might have incentives to manipulate the outcome of the mechanism through side contracts in order to achieve outcomes that are more favorable to them. If the designer is unable to prevent such side contracts, then the mechanism might fail to implement the desired outcome.

8.2 Overcoming Incentive Constraints by Linking Decisions

Thus far we have looked at individual social choice problems, and examined what implications incentive compatibility and individual rationality constraints have for the efficiency of the outcome of the given decision problem. We have seen through several examples how it could be impossible to implement a given social choice function due to the problem of incentive constraints. Namely, in many instances agents might have an incentive to lie or deviate from truthful reporting of their preferences, and as a result, something other than the desired social choice outcome could be an equilibrium of the given game form. In those cases, we said that the desired social choice function was not implementable. Let us illustrate this idea one more time using a voting problem.[8]

The decision problem d is binary such that $d = \{x, y\}$, and there are two agents, $i \in \{1, 2\}$, deciding between the two alternatives. Individual valuations for the given decision are described by a valuation function $v_i(d)$. The total utility of the decision problem to each agent depends on the valuation difference between alternatives x and y, such that $u_i = v_i(x) - v_i(y)$.

Clearly, when u_1 and u_2 have the same sign, it is easy to decide on the alternative, for any reasonable social choice function. Also, if $u_i = 0$ for each agent, then each agent is indifferent between alternatives and it is reasonable for the social choice to be random among the alternatives. However, there is one more possibility, and to us the most interesting case, where $u_i < 0$ and $u_j > 0$ for $i \neq j$. In such a case, it is ambiguous which alternative should be chosen and implemented by the society. We consider a possible resolution of this problem by the following social choice function.

Consider a case where u_i is i.i.d. (independently and identically distributed) and can take the values $\{-2, -1, 1, 2\}$ equiprobably, and consider the following social choice function, described by listing its value $f(u_i, u_j)$ for each possible pair (u_i, u_j). In words, this social choice function selects alternative x if $u_1 + u_2 > 0$, alternative y if $u_1 + u_2 < 0$, and

---

[8]The example is adapted from Jackson and Sonnenschein (2004), which is a longer version of Jackson and Sonnenschein (2007). This section is based on these papers.

randomizes the selection when $u_1 + u_2 = 0$.

$$f(2,2) = f(2,1) = f(1,1) = f(2,-1) = f(1,2) = f(-1,2) = x,$$
$$f(-2,-2) = f(-2,-1) = f(-1,-1) = f(-2,1) = f(-1,-2) = f(1,-2) = y,$$
$$f(-2,2) = f(-1,1) = f(1,-1) = f(2,-2) = \text{equiprobable lottery over } x \text{ and } y.$$

This social choice function is not incentive compatible. For each agent, the optimal choice is to always claim to be type $u_i = 2$ whenever their real type is $u_i = 1$. To see this, consider the case when agent 1 is type $u_1 = 1$ and agent 2 is type $u_2 = -1$. Assuming agent 2 tells the truth, it is best for agent 1 to lie and say that he is type $u_1 = 2$. This would guarantee his preferred alternative, x. If agent 1 reports truthfully, then there is a $1/2$ chance that the outcome chosen will be y, his less preferred alternative.

The main objective of this section is to examine if there is anything we could do about the restrictions that the incentive compatibility constraint imposes. As it turns out, when there is more than one decision problem, Jackson and Sonnenschein (2007) show that we may obtain positive results by linking the decision problems together. In addition, to obtain positive results, we shall allow the agents to declare that they are of one specific type on just one of the decisions. In other words, we ask the agents, "Which decision or alternative do you care more about?" Jackson and Sonnenschein (2007) show that if we were to link or combine a K-number of social decision problems and ask agents to report a K-vector of preferences, then each agent would find it in his best interest to report his vector of preferences truthfully. Such linking of mechanisms makes it possible to implement approximately the desired social choice function. The "trick" is that when agents are asked to report their preferences regarding a K number of linked independent social decision problems, as opposed to asking them to report their preferences about a single independent decision problem, they have to "budget" their representations. In other words, when we link decision problems and ask the agents to reveal their preferences over each problem, we are actually asking the agents to rank their preferences for the given set of problems.

We observe such linkings of decision problems in everyday life. For example, when a homeowner tries to sell a house that needs several repairs, and a homebuyer is interested in purchasing the house, the two agents will bargain over which items shall be repaired. The seller will rank the items and report which ones he prefers to repair, and the buyer will also rank the same items and report which ones he values the most. Naturally, the seller will prefer to repair those items that result in the lowest cost, and the buyer will prefer to have repaired the items that would cost the most. If both the buyer and the seller are very stubborn, they refuse to rank their preferences, and claim that all repairs are equally valuable and equally costly, respectively, then they might not be able to come to an agreement and the deal would fall through. The outcome of this type of negotiation is not very useful to either the buyer or the seller; it is inefficient.

However, consider what happens when we do not allow the buyer to claim that all of the items have one and the same high value to him. Likewise, we do not allow the seller to claim that all of the items have one and the same high repair cost. Instead, we ask the agents to rank their preferences and choose which items they regard as most important. Then we might be able to achieve an outcome more favorable to both the buyer and the seller; a more efficient outcome where the agents end up agreeing on specific repairs and signing a deal.

By linking decision problems and allowing the type of negotiation we have just described, Jackson and Sonnenschein (2007) show that we can overcome incentive constraints and achieve more efficient decisions or outcomes. Let us introduce some of the notation and definitions specific to this analysis, and then state the main theorem, which we apply to our voting problem.

8.2.1 Notation and Definitions

Define the decision problem as a triple (X, U, P), where X is the set of possible decisions or alternatives, $U = U_1 \times \cdots \times U_I$ is a set of possible profiles of utility functions $(u_1, \ldots, u_I)$ with $u_i : X \to \mathbb{R}$, and P is a profile of probability distributions with P_i being the distribution over U_i. For any finite set of alternatives X, we write $\Delta(X)$ for the set of probability distributions defined on X. A social choice function in this section has the form $f : U \to \Delta(X)$, which allows randomization over the decisions, which is why we use notation $\Delta(X)$. Let $f_x(u)$ denote the probability of choosing $x \in X$ given the profile of utility functions $u \in U$.

Definition 8.4 (*Ex Ante* Pareto Efficiency). A social choice function f on a decision problem (X, U, P) is *ex ante* **Pareto efficient** if there does not exist any social choice function f' on (X, U, P) such that

$$\sum_u \left[P(u) \sum_x (f'_x(u) u_i(x)) \right] \geq \sum_u \left[P(u) \sum_x (f_x(u) u_i(x)) \right]$$

for all i, and with strict inequality for some i.

This is the standard definition of *ex ante* Pareto efficiency. We expect the desired social choice function f to maximize the society's expected surplus when $f_x(u)$ denotes the probability of choosing $x \in X$ given the profile of utility functions $u \in U$. Therefore, there is no other social choice function that would be, *ex ante*, more desirable for any member of the given society. Recall that when X is a set and K a positive integer, X^K stands for the Cartesian product $X \times \cdots \times X$, with X appearing K times.

Definition 8.5 (Linking Mechanism). Given a decision problem (X, U, P) and a number K of linkings, a **linking mechanism** is a pair (M, g) of a message space $M = M_1 \times \cdots M_I$ and an outcome function $g : M \to \Delta(X^K)$.

Instead of having separate mechanisms for each decision problem, a linking mechanism is a single mechanism that we can apply to a number of linked decision problems. Notice that in a linking mechanism, an agent's message space M_i contains announcements of preferences for each decision problem. An agent's utility over a set of linked decision problems is the sum of utilities, $\sum_k u_i^k(x^k)$, that the agent gets from decisions $(x^1, \cdots, x^K) \in X^K$ given his preference profile $(u_i^1, \cdots, u_i^K) \in U_i^K$. We assume that the random variables u_i^k are independent across the K decision problems, for each i.

Since we are in the environment where incomplete information prevails, namely, agents know their own preferences, but have only probabilistic information about the preferences of other agents, the appropriate equilibrium solution concept is that of Bayesian equilibrium, which we discussed in chapter 4. Therefore, a strategy for agent i in a linking mechanism with K linkings and a decision problem (X, U, P) is a mapping $\sigma_i^K : U_i^K \to \Delta(M_i)$.

Definition 8.6. Given a decision problem (X, U, P) and a social choice function f defined on (X, U, P), a sequence of linking mechanisms defined on an increasing number of linked problems $\{(M^1, g^1), (M^2, g^2), \ldots, (M^K, g^K), \ldots\}$, and a corresponding sequence of Bayesian equilibria, $\{\sigma^K\}$, **approximate** the social choice function f if

$$\lim_{K \to \infty} \left[\max_{k \leq K} \operatorname{Prob} \left\{ g_k^K(\sigma^K(u)) \neq f(u^k) \right\} \right] = 0.$$

Therefore, a linking mechanism with its corresponding sequence of Bayesian equilibria will approximate the desired social choice function if, in the limit, the maximum probability that the outcomes of those equilibria do not coincide with the desired social choice function is zero.

Definition 8.7. Given a mechanism (M, g) on K linked decision problems, a strategy $\sigma_i : U_i^K \to M_i$ **secures** a utility level $\overline{u}_i$ for agent i if, for all strategies of the other agents σ_{-i},

$$\mathbb{E} \left[\sum_{k \leq K} u_i(g^k(\sigma_i, \sigma_{-i})) \right] \geq K \overline{u}_i.$$

We could interpret $K\overline{u}_i$ as agent i's reservation utility, and the inequality in the above definition as an individual rationality constraint. In other words, an agent is guaranteed to receive the payoff of $K\overline{u}_i$ for participating and playing strategy σ_i when all other agents are playing strategies σ_{-i}.

In the next definition we employ, for any finite set S, the notation $\#S$ to denote the number of members of S. Let P_i^K be an approximation to P_i such that $P_i^K(u_i)$ is a multiple of $1/K$ for each $u_i \in U_i$ and as close to P_i as possible.

Definition 8.8 (Approximate Truthfulness). Let M_i^K be agent i's strategy set such that

$$M_i^K = \left\{ \hat{u}_i \in U_i^K \quad \text{s.t.} \quad \# \left\{ k : \hat{u}_i^k = v_i \right\} = P_i^K(v_i)K \quad \text{for each} \quad v_i \in U_i \right\}.$$

A strategy $\sigma_i^K : U_i^K \to M_i^K$ is **approximately truthful** if

$$\# \left\{ k | \left[\sigma_i^K(u_i^1, \cdots, u_i^K) \right]^k \neq u_i^k \right\} \leq \# \left\{ k | m_i^k \neq u_i^k \right\}$$

for all $m_i \in M_i^K$ and all $(u_i^1, \cdots, u_i^K) \in U_i^K$.

An agent follows a strategy that is approximately truthful if the agent's announcements always involve as few lies as possible.

8.2.2 Results

You could be wondering at this point why we need approximately truthful strategies. Let us explain this starting with a consideration of K linked problems for which we use a linking mechanism to implement the desired social choice function. Agent i's strategy consists of reports of his utility functions regarding his preferences over the K-number of linked decision problems. The above definition states that if a strategy is to belong to agent i's strategy set, $m_i^k \in M_i^K$, each announcement made by agent i has to match the prescribed expected frequency distribution. In other words, we restrict the agent to announce a specific utility function, u_i, a limited number of times corresponding to $K \times P_i(u_i)$. When we impose such a constraint on an agent, we are forcing the agent to, in some instances, make false reports regarding his preferences, since his realizations of utility functions across the K-number of linked decision problems will not necessarily match a frequency P_i. Nonetheless, if we succeed in eliciting as many truthful reports as possible from the agent, then we can still obtain positive results, as the next theorem states.

Theorem 8.5 (Jackson and Sonnenschein, 2007). *Consider a decision problem* (X, U, P) *and an ex ante Pareto efficient social choice function f defined on it. There exists a sequence of linking mechanisms (M^K, g^K) on linked versions of the decision problem such that the following statements hold:*

- *There exists a corresponding sequence of Bayesian equilibria that are approximately truthful.*
- *The sequence of linking mechanisms together with these corresponding equilibria approximate f.*
- *Any sequence of approximately truthful strategies for an agent i secures a sequence of utility levels that converge to the ex ante target level $\bar{u}_i$.*

- *All sequences of Bayesian equilibria of the linking mechanisms result in expected utilities that converge to the ex ante efficient profile of target utilities of $\overline{u}$ per problem.*
- *For any sequence of Bayesian equilibria and any sequence of deviating coalitions, the maximal gain by any agent in the deviating coalitions vanishes along the sequence.*

Let us go back to the example from the beginning of the section and see how theorem 8.5 could be applied to implement the desired social choice function. Namely, we examine what would happen if we were to duplicate the original decision problem.

Example 8.2. (Jackson and Sonnenschein, 2004)

Let there be two agents, with two separate decision problems, $d_1 \in \{x_1, y_1\}$ and $d_2 \in \{x_2, y_2\}$, such that an agent's value over the two decision problems can be expressed as the sum of the values of the individual decision problems, $v_i(d_1, d_2) = v_{i1}(d_1) + v_{i2}(d_2)$. The preferences over a decision d_j are given by $u_{ij} = v_{ij}(x) - v_{ij}(y)$. We retain the assumption each u_{ij} is i.i.d. on $\{-2, -1, 1, 2\}$ with each occurring with equal probability.

Assume one agent has the type $(2, 1)$, which means in both cases he prefers x to y, and the other agent has the type $(-1, -2)$, which means that in both cases she prefers y to x. What would the outcome be if we were to ask the agents to vote over the two decision problems separately? In other words, we would hold two voting sessions: in the first session agents would vote over $\{x_1, y_1\}$, and in the second session agents would vote over $\{x_2, y_2\}$. Then, one agent's votes would be given by (x_1, x_2) and the other agent's votes would be given by (y_1, y_2). Then we would randomize over the four possible outcomes, (x_1, x_2), (y_1, y_2), (x_1, y_2), and (y_1, x_2). This is not efficient, since if we randomly select the outcome (y_1, x_2), we could improve both agents' utilities by selecting (x_1, y_2).

Now consider a linked mechanism that would handle both decision problems simultaneously. In a linked mechanism, we ask agents to rank their preferences for each problem by imposing the following constraint on their announcements. We require agents to report either $(-2, -1)$ or $(-1, -2)$, and $(2, 1)$ or $(1, 2)$, but in no case are they allowed to report $(-2, -2)$, $(-1, -1)$, $(1, 1)$ or $(2, 2)$. Then, if both agents report positive types, we choose alternative x, and if both agents report negative types, we choose alternative y. If one agent reports positive types, and the other agent negative, then we choose the alternative with a higher magnitude. And lastly, if there is a tie, then we randomize over the alternatives.

This mechanism has a Bayesian equilibrium where agents find it in their best interest to report truthfully if the magnitude of their preferences varies across the alternatives, and if the magnitudes are the same, the agents will randomize over the two choices. Even more, not only is this mechanism incentive compatible, but it also Pareto dominates the voting mechanism where agents report their preferences separately. To see this, notice that the probability of choosing less desirable alternatives in the separate voting mechanism was $1/2$, while this probability is $1/4$ in the linked mechanism. As an exercise, you should confirm that these probabilities indeed satisfy the property of Pareto dominance of the linked mechanism over the separate voting mechanism. ◇

8.3 Robust Mechanism Design

The standard approach to modeling information in the mechanism design literature is to use type spaces. Up until this point in the book, we have assumed that the relevant type space was such that the set of possible types an agent may have contained information regarding the agent's set of possible payoff types, which represent his preferences. In addition, we have assumed a common knowledge prior over this type space. This is the approach we have used in chapter 4. In this section, we turn to a different approach that considers a more general type space, the one originally proposed by John Harsanyi. Recall from section 4.1 that John Harsanyi argued that all the uncertainty about a game with incomplete information can be reduced to a construction in which we imagine that each player has a set of types. These types reflect the agent's characteristics, the agent's beliefs about the characteristics of the other agents, the agent's beliefs about the beliefs of the other agents, and so on. This kind of type space is much richer than the payoff type space often used in the mechanism design literature. It also is very much larger, leading to a problem when applied economists use a small type space together with the assumption that each agent's type space and each agent's beliefs over the types of other agents are common knowledge among the agents.

Why are we interested in altering the way we model information encompassed by type spaces? We want to weaken some of the common knowledge assumptions in order to examine the robustness properties of our mechanisms. In other words, we would like to bring the theory closer to what we expect to observe in the real world. Before we look at some examples, let us explore the meaning of *robust mechanism design*. *Webster's Online Dictionary* defines the word *robust* as "capable of performing without failure under a wide range of conditions." This is precisely how we would like our mechanisms to be—"more robust or less sensitive to the assumed structure of the environment" (Bergemann and Morris, 2005, page 1771). In other words, we would like our mechanisms to perform well, and generate the desired results even when we weaken some of our assumptions. Bergemann and Morris (2005) present a wonderful exposition of the theory regarding robust mechanism design. Before we state their main results, it is important to review the differences between *ex ante*, *interim*, and *ex post* implementation.[9]

We base the distinction between the concepts of *ex ante*, *interim*, and *ex post* implementation on the time the information becomes available to the mechanism participants. The information that we are interested in includes the agents' preferences over the set of possible alternatives, and also their beliefs regarding other agents' preferences over the

---

[9]These concepts were introduced in chapter 4 in the context of voluntary participation constraints.

same set of possible alternatives. For the case of ***ex ante*** implementation, we consider whether it is possible to implement a certain mechanism before the agents have received any private information. The case of ***interim*** implementation assumes that each agent has received and knows his private information, but does not know the other participants' information. When the information state is public knowledge, that is, all the information is known to all of the agents, we have the case of ***ex post*** implementation. In other words, in the case of *ex post* implementation, we are exploring the possibility of using a mechanism to implement the desired social choice function given that all agents have complete information.

Let us be clear on the connection between dominant strategy implementation and *ex post* implementation. Recall our discussion of a private values auction model in chapter 4, where bidders' valuations were continuous random variables distributed independently of each other. If *ex post* implementation considers a situation where the information state is public knowledge, and a participant's state is independent of other participants' states, which is the private value case,[10] then *ex post* implementation is equivalent to dominant strategy implementation.

This section is based on Bergemann and Morris (2005), who examine what happens to the implementation problem when we modify our assumption regarding type spaces. They assume that an agent's type implicitly contains a description of not only his payoffs or preferences, but also his beliefs. In other words, they model information by using a broader type space than we generally observe in the mechanism design literature. This assumption is necessary if one wants to allow agents to have all possible beliefs about other agents' types while maintaining that the payoff environment is common knowledge. Before we can formally state the Bergemann and Morris (2005) results, let us introduce some notation and definitions.

8.3.1 Notation and Definitions

The **payoff environment**, which we have used throughout the book, includes the set of agents $\mathcal{I} = \{1, 2, \dots, I\}$, where each agent i has a set of possible *payoff types* Θ_i, which we assume to be finite. A set of possible outcomes is X, which affect agent i's utility function $u_i : X \times \Theta \to \mathbb{R}$. There is a social choice correspondence $F : \Theta \to\to X$, such that if the agents' true type profile is θ, the designer would like to implement the set of alternatives $F(\theta)$. We assume that this payoff environment is common knowledge, and we allow for interdependence of types, so that one agent's utility from outcome $x \in X$ depends on the other agents' types.

In addition to this standard payoff environment, we would like to allow the agents to possess all possible beliefs about the other agents' types. In other words, we do not want

---

[10]How much an individual values some object or some alternative does not depend on how much other individuals value the same object or alternative.

to assume a common prior for all agents. Modeling this requires a richer type space than the payoff type we defined in the previous paragraph. Let us now formally define this concept.

Definition 8.9 (Type Space). A **type space** is a collection $(T_i, \widehat{\theta}_i, \widehat{\pi}_i)_{i=1}^I$, where agent i's *type* is $t_i \in T_i$, which includes agent i's description of his *payoff type* $\widehat{\theta}_i(t_i)$ and agent i's beliefs $\widehat{\pi}_i(t_i)$ when his type is t_i.

Notice that the payoff type in this definition is a function $\widehat{\theta}_i : T_i \to \Theta_i$ that associates agent i's type with his payoff type, such that agent i's payoff type is $\widehat{\theta}_i(t_i)$ when his type is t_i. Also, agent i's beliefs is a function $\widehat{\pi}_i(t_i) : T_i \to \Delta(T_{-i})^{11}$ that associates i's type with his beliefs regarding the other agents' types. When the set of types is finite, we say that $\widehat{\pi}_i(t_i)[t_{-i}]$ is the probability that type t_i of agent i assigns to other agents' types, t_{-i}. Therefore, agent i's type includes specific information regarding both the agent's payoff type and his beliefs about the other agents' types. This type space is much richer than the payoff type we generally use in mechanism design, where, usually, when describing a decision problem, we use payoff types: we fix agents' types using their preference profiles, and then we add their beliefs using a common prior for all agents. We now define formally the concepts of *interim* and *ex post* implementation.

Definition 8.10 (Interim Incentive Compatibility). A direct mechanism $f : T \to X$, is **interim incentive compatible** on type space $(T_i, \widehat{\theta}_i, \widehat{\pi}_i)_{i=1}^I$, if

$$\int_{t_{-i} \in T_{-i}} u_i \left(f(t_i, t_{-i}), \widehat{\theta}(t_i, t_{-i}) \right) d\widehat{\pi}_i(t_i) \geq \int_{t_{-i} \in T_{-i}} u_i \left(f(t_i', t_{-i}), \widehat{\theta}(t_i, t_{-i}) \right) d\widehat{\pi}_i(t_i),$$

for all i, $t \in T$ and $t_i' \in T_i$.

Interim incentive compatibility requires that after agent i has received only his private information, and has no insight into the other agents' private information other than his own beliefs, agent i will choose to report his type truthfully since this truthful reporting will give him at least as much utility as any other report. When we assume a common prior, interim incentive compatibility is equivalent to Bayesian incentive compatibility.

Definition 8.11. A social choice correspondence F is **interim implementable** on type space $(T_i, \widehat{\theta}_i, \widehat{\pi}_i)_{i=1}^I$, if there exists a direct mechanism $f : T \to X$ such that f is **interim incentive compatible** on $(T_i, \widehat{\theta}_i, \widehat{\pi}_i)_{i=1}^I$ and $f(t) \in F(\widehat{\theta}(t))$, for all $t \in T$.

---

[11] $\Delta(T_{-i})$ is the space of probability measures on the Borel field of the measurable space T_{-i}. If you do not know what a Borel field is, do not worry; any book on measure theory covers the topic. Also, if we take T_{-i} to be finite, then $\Delta(T_{-i})$ is simply the set of probability distributions over T_{-i}. In that case, all the integrals in this section simplify to sums.

We may think of *interim* implementation as partial Bayesian equilibrium implementation without a common prior, since *interim* implementation would be equivalent to Bayesian equilibrium implementation if we assumed a common prior for all agents. Compare with definition 4.4. and note that interim implementation is not full implementation.

Definition 8.12 (Ex Post Incentive Compatibility). A direct mechanism $f : T \to X$ is **ex post incentive compatible** if, for all $i \in \mathcal{I}$, $\theta \in \Theta$, and $\theta'_i \in \Theta_i$, $u_i(f(\theta), \theta) \geq u_i(f(\theta'_i, \theta_{-i}), \theta)$.

In order for the *ex post* incentive compatibility to be satisfied, agent i must prefer to tell the truth when his type is θ if he expects all other agents to report their true types as well. However, recall that dominant strategy implementation requires that agent i prefers to tell the truth in all circumstances, or for all possible reports of other agents, truthful or not.

Definition 8.13 (Dominant Strategy Incentive Compatibility). A direct mechanism $f : T \to X$ is **dominant strategy incentive compatible,** if for all $i \in \mathcal{I}$, $\theta \in \Theta$, and $\theta' \in \Theta$, $u_i(f(\theta_i, \theta'_{-i}), \theta) \geq u_i(f(\theta'), \theta)$.

In the case of private values, where each $u_i(x, \theta)$ depends on θ only through θ_i, *ex post* incentive compatibility is equivalent to dominant strategy incentive compatibility.

Definition 8.14 (Ex Post Implementation). A social choice correspondence F is **ex post implementable** if there exists $f : T \to X$ such that f is *ex post* incentive compatible and $f(\theta) \in F(\theta)$ for all $\theta \in \Theta$.

8.3.2 Results

Bergemann and Morris (2005) prove that ex post implementation implies interim implementation on all type spaces. We now formally state and prove this result.

Theorem 8.6 (Bergemann and Morris, 2005). *If a social choice correspondence F is ex post implementable, then F is interim implementable on any type space.*

Proof. According to definitions 8.12 and 8.14, if F is *ex post* implementable, then there must exist some $f^e : \Theta \to X$ with $f^e(\theta) \in F(\theta)$ for all $\theta \in \Theta$, such that for all i, $\theta \in \Theta$, and $\theta'_i \in \Theta_i$, $u_i(f^e(\theta), \theta) \geq u_i(f^e(\theta'_i, \theta_{-i}), \theta)$.

Let there also be some arbitrary type space $(T_i, \widehat{\theta}_i, \widehat{\pi}_i)_{i=1}^{I}$ with the direct mechanism $f : T \to X$ and $f(t) = f^e(\widehat{\theta}(t))$. Then, according to definition 8.10 *interim* incentive compatibility requires that

$$t_i \in \arg\max_{t'_i \in T_i} \int_{t_{-i} \in T_{-i}} u_i \left(f(t'_i, t_{-i}), (\widehat{\theta}(t_i), \widehat{\theta}_{-i}(t_{-i})) \right) d\widehat{\pi}_i(t_i) =$$

$$\arg\max_{t'_i \in T_i} \int_{t_{-i} \in T_{-i}} u_i \left(f^e(\widehat{\theta}(t'_i), \widehat{\theta}_{-i}(t_{-i})), (\widehat{\theta}(t_i), \widehat{\theta}_{-i}(t_{-i})) \right) d\widehat{\pi}_i(t_i).$$

This in turn implies

$$\widehat{\theta}_i(t_i) = \arg\max_{\theta_i \in \Theta_i} \int_{t_{-i} \in T_{-i}} u_i\left(f^e(\theta_i, \widehat{\theta}_{-i}(t_{-i})), (\widehat{\theta}(t_i), \widehat{\theta}_{-i}(t_{-i}))\right) d\widehat{\pi}_i(t_i) =$$

$$\arg\max_{\theta_i \in \Theta_i} \sum_{\theta_{-i} \in \Theta_{-i}} \left(\int_{\{t_{-i}:\widehat{\theta}_{-i}(t_{-i})=\theta_{-i}\}} d\widehat{\pi}_i(t_i)\right) u_i\left(f^e(\theta_i, \theta_{-i}), (\widehat{\theta}_i(t_i), \theta_{-i})\right).$$

Recall that *ex post* incentive compatibility in definition 8.12 is directly defined on the payoff type space. But this is the same as requiring *ex post* incentive compatibility on any type space where all payoff types are possible, since the range of each $\widehat{\theta}_i$ is Θ_i. Also, recall that from definition 8.14 *ex post* implementability requires truthful reporting by i for any profile θ_{-i}. Therefore, truthful reporting by i remains a best response for arbitrary expectations over Θ_{-i}.   QED

We now present an example that shows that the converse of theorem 8.6 is not true, and clarifies the main concepts we are discussing. Namely, if a social choice correspondence is *interim* implementable in all type spaces, it may not be *ex post* implementable. Nonetheless, under certain conditions, such as in separable environments, *interim* implementation in all type spaces implies *ex post* implementation. To conserve space, we refer you to (Bergemann and Morris, 2005, Section 4) for further discussion of this topic and to that paper as a whole for a comprehensive treatment of robust implementation.

Example 8.3. (Bergemann and Morris, 2005)
Let there be two agents, $i = 1, 2$. Each agent can have two possible types, θ and θ', such that $\Theta_1 = \{\theta_1, \theta_1'\}$ and $\Theta_2 = \{\theta_2, \theta_2'\}$. There are three possible outcomes: $X = \{a, b, c\}$. The relevant payoffs are given in the following three tables, where the first payoff belongs to agent 1 and the second payoff belongs to agent 2.

a	θ_2	θ_2'
θ_1	$1,0$	$-1,2$
θ_1'	$0,0$	$0,0$

b	θ_2	θ_2'
θ_1	$-1,2$	$1,0$
θ_1'	$0,0$	$0,0$

c	θ_2	θ_2'
θ_1	$0,0$	$0,0$
θ_1'	$1,1$	$1,1$

The social choice correspondence is defined as follows:

F	θ_2	θ_2'
θ_1	$\{a, b\}$	$\{a, b\}$
θ_1'	$\{c\}$	$\{c\}$

In order to verify that this social choice correspondence is not *ex post* implementable, notice that when agent 1 is type θ_1', he finds it optimal to report truthfully because that maximizes his utility. In that case, agent 2 finds it optimal to report his type truthfully as well because that maximizes his utility. Hence, the agents agree that when agent 1 is type θ_1' the optimal choice is c.

Consider agent 1 being type θ_1. *Ex post* implementation requires that he knows with certainty that agent 2 is, for example, type θ_2. Then agent 1's optimal strategy is to truthfully report his type if and only if the social outcome is a. In that case, truthful reporting maximizes his utility and gives him the payoff of 1 instead of the payoff of -1 or 0. Similarly, if agent 1 is type θ_1, and he knows with certainty that agent 2 is type θ_2', then his optimal strategy is to truthfully report his type if and only if the social outcome is b. In that case, truthful reporting maximizes his utility and gives him the maximum payoff of 1 instead of the payoff of -1 or 0. In summary, agent 1's *ex post* incentive constraints require that

f	θ_2	θ_2'
θ_1	$\{a\}$	$\{b\}$
θ_1'	$\{c\}$	$\{c\}$

Next, we show that the above violates agent 2's *ex post* incentive constraints, which imply the following.

f	θ_2	θ_2'
θ_1	$\{b\}$	$\{a\}$
θ_1'	$\{c\}$	$\{c\}$

If the social outcome is a when types reported are (θ_1, θ_2), and b when types reported are (θ_1, θ_2'), then agent 2 will have an incentive to misrepresent his preferences because that would increase his payoff from 0 to 2. Therefore, the correspondence F is not *ex post* implementable.

We can show that the social choice correspondence in this example is *interim* implementable in any type space by letting the mechanism depend on agent 1's beliefs regarding agent 2's type, and by asking agent 1 to pick the social outcome. Specifically, if agent 1 believes that agent 2 is type θ_2 with probability at least $1/2$, then, if agent 1's type is θ_1, his expected utility is maximized when he picks outcome a. On the other hand, if agent 1 believes that agent 2 is type θ_2 with probability less than $1/2$, and agent 1 is type θ_1, then agent 1 will pick outcome b. Outcome c will be picked whenever agent 1 is type θ_1'. Therefore, the social choice correspondence is *interim* implementable.   ◇

8.4 The Limits of Ex Post Implementation

In section 8.3, we have seen that under certain conditions, *ex post* implementation is equivalent to dominant strategy implementation. Implementation in dominant strategies is considered the most robust form of implementation, and as such, we would like to use it as often as possible. However, recall that Gibbard and Satterthwaite showed that there exist serious limitations to implementation in dominant strategies. Therefore, we consider instances where *ex post* implementation is equivalent to dominant strategy implementation not very encouraging.

Nonetheless, this equivalence requires that we assume independence among agents' preferences, or what is known as private values case, which oftentimes is a restrictive and unrealistic assumption. In most cases, agents' preferences will be interdependent. The most robust form of implementation in environments where agents' valuations are interdependent is *ex post* implementation. In section 8.3, we have already presented some of the characteristics of *ex post* implementation. This section builds upon section 8.3 and is based on Jehiel et al. (2006).

Jehiel et al. (2006) present and prove an impossibility theorem, which shows that there are serious limitations to *ex post* implementation of deterministic social choice functions. Their theorem states that, assuming an environment with quasilinear, interdependent preferences, multidimensional types, and generic valuation functions, we will be able to *ex post* implement only constant deterministic social choice rules.

8.4.1 Notation and a Result

Agents hold private information, which is embedded in a private exogenously determined signal $\theta_i \in \Theta_i$, which is here the agent's type. Joining all of the private signals $(\theta_i)_{i \in I}$ gives the state of the world $\theta \in \Theta$, such that $\Theta = \prod_{i \in I} \Theta_i$ and $\theta = (\theta_i, \theta_{-i})$ is the same notational convenience we have used before. For each $i \in \mathcal{I}$, let the positive integer $d_i \geq 1$ stand for the number of dimensions of agent i's signal. We assume $\Theta_i = [0,1]^{d_i}$. The multidimensionality of types and the uncountably infinite number of them is a very important assumption that makes the analysis in this section deeply different than the one of the previous section, where each Θ_i was assumed to be a finite set.

We assume that agent i's utility function $u_i : X \times \Theta \to \mathbb{R}$ is given by quasilinear preferences such that $u_i(x, \theta) = v_i^x(\theta) - t_i(\theta)$, where $x \in X$, and such that every function $v_i : \Theta \to \mathbb{R}$ is smooth, i.e., has partial derivatives of every order. The functions v_i are in fact functions of the arguments x and θ, but by putting x as a superscript we emphasize that θ contains the relevant variables for the derivatives we will be taking shortly. In addition, we limit our attention to an environment where there are only two agents, $1, 2 \in \mathcal{I}$, and two alternatives, $x, y \in X$. Since any environment with more agents and alternatives has an environment with just two of each embedded in it, the negative result we will see extends to all such environments with any number of agents and alternatives more than two.

Let D_v be the **directional derivative** operator in direction $v \in \mathbb{R}^{d_i}$ (see section A.2 on page 256). Two vectors, $x, y \in \mathbb{R}^d$, are said to be **co-directional** if $x = \lambda y$ for some $\lambda \geq 0$. If we drew two co-directional vectors with their starting points at the origin, they would be on the same line.

We consider a social choice function, $f : \Theta \to X$ with $t_i : \Theta \to \mathbb{R}$. We say that a social choice function is **trivial** if it is constant on the interior intΘ of the type space.

Let us now define *ex post* implementation in the context of current analysis. Its interpretation is as in the preceding section.

Definition 8.15 (Ex Post Implementation). The social choice function f is **ex post implementable** if truthful reporting is an *ex post* equilibrium of the direct revelation mechanism such that

$$v_i^{f(\theta)}(\theta) - t_i(\theta) \geq v_i^{f(\tilde{\theta}_i, \theta_{-i})}(\theta) - t_i(\tilde{\theta}_i, \theta_{-i}),$$

for all $\theta_i, \tilde{\theta}_i \in \Theta_i$ and $\theta_{-i} \in \Theta_{-i}$.

It turns out to be easier to use relative valuations and relative transfers.

Definition 8.16 (Relative Valuations and Transfers). For every $\theta \in \Theta$ and every $i \in \mathcal{I}$, the **relative valuation** is $\mu_i(\theta) = v_i^x(\theta) - v_i^y(\theta)$, and the **relative transfers** are $\tau_i(\theta_{-i}) = t_i^x(\theta_{-i}) - t_i^y(\theta_{-i})$.

We assume that $D_{\theta_i}\mu_i(\theta) \neq 0$ for all $\theta \in \Theta$ (D_{θ_i} denotes the d_i-dimensional vector of derivatives with respect to θ_i). This means that for each agent i, i's relative valuation is responsive to the signal of i at every signal vector θ. For the next definition, we recall that if a set S is a subset of a topological space, then $\overline{S}$ stands for the closure of S, which is the smallest closed set that contains S.

Definition 8.17 (Indifference Set). The **indifference set** K of a social choice function f is defined by $K = \overline{f^{-1}\{x\}} \cap \overline{f^{-1}\{y\}} \cap \text{int}\Theta$. For an indifference signal $\widehat{\theta} \in K$, define the **indifference set with fixed** $\widehat{\theta}_i$ by $K_i(\widehat{\theta}) = \left\{ \theta \in K : \theta_i = \widehat{\theta}_i \right\}$.

The indifference set is the set of signal vectors θ that are in the interior of Θ (so they contain no 0 or 1 coordinates), and are in the set that separates the areas of Θ where the two alternatives x and y are chosen.

We can now state the geometric condition that is at the heart of the analysis of Jehiel et al. (2006).

Theorem 8.7 (The Geometric Condition; [Jehiel et al., 2006]). *Let the mechanism (f, t) be nontrivial and* ex post *incentive compatible.*

- If the relative transfers τ_i are continuous on $\mathrm{int}\Theta_{-i}$ for all $i \in \{1,2\}$, then there exist an indifference signal $\widehat{\theta} \in K$ and a vector $z \in \mathbb{R}^{d_i}$ such that $D_{\theta_i}\mu_i(\theta)$ and $(D_{\theta_i}\mu_{-i}(\theta) - z)$ are co-directional for every $\theta \in K_i(\widehat{\theta})$.

- If relative transfers τ_{-i} are discontinuous at a signal $\widehat{\theta}_i$ for some $i \in \{1,2\}$, then agent i's incentives are locally independent of θ_{-i}. That is, there exist a vector $z \in \mathbb{R}^{d_i}$ and a non-empty open set $Q \subseteq \Theta_{-i}$ such that $D_{\theta_i}\mu_i(\widehat{\theta}_i, q)$ and z are co-directional for every $q \in Q$.

8.4.2 An Illustration of the Geometric Condition

Theorem 8.7 can be used to illustrate that in a simple case of bi-linear valuations and two-dimensional signals, a geometric condition on the coefficients of the valuation functions has to be satisfied, if we desire to implement a non-trivial social choice function. The example is adapted from (Jehiel et al., 2006, page 592).

Let the signals be given by $\theta_i = (\theta_i^x, \theta_i^y) \in [0,1]^2$, define valuations by

$$v_i^x(\theta) = k_i^x \theta_i^x + l_i^x \theta_i^x \theta_{-i}^x \text{ and}$$
$$v_i^y(\theta) = k_i^y \theta_i^y + l_i^y \theta_i^y \theta_{-i}^y,$$

and assume that the parameters $k_i^x, k_i^y, l_i^x, l_i^y$ are all non-zero.

We can express these valuation functions in terms of relative valuation functions by recalling definition 8.16.

$$\begin{aligned}
\mu_i(\theta) &= v_i^x(\theta) - v_i^y(\theta) \\
&= k_i^x \theta_i^x + l_i^x \theta_i^x \theta_{-i}^x - k_i^y \theta_i^y - l_i^y \theta_i^y \theta_{-i}^y \\
&= \theta_i^x (k_i^x + l_i^x \theta_{-i}^x) - \theta_i^y (k_i^y + l_i^y \theta_{-i}^y).
\end{aligned}$$

Similarly,

$$\begin{aligned}
\mu_{-i}(\theta) &= v_{-i}^x(\theta) - v_{-i}^y(\theta) \\
&= k_{-i}^x \theta_{-i}^x + l_{-i}^x \theta_{-i}^x \theta_i^x - k_{-i}^y \theta_{-i}^y - l_{-i}^y \theta_{-i}^y \theta_i^y \\
&= \theta_{-i}^x (k_{-i}^x + l_{-i}^x \theta_i^x) - \theta_{-i}^y (k_{-i}^y + l_{-i}^y \theta_i^y).
\end{aligned}$$

Since D_{θ_i} denotes the d_i-dimensional derivative vector operator with respect to θ_i, and in this example $d_1 = d_2 = 2$, we have

$$D_{\theta_i}\mu_i(\theta) = \begin{pmatrix} k_i^x + l_i^x \theta_{-i}^x \\ -k_i^y - l_i^y \theta_{-i}^y \end{pmatrix}.$$

For any arbitrary vector $z \in \mathbb{R}^2$, write $z = \begin{pmatrix} z^x \\ z^y \end{pmatrix}$, so that

$$D_{\theta_i}(\mu_{-i}(\theta) - z) = \begin{pmatrix} l_{-i}^x \theta_{-i}^x - z^x \\ -l_{-i}^y \theta_{-i}^y - z^y \end{pmatrix}.$$

If f is to be a nontrivial *ex post* incentive compatible social choice function with a continuous relative transfer function τ, then theorem 8.7. calls for $D_{\theta_i}\mu_i(\theta)$ and $D_{\theta_i}(\mu_{-i}(\theta) - z)$ to be collinear for every $\theta \in K_i(\widehat{\theta})$.[12] In other words, for the two vectors, $D_{\theta_i}\mu_i(\theta)$ and $D_{\theta_i}(\mu_{-i}(\theta) - z)$, to be collinear, their cross-product must vanish. Specifically,

$$(k_i^x + l_i^x \theta_{-i}^x)(-l_{-i}^y \theta_{-i}^y - z^y) - (-k_i^y - l_i^y \theta_{-i}^y)(l_{-i}^x \theta_{-i}^x - z^x) = 0. \tag{8.1}$$

Given our assumptions,[13] when we vary θ_{-i}^x and θ_{-i}^y, this condition is satisfied when $l_i^y l_{-i}^x - l_i^x l_{-i}^y = 0$. To prove this, we can parameterize the indifference set $K_i(\widehat{\theta})$ by

$$\theta_{-i}^x = \frac{\mu_{-i}(\widehat{\theta})}{k_{-i}^x + l_{-i}^x \widehat{\theta}_i^x} + \frac{k_{-i}^y + l_{-i}^y \widehat{\theta}_i^y}{k_{-i}^x + l_{-i}^x \widehat{\theta}_i^x} \theta_{-i}^y.$$

Substituting this θ_{-i}^x into (8.1), we observe that this equation holds if

$$\frac{k_{-i}^y + l_{-i}^y \widehat{\theta}_i^y}{k_{-i}^x + l_{-i}^x \widehat{\theta}_i^x}(l_i^y l_{-i}^x - l_i^x l_{-i}^y) = 0.$$

Therefore, given our assumptions, this implies that $(l_i^y l_{-i}^x - l_i^x l_{-i}^y) = 0$.

Finally, theorem 8.7. states that if the relative transfer function τ_i is not continuous, then we have to require $l_i^x = l_i^y = 0$, so that the algebraic condition $(l_i^y l_{-i}^x - l_i^x l_{-i}^y) = 0$ is satisfied and theorem 8.7. still holds.

This condition is nongeneric, and we should not expect it to be satisfied for generic utility functions. It is easy to see why there are eight parameters of the problem, and the condition $(l_i^y l_{-i}^x - l_i^x l_{-i}^y) = 0$ imposes a restriction that removes one dimension, so the set of eight-dimensional parameter vectors that satisfy the condition is at most a seven-dimensional set, which has volume zero in eight-dimensional parameter space.

Jehiel et al. (2006) show in their main result that this geometric condition is not satisfied for generic utility functions. Therefore, when we assume quasilinear and interdependent preferences and multidimensional types, and we have some non-constant deterministic social choice function, then we cannot achieve *ex post* implementation since the

---

[12]If two non-zero vectors x and y are collinear, and $x = \lambda y$, then it must be that $\lambda \neq 0$.

[13]We have assumed $k_i^x, k_i^y, l_i^x, l_i^y \neq 0$, and we can also assume without loss of generality that $(k_{-i}^a + l_{-i}^a \widehat{\theta}_i^x, (k_{-i}^y + l_{-i}^y \widehat{\theta}_i^y) \neq 0$.

geometric condition will be violated. In other words, given our assumptions regarding the specifications of the relevant environment, we will be able to *ex post* implement only constant deterministic social choice rules. To conserve space, we do not formally state and prove this theorem.

The requirement of multidimensionality of types is an important assumption for the current analysis. Cremer and McLean (1985) show that if we require types to be single-dimensional, and if the single-crossing property is satisfied and valuations are interdependent, then efficient *ex post* implementation is possible.

8.5 Exercises

Exercise 34: Endogenous Mechanisms

Consider the problem of voluntary contributions in the example of section 8.1.2.
- Show that in order to ensure a unique Nash equilibrium in the underlying game without transfers, the specified normalization, that is, $\sum \theta_i = 1$, is required.
- Show that when Amy's solo transfer is introduced, the solution to the problem is indeed a corner solution with $m_A = 0$ and $m_B = 1$.
- Verify that when Bill's solo transfer is introduced, his optimal strategy is $m_B = 0$.

Exercise 35: Endogenous Mechanisms (*Jackson and Wilkie, 2005*)

Consider a Cournot duopoly game where each firm i has to decide how much of an output m_i to produce. In other words, each firm has to choose an action $m_i \in \mathbb{R}_+$. Let the inverse demand function for each firm's product be $p(m_i) = a - \sum_i m_i$, and assume that each firm's costs of production are zero, i.e. $c(m_i) = 0$. Then we can represent firm i's profit via payoff function $v_i(m) = (a - \sum_i m_i)m_i$.
- Calculate the Cournot equilibrium quantities and the resulting profits for each firm.
- How would your answers differ if the two firms colluded and formed a monopoly in order to maximize their joint profits?
- Investigate whether this pair of "monopoly" profits is supportable.

Hint: Apply theorem 8.2. and check that the sum of the solo payoffs exceeds the sum of the maximal possible profits. Consider symmetric transfers $t_i(m_i', 0) = (a - m_i)^2/4$, and $t_i(m) = a^2$ if $m_i \neq m_i'$, and $t_i(m) = 0$ otherwise.

Exercise 36: Linking Decisions (*Jackson and Sonnenschein, 2004*)

Consider a township consisting of I citizens trying to decide whether or not to build a new public swimming pool. The cost of building the pool is $c > 0$. Citizen i has a personal valuation v_i for the new swimming pool that falls in the set $\{0, 1, \ldots, m\}$ for all $i = 1, 2, \ldots, I$. Let v denote the vector of valuations. Assuming that the township uses Pareto efficiency to decide whether or not the swimming pool should be built, then the pool should be built when $\sum_i v_i \geq c$. Otherwise, the pool should not be built. The citizens are willing to pay a share $c_i(v)$ of the total cost as long as their share does not exceed their valuation such that $c_i(v) \leq v_i$, and $\sum_i c_i(v) = c$. If $\sum_i v_i < c$ then $c_i(v) = 0$.

- Show that the target decision rule will generally not be incentive compatible.
- Construct the second best incentive compatible mechanism that satisfies voluntary participation and achieves the maximal efficiency.

Now consider what happens when the township is making decisions on two different projects at once; namely, building the swimming pool and a new public library. Assume that the citizens' valuations are independent across the two problems. If we do not link the decisions across the two problems, the best we can do is repeat the second best mechanism twice. Can we have an improvement if we link the decisions? Require the citizens to act as if they have a valuation $v_i = 0$ on one of the problems and $v_i = 1$ on the other problem.

- Will the linked mechanism result in the efficient decision in all instances? What about the situation where all citizens' true valuations for the two projects are 0,0?
- When is the voluntary participation constraint violated? How could we resolve this problem?

Exercise 37: Linking Decisions

Consider example 8.2. Show that the probability of choosing less desirable alternatives in the separate voting mechanism is $1/2$, while the same probability in the linked mechanism is $1/4$. In other words, confirm that these probabilities satisfy the property of Pareto dominance of the linked mechanism over the separate voting mechanism.

Exercise 38: Robust Mechanism Design (*Bergemann and Morris, 2005*)

Let there be two agents, with the first agent having three possible types and the second agent two possible types. There are eight possible allocations. Lotteries are allowed, hence $X = \Delta(\{a, b, c, d, a', b', c'd'\})$. The agents have private values.[14] The agents' private values payoffs are as follows.

u_1	a	b	c	d	a'	b'	c'	d'
θ_1	1	-1	$1/2$	-1	-1	-1	-1	$1/2$
θ_1'	0	0	1	0	0	0	1	0
θ_1''	0	0	0	1	0	0	0	1

[14]Recall that the example in the chapter considers interdependent valuations.

u_2	a	b	c	d	a'	b'	c'	d'
θ_2	0	1	0	0	0	1	-1	-1
θ_2'	1	0	-1	-1	1	0	0	0

The social choice correspondence is described by the following table.

	θ_2	θ_2'
θ_1	$\{a,b\}$	$\{a',b'\}$
θ_1'	$\{c\}$	$\{c'\}$
θ_1''	$\{d\}$	$\{d'\}$

Show, by contradiction, that this social choice correspondence is not *ex post* implementable.

Hint: Let q be the probability that a is chosen at profile (θ_1, θ_2), and let q' be the probability that a' is chosen at profile (θ_1, θ_2').

Exercise 39: Limits of Ex Post Implementation (*Jehiel et al., 2006*)

Consider two bidders competing for one object. The bidders' valuations are given by the valuation function $v_i(\theta_i, \theta_{-i}) = p_i + c_i c_{-i}$ with $\theta_i = (p_i, c_i) \in [0,1]^2$ and $i \in \{1,2\}$.

- Consider a setting where the seller is not allowed to keep the object. Explore whether the first geometric condition stated in theorem 8.7. is satisfied.
- Now examine whether the second condition stated in the same proposition is satisfied.

Chapter 9

Matching Models: Theory and Applications

Matching theory studies an economic domain where there are two sides in a market, and each side has discrete members. A member can be a house that can be owned by an agent, a worker who seeks employment, or a man who seeks marriage. Corresponding members on the other side of the matching market would be house-buyers, firms looking to hire workers, and women looking to be married to men. We did not say "agents" for "members," since matching allows in some cases members such as houses, who do not have preferences over the outcome of the matching and do not take actions in the matching process.

In the economic domains of exchange and of public goods, we only considered goods that can be well modeled as continuous quantities. We also restricted our attention to agents consuming bundles of goods. The matching domain covers many important real-life problems, such as the matching of husbands to wives, of individuals to houses, of medical residents to hospitals, of workers to firms, of school students to schools, and of kidney donors to patients who need kidney transplants. These problems do not fit in economic domains as we have studied them in the rest of this book. In this chapter we give an overview of matching theory and present its application to these problems. While the context and some of the notation in this chapter are different from before, the objective is to study mechanisms in the matching domain and their performance, as in the rest of the book.

9.1 What Is Matching?

Matching theory studies the case when there are two distinct sides to a market and members from one side can only be matched with members from the other side of the market. Members may be individuals, goods or institutions. Matching theory is particularly concerned with matching members when the agents or goods are heterogeneous and indivisible. A matching may be either one-sided or two-sided.

One-sided matching occurs when one side of the market does not have preferences. This means that agents, on one side, are matched with objects on the other side. Examples include the classic Shapley and Scarf (1974) house market, college dorm placement and kidney exchange. Two-sided matching occurs when both sides of the market have preferences and strategies. Examples include job matching, including labor market clearinghouses (such as those for resident doctors), and school choice mechanisms. Most of the theoretical work to date deals with two-sided matching theory on which we will mainly focus in this chapter. Most of the results of matching models deal with efficient and stable matchings and core allocations. In addition, many discuss whether the true preferences are revealed by both sides of the market, which is the main concern of incentive compatibility that we have looked at extensively in this book.

The original motivation for matching theory was to explain college admissions (which is a two-sided matching theory problem). David Gale was one of the pioneers of matching theory. As Gale (2001) explains, he originally was intrigued by the college admissions problem due to a September 10, 1960 article in the *New Yorker* magazine. The *New Yorker* article questioned the effectiveness of the college admissions process, citing how the incentives of both the applicants and college admissions officers lead to a non-optimal solution. Gale and Shapley (1962) was the first article that attempted to model this matching problem. However, it was later realized that a centralized clearinghouse to place medical interns, known as the National Resident Matching Program (NRMP), which began in the early 1950s, was already using a similar algorithm to solve a matching problem. The NRMP matches medical students (workers) with residency programs (employers).[1]

A full description of matching theory is beyond the scope of this book. We refer the interested reader to the many detailed surveys that exist about matching theory. These include Gale (2001), Niederle et al. (2008) and Roth (2008a). Another survey by Roth (2008b) discusses the applications and results of the use of matching algorithms in market design.

We now turn to the matching problem and the insights that mechanism design gives us about it.

9.1.1 Notation and Definitions

In a matching problem there are two disjoint sets of agents. Let $M = \{m_1, \ldots, m_n\}$ denote the set of men, colleges or firms. Let $W = \{w_1, \ldots, w_p\}$ denote the set of women, students or workers. Then m_i and w_j represents the typical man (college or firm) and woman (student or worker), respectively. We denote a match by $m_i w_j$.

---

[1] According to the *Shorter Oxford English Disctionary*, an algorithm is "[a] procedure or a set of rules for calculation or problem-solving, now esp. with a computer." In the domain of matching problems, an algorithm specifies a mechanism in the sense we have been using the term "mechanism." As we will see, algorithms typically have many stages, as opposed to most of the mechanisms that we consider in the rest of this book.

Each agent has a complete and transitive preference ordering on the members of the opposite set. In addition, these preferences allow agents to prefer to match with themselves, that is, remain single. Formally, the preferences of each m_i is represented by the preference ranking R^{m_i} on the set $W \cup \{m_i\}$ and the preferences of each w_j is represented by the preference ranking R^{w_j} on the set $M \cup \{w_j\}$.

Every man, college or firm has a **quota**, which is denoted by q_{m_i}. The quota profile is $q = (q_{m_1}, \ldots, q_{m_n})$. When $q_{m_i} = 1$, then m_i may only match with at most one agent on the other side of the market; when $q_{m_i} = 2$, then m_i may match with at most two agents on the other side of the market; and so on. Quotas represent the matching capacities of the agents.

The economy is a four-tuple $e = (M, W, \mathcal{R}^I, q)$ on the domain $\mathcal{E}$, where $\mathcal{R}^I$, $I = M \cup W$, is the associated preference profiles of the sets of men M and women W and q is their quotas.

In general, a **matching** $\mu : M \cup W \to M \cup W$ is such that $m_i \in \mu(w_j)$ if and only if $w_j \in \mu(m_i)$. If $\mu(m_i) = m_i$, for $m_i \in M$, then m_i is matched with himself. Likewise, if $\mu(w_j) = w_j$, for $w_j \in W$, then w_j is matched with herself.

A matching is said to be **blocked by an individual agent** if the agent k prefers not to be matched with some agent under the matching μ; that is, prefers to be matched with himself than being matched with $\mu(k)$. A matching μ is said to be **individually rational**[2] if it is not blocked by any individual agent. In addition, a matching μ is said to be **blocked by a pair of agents** $m_i w_j$ when μ does not match the m_i and w_j who prefer each other to their match under μ.

Definition 9.1. A matching μ is **stable** if it is not blocked by any individual or any pair of agents.

In addition, a matching μ is in the core if no coalition of agents can improve upon the matching, such that at least one agent in the coalition is strictly better off and no agents are worse off. See chapter 1 for the formal definition of the core.

9.2 Two-Sided Matching

Two-sided matching theory is concerned with the matching of agents in markets with heterogeneous and indivisible goods; such matchings include those between women and men, employees and firms, and students and colleges. Much of the theory manifests itself in centralized matching mechanisms, called clearinghouses. Some examples of clearinghouses are the NRMP, Medical Specialties Matching Program (MSMP), British National

---

[2]Here we say individually rational as this is the common terminology in matching theory. However, recall that this is the same as voluntary participation.

Health Service clearinghouse and school choice matching mechanisms. Clearinghouses utilize *deferred acceptance algorithms*, some of which will be discussed in this chapter.

9.2.1 One-to-One Matching

Our first model of the one-to-one matching problem is when every agent matches with at most one other agent (i.e., $q_{m_i} = 1$ for all $m_i \in M$) and once the match of two agents is made, those two agents are no longer available to match with any other agent. A **feasible one-to-one matching** $\mu : M \cup W \rightarrow M \cup W$ is a set of compatible matches $m_i w_j$ where each m_i and w_j occur in at most one matching; that is, $m_i = \mu(w_j)$ if and only if $w_j = \mu(m_i)$.

The first major contribution to this theory was the Gale-Shapley Marriage Market Model by Gale and Shapley (1962). In the Gale-Shapley Marriage Market Model, the two disjoint sets of agents are the set of men M and of women W. Each agent has complete and transitive preferences. Each man lists his preferences in a list of **acceptable** choices such that any woman listed after the choice of the agent himself is not acceptable and the man would prefer to remain unmatched. In addition, each woman lists her preferences in a list of **acceptable** choices such that any man listed after the choice of the agent herself is not acceptable and the woman would prefer to remain unmatched. The outcome is a matching μ such that agents are either matched with an agent on the other side of the market or matched with themselves.

Theorem 9.1 (Existence Theorem [Gale and Shapley, 1962]). *In the Gale-Shapley marriage market, there always exists a stable matching.*

Proof. A matching is found by using the following deferred acceptance algorithm. Note that if agents' preferences are not strict, then ties are broken arbitrarily by a preselected ordering.

Step 1 a: Each m_i proposes to the most preferred w_j in his list of acceptable choices (if any w_j are acceptable).

Step 1 b: Each w_j temporarily accepts (holds) the proposal of the m_i that she most prefers, rejecting all others if she receives more than one proposal, and rejects any unacceptable proposal.

Step k a: Each m_i who has been rejected in the previous step $k-1$ proposes to his next most preferred choice, a w_j who has not yet rejected him. If no w_j remains in m_i's list of acceptable choices, m_i makes no proposal.

Step k b: Each w_j holds her most preferred proposal to date and rejects all others.

This algorithm stops when no further proposals are made. The outcome is to match each m_i with the w_j (if any) who is holding his proposal. Thus each m_i is either matched with a w_j with whom he proposed or has been rejected by all w_j in his list of acceptable choices, thus remaining single or unmatched. In addition, any w_j, who did not receive any acceptable proposals, also remains single or unmatched.

We can see that the algorithm always results in a stable matching because if some man preferred a woman other than the one he is matched to, then he must have previously proposed to that woman and she must have rejected him. Then it must be true that the woman is matched with another man that she strictly prefers. Therefore, the two cannot form a blocking pair and the matching is stable.   QED

Example 9.1. Deferred Acceptance Algorithm

Let there be three men and three women with the following preferences.

R^{m_1}	R^{m_2}	R^{m_3}	R^{w_1}	R^{w_2}	R^{w_3}
w_1	w_3	w_3	m_3	m_3	m_2
w_2	w_1	w_1	m_1	w_2	m_1
m_1	w_2	m_3	w_1	m_2	m_3
w_3	m_2	w_2	m_2	m_1	w_3

Suppose every agent reports his preferences as stated above and the men propose in the deferred acceptance algorithm, which takes the following steps.

Step 1 a: m_1 proposes to w_1; m_2 and m_3 propose to w_3.
Step 1 b: w_1 holds m_1's proposal; w_3 rejects m_3's proposal and holds m_2's proposal.
Step 2 a: m_3 proposes to w_1.
Step 2 b: w_1 rejects m_1's proposal and holds m_3's proposal.
Step 3 a: m_1 proposes to w_2.
Step 3 b: w_2 rejects m_1's proposal.

No further proposals are made and the outcome is the following stable matching μ:
$\mu(m_1) = m_1$, $\mu(m_2) = w_3$, $\mu(m_3) = w_1$, $\mu(w_1) = m_3$, $\mu(w_2) = w_2$ and $\mu(w_3) = m_2$. $\Diamond$

Notice that both m_1 and w_2 remain unmatched in the above example. This is the case because although m_1 prefers to be matched with w_2 than to be unmatched, w_2 prefers to be unmatched than to be matched with m_1. Therefore, w_2 rejects m_1's proposal.

Gale and Shapley (1962) found that the side of the market who makes the proposals in the algorithm affects the outcome of the game. We see that the side of the market, which proposes in the deferred acceptance algorithm receives the outcome that is best for the members of that side. This is stated in the following theorem. First, let the **M-optimal** stable matching be a stable matching in which no man prefers another stable matching, while the **W-optimal** stable matching be a stable matching in which no woman prefers another stable matching.

Theorem 9.2 (First Optimality Theorem [Gale and Shapley, 1962]). *An M-optimal stable matching always exists when men propose in the deferred acceptance algorithm and all agents have strict preferences. Additionally, an W-optimal stable matching always exists when women propose in the deferred acceptance algorithm and all agents have strict preferences.*

In addition, theorem 9.2. holds independently of the order in which the proposing side proposes. A mechanism in this case specifies which side proposes and then that the algorithm we described takes place. The next example shows how the optimal stable matching may be different when a different side of the market proposes, so the men-proposing and women-proposing mechanisms may result in different outcomes.

Example 9.2. Deferred Acceptance Algorithm: M-optimal Versus W-optimal
Let there be four men and three women with the following preferences.

R^{m_1}	R^{m_2}	R^{m_3}	R^{m_4}	R^{w_1}	R^{w_2}	R^{w_3}
w_1	w_3	w_2	w_1	m_2	m_4	m_1
w_3	w_1	m_3	w_2	m_1	m_2	m_4
w_2	w_2	w_1	w_3	m_4	m_3	m_2
m_1	m_2	w_3	m_4	w_1	m_1	m_3
				m_3	w_2	w_3

Suppose every agent reports his preferences as stated above and the men propose in the deferred acceptance algorithm, which takes the following steps.
Step 1 a: m_1 proposes to w_1; m_2 proposes to w_3; m_3 proposes to w_2; and m_4 propose to w_1.
Step 1 b: w_1 rejects m_4's proposal and holds m_1's proposal; w_2 holds m_3's proposal; and w_3 holds m_2's proposal.
Step 2 a: m_4 proposes to w_2.
Step 2 b: w_2 rejects m_3's proposal and holds m_4's proposal.
Step 3 a: m_3 proposes to w_3.
Step 3 b: w_3 rejects m_3's proposal.
Step 4 a: m_3 proposes to w_1.
Step 4 b: w_1 rejects m_3's proposal.
No further proposals are made and the outcome is the following M-optimal stable matching μ^M: $\mu^M(m_1) = w_1$, $\mu^M(m_2) = w_3$, $\mu^M(m_3) = m_3$, $\mu^M(m_4) = w_2$, $\mu^M(w_1) = m_1$, $\mu^M(w_2) = m_4$, and $\mu^M(w_3) = m_2$.
Now suppose the women propose in the deferred acceptance algorithm, which takes the following steps:
Step 1 a: w_1 proposes to m_2; w_2 proposes to m_4; and w_3 proposes to m_1.

Step 1 b: m_1 holds w_3's proposal; m_2 holds w_1's proposal; and m_4 holds w_2's proposal. No further proposals are made and the outcome is the following W-optimal stable matching μ^W: $\mu^W(m_1) = w_3$, $\mu^W(m_2) = w_1$, $\mu^W(m_3) = m_3$, $\mu^W(m_4) = w_2$, $\mu^W(w_1) = m_2$, $\mu^W(w_2) = m_4$, and $\mu^W(w_3) = m_1$.

We can see that $m_4 w_2$ is matched in both the M-optimal and W-optimal stable matchings. However, m_1 is matched with w_1 in the M-optimal stable matching, while he is matched with w_3 in the W-optimal stable matching. On the other hand, m_2 is matched with w_3 in the M-optimal stable matching, while he is matched with w_1 in the W-optimal stable matching. In addition, m_3 remains unmatched in both stable matchings. $\diamond$

Next, we see that not only do an M-optimal and W-optimal stable matching exist when all agents have strict preferences, but by the next theorem and corollary each is the worst stable matching for the other side of the market when all agents have strict preferences. That is, the M-optimal stable matching is the worst stable matching for women, while the W-optimal stable matching is the worst stable matching for men.

Theorem 9.3 (Knuth, 1976). *If all agents have strict preferences, then the common preferences of each side of the market are opposed on the set of stable matchings. That is, if μ and μ' are stable matchings, then all men like μ at least as well as μ' if and only if all women like μ' at least as well as μ.*

Corollary 9.1. *If all agents have strict preferences, then the M-optimal stable matching matches each woman to her least preferred acceptable choice. In addition, the W-optimal stable matching matches each man to his least preferred acceptable choice.*

Structural Properties of the Marriage Market Model

Here we will describe the mathematical structure of the set of stable matchings in the marriage market. The first theorem states that in the marriage market, no coalition can form, which would wish to block any stable matching.

Theorem 9.4 (Core in the Marriage Market [Roth and Sotomayor, 1990, page 55]). *In every economy in the domain $\mathcal{E}$, the core of the marriage market is equal to the set of stable matchings.*

The optimality theorems introduced in the previous section lead us to the idea that the set of stable matchings has an algebraic structure called a *lattice*. However before we proceed to this finding, we first need some new notation and definitions.

A **partially ordered set** or **poset** $(X, \succ)$ consists of a set of alternatives X and a partial order relation $\succ$ defined on X. Here a **partial order** relation $\succ$ is reflexive, transitive and **antisymmetric**. When $x \succ y$, we say x is at least as good as y or x dominates y. A relation is **antisymmetric** if $\forall a, b \in X$, $a \succ b$ and $b \succ a \Rightarrow a = b$.

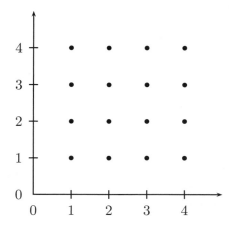

Figure 9.1: Example 9.3. A Lattice

An element $x \in X$ is an **upper bound** for a nonempty subset A of X if $x \succ a$ for every $a \in A$. Then a **least upper bound** for $A \subseteq X$ is an element $x \in X$ that is dominated by every upper bound in A. On the other hand, an element $x \in X$ is a **lower bound** for a nonempty subset A of X if $a \succ x$ for every $a \in A$. Then a **greatest lower bound** for $A \subseteq X$ is an element $x \in X$ that dominates every lower bound in A.

We can now formally define a lattice.

Definition 9.2. A **lattice** L is a partially ordered set in which every pair of elements has a least upper bound and a greatest lower bound.

Denote $x \vee y$ as the least upper bound of any two elements x and y in a lattice L, where $x \vee y$ is an element of L called the **join** of x and y. Denote $x \wedge y$ as the greatest lower bound of any two elements x and y in a lattice L, where $x \wedge y$ is an element of L called the **meet** of x and y. Join and meet are analogous to set union and intersection. That is, for any two sets X and Y, their join is $X \vee Y = X \cup Y$, their union, and their meet is $X \wedge Y = X \cap Y$, their intersection.

Example 9.3. This example is similar to example 1.34 of Carter (2001, page 26).

Let $X = \{1, 2, 3, 4\}$. Then the partially ordered set $L = X \times X$ is a lattice. Here the join and meet of any two elements (x_1, x_2) and (y_1, y_2) in L are defined as

$$(x_1, x_2) \vee (y_1, y_2) = (\max\{x_1, y_1\}, \max\{x_2, y_2\}),$$
$$(x_1, x_2) \wedge (y_1, y_2) = (\min\{x_1, y_1\}, \min\{x_2, y_2\}).$$

See figure 9.1. The least upper bound and the greatest lower bound of $(3, 1)$ and $(2, 2)$

are given as follows.

$$(3,1) \vee (2,2) = (\max\{3,2\}, \max\{1,2\}) = (3,2),$$
$$(3,1) \wedge (2,2) = (\min\{3,2\}, \min\{1,2\}) = (2,1)$$

$$\Diamond$$

Returning to our matching model, if every man is at least as well off under the matching μ as under μ', then we write $\mu\ R^M\ \mu'$. Similarly, if every woman is at least as well off under the matching μ as under μ', we write $\mu\ R^W\ \mu'$. Then the lattice theorem, which is attributed to John Conway in Knuth (1976), can be stated as follows:

Theorem 9.5 (Lattice Theorem; John Conway). *The set of stable matchings ordered by R^M and set of stable matchings ordered by R^W are lattices. In addition, the M-lattice and the W-lattice are opposite in the sense that if $\mu\ R^M\ \mu'$, then $\mu'\ R^W\ \mu$.*

Three additional structural properties, which follow from the matching lattice property, were found by Gale and Sotomayor (1985).

Theorem 9.6 (Invariance Theorem [Gale and Sotomayor,1985]). *Each man or woman matched under one stable matching is matched under all stable matchings.*

Theorem 9.7 (Comparative Statics Theorem [Gale and Sotomayor,1985]). *When a new man enters the market, then no woman is worse off in either the M-optimal matching or the W-optimal matching. When a new woman enters the market, then no man is worse off in either the M-optimal matching or the W-optimal matching.*

Finally, the third structural property shows that no matching exists, whether it is stable or not, such that every man can be made better off than in the M-optimal stable matching. The same can be said for the women. Formally, this is stated in the following theorem.

Theorem 9.8 (Second Optimality Theorem [Roth, 1982a]). *The M-optimal stable matching μ^M is weakly Pareto optimal for each man in the set of all matchings. In other words, there is no matching μ in which every man is made strictly better off than if he is under the M-optimal stable matching μ^M. In addition, the W-optimal stable matching μ^W is weakly Pareto optimal for each woman in the set of all matchings. In other words, there is no matching μ in which every woman is made strictly better off than if she is under the W-optimal stable matching μ^W.*

Strategies in the Marriage Market Model

The next question is whether a mechanism can be designed such that all agents wish to report their true preferences. To answer this question, Roth (1982a) found that there is no mechanism in which it is a best response for all agents to report their preferences truthfully. However, Dubins and Freedman (1981) and Roth (1982a) found that a mechanism may be designed in which one side of the market does wish to truthfully report their preferences. These findings are stated in the following two theorems.

Theorem 9.9 (Impossibility Theorem [Roth, 1982a]). *No stable matching mechanism exists such that stating the true preferences is a dominant strategy for every agent.*

Example 9.4. Dominant Stategies: Truthful or Not?

Let there be three men and three women that submit truthfully the following preferences.

R^{m_1}	R^{m_2}	R^{m_3}	R^{w_1}	R^{w_2}	R^{w_3}
w_1	w_3	w_2	m_3	m_1	m_3
w_2	w_1	w_1	m_2	m_3	m_2
w_3	w_2	w_3	m_1	m_2	m_1
m_1	m_2	m_3	w_1	w_2	w_3

Suppose every agent reports his preferences as stated above and the men propose in the deferred acceptance algorithm, which takes the following steps.

Step 1 a: m_1 proposes to w_1; m_2 proposes to w_3; and m_3 propose to w_2.

Step 1 b: w_1 holds m_1's proposal; w_2 holds m_3's proposal; and w_3 holds m_2's proposal. No further proposals are made and the outcome is the following stable matching μ: $\mu(m_1) = w_1$, $\mu(m_2) = w_3$, $\mu(m_3) = w_2$, $\mu(w_1) = m_1$, $\mu(w_2) = m_3$, and $\mu(w_3) = m_2$.

However, we will see that w_1's best response to the truthful reports of all other agents is to report an untruthful preference ordering such that $m_3\ P^{w_1}\ m_2\ P^{w_1}\ w_1\ P^{w_1}\ m_1$. With this untruthful reporting of preferences by w_1, the men-proposing deferred acceptance algorithm takes the following steps resulting in a different matching μ', which is a strictly better outcome for w_1.

Step 1 a: m_1 proposes to w_1; m_2 proposes to w_3; and m_3 propose to w_2.

Step 1 b: w_1 rejects m_1's proposal; w_2 holds m_3's proposal; and w_3 holds m_2's proposal.

Step 2 a: m_1 proposes to w_2.

Step 2 b: w_2 rejects m_3's proposal and holds m_1's proposal.

Step 3 a: m_3 proposes to w_1.

Step 3 b: w_1 holds m_3's proposal.

No further proposals are made and the outcome is the following stable matching μ'. $\mu'(m_1) = w_2$, $\mu'(m_2) = w_3$, $\mu'(m_3) = w_1$, $\mu'(w_1) = m_3$, $\mu'(w_2) = m_1$ and $\mu'(w_3) = m_2$. $\diamond$

The next result shows that the fact that a woman and not a man has an incentive to misreport her preferences when men propose should not be too surprising.

Theorem 9.10 (Dominant Strategies; Dubins and Freedman [1981]; Roth [1982a]). *The mechanism that yields the M-optimal stable matching, in terms of stated preferences, makes it a dominant strategy for each man to state his true preferences. On the other hand, the mechanism that yields the W-optimal stable matching, in terms of stated preferences, makes it a dominant strategy for each woman to state her true preferences.*

Note that when a mechanism, which implements the best outcome for an agent, is employed, then that agent would have no incentive to state anything other than his or her true preferences. Therefore, when a mechanism resulting in the M-optimal stable matching is employed, every man chooses to state his true preferences. Also, when a mechanism resulting in the W-optimal stable matching is employed, every woman chooses to state her true preferences.

We can view this result as a echo of the Gibbard-Satterthwaite theorem (theorem 1.3 on page 17). That theorem said that the only way to make an agent always report truthfully is to make the agent a dictator. Here, the privileged side of the market has no incentive to misreport. While the agents on the privileged side are not dictators, they are treated better by the mechanism than the other agents. The mechanism designer can ensure truthful reporting of preferences only on the side she chooses to privilege—the battle of the sexes is not settled by this theorem.

9.2.2 Many-to-One Matching

One-to-one matching works well for the marriage problem. However, this type of matching does not solve the college admissions or job matching problems where each college or firm may have matches with multiple individual agents, but each individual agent may match with only one college or firm. This is called the many-to-one matching problem.

In many-to-one matching problems, each agent from the set W may match with only one agent from the set M, while every agent from the set M may match with more than one agent from the set W. Thus, the quota of each m_i may be greater than one, i.e., $q_{m_i} \geq 1$ for all $m_i \in M$). A **feasible many-to-one matching** is a correspondence $\mu : M \cup W \rightarrow\rightarrow M \cup W$ such that $w_j \in \mu(m_i)$ if and only if $\mu(w_j) = m_i$.

We will see how theorem 9.2 fares in the many-to-one matching problem. That is, in college admission or job matching models there are college- or firm-optimal (M-optimal) stable matchings and student- or worker-optimal (W-optimal) stable matchings. However, while it is still true that the W-optimal stable matching is the best outcome for the students or workers, it does not hold that the M-optimal stable matching is necessarily the best outcome for the colleges or firms. Nevertheless, it is still true that which side of the market receives their optimal outcome depends on which side is the first to take action.

In addition, in the many-to-one problem there no longer exists a mechanism that makes it a dominant strategy for colleges or firms to state their true preferences. However, it is still possible to design a mechanism that makes it a dominant strategy for students and workers to state their true preferences.

Note that in the following sections colleges and firms are denoted by m_i, while students and workers are denoted by w_j.

College Admissions Problem

The original college admissions model was introduced by Gale and Shapley (1962) as an extension to their marriage market model. They extended that model by allowing each college to accept at most its quota q of students in each round of the algorithm according to its preferences, and to reject all others. Gale and Sotomayor (1985) in turn extended the Gale and Shapley marriage market model through the replication technique that we describe next.

Let each college m_i have a quota q_i of how many students it may admit. Then through replication, each college is represented by q_i agents each with the same preferences over the students. At the same time, each student lists each of the q_i replicated agents in a consecutive list on her preference ordering over colleges. By representing the college admissions model through replication, it is easier to compare the results found for the marriage market model to the college admissions model.

To compare the results of the marriage market model and the college admissions model, Roth introduced **responsive** preferences, which restricts the admissible preferences of colleges in the domain. Such preferences state that students are substitutes rather than complements in the colleges' preference rankings. That is, if a college m_i faces a set of students S such that the number of students in the set is less than the quota of the college q_{m_i}, and m_i has the choice of adding one of two students w_j or w_k to S, then m_i prefers S to contain the more preferred student as long as m_i prefers to be matched with the student rather than leaving a position open. Formally this is stated as follows.

Definition 9.3 (Responsive Preferences). Each college m_i has preferences over sets of students, such that for any set $S \subseteq W$ where $|S| < q_i$, and any students w_j and w_k not in S, m_i prefers $S \cup \{w_j\}$ to $S \cup \{w_k\}$ if and only if $w_j\ P^{m_i}\ w_k$, and prefers $S \cup \{w_j\}$ to S if and only if w_j is acceptable[3] to m_i.

Roth (1985) finds that when colleges have responsive preferences both theorem 9.1. and theorem 9.2. hold. However, the following theorem differs from theorem 9.8. as Roth proves that the M-optimal stable matching may no longer be the best outcome for the colleges.

Theorem 9.11 (Roth, 1985). *If all agents have strict preferences, then the W-optimal stable matching is weakly Pareto optimal for the students. However, when colleges have responsive preferences, the M-optimal stable matching need not be even weakly Pareto optimal for the colleges.*

We prove that there may exist a solution other than the M-optimal stable matching that every college may strictly prefer by following the proof by example that Roth (1985) presents in his paper.

Proof. Let there be three colleges and four students with the following preferences.

R^{m_1}	R^{m_2}	R^{m_3}	R^{w_1}	R^{w_2}	R^{w_3}	R^{w_4}
w_1	w_1	w_3	m_3	m_2	m_1	m_1
w_2	w_2	w_1	m_1	m_1	m_3	m_2
w_3	w_3	w_2	m_2	m_3	m_2	m_3
w_4	w_4	w_4	w_1	w_2	w_3	w_4
m_1	m_2	m_3				

Let each college face the following quotas: $q_{m_1} = 2$, $q_{m_2} = 1$, and $q_{m_3} = 1$. The M-optimal stable matching μ^M is as follows: $\mu^M(m_1) = (w_3, w_4)$, $\mu^M(m_2) = w_2$, $\mu^M(m_3) = w_1$, $\mu^M(w_1) = m_3$, $\mu^M(w_2) = m_2$, $\mu^M(w_3) = m_1$, and $\mu^M(w_4) = m_1$.

Next consider the feasible outcome μ' such that $\mu'(m_1) = (w_2, w_4)$, $\mu'(m_2) = w_1$, $\mu'(m_3) = w_3$, $\mu'(w_1) = m_2$, $\mu'(w_2) = m_1$, $\mu'(w_3) = m_3$, and $\mu'(w_4) = m_1$. The outcome μ' gives colleges m_2 and m_3 each their first choice student, which they both strictly prefer to their outcomes under μ^M. Since college m_1 has responsive preferences, it strictly prefers μ', which assigns m_1 its second and fourth choice as opposed to being assigned its third and fourth choice as in μ^M. Thus every college strictly prefers μ' to μ^M.   QED

Roth then answers the strategic question of whether a mechanism can be designed in a way that the students and colleges have incentives to truthfully reveal their preferences over the other side of the market. He finds that the impossibility theorem 9.9 holds in the

---

[3]See page 205 for the definition of "acceptable."

college admissions problem, but theorem 9.10 no longer holds for colleges. When colleges have responsive preferences, it is no longer the case that the M-optimal stable matching makes it a dominant strategy for each college to state its true preferences. In fact, as the following theorem states, no stable matching mechanism induces every college to state its preferences truthfully.

Theorem 9.12 (Roth, 1985). *The mechanism that yields the W-optimal stable matching in the college admissions problem makes it a dominant strategy for every student to state her true preferences. However, when colleges have responsive preferences, no stable matching mechanism exists that makes it a dominant strategy for every college to state its true preferences.*

In addition, each college has the private information of how many students they may admit. Sönmez (1997) finds that although colleges prefer to fill their quotas if they can get the students that they prefer, he proves the following impossibility result.

Theorem 9.13 (Sönmez, 1997). *No stable matching mechanism exists such that it is a dominant strategy for every college to always state its true quota.*

Sönmez (1997) proved this theorem for a hospital-intern match, which is analogous to the college-student match. The following proof, given by Sönmez (1997), begins by proving the theorem for two hospitals (colleges) and three interns (students).

Proof. Let there be two colleges and three students with the following responsive preferences.

R^{m_1}	R^{m_2}	R^{w_1}	R^{w_2}	R^{w_3}
$\{w_1, w_2, w_3\}$	$\{w_1, w_2, w_3\}$	m_2	m_1	m_1
$\{w_1, w_2\}$	$\{w_2, w_3\}$	m_1	m_2	m_2
$\{w_1, w_3\}$	$\{w_1, w_3\}$	w_1	w_2	w_3
w_1	w_3			
$\{w_2, w_3\}$	$\{w_1, w_2\}$			
w_2	w_2			
w_3	w_1			
m_1	m_2			

Let each college face the following quotas: $q_{m_1} = q_{m_2} = 2$ and $q'_{m_1} = q'_{m_2} = 1$.

Let both colleges state a quota of $q_{m_i} = 2$. Whether the college-proposing deferred acceptance algorithm or the student-proposing deferred acceptance algorithm is employed, the stable matching is μ, the M-optimal and W-optimal stable matching $\mu^M = \mu^W = \mu$, defined by: $\mu(m_1) = (w_2, w_3)$, $\mu(m_2) = w_1$, $\mu(w_1) = m_2$, $\mu(w_2) = m_1$, and $\mu(w_3) = m_1$.

Let m_1 state a quota of $q_{m_1} = 2$, while m_2 states a quota of $q'_{m_2} = 1$. Then the W'-optimal stable matching is the same as the W-optimal stable matching, which is μ. However, the M'-optimal stable matching $\mu^{M'}$ is: $\mu^{M'}(m_1) = (w_1, w_2)$, $\mu^{M'}(m_2) = w_3$, $\mu^{M'}(w_1) = m_1$, $\mu^{M'}(w_2) = m_1$ and $\mu^{M'}(w_3) = m_2$.

Let both colleges state a quota of $q'_{m_i} = 1$. Again the M''-optimal and W''-optimal stable matchings are the same or $\mu^{M''} = \mu^{W''} = \mu''$, which is as follows: $\mu''(m_1) = w_1$, $\mu''(m_2) = w_3$, $\mu''(w_1) = m_1$, $\mu''(w_2) = w_2$ and $\mu''(w_3) = m_2$.

Suppose that when m_1 states $q_{m_1} = 2$ and m_2 states $q'_{m_2} = 1$, the student-proposing deferred acceptance algorithm is employed, which results in the stable matching μ. Then m_2 states its true quota, m_1 is better off by underreporting its quota as $q'_{m_1} = 1$ because m_1 strictly prefers μ'' to μ; that is, $w_1 \, P^{m_1} \, \{w_2, w_3\}$.

Otherwise, if when m_1 states $q_{m_1} = 2$ and m_2 states $q'_{m_2} = 1$, the college-proposing deferred acceptance algorithm is employed, the stable matching is $\mu^{M'}$. Then if m_2's true quota is $q_{m_1} = 2$, m_2 is better off by underreporting its quota as $q'_{m_2} = 1$ because m_2 strictly prefers $\mu^{M'}$ to μ; that is, $w_3 \, P^{m_2} \, w_1$.

To conclude the proof, the above argument is generalized to markets with more than two colleges and three students by including colleges whose top choice is to keep all their positions vacant and students whose top choice is not to go to college. QED

School Choice Problem

Closely related to the college admissions problem is the school choice problem. In this problem, city students are being matched to public schools. Here each student w_j may be matched to only one school m_i, while each school m_i may match with many students up to its quota q_{m_i} or maximum number of seats available. Every student has strict preferences over all the schools and each school has a strict priority ordering over students. However, the priority ordering of students does not represent school preferences, instead it represents the state or local laws that are imposed on the schools. This is the main difference between the school choice and college admissions problems. The school choice problem utilizes a clearinghouse (student assignment mechanism) to match every student to a school.

Abdulkadiroğlu and Sönmez (2003) compare the Boston student assignment mechanism, the Gale-Shapley student-optimal (W-optimal) stable mechanism and the Top Trading Cycles (TTC) mechanism.

In the Boston student assignment mechanism every student submits her preference ordering of the schools and every school submits its priority ranking of students as determined by the state and local laws. Given the submissions of the students and schools the mechanism is as follows:

Round 1: For each student, only her first choice school is considered. For each school, consider every student who has listed it as her first choice and match those students to the school one at a time following the school's priority order until either there are no seats left or there is no student left who listed the school as her first choice.

Round 2: For each remaining unmatched student, only her second choice school is considered. For each school with seats remaining available, consider every student who has listed it as her second choice and match those students to the school one at a time following the school's priority order until either there are no seats left or there is no student left who listed the school as her second choice.

Round k: For each remaining unmatched student, only her kth choice school is considered. For each school with seats remaining available, consider every student who has listed it as her kth choice and match those students to the school one at a time following the school's priority order until either there are no seats left or there is no student left who listed the school as her kth choice.

The Boston student assignment mechanism is not strategy-proof.

The Gale-Shapley W-optimal stable mechanism applies the Gale-Shapley deferred acceptance algorithm by interpreting the priority ordering as preferences and is as follows.

Step 1 a: Each w_j proposes to the most preferred m_i in her list of acceptable choices.

Step 1 b: Each m_i temporarily accepts (holds) the proposals of each w_j one at a time following its priority ordering. Any remaining proposers are rejected.

Step k a: Each w_j who has been rejected in the previous step $k-1$ proposes to her next most preferred choice, an m_i who has not yet rejected her.

Step k b: Each m_i considers the students it has been holding and its new proposers and holds each w_j one at a time following its priority ordering. Any remaining proposers are rejected.

This algorithm stops when no student proposal is rejected and each student is matched with the school that is holding her proposal in the final step.

As theorem 9.10 states, the Gale-Shapley W-optimal stable mechanism is strategy-proof. However, the Gale-Shapley W-optimal stable mechanism may not be Pareto efficient.

The TTC mechanism finds matches using the TTC algorithm, which is attributed to David Gale. In each step, at least one *cycle* exists, which is first defined as follows:

Definition 9.4. A cycle $(m_{i_1}, w_{i_1}, m_{i_2}, \ldots, m_{i_k}, w_{i_k})$ is an ordered list of schools and students, where m_{i_1} announces w_{i_1}, w_{i_1} announces m_{i_2}, $\ldots$, m_{i_k} announces w_{i_k}, w_{i_k} announces m_{i_1}.

Then the TTC algorithm is as follows:

Step 1: Each school is assigned a counter that keeps track of how many seats it has left, which is initially set at its quota. Each student announces her most preferred school. Each school announces the student who has the highest priority for the school. For each cycle, every student in the cycle is assigned a seat to the school she announces and the counter of the school is reduced by one. When the counter of a school reduces to zero, the school is removed.

Step k: Each unassigned student announces her most preferred school among the remaining schools. Each remaining school announces the student with the highest priority among the remaining students. For each cycle, every student in the cycle is assigned a seat to the school she announces and the counter of the school is reduced by one. When the counter of a school reduces to zero, the school is removed.

This algorithm stops when all students are matched to a school.

Abdulkadiroğlu and Sönmez (2003) find that the TTC mechanism is Pareto efficient and strategy-proof.

Job Matching Problem

A frequently cited job matching model is that of the Kelso and Crawford (1982) salary-adjustment process. In their model, the two disjoint sets of agents are firms $M = \{m_1, \ldots, m_n\}$ and workers $W = \{w_1, \ldots, w_p\}$. While each firm m_i can hire as many workers as it wishes, each worker w_j can only work for one firm and receives the salary $s_{m_i w_j}$. Each m_i has a production function $y_{m_i}(C_{m_i})$, where C_{m_i} is the set of workers hired by m_i. The three main assumptions employed by Kelso and Crawford are marginal product (MP), "no-free-lunch" (NFL), and gross substitutes (GS), which are as follows:

MP a worker's marginal product to a firm must be greater than the lowest salary that she is willing to accept from the firm;

NFL a firm who has no workers produces nothing; and,

GS workers are gross substitutes in that "increases in other workers' salaries can never cause a firm to withdraw an offer from a worker whose salary has not risen."

Then the salary-adjustment process (or firm-proposing deferred acceptance algorithm) presented by Kelso and Crawford has five rounds where offers can be held over many periods before rejecting or firmly accepting, such that

1. Each firm learns the minimum acceptable salary for each agent to work and makes this offer to each agent.

2. Each firm makes offers to its favorite set of agents which maximize its profit function

$$\pi_{m_i}(C_{m_i}, s_{m_i}) \equiv y_{m_i}(C_{m_i}) - \sum_{w_j \in C_{m_i}} s_{m_i w_j}, \tag{9.1}$$

where $s_{m_i} = (s_{m_i w_1}, \ldots, s_{m_i w_1})$ is the vector of salaries paid by m_i.

3. Each worker rejects all but one offer which she tentatively accepts.

4. Offers that were not previously rejected do not change. However, firms have the option of increasing an offer by one unit if it was rejected in the previous round.

5. The process stops when there are no rejections and each worker accepts the offer that she has not previously rejected.

Two main results of Kelso and Crawford are the following two existence theorems.

Theorem 9.14 (Kelso and Crawford, 1982). *The salary-adjustment process converges in finite time to a core allocation in the market with discrete integer salaries.*

Theorem 9.15 (Kelso and Crawford, 1982). *Every market with a continuous measurement of salaries has a strict core allocation.*

Decentralized Matching Mechanisms

Thus far, the models discussed are centralized matching mechanisms. However, decentralized models better reflect the reality of many college admission and job matching problems where a centralized model does not work. Recent decentralized models were presented by Haeringer and Wooders (2007) and Niederle and Yariv (2007).

The model by Haeringer and Wooders is a sequential game of complete information where agents make their decisions independently of other agents and a worker is not required to hold an offer even though she prefers the offer to having no job in the end of the game. In addition, their model does not allow workers to hold offers and each worker's acceptance decision is irreversible. In their job market game agents do not act simultaneously and each time period has two stages as follows:

First Stage In each subsequent time period, firms that have not been matched sequentially make offers to at most one worker the firm had not made an offer to yet.

Second Stage In each time period, each worker may reject all offers made to her or accept only one of the offers.

When an offer is accepted, the worker and firm are matched and leave the market.

Haeringer and Wooders show that the W-optimal matching is the unique subgame perfect equilibrium outcome.

Theorem 9.16 (Haeringer and Wooders, 2007). *The subgame perfect equilibrium outcome of the job market game is the W-optimal matching.*

Niederle and Yariv (2007) study when firms allow agents to hold offers from period to period (perhaps waiting for a better offer) and when firms can make **exploding offers** (where agents must accept or reject the offer immediately). Additional assumptions include (1) an agent is not allowed to reject an offer if that offer is preferable to being unmatched, and (2) offer acceptances are irreversible.

In addition, Niederle and Yariv study both complete and incomplete information models. Here a complete information (CI) model is a model where every agent knows his own utilities from the possible matches and those of every other agent. A complete private information (CPI) model is a model where every agent knows only his own utilities from the possible matches. Finally, an incomplete private information (IPI) model is a model where every firm knows only its own utilities from the possible matches, while every worker does not know her own utility from a match with a firm until she receives an offer from the firm.

The job market game introduced by Niederle and Yariv has an infinite time horizon and in each period there are two stage such that at each time the following occurs:

First Stage All firms simultaneously determine which offers to make to the workers. Each offer made by a firm includes a deadline by which the offer must be accepted or rejected.

Second Stage Each worker who receives an offer, decides whether to accept or reject the offer, only being able to hold the offer until the end of the deadline specified by the firm making the offer.

Once offers are accepted the worker and firm are matched and both leave the market. In each period that a firm has not yet hired and has no offers being held by a worker, the firm may make only one offer to an unmatched worker. In addition, both firms and workers can choose to leave the market at any time and remain unmatched.

Niederle and Yariv (2007) find that there is a unique stable matching for their model. They then state the following propositions about how the unique stable matching is implemented. We present these propositions here without proof to give you an idea of the scope of this model; Niederle and Yariv (2007) has proofs and discussion.

Proposition 9.1 (Complete Information [Niederle and Yariv, 2007]). For any economy, for a sufficiently high discount rate, in the market game with offers of any length (exploding or not), any Nash equilibrium in weakly undominated strategies generates a matching that coincides with the unique stable matching.

Proposition 9.2 (CPI with Open Offers [Niederle and Yariv, 2007]). For any economy, for a sufficiently high discount rate, in the market game with complete private information and open offers, any Bayesian equilibrium in weakly undominated strategies generates a matching that coincides with the unique stable matching for each utility realization.

Proposition 9.3 (CPI with Exploding Offers [Niederle and Yariv, 2007]). For any economy, for a sufficiently high discount rate, in the market game with complete private information and exploding offers, there exists a Bayesian equilibrium in weakly undominated strategies that implements the unique stable matching for each utility realization.

Proposition 9.4 (IPI with Open Offers [Niederle and Yariv, 2007]). For any economy, for a sufficiently high discount rate, in the market game with incomplete private information and open offers, there is a Bayesian equilibrium in weakly undominated strategies that generates the unique stable matching.

Finally, Niederle and Yariv find that when firms can make exploding offers and agents do not have complete information, then there may not be any equilibrium outcomes that lead to the unique stable matching. First, they define a **rich** economy as one in which all agents prefer a match to exiting the market and with positive probability there can be any possible combination of match utility preferences.

Proposition 9.5 (IPI: Thin Competition [Niederle and Yariv, 2007]). For any rich economy with at most three firms, for a sufficiently high discount rate, in the market game with incomplete private information and exploding offers, there is a Bayesian equilibrium in weakly undominated strategies that generates the unique stable matching.

Proposition 9.6 (IPI: Thick Competition [Niederle and Yariv, 2007]). For any rich economy with at most four firms and two workers, for any discount rate, in the market game with incomplete private information and exploding offers, there is no Bayesian equilibrium in weakly undominated strategies that generates a stable matching.

9.3 One-Sided Matching

One-sided matching theory is concerned with the matching of agents to an indivisible good, which has no preferences; that is, agents are matched with objects. In a one-sided matching problem, the matching μ is a matching of agents with the goods where each agent is matched with one and only one good.

9.3.1 The Shapley and Scarf House Market

Shapley and Scarf (1974) introduced a basic matching markets model where each agent in the market owns one (and only one) indivisible good called a house. In this model, each agent also has preferences over all of the houses in the market. Additionally, trade is only possible in houses, which means there is no money in this market.

In the Shapley and Scarf house market a matching μ is such that each agent is matched with at most one house. The matching μ is in the core if no coalition of agents exists, which can improve upon μ by trading their own houses. To find the core matching for any housing market, Shapley and Scarf use the **Top Trading Cycles** (TTC) algorithm. Here the definition of a cycle is slightly different then the definition previously stated.

Definition 9.5. A **cycle** is an ordered list of agents with each successive agent announcing the next agent in the list; that is, $(m_{i_1}, m_{i_2}, \ldots, m_{i_k})$ is a cycle, where m_{i_1} announces m_{i_2}, m_{i_2} announces $m_{i_3}, \ldots, m_{i_k}$ announces m_{i_1}.

The TTC algorithm is described as follows:

Step 1: Each agent in the market announces the owner of his most preferred house, which could be himself. At least one cycle exists. In each cycle, the exchange of houses occurs and every agent in the cycle is removed along with his house.

Step k: Each of the remaining agents announce the owner of his most preferred house among all of the remaining houses. There exists at least one cycle where the exchange of houses occurs and every agent in each cycle is removed along with his house.

The TTC algorithm ends when every agent is matched to one house.

Example 9.5. Let there be six agents with the following preferences over each agent's house:

R^{m_1}	R^{m_2}	R^{m_3}	R^{m_4}	R^{m_5}	R^{m_6}
m_3	m_4	m_1	m_5	m_1	m_3
m_2	m_5	m_6	m_1	m_6	m_4
m_6	m_2	m_2	m_6	m_4	m_6
m_5	m_6	m_3	m_3	m_2	m_1
m_4	m_3	m_5	m_4	m_5	m_2
m_1	m_1	m_4	m_2	m_3	m_5

Suppose every agent reports his preferences as stated above, then the TTC algorithm takes the following steps:

Step 1: Agent m_1 announces m_3; m_2 announces m_4; m_3 announces m_1; m_4 announces m_5; m_5 announces m_1; and, m_6 announces m_3. The only cycle that exists is $(m_1 m_3)$. Thus, m_1 and m_3 trade their houses.

Step 2: Agent m_2 announces m_4; m_4 announces m_5; m_5 announces m_6; and m_6 announces m_4. The only cycle that exists is (m_4, m_5, m_6). Here the exchange occurs such that m_4 trades for m_5's house, m_5 trades for m_6's house and m_6 trades for m_4's house.

Step 3: Agent m_2 is the only remaining agent and is thus matched with his own house. The matching μ in this house market is as follows: $\mu(m_1) = m_3$, $\mu(m_2) = m_2$, $\mu(m_3) = m_1$, $\mu(m_4) = m_5$, $\mu(m_5) = m_6$, and $\mu(m_6) = m_4$.   ◇

Theorem 9.17 (Core in the House Market [Shapley and Scarf, 1974]). *The TTC algorithm results in a matching in the core for each housing market.*

Roth (1982b) later found that all agents have the incentive to truthfully report their preferences when the TTC algorithm is used to find the matching in the house market.

Theorem 9.18 (Truth-telling in the House Market [Roth, 1982b]). *When agents have strict preferences over houses, the TTC algorithm is strategy-proof; that is, truth-telling is a dominant strategy for all agents when the TTC algorithm is used to produce the matching in the house market.*

9.3.2 House Allocation Problems

In house allocation problems, agents are matched to at most one object (house) from a set of houses, where some agents may have a prior claim to a particular house. Examples include matching students to college dormitories, workers to office spaces and workers to tasks.

In the case of college dormitories (dorms), each year students are placed into dorm rooms, which they have preferences over. While returning students have lived in a particular dorm room the prior year, new students have never lived in any of the dorm rooms. Therefore, a matching in this case must take into account the claim a returning student has on the dorm room he resided in the prior year. Additionally, the set of dorms include both empty rooms and rooms that are claimed by returning students.

Abdulkadiroğlu and Sönmez (1999) define the house allocation problem with existing agents (tenants) as a five-tuple, which includes a finite set of existing tenants, a finite set of newcomers, a finite set of occupied houses, a finite set of vacant houses and a list of strict preference orderings. Each tenant, who currently occupies a house, is entitled to keep the house, which is called squatter's rights. Every tenant has strict preferences over the houses and has use for only one house.

Note that the Shapley and Scarf house market is a special case of the house allocation problem where there are only existing tenants and occupied houses. On the other hand, the house allocation problem without existing tenants (Hylland and Zeckhauser, 1979) is where there are only newcomers and vacant houses.

In the house allocation problem, a lottery mechanism is often used, which selects a lottery for each house allocation problem. A **lottery** is a probability distribution over all matchings. When a house allocation mechanism gives positive probabilities to only Pareto efficient house allocations, then the mechanism is *ex post* Pareto efficient. If every existing tenant receives a house at least as good as the one he currently occupies, then the mechanism is *ex post* individually rational.

The first mechanism we will discuss is called **Random Serial Dictatorship with Squatting Rights**. This mechanism is widely used by colleges to assign their students to dormitories. The mechanism is as follows.

Step 1: Every existing tenant decides whether he will enter the housing lottery or keep his current house. Each tenant who wishes to keep his house is assigned it. All others become available for allocation in the lottery.

Step 2: Every agent in the lottery reports his preferences over the available houses.

Step 3: An ordering of agents in the lottery is randomly chosen from a given distribution of orderings.

Step 4: Given the ordering of the agents, each agent is assigned his top preference among the remaining available houses.

This mechanism is neither individually rational nor Pareto efficient because the lottery does not guarantee that existing tenants will receive a house at least as good as their current house and thus some tenants will select not to enter the lottery.

Abdulkadiroğlu and Sönmez (1999) introduce the next mechanism by modifying the TTC algorithm. In the mechanism every agent, existing tenants and newcomers, reports his preferences over all the houses, occupied and vacant. An ordering of all agents is randomly chosen from a given distribution of orderings. Then the following **you request my house—I get your turn** (YRMH—IGYT) algorithm is run.

Step 1: Given the ordering of the agents, each agent is assigned his top preference among the remaining available houses, until someone requests the house of an existing tenant.

Step 2: If the existing tenant of the house that is requested is already assigned a different house, then continue with the given ordering. Otherwise, change the remainder of the ordering by moving the existing tenant of the house requested to the top of the line before the requester and continuing with this new ordering.

Step 3: Every time someone requests the house of an existing tenant who has not yet been assigned a different house, reorder the remaining ordering by moving the existing tenant to the top of the line.

Step 4: If a cycle as defined in section 9.3.1 of existing tenants forms, then assign the houses to the agents in the cycle and proceed with the remainder of the ordering.

By moving an existing tenant to the top of the ordering when his house is requested, this algorithm ensures that the mechanism is individually rational. In addition, this mechanism is also Pareto efficient and strategy-proof.

9.3.3 The Kidney Exchange Problem

The best option for individuals with certain kidney diseases is to have a kidney transplant. Kidneys may be transplanted from either cadavers or live donors. Sometimes a patient in need of a kidney transplant may have a willing living donor. However, the donor's kidney may not be compatible with the patient and thus the kidney transplant is considered infeasible. In this case, the patient-donor pair may be able to exchange with another patient donor pair or with a patient on the cadaver waiting list.

Let the patient be denoted by m_i, the donor by w_j, and the patient-donor pair by (m_i, w_i). A **pairwise kidney exchange** occurs when there are two patient-donor pairs, both of whom the transplant from the donor to the intended patient is infeasible, such that each patient can feasibly receive a kidney transplant from the donor in the other pair. On the other hand, an **indirect kidney exchange** occurs when there is one patient-donor pair, for whom the transplant from the donor to the patient is infeasible, such that the patient in the pair receives high-priority on the cadaver list in exchange for his donor donating her kidney to a patient already on the cadaver waiting list.

Roth et al. (2004) introduce a kidney exchange model using the **Top Trading Cycles and Chains** (TTCC) algorithm, which extends the TTC algorithm used in house allocation problems. In their model, there is a set of living donors W that come from the patient-donor pairs. Each patient m_i from patient-donor pair (m_i, w_i) has strict preferences over the subset of donors who are compatible with him $K_{m_i} \subseteq K$, his own donor (who may or may not be compatible) w_i, and the option of being on the cadaver waiting list, c. The matching is such that every patient is matched to either a donor or the cadaver waiting list and each donor can be matched with at most one patient although more than one patient may be matched to the cadaver waiting list.

In the TTCC algorithm, cycles and c-chains are used. The definition of a cycle is as it was defined in section 9.3.1, such that every agent announces the patient whose paired donor he wishes to match with.

Definition 9.6. A **c-chain** is an ordered list of patients with each successive patient announcing the next patient in the list; that is, $(m_{i_1}, m_{i_2}, \ldots, m_{i_k})$ is a c-chain, where m_{i_1} announces m_{i_2}, m_{i_2} announces m_{i_3}, $\ldots$, m_{i_k} announces c.

The TTCC algorithm is described as follows.

Step 1: Each patient in the market announces the patient from the patient-donor pair of his most preferred donor, which could be himself, or the cadaver waiting list.

Step 2: There is either a cycle, or a c-chain, or both.

    (a) If no cycle exists, proceed to step 3. Otherwise, for each cycle, the kidney exchanges should occur. Then remove all patient-donor pairs in the cycle.

    (b) Each of the remaining patients announce the patient from the patient-donor pair of his most preferred donor among all of the remaining patient-donor pairs. For all cycles, the kidney exchanges should occur. Repeat this until no cycle exists.

Step 3: If there are no patient-donor pairs remaining, then the TTCC algorithm ends. Otherwise, each remaining pair is the end of a c-chain. Using a **chain selecion rule**, a rule that determines which c-chain is selected, select only one c-chain. In the selected c-chain, the kidney exchanges occur, the patient at the end of the chain goes onto the cadaver waiting list, and the chain selecion rule determines whether the donor paired with the first patient in the c-chain is immediately assigned to a cadaver waiting list patient or is kept in the algorithm.

Step 4: After each c-chain is selected, new cycles may form. Repeat steps 2 and 3 with the remaining patient-donor pairs and unassigned donors until no patient remains.

Roth et al. (2004) find that when any chain selection rule is employed that allows the donor who is not assigned a patient in a c-chain to remain in the algorithm, the TTCC algorithm is efficient. Additionally, they find that there exists chain selection rules such that the TTCC algorithm is Pareto efficient and strategy-proof. These findings are formally stated in the following theorems.

Theorem 9.19 (Roth et al., 2004). *The TTCC algorithm is efficient when the chain selection rule is set such that at any nonterminal round, the unassigned donor in a c-chain remains available for the next round of the algorithm.*

Theorem 9.20 (Roth et al., 2004). *There exists a TTCC algorithm that is Pareto efficient and strategy-proof.*

9.4 Exercises

Exercise 40: Deferred Acceptance Algorithm

Suppose there are three men and four women with the following preferences.

R^{m_1}	R^{m_2}	R^{m_3}	R^{w_1}	R^{w_2}	R^{w_3}
w_2	w_3	w_1	m_2	m_2	m_3
w_1	w_2	w_3	m_3	m_3	m_1
w_3	m_2	w_2	m_1	m_1	w_3
m_1	w_1	m_3	w_1	w_2	m_2

Using the deferred acceptance algorithm, find a stable matching when the men make the proposals and show the steps of the algorithm.

Exercise 41: First Optimality Theorem

Prove by contradiction theorem 9.2—First Optimality Theorem (Gale and Shapley, 1962).

Exercise 42: Lattice

Using the lattice L in example 9.3., find the least upper bound and the greatest lower bound for each of the following pairs of elements in L.

1. $(2, 2)$ and $(1, 3)$
2. $(3, 2)$ and $(4, 1)$
3. $(3, 2)$ and $(2, 3)$
4. $(3, 4)$ and $(4, 3)$

Exercise 43: College Admissions Problem

Verify the M-optimal stable matchings μ^M found in the proof of theorem 9.11.

Exercise 44: School Choice Problem

Suppose there are three public schools and five students with the following preferences.

R^{m_1}	R^{m_2}	R^{m_3}	R^{w_1}	R^{w_2}	R^{w_3}	R^{w_4}	R^{w_5}
w_1	w_2	w_3	m_1	m_3	m_2	m_2	m_2
w_5	w_3	w_5	m_2	m_2	m_3	m_3	m_1
w_4	w_5	w_4	m_3	m_1	m_1	m_1	m_3
w_2	w_1	w_2					
w_3	w_4	w_1					

In addition, let each public school have the following quota: $q_{m_1} = 2$, $q_{m_2} = 2$, and $q_{m_3} = 1$.

Find the matchings from each of the following mechanisms:

1. the Boston student assignment mechanism;
2. the Gale-Shapley W-optimal (student-optimal) stable mechanism; and
3. the Top Trading Cycles (TTC) mechanism.

Exercise 45: YRMH—IGYT Algorithm

Let $M_E = \{m_1, m_2, m_3, m_4\}$ be the set of existing tenants, $M_N = \{m_5, m_6, m_7\}$ be the set of newcomers, $W_O = \{w_1, w_2, w_3, w_4\}$ be the set of occupied houses and $W_V - \{w_5, w_6, w_7\}$ be the set of vacant houses. Here for each existing tenant $m_i \in M_E$, w_i is his current house. The agents have the following preferences over the houses:

R^{m_1}	R^{m_2}	R^{m_3}	R^{m_4}	R^{m_5}	R^{m_6}	R^{m_7}
w_1	w_4	w_7	w_7	w_6	w_3	w_4
w_2	w_5	w_3	w_6	w_1	w_2	w_7
w_3	w_2	w_2	w_4	w_3	w_7	w_6
w_4	w_1	w_5	w_1	w_2	w_1	w_3
w_5	w_3	w_4	w_3	w_5	w_6	w_1
w_6	w_6	w_1	w_2	w_4	w_4	w_5
w_7	w_7	w_6	w_5	w_7	w_5	w_2

Now let the ordering of the agents be as follows: $(m_3, m_7, m_2, m_5, m_6, m_4, m_1)$. Find the matching that results when the YRMH—IGYT algorithm is employed.

Chapter 10

Empirical Evidence on Mechanisms

10.1 Introduction

Economic design theory has influenced telecommunication spectrum auctions, electricity markets, and the markets for medical residents, to name a few. But relative to the size of the theoretical literature, there have been few real-world economic design applications, and the size of the empirical literature is still small. Economic designers have recently started carefully documenting the ways in which real-world economic situations depart from their simplifying assumptions of mistake-free, rational optimizing behavior in common knowledge, complete information environments.

In an early survey of the implementation theory literature, Laffont (1987) wrote "...any real applications will be made with crude approximations to the mechanisms obtained here ...considerations such as simplicity and stability to encourage trust, goodwill and cooperation, will have to be taken into account." Indeed, many mechanisms presented in this book are complicated, have high operating costs, or make unrealistic assumptions about human behavior. Many were designed to satisfy sufficiency proofs for implementability.

Many mechanisms exist in the abstract, and many theories of implementation have yet to be tested by formal observation. Studies of the private provision of public goods focus on the voluntary contribution mechanism and its close cousin, the provision point mechanism, described in section 10.2. Neither mechanism is incentive compatible, but both are easy to understand and used in the real world. For those and other more complicated mechanisms, much of the evidence comes from laboratory experiments. In experiments researchers can control agents' preferences, information, and payoffs while accurately recording their choices of strategy.

This chapter summarizes empirical research geared specifically toward mechanism design and implementation theory. We argue in chapter 1 and elsewhere that the study of market exchange may be viewed as a subset of this framework. This implies that markets should be included in this chapter. However, since the bulk of economics education and research is composed of the study of markets,[1] we will leave readers to rely on their own

---

[1] At least in the United States, where this was written.

resources for insights into that branch of the field. We also recognize that numerous empirical studies have been conducted on auctions, games and matching mechanisms. Those topics are also a subset of economic design, but they have become mini-fields in their own right with published surveys of their own.[2] The focus in this chapter will be on the evidence related to public good provision.

Of those areas, by far the largest literature relates to public goods. That area is surveyed in this chapter first, with emphasis on private provision through the voluntary contribution mechanism and several of its variants. Following that are sections on the observed incentive compatibility of some mechanisms, research on mechanism dynamics and tests of implementation concepts. In section 10.6, we discuss the experience of two researchers, Paul Milgrom and Alvin Roth, who have successfully applied economic design theory in practice. In that section we also examine two studies that illustrate how the principles of economic design may be used to understand real-world phenomena and address problems in resource allocation. The closing section highlights a few new areas of research, points out some open questions and examines the relationship of theory to practice.

10.2 Voluntary Contribution Mechanisms for Public Goods

We dare say some economists dream at night of producing bridges, park land and other non-rivalrous, non-excludable goods while eliminating free-riding. When we ask individuals to contribute some of their resources for a public good, there is a well-known tendency toward a less-than-optimal outcome. Unfortunately, the simple voluntary contribution mechanism for the provision of public goods lacks incentive compatibility.

The voluntary contribution mechanism's failure in theory to privately provide any resources to the production of non-excludable public goods, as demonstrated in Samuelson (1954), helped spur interest in economic design. In practice, however, the voluntary contribution mechanism fails only partially. The prediction that it will produce zero contributions and zero production of the public good has been refuted again and again in experiments and the real world (Ledyard, 1995). To understand human behavior in the production of public goods, we must relax some of Samuelson's implicit and

---

[2]For a survey of auction theory, real-world auctions and a discussion of the mechanism design approach in relation to real-world auction design, see Milgrom (2004, Chapter 1). Laffont (1997) surveys experimental research on auctions and Athey and Haile (2006) present econometric models of auctions. The *Handbook of Experimental Economics* (Kagel and Roth, 1995) contains surveys of experimental results for a variety of strategic economic interactions described by game theory and auction theory. Goeree and Holt (2001) give an entertaining overview of some of game theory's empirical successes and failures. For a survey of empirical results on game theory from a behavioral perspective, see Camerer (2004). To learn more about applied and empirical work in matching, see Niederle et al. (2008).

explicit assumptions: purely rational, selfish agents[3]; common knowledge of rationality and selfishness; one round of play; no communication among players; and no monitoring or punishment of free riders. Recent research on the voluntary contribution mechanism tests these assumptions and finds them to be too narrow.

In the field we see numerous examples of public goods provided wholly or partially through voluntary contributions: Charitable foundations, private colleges and office coffee clubs are just a few examples. Laboratory work by economists and other social scientists has produced important insights into how and why public goods are produced in spite of the incentive to free-ride. Ledyard (1995) provides a thorough and oft-cited survey of experimental research on the voluntary contribution mechanism up to 1995. He reports that the following conclusions may be drawn from the literature:

- Experimental subjects have not been found to fully meet the Nash equilibrium prediction of zero contribution.
- Results are sensitive to the payoff structure and design of the experiment.
- Subjects who can see each other and communicate with each other tend to contribute more to the public good.
- Contributions decline with repetition, often to the Nash equilibrium prediction of zero contribution.

The last item—contributions decline with repetition—has been found to be sensitive to the ability of players to punish free-riding. Several experiments have maintained high levels of contributions for multiple rounds by allowing punishment of free riders. Some experiments have found subjects are willing to punish free-riding at a cost to themselves. While humans have a tendency to free-ride, we also appear to "have a strong aversion against being the 'sucker'," as Fehr and Gächter (2000) put it in the introduction to a public goods study.

In that study, Fehr and Gächter conduct experiments on non-excludable public goods to learn what people will do if they have been contributing to a public good while other members of their group have enjoyed its benefits without contributing. In each of their experimental treatments, Fehr and Gächter's subjects play ten rounds of a voluntary contribution mechanism. The authors perform one set of experiments using a simple mechanism. Each of four players is endowed with some tokens. Each player chooses how many tokens to contribute to the public good. The payoff to each subject is the sum of the tokens they keep plus the benefit of the public good produced using the contributed tokens. Fehr and Gächter compare behavior in that mechanism to another scheme in which there is a second stage. In the second stage, players each learn what the other three players contributed. They are then given the option to, for a fee, punish any or all of their opponents by knocking 10 percent off their opponents' final payoffs. Fehr and Gächter set the fee so high that a rational, payoff-maximizing player would not find

---

[3]By selfish, we mean that their utility functions do not account for utility from altruistic choices.

it worthwhile to punish anyone. Because there should rationally be no repercussions to free-riding, the subgame perfect equilibrium is for all players to contribute nothing to the public good in both the one-stage and two-stage games.

Fehr and Gächter report that subjects playing the mechanism without punishment play free-riding or nearly free-riding strategies by the tenth round. In the mechanism with punishment, subjects contribute significant amounts to the public good for all ten rounds. When subjects play with the same partners for all ten rounds, their strategies come close to full contribution to the public good. Subjects punish opponents even when they are reassigned to new groups at each stage and should expect no future benefit to themselves from the punishment. The punishment option is used overwhelmingly on free-riders rather than agents who contribute a significant amount to the public good. Multiple studies support Fehr and Gächter's findings. They include Carpenter and Matthews (2002), Fehr and Gächter (2002), Masclet et al. (2003), Falk et al. (2005), Page et al. (2005), and Sefton et al. (2006).

Anderson and Putterman (2006) test whether punishment is better modeled as a rational choice by agents with pro-social preferences or as irrational anger. By randomly varying the cost of punishing other group members from round to round in a voluntary contribution mechanism, Anderson and Putterman find that people punish less if it costs more. This is consistent with pro-social preferences rather than irrational anger; an irrationally angry player would not consider the cost of punishment.[4]

Allowing punishment of free-riders is one way to get people to contribute to a public good. Another way is to cancel the good's production and give agents their money back if the mechanism operator does not collect enough contributions to cover the cost. Bagnoli and Lipman (1989) explore the theoretical properties of this "provision point" mechanism in the context of providing a non-excludable, though perhaps rivalrous, public good. In Bagnoli and Lipman's model, the group of economic agents has a well-defined membership. Each group member knows the public good's cost, the public good's payoff to all other group members, and all group members' wealth.

More formally, the provision point mechanism assumes I agents indexed by i. Let C represent the project's cost, w the profile of all agents' wealth, m the profile of all agents' strategies, and m_i agent i's strategy. Strategies are contributions to the payment of the cost of the public good. In the case of projects for which there are only two outcomes—the public good is produced or it is not—the provision point mechanism's outcome function

---

[4]The finding also implies that punishment acts like a good that follows the law of demand. Carpenter (2007) estimates a demand curve for punishment and studies income and wealth effects. Carpenter concludes punishment behaves like an ordinary inferior good that is inelastic with respect to price and income.

$O(m)$ is

$$O(m) = \begin{cases} (0, w) & \text{if } \sum_i m_i < C; \\ (1, w - m) & \text{otherwise.} \end{cases} \tag{10.1}$$

Bagnoli and Lipman prove the mechanism generates a Pareto efficient Nash equilibrium. In this equilibrium, each group member contributes his or her true value, and the public good is purchased if it provides a net social benefit. Furthermore, the group as a whole will voluntarily contribute exactly the amount necessary for the good's provision. The mechanism gives agents more incentive to contribute to the public good, because it eliminates outcomes in which agents lose wealth and receive no public good.

Other, less desirable Nash equilibria are possible, too. Which equilibrium arises empirically is a question explored experimentally by Bagnoli and McKee (1991). In 85 of 98 experimental rounds of play, the public good is provided. The exact level of contribution needed to provide the public good is achieved in 52 of 98 cases. This happens even though the authors make sure the exact contribution is not a round number in order to mitigate the focal point effect. Bagnoli and McKee find that groups for which the differences in wealth or public good valuations are large are as likely to provide the public good as a group comprised of individuals with identical wealths and valuations. They also find that increasing the number of persons in the group slows the rate at which the group reaches equilibrium.

Bagnoli and Lipman's result depends in part on the assumption of common knowledge of wealth and other players' values. These assumptions seem strict. But Bagnoli and McKee identify several real-world campaigns that succesfully provided public goods using the provision point mechanism in which the assumptions may hold. A professors' association in the U.S. state of Oregon used the mechanism to raise funds to hire a lobbyist. The lobbyist sought higher salaries for the professors from the state legislature. Presumably university professors have a good, though imprecise, idea of what their colleagues earn and what a raise would mean to them. In the Canadian province of Manitoba, the New Democratic Party used the provision point mechanism to raise campaign funds from previous donors of large sums. Large campaign donors to a political party would probably have a reasonably good estimate of their fellow donors' wealth and values. In the U.S. state of Colorado, a club raised money with the provision point mechanism to maintain cross-country skiing trails abandoned by a bankrupt resort. Members of a ski club share a common interest and probably similar demographics.

Alston and Nowell (1996) put the provision point mechanism to another field test. Imitating their peers in Oregon, Alston and Nowell try to use it to raise money for the Utah Association of Academic Professionals to hire a lobbyist. The key word here is "try," because the effort fails. Alston and Nowell conclude that unexpected transactions costs caused the mechanism to fail in their application. A rational agent with a positive but low value for a lobbyist would not participate, they argue. On the basis of follow-up, in-person interviews, the authors estimate about 30 percent of the faculty who received solicitation letters in the mail threw them away without opening them. A strong majority of the rest tell interviewers they place some value on a lobbyist.[5] To reconcile their results with theory, Alston and Nowell hypothesize that professors with positive but low valuations did not want to spend time filling out forms, thinking about how much they want to donate, and mailing checks. Of course this did not prevent the professors in Oregon from raising the money needed for their lobbyist. Perhaps professors in Utah attach a stigma to lobbying that is not present in Oregon. Perhaps having no lobbyist is the efficient outcome in Utah!

Rondeau et al. (2005) compare variants of the voluntary contribution mechanism and the provision point mechanism using evidence from experiments and the field. In their voluntary contribution mechanism, subjects receive payoffs that increase as the level of funding for a public good increases up to a threshold. This is analogous to a fundraiser that solicits contributions and produces a fraction of the desired public good if the full funding level is not achieved. Rondeau et al. were inspired by a voluntary contribution mechanism used in a study by Champ et al. (2006) in which funds were raised to remove 215 miles of unwanted roads in the United States' Grand Canyon National Park. Donors were told each dollar they contributed would pay for the removal of eight feet of road. The total amount of road removed would be proportional to the amount of money raised.

Rondeau et al. compare the voluntary contribution mechanism to another, slightly different provision point mechanism for a non-divisible public good. In the provision point mechanism, donors receive their money back if the provision threshold is not reached. Money beyond the threshold is returned in proportion to each donor's share of initial contributions.

Rondeau et al. let their subjects know two things: Their private payoff from the public good, and that all subjects have the same endowment. Their subjects know neither the others' values nor the precise size of the group.[6] This resembles field conditions in which players know they have similar incomes but values and group size are not common knowledge. Rondeau et al.'s subjects play this mechanism for one round. Every player's endowment is greater than their assigned value, allowing the authors to analyze the results not just in terms of contributions but also in terms of the players' cost-benefit ratios. Because the subjects are neither aware of others' values nor the precise group size, the authors are able to use the statistical technique of bootstrapping to simulate a much larger number of experiments. Greene (2003, Appendix E) briefly explains bootstrapping.

The modified provision point mechanism provides higher net benefits on average than the voluntary contribution mechanism, Rondeau et al. find. Agents consistently

---

[5]Alston and Nowell (1996) do not discuss the possibility that interviewees were placating their interviewers.

[6]Because subjects were drawn from introductory economics lecture classes, they could have formed a rough estimate of the group size if they thought about it.

contribute a higher fraction of their assigned values in the provision point mechanism. The mechanism never overprovides the public good. The provision point mechanism is more efficient than the voluntary contribution mechanism when the cost of the project is greater than the total benefit to all players because it returns contributions when the project is not undertaken. It is also more efficient when the total benefit is more than 1.4 times the cost. But in some respects the voluntary contribution mechanism outperforms the provision point. About 24 percent of the time, the provision point mechanism fails to provide any good. The voluntary contribution mechanism always provides at least some. And the voluntary contribution mechanism provides more surplus when the benefit is between 1 and 1.4 times the cost.

Rondeau et al. also perform a field comparison of the two mechanisms. They ask Cornell University alumni on a weekend visit to campus to fund a $1,000 undergraduate award for environmental research. Alumni make two pledges, one for each mechanism. The authors then flip a coin to choose the mechanism. The provision point mechanism draws a higher dollar value of pledges but not enough to reach the provision threshold.[7] The authors compare public good demand curves observed in the field and lab experiments and find they are remarkably similar to each other. This suggests the provision point mechanism would work better in repeated real-world applications because on average it would attract more contributions. But as the field test shows, the provision point mechanism carries the risk of providing nothing. The authors report charities are reluctant to use the provision point mechanism for this reason.

With simplicity in mind, Falkinger (1996) proposes a theoretically Nash-efficient public goods mechanism. The mechanism assesses penalties and rewards depending on each agent's deviation from the mean contribution. A player who provides less than the mean pays a penalty that increases linearly as the deviation increases. A player who provides more than average receives a subsidy that increases the same way.[8]

Falkinger et al. (2000) conduct an experiment in which they compare the behavior of individuals contributing to a public good with the Falkinger (1996) mechanism and the standard voluntary contribution mechanism. They vary the group size and the players' payoff functions. Regardless of the variations, the Falkinger mechanism causes immediate, large increases in contributions relative to the voluntary contribution mechanism. The additional contributions bring outcomes closer to the efficient level of public good provision. They also find that Nash equilibrium is a good predictor of behavior in the mechanism, particularly when it is a boundary solution.[9]

---

[7] The authors report the coin toss went in favor of the voluntary contribution mechanism, eliminating a potential ethical dilemma.

[8] For comparison, the Groves-Ledyard mechanism levies taxes on each player proportional to the cost of the public good plus an amount proportional to each agent's deviation from the average and an amount proportional to the standard error of the average.

[9] By boundary solution, we mean players contribute the maximum or minimum possible amount in Nash

So far we have covered research on the production of public goods that are either non-excludable or both non-rivalrous and non-excludable. A large body of field evidence also investigates the distribution of another type of public good, common-pool resources. Common-pool resources are existing public goods that are rivalrous but non-excludable. They include natural resources that can be accessed by all but will be depleted if overused, such as fisheries and bodies of water. Many field studies of common-pool resource provision have been conducted, organized or collected by the political scientist Elinor Ostrom and her colleagues. These studies show that people have been devising successful ways of balancing the conflicting forces of individual rationality, incentive compatibility, budget balance and efficiency for thousands of years.

What lessons can economic designers learn from these studies? Ostrom (2000) reports five common features of long-lasting, self-organized regimes for common-resource management:

1. Clear boundaries defining who is part of the community using and managing the resource.
2. Rules take local conditions into account and allocate benefits to participants proportional to their input.
3. Most individuals affected by the regime can participate in rule-making.
4. Users select their own monitors, and the monitors are accountable to the users themselves.
5. Sanctions for free-riding or other rules violations are proportional to the seriousness of the offense.

Ostrom concludes that common resources are successfully managed when the participants themselves invest substantial resources in monitoring and sanctioning to reduce free-riding. Most people have an innate ability to learn social norms and are willing in many cases to conform to norms rather than act entirely in their own self-interest, Ostrom argues.

Non-rivalrous, excludable public goods receive attention in Gailmard and Palfrey (2005). An example of such a good is a public park that requires a fee for entry. Gailmard and Palfrey focus on threshold mechanisms, mechanisms that only provide the public good if members commit to paying the cost of producing it before it is produced. The provision point mechanism discussed above is an example of a threshold mechanism.

The authors compare the experimental performance of the serial cost sharing mechanism of Moulin (1994) to two versions of the provision point mechanism.[10] In serial cost sharing, agents bid what they are willing to pay toward the cost of the public good. The public good is produced if there is a subgroup of bidders that can split the cost of the good

---

equilibrium.

[10]Gailmard and Palfrey call the two versions of the provision point mechanism voluntary cost sharing with proportional rebates (abbreviated PCS) and voluntary cost sharing with no rebates (abbreviated NR).

evenly and the cost to each member subgroup is less than his or her reported value. Those bidders who are not in the subgroup pay nothing but are not allowed to use the public good.

In formal terms, the serial cost share mechanism tested by Gailmard and Palfrey has I agents indexed by i. Let C represent the public good's cost, w the profile of all agents' wealth, m the profile of all agents' strategies arranged in decreasing order of magnitude, m_i agent i's strategy, and S_i agent i's payment. Strategies are reported valuations of the public good. If $\sum_i m_i < C$ the good is not produced, and all agents pay $S_i(m) = 0$. If $\sum_i m_i \geq C$ and there is an integer k such that $m_k \geq C/k$, then the good is produced. Agents $j \in \{1, \ldots, k^*\}$ consume the public good and pay $S_j(m) = C/k^*$, where k^* is the largest integer such that $m_k \geq C/k$. Agents $i \in \{k^* + 1, \ldots, I\}$ do not consume the public good and pay $S_i(m) = 0$. If $\sum_i m_i \geq C$, and there is not an integer k such that $m_k \geq C/k$, then the good is not produced and all agents pay $S_i(m) = 0$.

In one of Gailmard and Palfrey's tests of the provision point mechanism, the good is produced if the sum of the bids is greater than or equal to the cost of the good. The cost is then divided proportionally, according to the size of the bids. Thus if two people bid and one bid is twice as high as the other, the high bidder pays twice as much as the low bidder. Excess funds are returned to the bidders in proportion to their bids. Formally, agents submit bids, b_i. If $\sum_i b_i \geq C$, all agents consume the good, and agent i's cost share is $Cb_i / \sum_i b_i$. Otherwise no agents consume the good and no agents pay any fee.

In Gailmard and Palfrey's second, "no-rebate," version of the provision point mechanism, players simply pay their bid if the sum of bids equals or exceeds the good's cost. Symbolically, $s_i = b_i$ if $\sum_i b_i \geq C$, and $s_i = 0$ if $\sum_i b_i < C$.

The serial cost sharing mechanism is incentive compatible, while the provision point mechanisms are not. In theory, serial cost sharing is more efficient than any other strategy proof mechanism for providing an excludable public good. Gailmard and Palfrey find the serial cost share mechanism induces truthful bids 85 percent of the time. But they find that the provision point mechanisms induced higher bids. In terms of efficiency, Gailmard and Palfrey find the provision point mechanism that gives rebates performs best. It extracts a higher percentage of available surplus and makes the efficient decision to provide the good more often.

Numerous other interesting studies have been conducted on the private provision of public goods. We point the reader here to some, though this is not a complete list. Blackwell and McKee (2003) examine the possibility that people are biased toward contributing to public goods that benefit local groups rather than global communities. They find that when the average per capita return of a global public good exceeds the average per capita return of a local public good, individuals will substitute contributions to the global public good for contributions to the local public good. Cadsby and Maynes (1998a) find that in a voluntary contribution mechanism, nursing students contribute significantly more to public goods than economics and business students. Cadsby and Maynes (1998b) find significant gender differences in contributions to voluntary public goods mechanisms. Women initially contribute more than men, but the differences fade in repeated play. A more persistent difference is that women are more likely to reach an equilibrium, perhaps due to a greater tendency to imitate each other. Rose et al. (2002) investigate the successful use of the provision point mechanism to fund a renewable energy program in New York State. The August 2005 issue of the *Journal of Public Economics* is devoted entirely to public goods experiments.

10.3 Tests of Incentive Compatibility

In spite of their theoretical properties, some incentive compatible mechanisms do not induce truth-telling in practice. Agents who can do no worse than tell the truth do not necessarily tell the truth. Failure to induce truth-telling by incentive compatible mechanisms has been traced to two factors: a failure to consistently and sufficiently punish agents for misrepresenting preferences, and less-than-complete information about the mechanism's payoffs.[11]

In Harstad (2000), experimental subjects fail to adopt the truth-telling dominant strategy in second-price, sealed-bid, or Vickrey, auctions for private goods. (For a description of Vickrey auctions, see section 2.5.) Instead, subjects tend to bid more than their true values. The overbidding increases as players participate in more Vickrey auctions. In contrast, Harstad finds subjects in first-price, open-bid, or English, auctions largely bid their true values. Subjects with experience in English auctions also overbid significantly less in Vickrey auctions. This is somewhat puzzling, because under certain conditions the English and Vickrey auctions are strategically equivalent. In both types of auctions, bidders have a dominant strategy of bidding their true values. One explanation is that the feedback to overbidding in English auctions is strong and transparent. If subjects bid above their true values and win the object, they suffer a penalty. In a second-price auction, winning subjects can bid above their true values, win the object and still pay prices below their true values.

The second-price sealed-bid auction is one version of the Vickrey-Clarke-Groves mechanism. Another version, the pivotal mechanism of Clarke (1971),[12] decides whether to build a fixed-size public good based on the sum of the participants' reported values. The pivotal mechanism requires an agent to pay a tax equal to her effect on the other agents' welfare. If an agent's reported value changes the project decision so the other agents suffer a welfare loss valued at $100, that agent must pay a $100 tax. If an agent's reported value does not change the project decision, she pays no tax. When preferences are quasilinear, truth-telling is a weakly dominant strategy in the pivotal mechanism.

---

[11]We discuss empirical work on this issue from the perspective of implementation theory in section 10.5.
[12]See also chapter 2 in this book.

In experiments, however, the pivotal mechanism has not induced truth-telling of players' values. Attiyeh et al. (2000) test the mechanism by randomly assigning players values for a public good. Subjects report their true values about 10 percent of the time. Nevertheless, they make the efficient choice 70 percent of the time.[13] A majority voting rule also produces the efficient outcome 70 percent of the time.

Attiyeh et al. provide no explicit information on the payoffs that would result from each strategy. Kawagoe and Mori (2001) suspect more information on the payoff structure will increase truth-telling and efficiency in the pivotal mechanism. They test this hypothesis in three information environments. In the first environment, subjects play repeated rounds with private values that remain fixed each round. In the second environment, the subjects are assigned private values that vary each round. This lets the authors see if subjects learn the consequences of misrepresentation as they experience them with several different values. In the third environment, Kawagoe and Mori give subjects values that remain fixed each round. But the subjects also receive tables listing the payoffs from each possible strategy when combined with the aggregates of other players' possible strategies.

Kawagoe and Mori conclude their subjects play the truth-telling dominant strategy more when there is more information. The authors find statistically significant improvements in the mechanism's performance in the third environment, when the players have payoff tables. In that environment, subjects tell the truth significantly more often than in the privately held variable value environment and the privately held fixed-value environment (47 percent to 14 percent to 17 percent). These results support the hypothesis that players are more likely to choose weakly dominant strategies if they know the consequences of failing to choose them. One should note, however, that even with improved information subjects play the truth-telling strategy only about half the time.

In a continuous public goods setting, Chen and Plott (1996) find penalizing misrepresentation is crucial to inducing truth-telling in the mechanism of Groves and Ledyard (1977). In that mechanism, agents announce the amount they wish to contribute to a public good. They pay an equal share of the good's total cost plus a penalty that increases the more they deviate from the average contribution. The penalty is adjusted further based on the variance of other agents' contributions. The higher the variance, the higher the penalty.

Formally, let there be I players, with y the level of public good, m the vector of all agents contributions, m_i agent i's contribution, τ_i agent i's penalty, κ the per-unit cost of the public good, μ_{-i} the mean of all other agents' contributions and σ^2_{-i} the variance

---

[13]The efficient choice is to produce the public good if the sum of true values exceeds its cost. If the sum of true values is less than the cost, the efficient choice is to not produce it.

of all others' contributions. The Groves-Ledyard mechanism's outcome functions are:

$$y(m) = \sum_i m_i, \qquad \tau_i(m) = \frac{\kappa y(m)}{I} + \frac{\gamma}{2}\left[\frac{I}{I-1}(m_{-i} - \mu_{-i}^2) - \sigma_{-i}^2\right]. \qquad (10.2)$$

Here, γ determines the severity of the penalty for deviation, and is called the "punishment parameter." Groves and Ledyard show that as long as the punishment parameter is positive—as long as agents pay a price for contributing less than the group average—a truth-telling, efficient Nash equilibrium exists.

Chen and Plott test the Groves-Ledyard mechanism with low and high punishment parameters. When the punishment parameter is low, the mechanism produces an inefficiently low level of the public good. When the punishment parameter is high, individuals are more likely to tell the truth. The mechanism provides a higher level of the public good and a higher level of efficiency than when the punishment parameter is low. The result spurs Chen and Plott to formulate a rule they call "the general incentive hypothesis": The higher the cost of deviating from the best response function, in this case telling the truth, the more accurate the game theoretic model will be in practice.

10.4 Research on Mechanism Dynamics

Abundant empirical evidence shows that people often do not play equilibrium strategies the first time they play a game. In many experiments, for example, players often choose non-equilibrium strategies the first several times they play a mechanism's game form before converging on strategies consistent with Nash equilibrium or other equilibrium concepts. Given that real-world environments typically require players to interact repeatedly and learn as they play, Chen (2005) argues that the fundamental question concerning real-world implementation is whether mechanisms will converge to the stable equilibria predicted by theory, given a dynamic, decentralized learning process.

Empirical research indicates a property called *supermodularity* helps determine whether strategies converge to Nash equilibrium.[14] In games, supermodularity means players' actions are strategic complements. Strategic complements are strategies that increase as other players' strategies increase. To be strategic complements, strategies must be ordered. Games in which players must choose contributions, bids, prices or output have ordered strategies. Games in which players choose "Confess" or "Deny" do not.

More formally, define M as the set of possible strategy profiles, m_i as player i's strategy, m_{-i} as the strategies of all players except i, u as the set of possible payoff function profiles, and u_i as player i's payoff function. A game (M, u) is **supermodular** if for each player i:

---

[14]For an introduction to the theory of supermodular games, see Topkis (1998).

- M_i is a compact subset of $\mathbb{R}$;
- u_i is upper semi-continuous in (m_i, m_{-i});
- u_i has increasing differences in (m_i, m_{-i}).

Many commonly encountered strategic situations can be modeled as supermodular games. In a banking crisis, an individual depositor is better off taking more money from her bank if everyone else takes more money from their bank. A country reaps more benefit from building another missile when its enemy's missile stockpile grows. In the case of providing a public good, a game form would be supermodular when the marginal benefit of contributing to the public good increases as others contribute more. If one player reports a higher value for a public good, other players have greater incentive to report higher values for the good.

In some games, supermodularity depends on the values of the payoff functions' parameters. Over some ranges of parameter values, the game may be supermodular while over other ranges it is not. Chen (2004, 2005) shows that, given quasilinear utility functions, the Groves-Ledyard mechanism is supermodular when the punishment parameter is above a certain threshold. This is because the penalty for free-riding grows as the average level of contributions increases. Hence the incentive to report higher values increases as average contributions increase. Chen also shows the mechanism of Falkinger (1996) (see section 10.2) is supermodular, while the Walker (1981) mechanism is not. (See section 6.3 for a description of the Walker mechanism.) In a survey of eight experiments on public goods mechanisms, Chen finds that mechanisms that have supermodular game forms converge to unique Nash equilibria. The others do not. Chen concludes that supermodularity provides a sufficient but not necessary condition for convergence under a wide range of learning dynamics.

Chen and Gazzale (2004) perform an experimental study to isolate the effect of supermodularity on mechanism performance. They use the two-player version of the generalized compensation mechanism of Cheng (1998).[15] This mechanism can be supermodular or not, depending on the values of two easy-to-vary punishment parameters. It has two stages and two players. Player one produces a good for which she can receive payment, while player two suffers an externality from the good. In the first stage, each player offers to compensate the other for the cost of the efficient choice. In the second stage, player one chooses the level of production. They pay fines proportional to the squared difference between the levels of compensation they propose in the first round. This gives incentive to choose similar punishments in the first stage. But whether the game is supermodular depends on the weight given to the squared difference in compensations. A heavy weight makes the game supermodular. A light weight means the game is not supermodular.

In their experiments, Chen and Gazzale find that supermodular and near-supermodular versions of the generalized compensation mechanism converge to efficient Nash equilibria

---

[15]This is a generalized version of the compensation mechanism proposed by Varian (1994).

faster and more frequently than a version that is far from supermodular. The performance of supermodular and near-supermodular mechanisms are not significantly different in the statistical sense. These results are consistent with those of Chen and Tang (1998). In that paper, the authors test a low punishment parameter Groves-Ledyard mechanism, a high punishment parameter Groves-Ledyard mechanism and the Walker mechanism. They find the high punishment parameter Groves-Ledyard mechanism produces more efficient outcomes and reaches those outcomes in fewer rounds of play than the low punishment parameter Groves-Ledyard mechanism. Both Groves-Ledyard mechanisms produced more efficient outcomes in fewer rounds of play than the Walker mechanism. Healy (2007) reports more experimental evidence showing supermodular game forms converge quickly to unique Nash equilibria.

10.5 Tests of Implementation Concepts

Up to this point in the chapter, we have surveyed empirical studies from the perspective of mechanism design. Some empirical work has sought to examine the other side of economic design—implementation theory. Implementation theory predicts which societal goals can be achieved according to equilibrium concepts such as Nash equilibrium or dominant strategy equilibrium.

At the heart of implementation theory are Maskin's (1999) necessary and sufficient conditions for implementing social choice rules in Nash Equilibrium discussed in section 3.2. Cabrales et al. (2003) test a modified version of the canonical mechanism (see also section 3.2.) used to prove the result. The canonical mechanism has been criticized for its complexity and logic. Cabrales et al. simplify it considerably. Their environment has three players, three possible states of the world, three possible outcomes and three integers from which to choose. The true state of the world is the hidden information in which the planner is interested. They require subjects to announce the state, an outcome and an integer. If everyone announces the same state or if there is only one dissident, the integer does not play a role in determining the outcome. If there is more than one departure from unanimity, then the mechanism selects the outcome according to the reported integers. The authors remove the incentive to report the highest number possible by taking the sum of reports, dividing by three and using the remainder to determine the winner. That is, they use the modulo game form of the canonical mechanism described in section 3.2.

In the experimental setting, the modulo mechanism implements a simple social choice function 68 percent of the time. When the authors added a fine for being a dissident, the implementation rate increased to 80 percent. But many of the successful implementations did not involve all subjects playing the truth-telling Nash equilibrium strategies. Frequently the subject least likely to benefit from the Nash equilibrium outcome misrepresented the state. This misrepresentation declined significantly when such dissidents were also fined. Cabrales et al. admit their environment is not general, but they interpret their results as evidence that the canonical mechanism has potential for practical implementation.

Cason et al. (2006) use experiments to study the concept of secure implementation proposed in Saijo et al. (2007).[16] A social choice function is securely implementable if (1) a mechanism exists that implements it in dominant strategy equilibria, and (2) that mechanism's Nash equilibria coincide with the dominant strategy equilibria.[17] A mechanism that securely implements a social choice function deters players from using untruthful strategies that are part of an undesirable Nash equilibrium. Saijo et al. identify a number of prominent mechanisms that do not securely implement standard social choice rules. They include the Vickrey auction for an indivisible private good in a complete information environment (section 2.5), serial cost sharing for excludable public goods (section 10.2), the pivotal mechanism for a non-excludable public good, the Condorcet winner with single-peaked preferences (section 1.5) and the uniform allocation rule (section 2.3) with single-peaked preferences.

Cason et al. perform public goods experiments on two mechanisms in a complete information environment. One mechanism is the pivotal mechanism, which is strategy-proof but does not provide secure implementation. The other mechanism is a Groves mechanism with single-peaked preferences that is both strategy-proof and provides secure implementation. They find players use truth-telling dominant strategies significantly more often in the secure Groves mechanism. In light of the findings and the fact that second-price sealed-bid auctions do not securely implement efficient outcomes in a complete information environment, the authors suggest performing lab tests that replicate the information environment expected in the field before recommending a second-price auction.

Some mechanisms implement desired outcomes in Nash equilibrium, but they are not robust to small deviations in strategies. Some theorists have addressed these shortcomings with concepts such as implementation in subgame perfect equilibrium (section 5.1) and virtual implementation (section 5.4). Implementation in subgame perfect equilibrium implies the mechanism induces the desired outcome in Nash equilibrium of each of its subgames. Virtual implementation requires the outcomes induced by a mechanism to be close to the outcome chosen by the desired social choice rule.

Abreu and Matsushima (1992a) propose a mechanism that virtually implements a broad range of social choice functions through the iterative elimination of strictly dominated strategies.[18] The Abreu-Matsushima mechanism works by dividing games into

---

[16]A version of Saijo et al. (2007) was first posted as a working paper in 1998.

[17]This is a form of double implementation. See also section 5.3. for a discussion of double implementation using Nash and strong Nash equilibria.

[18]Iterative elimination of strictly dominated strategies means players choose strategies that are not strictly dominated in the game that results when all of their strictly dominated actions are eliminated and all of their opponents' strictly dominated actions are eliminated. Strictly dominated strategies are strategies

many segments and fining players a small amount for every segment in which they play strategies the planner does not want them to play. For instance, in a game where players choose Confess or Deny, the Abreu-Matsushima mechanism would require the players to choose Confess or Deny for ten sequential game segments at one time. If the fine is large enough, a rational player will avoid the fine by playing the planner's desired strategy. But to determine this is the best strategy, a player must eliminate dominated strategies. The more rounds into which the game is divided, the more times the players must eliminate dominated strategies.

Sefton and Yavas (1996) find the Abreu-Matsushima mechanism fails to implement predicted equilibrium outcomes in two tests. In one test, subjects play a game with two Nash equilibria, one that is best for the players individually and efficient for them as a group, and one that is not. Sefton and Yavas use the Abreu-Matsushima mechanism to see if it induces play at the inefficient equilibrium. It does not. In the other test, the authors use a game that has a risk-dominant equilibrium outcome, one in which the players act as if they are worried about the other player failing to cooperate. The other equilibrium outcome is Pareto dominant. Previous experiments had shown players tend to play the risk-dominant equilibrium in such games. Sefton and Yavas checked to see if the Abreu-Matsushima mechanism could get them to play the Pareto-dominant outcome. It did not. Those outcomes and other data were consistent with the notion that people carry out iterated domination arguments for only three or four iterations. This is consistent with other studies such as McKelvey and Palfrey (1992) and Costa-Gomes et al. (2001) that have tested whether humans eliminate dominated strategies to reach predicted equilibria.

Glazer and Perry (1996) proposed a mechanism that virtually implements a broad range of social choice functions in subgame perfect equilibrium. They modify the Abreu-Matsushima mechanism by requiring players to choose their strategies at sequential points in time rather than simultaneously. So rather than having to choose between Confess and Deny in ten game segments at the same time, the players must play ten separate rounds in which they choose Confess or Deny and observe their opponents' choice after each round. Glazer and Perry's mechanism requires players to determine their best strategy using backward induction.[19] Glazer and Perry argue their mechanism is simpler and more intuitive for players than the Abreu-Matsushima mechanism.

Katok et al. (2002) test the Abreu-Matsushima and Glazer-Perry mechanisms by applying them to the same implementation task. They note that elimination of strictly dominated strategies and backwards induction share some of the same problems as implementation concepts. Both may fail due to lack of common knowledge, bounded rationality and uncontrolled preferences. The authors find the majority of outcomes conform neither to the prediction of iterative strict dominance nor to the prediction of backward induction.

---

for which there exists at least one alternative strategy that always produces a strictly preferred outcome. Strict dominance is a stronger concept than weak dominance discussed in section 5.2.

[19] Section 5.1. contains a description of backward induction.

They obtain no evidence the Glazer-Perry mechanism implements the desired outcome more often than the Abreu-Matsushima mechanism. Despite the mechanisms' failures to produce their predicted outcomes, Katok et al. see some promising results. The experimental players use undominated strategies, indicating they are aware of the incentives to avoid fines. And as subjects repeatedly participate in the mechanism, they tend to apply more steps of dominance and backwards induction.

10.6 Applied Economic Design: Notes from the Field

Perhaps some day economic design will be a business like architecture and interior design. After they have hired architects to build them new headquarters and interior designers to outfit their offices with tasteful curtains and furniture, business executives will contract with economic design firms to help them devise solutions to thorny problems of free-riding, allocation of unique, indivisible goods, the sale of unwanted assets, and the unintended consequences of their bureaucracies. And perhaps some day, the field of economic design will develop to a state in which economists routinely devise mechanisms that balance individual rationality, incentive compatibility and efficiency.

Thoughts from some pioneering economic designers may help guide the application of this theory. Though their experiences are outside the scope of this chapter, Paul Milgrom and Alvin Roth's work on auctions and matching respectively have produced lessons that may be applied to the branches of economic design covered here.[20] We present their thoughts for those who find themselves attempting real-world applications of economic design. We follow our discussion of Milgrom and Roth with discussions of two articles that further illustrate how the tools of economic design may be used to address real-world economic problems and heighten our understanding of economic issues. Healy et al. (2006) study a problematic real-world system in an attempt to devise an improvement. Casari and Plott (2003) study a case in which real-world agents have successfully managed a common-pool resource to determine what made the system work.

Although he is one of the leading theorists in auctions and mechanism design, Milgrom writes in *Putting Auction Theory to Work* (Milgrom, 2004) that he finds several assumptions of mechanism design theory "fragile." These include the assumptions that bidders in auctions have well-formed beliefs, that differences in bidder beliefs reflect differences in information, that bidders maximize their payoffs and that bidders believe all other bidders maximize payoffs. Milgrom further points out that theoretical models often skirt many issues that are important in the field such as: What to sell? Should the object

---

[20]Another paper in the same vein is Wilson (2002). Wilson discusses the issues involved in designing markets for wholesale electricity, where technological constraints play an important role. Binmore and Klemperer (2002) describe the experience of developing a successful auction of telecommunications spectrum in the United Kingdom. Vulkan (2003) gives advice grounded in economic design theory to businesses considering e-commerce strategies.

be sold as a single unit or broken into multiple units? To whom and when to sell the object? How much time should be given to bidders to prepare? Who should be allowed to participate? Are the items substitutes or complements? Would direct negotiations be better due to the complicated nature of the object? What is the likelihood of collusion and mergers, and re-sale of the object after the auction? Other issues arise in the execution of an auction. The auctioneer must advertise enough to attract all interested parties. Bidders may refuse to participate in designs they consider strange or unfair. How does one make it less likely for players to make a typo and bid $10 million when they actually want to bid $1 million? How does one keep bidders from sending collusive messages or threats through their bids?

Milgrom still takes the mechanism design approach in his book, because he finds it useful for identifying design issues and the effects of design decisions. The theory helps to determine what information to reveal, how to create rules in which bids are evaluated in dimensions other than price and how to handicap some participants, so one might promote small businesses, or minority-owned businesses, for instance. His writings imply that successful auctions and successful mechanisms must be well designed in all respects, of which theory is just one.

Roth (2002) focuses on market design, particularly his experience with the matching mechanism for hospitals and medical residents. He reports that none of the available theory could be directly applied to that market. But he found theory to be a good guide and a source of intuition. The designer must study the history of the markets, he writes, as well as the complications that do not match theory. Experiments can be used to answer questions that theory has not answered or cannot answer. Computer simulations can complement experiments. The designer must also be sensitive to the politics surrounding the market he is contracted to improve. Roth had to address the concerns of both hospitals and medical students who would be affected by his decisions.

Roth notes three common features of recent real-world economic design efforts. First, all had to be designed within about one year. Second, all required the designer to learn about the particular market's history and early efforts toward a market design. Third, all of the design-selection processes were at least partly political. From these observations we can conclude that economic designers must be sensitive to more than economic efficiency and logical consistency when they apply their theories.

Healy et al. (2006) take a step in that direction in a conventional journal article format. They tackle the economics of mission development for the U.S. government's National Aeronautics and Space Administration (NASA). Under its current system, NASA headquarters regularly posts a list of scientific missions in space that it wants to undertake. Several offices, or implementing centers, within NASA then offer estimates of the cost of developing each mission. On the basis of the submitted estimates, headquarters awards a contract to one implementing center for each mission. The winning implementing centers gather more information on each project and submit new cost estimates. If the new estimates fit into NASA's budget, the projects are approved. But NASA also sets a limit, or cap, on the cost of each project. Headquarters reimburses the implementing center up to the cost cap, no more.

The system creates several problems stemming from adverse selection and moral hazard. Implementing centers that bid too high do not win projects. If they bid too low, they are more likely to reach their cost cap before finishing the project. If a project hits its cost cap before completion, NASA must either cancel the project, transfer funds to it from another project or ask Congress for more money—something no one in NASA wants to do. In practice, implementing centers often bid low and win projects they cannot afford, Healy et al. report. The implementing centers then cut vital parts of the project to stay under the cost cap. This increases the likelihood that missions will fail. Healy et al. write that the 1999 failures of the Mars Climate Orbiter and the Mars Polar Lander are blamed partly on pressures created by cost caps.

The standard optimal principal-agent theory (see Laffont and Tirole, 1993) addresses situations when the principal cannot observe the true project cost and the agents' efforts are not observable. The optimal solution is for the principal to ask agents to submit estimates of the project cost. The principal awards the contract to the agent who submits the lowest estimate and pays that agent the estimated cost. The agent keeps savings below the estimate or pays for overruns above it. As long as the agents have standard payoff functions, this procedure induces agents who can develop the project for a low cost to bid low and agents with high costs to bid high.

The standard theory's assumptions do not all hold in NASA's procurement environment. The standard theory assumes agents know the true cost of projects from the start. While this may be true of common public works projects such as street repairs, it does not hold for pioneering scientific research in outer space. In the standard theory, greater effort lowers costs. That is not always the case in scientific research. In the standard theory, principal and agent have conflicting preferences. But in the case of NASA and its implementing centers, preferences are nearly aligned between headquarters and implementing centers. Both place a high priority on making scientific discoveries. Headquarters wants scientific discoveries it can show Congress and the public. Engineers and scientists use findings from NASA missions in their own research.

Healy et al. design a contracting mechanism called the Multicontract Cost Sharing System. At the start of the multicontract cost sharing process, the implementing centers see the NASA budget and form initial cost estimates for a set of projects. Through a mixture of bids and negotiations, NASA awards implementing centers contracts that set a baseline project cost. The implementing center is allowed to keep a percentage of cost savings. If the project cost goes over budget, the cost center must pay a percentage of the overrun. NASA then creates two other contracts. One sets a higher project cost and a smaller percentage for cost savings or overruns. The other sets a low cost and a higher percentage for savings or overruns. The implementing centers work on the project for one period, learn more about the projects' true cost, and then choose one of the three contracts. That contract binds for the rest of the project development process.

This system ensures all implementing centers will receive enough funding to finish the projects while approximately maintaining incentive compatibility. Low cost implementing centers have no reason to "gold plate" projects, and high cost centers know they will be paid for their higher expenses. The ability to select from a menu of contracts reduces the risk borne by the implementing centers in the initial round of bidding. The sharing of cost-savings and cost-overruns also encourages implementing centers to try risky innovations that could save money and increase their projects' scientific output. The multicontract cost sharing process lets implementing centers carry over their earnings from a project to the next period. This lets implementing centers self-insure against surprise costs.

The authors do not have a well-developed theory to give them precise predictions on how well their contracting system will work. They perform experiments using a simplified version of the Multicontract Cost Sharing System. Purdue University graduate students take the place of NASA headquarters and implementing center employees as experimental subjects. The experimenters award subjects points based on the scientific output of their projects. Those points are converted to cash at the end of experimental sessions. The success of projects is randomly determined by a computer, but the probability of success increases according to the spending choices made by the subjects. The authors program exogenous "luck shocks" into some stages of the experiment to replicate the surprise costs encountered by real-world mission developers.

The result of the experiments is that payoffs are significantly higher for both headquarters and implementing centers under Healy et al.'s Multicontract Cost Sharing System. The Multicontract Cost Sharing System performs better regardless of the number of implementing centers, the strength of the luck shocks and the subjects' experience using the mechanism. The authors think there is a good chance NASA will field test the Multicontract Cost Sharing System.

Healy et al. present their process as a possible roadmap for using experiments to design real-world applications. Theory does not provide a complete solution to NASA's problem. The authors of this paper, three of whom are NASA employees, interview the people involved in NASA's science projects to determine the existing system's strengths, weaknesses and incentives. They develop a relatively simple approximate solution and test it in the lab to determine if it worked satisfactorily. Given satisfactory performance in the lab, they feel confident recommending it. Their experience is consistent with Roth's observations that applied economic designers must learn from the participants about the economic environment and how it relates to theory.

Healy et al. use economic design and experiment to address a modern application. Casari and Plott (2003) show similar methods can be used to learn from economic history. The authors were intrigued by the successful operation from the early 1200s to the early 1800s of a common resource management system in the Italian Alps called the Carte di

Regola. A Carte di Regola outlined a system for monitoring and punishing persons found to have used common forests and pastures above a level agreed upon by the villagers. It was developed by the population of a village and approved by the regional government. The system gave individual villagers the authority to report violations. An independent court would rule on the charges and fine violators. Villagers who brought successful charges received a share of the fine, giving them an incentive to monitor overuse.[21]

Casari and Plott want to learn why such charters succeeded in preventing overuse of forests and pastures. They also want to explain a paradox found in previous experiments on common-pool resources and public good provision (Andreoni, 1995; Isaac et al., 1994; Walker et al., 1990). In these studies, when the object is to produce a public good, subjects cooperate more than predicted by a Nash equilibrium involving classical rational, selfish agents. In studies of existing common-pool resources, cooperation levels fall *below* the classical Nash equilibrium. In the public goods experiments, people appear to show altruistic preferences. They appear to enjoy higher utility when others in the group enjoy higher payoffs. In the common-pool resources experiments, people seem to show spiteful preferences. They appear to enjoy higher utility when others in the group suffer lower payoffs.

One explanation is that some people are spiteful, some are altruistic and some are not concerned about others' well-being either way. Different environments might lead to different expressions of these characteristics. Casari and Plott devise two theoretical models of common-pool resource users. One has homogeneous agents of the classical economic sort who do not have other-regarding preferences. The other model has heterogeneous agents with all three types of preferences: classical, spiteful and altruistic. They calculate Nash equilibrium predictions for the outcomes of common-pool resource games with no sanctions, weak sanctions and strong sanctions. In the no-sanction environment, there is no point to inspecting the behavior of other agents because it is impossible to punish them. In the weak-sanction environment, it is unprofitable to inspect when use of the commons is below the classical model equilibrium. Any agent performing an inspection would either be irrational, mistaken or spiteful. In the strong-sanction environment, spiteful agents, classical agents and weakly altruistic agents would gain satisfaction from inspecting.

The experimental results show the Carte di Regola mechanism improves efficiency of resource use. The authors measure efficiency as the percent of the maximum possible payoff that the group could earn from the system. Efficiency was about 28.4 percent with the no-sanction environment. This efficiency was below the classical model prediction of 39.5 percent efficiency but consistent with heterogeneous, other-regarding behavior. With weak sanctions, efficiency rose to 48.3 percent. With strong sanctions, efficiency

---

[21]The system met its end in 1805 at the hands of Napoleon, who had conquered the region a few years earlier. For a more thorough account, see Casari (2007).

improved to 76.9 percent. If one does not count the costs of inspection, the efficiency in the stronger sanction environment is 94 percent.

The results from the no-sanction environment help explain why people appear altruistic in public goods settings and spiteful in common-pool resource settings. In common-pool resource settings, more spiteful strategies are available. One can lower others' payoffs by using more of the resource. In a public goods setting, spiteful agents can only lower others' payoffs by not contributing. They cannot reduce the level of public good any further. This setting also gives altruistic agents more relative power to raise others' payoffs.

Casari and Plott find in the weak-sanction environment, the most intense resource users conduct the most inspections. In the strong-sanction environment, the least intense users conduct the most inspections. The classical model does not explain this, but the model with heterogeneous, other-regarding agents does. Spiteful agents are always more aggressive inspectors than altruistic agents. It gives them a chance to lower others' payoffs. Spiteful agents' use levels are very sensitive to the level of sanctions because part of their penalty makes another player better off. In a strong-sanction environment, spiteful agents use the resource less both to avoid penalties and to keep inspectors from collecting them.

Casari and Plott identify five features that may explain the Carte di Regola system's success:

1. It uses the agents' heterogeneity in a socially beneficial way. Spiteful people who enjoy punishing others help the system by conducting more inspections.
2. The system channels irrational behavior to useful ends. Mistaken or impulsive inspections tell potential overusers that they have a better chance of being inspected.
3. The large number of monitors and the transfer of fines to monitors reduces the chance that monitors will be bribed. An overuser could bribe the monitor who detects the overuse, but that bribe would not stop other monitors from inspecting.
4. The incentives do not depend on repeated rounds of play.
5. Even if agents had no preference for fairness nor regard for others, the possibility of punishment would still produce a more efficient outcome than allowing open access to the commons.

Casari and Plott's research provides another model for studying real-world economic design. They use game theory to model the behavior of two sets of agent types to form specific predictions about their behavior. The controlled setting of a laboratory allows them to record more data than are available in the real world. They then compare theoretical predictions, laboratory data and real-world data. This allows them to find a positive correlation between overuse and inspections in the weak sanction environment and a negative correlation between overuse and inspections in the strong sanction environment.

We should remember that this experimental environment makes some important assumptions. It assumes an ability to collect perfectly accurate data on resource use as well as an unbiased and competent judiciary. In the lab, the experimenters know with certainty what all agents do, so there is a 100 percent chance of an accurate ruling on accusations. There is no cost in collecting penalties from violators, no corruption in distributing penalties and no corruption in the rulings.

10.7 Conclusion

In this closing section we discuss some possible directions for future empirical research in economic design. We point out some areas that have not been well explored but hold exciting potential. They include the private goods domain, voting games, networks, endogenous mechanism choice and field research. We close with some thoughts on the current body of empirical research in economic design and the future of this approach to economics.

As the length of section 10.2. suggests, volumes of research are devoted to mechanisms designed to produce and allocate public goods. Private goods have received less attention outside the field of auctions. One exception is a study by Ponti et al. (2003) that compares the performance in experiments of two mechanisms devised for handling Solomon's Dilemma. Solomon's Dilemma is the problem of distributing an indivisible private good between two agents who have differing private values for the good. The name comes from the biblical story of King Solomon, who must referee a dispute between two women claiming to be the mother of the same baby.[22]

The mechanism of Glazer and Ma (1989) directs the two women to sequentially announce the identity of the baby's true mother. If both claim to be the true mother, the first woman pays a penalty while the second gets the baby subject to a lump-sum transfer to Solomon.[23] The unique subgame perfect equilibrium is for the impostor to say the baby is not hers. This is the first-best socially efficient outcome; the true mother gets the baby with no payment going to Solomon. But Glazer and Ma's game has socially inefficient Nash equilibria, Ponti (2000) shows. Ponti argues it is possible Glazer and Ma's mechanism could result in these inefficient equilibria. In an alternative mechanism proposed in Ponti (2000), if both women claim to be the true mother, Solomon holds a lottery that gives each woman a 50 percent chance of winning the object. The lottery winner is required to make a payment to Solomon. Ponti's mechanism implements the first-best efficient outcome in subgame perfect equilibria. Ponti et al. (2003) find the two mechanisms produce the first-best outcome with nearly identical frequency in their experiments. The Ponti mechanism produces the second-best outcome (getting the baby to the true mother with a payment going to Solomon) more often.

---

[22]The Bible reports that Solomon determined the true mother by threatening (credibly) to slice the baby into two pieces to be distributed among the two women. Guiding Solomon's action was the premise that the true mother would respond to this threat in a noticeably more emotional manner than the impostor.

[23]These mechanisms can be generalized by substituting the terms "planner," "agents," and "object" for "Solomon," "women," and "baby." The true mother is the agent with the higher valuation for the object.

In one of the few papers in the empirical economic design literature on voting mechanisms, Casella et al. (2003) test the storable vote mechanism of Casella (2003) in the lab. The storable vote mechanism is designed for committees that meet periodically to consider "binary" decisions – votes over two choices. It lets voters store votes by opting not to vote on some matters and allows them to use multiple stored votes on others. This allows voters to spend more resources on issues that matter more to them. Casella's model predicts efficiency improvements. Those improvements were observed in experiments, although voters did not behave as predicted to achieve them.

Networks will likely provide a fruitful and interesting area of research for years to come. Callander and Plott (2002) report results from what are likely the first economic experiments on networks. They find that networks arise for economic reasons, their outcomes stabilize and that the principles of game theory describe important parts of what they observe. Network dynamics do not monotonically enhance efficiency. The institutions that characterize the environment influence network dynamics. Callander and Plott suggest future research should study the importance of institutions for network development and the sensitivity of network performance to changes in the parameters governing their formation.

Another area that has the potential to produce interesting research is endogenous mechanism choice. In one of the first experimental studies of the issue, Kugler et al. (2005) test the factors that influence agents' mechanism choice. They study the choice of conducting exchange by way of decentralized bargaining versus exchange in a centralized market. They find different types of buyers and sellers prefer different mechanisms. When buyers have a relatively high willingess to pay and sellers have relatively low production costs, the two groups tend to prefer a centralized market to decentralized bargaining.

We point out these few papers on private goods, voting, networks and mechanism choice because they promise to provide important insights into the theories presented in this book. Economic design encompasses a wide range of resource allocation questions.

Economic design would also benefit from more studies of real-world institutions like those Ostrom and her colleagues have compiled on common-pool resources (see section 10.2.). Experimental studies have proven to be valuable, but they have limits. Experiments give limited information on the voluntary participation qualities of mechanisms. The participants in such experiments are usually undergraduate students who may view the experiment as an opportunity to earn some money in return for relatively little effort.[24] To be sure, many experiments have given agents endowments and the opportunity to stay out of mechanisms once they are in the lab. But these experiments do not tell us if real-world agents would take part in unfamiliar schemes that subject their income and assets to the outcomes of games that involve difficult calculations. People operating outside of a lab may be inclined to seek mechanisms that seem familiar, even if economists can

---

[24]And, no doubt, by the chance to play a role in the advancement of the social sciences.

mathematically prove those mechanisms to be less efficient. In addition, experimental subjects make their choices isolated from all of the other choices they make in their lives. They deal with people with whom they have little or no past history or emotional involvement. And as a whole, past economics experiments have not replicated transactions costs and mechanism operating costs well.

We suspect the relative cost and uncertainty of conducting field studies has led to only a few of them being performed. But they could produce valuable information on how real-world agents deal with incentive issues. They could also give us information on the costs of operating mechanisms and what role that plays in the agents' choice of mechanism. Experimental economists have low opportunity costs for operating their mechanisms because it is their job. They do not tell us the cost of getting people informed about a mechanism and making it appear attractive to them. In the real world, if you want a mechanism that assesses taxes on pivotal agents, you need to pay for tax computation and collection.

On the basis of this chapter's review of empirical evidence on mechanism design and implementation theory, we offer a few observations to stimulate thought and future research in the field:

1. Models with perfectly informed, fully rational and fully selfish agents operating with complete information are rough approximations at best. As the studies of public good contribution mechanisms featured in section 10.2 indicate, there are situations in which people find contributing to the greater good desirable. The studies of backward induction discussed in section 10.5 show there are optimization problems many people do not appear able to solve. The studies of the pivotal mechanism surveyed in section 10.2 indicate that players behave differently when experimenters aid their calculations by giving them additional information about the mechanisms' possible outcomes. And it should be apparent to us that real life consumers, firms and voters are not always operating with the most accurate or most complete information related to their decisions. It follows that applied economic designers should take seriously other-regarding preferences, bounded rationality and limited information.

2. Models involving one-round games are also imperfect approximations. The experiments by Chen and others demonstrate that understanding the dynamic behavior of mechanisms in repeated play is crucial to predicting their performance. The dynamics of learning and repeated play in mechanisms warrant continued study and application in economic design.

3. Many of our models and empirical studies focus on a single public good. But the members of our societies compete to determine the production of a large menu of public goods. Decisions to build highways depend in part on values for highways versus money. But in real-world legislatures, these decisions also depend on preferences for highways versus mass transportation, education, military spending, police

protection and a whole host of other public goods. Likewise, donors choose among numerous charities. The allocations of resources to a menu of multiple public goods seems to be an area that would have many applications.

4. Both theoretical and empirical mechanism design researchers almost always analyze outcomes relative to Pareto efficiency. But one advantage of the mechanism design approach is that it gives us more flexibility in defining what society as a whole finds desirable. We can use the mechanism design toolbox to consider goals other than Pareto efficiency, such as equal, envy-free, and winner-take-all outcomes. But to date, few economists have taken advantage of this flexibility.

In this book, we have proposed the economic design approach as a superior alternative to the economics-equals-markets approach. In doing so, we cast a more skeptical eye than classical economics on markets and the concept of rational, selfish, optimizing agents. We even use the construct of a central planner in our models. But we do not make the mistake of other central planning schemes by overlooking the roles of incentives and information. Incentives still matter in economic design. The beauty of economic design is that it offers us more flexibility in modeling those incentives and studying human economic behavior. The challenge for economic designers is to identify what people's preferences actually are in various situations, the strategies people follow to pursue their interests in different environments and the ultimate outcomes in which people are interested. With that knowledge we can best use our economic design toolbox to help us achieve those ends.

Appendix A

Mathematics Review and More on Economic Domains

This appendix provides a synopsis of some mathematical terms and results used in the book, and a somewhat extensive review of economies with private and public goods, as they are not covered sufficiently in standard microeconomics textbooks. The mathematics review is definitely a bare-bones one, as it would require a thick separate volume to do the subject justice. It is not intended to teach you the subject in depth, it is rather intended to remind you of concepts you may have half-forgotten and to give some pointers for further study. A good place to start studying the mathematics we refer to here more deeply is Simon and Blume (1994), and the Mathematical Appendix of Mas-Colell et al. (1995) is also a great repository of mathematical results and pointers to sources for further study.

A.1 Sets, Correspondences, Functions, Intervals

A **set** is a collection of items, the **members** of the set. We write $x \in S$ to mean "x is a member of the set S" or "x belongs to set S." A set S of members that share a common property P is written as $S = \{x \mid x \text{ has property } P\}$. We read this as "the set of members x such that x has property P." A set S is a **subset** of a set T if for each $x \in S$ we have $x \in T$. If S is a subset of T we write $S \subseteq T$. Two sets S and T are **equal** if we have both $S \subseteq T$ and $T \subseteq S$. If $S \subseteq T$ and $S \neq T$, then we say S is a **proper subset** of T and we write $S \subset T$. For any two sets S and T, the **intersection** of S and T is the set $S \cap T \equiv \{x \mid x \in S \text{ and } x \in T\}$ and the **union** of S and T is the set $S \cup T \equiv \{x \mid x \in S \text{ or } x \in T\}$. We use "$\equiv$" for "is defined by being set equal to," and we take "or" to mean "and/or."

An **ordered pair** is a set with two members with the additional property that one of the members is considered first and the other second. Such order considerations are not applied to sets in general. The standard notation for an ordered pair is (x, y), which employs regular parentheses to distinguish the ordered pair from the set $\{x, y\}$ in which order does not matter. Let S and T be two nonempty sets. The **Cartesian product** $S \times T$ is the set $\{(s,t) \mid s \in S, t \in T\}$.

Let S and T be two nonempty sets. A **correspondence** from S to T is a subset of the Cartesian product $S \times T$. A correspondence is also called a **relation**, as in "preference relation." We write a correspondence F on $S \times T$ as $F : S \rightarrow\rightarrow T$, even though it is a set of ordered pairs. The idea is that if (s,t) is a member of a correspondence F, t stands in a particular relation to s, which often is made clearer by writing $t \in F(s)$. We call S the **domain** of the correspondence F, T the **range** of the correspondence F, and, for any $s \in S$, $F(s)$ the **image** of s by the correspondence F.

As an example of a correspondence, consider the set $X = \{x, y, z\}$ that has three alternatives as members, and the correspondence $F \subseteq X \times X$ that describes an agent's preferences by listing every pair of members of X such that the first member is considered at least as good as the second. Suppose that this agent strictly prefers x to y and to z, and considers y and z indifferent to each other. Then $F = \{(x,y), (x,z), (y,z), (z,y)\}$, or $F(x) = \{y, z\}$, $F(y) = \{z\}$ and $F(z) = \{y\}$. When, as in this example, we want a correspondence to represent a preference relation, it is easier to write it, as we did in chapter 1, using the symbol R as in writing $x \, R \, y$ to mean "x is at least as good as y." But in other cases, the notation $F(x)$ for the images of a correspondence is more intuitive. This is particularly true for social choice correspondences, where $F(\theta)$ stands for "the set of alternatives that the social choice correspondence selects for an environment with type profile θ."

A **function** is a relation f between two nonempty sets S and T such that for each $s \in S$, each $t \in T$ and each $t' \in T$, if $(s,t) \in f$ and $(s,t') \in f$, then $t = t'$. A function is a correspondence such that every member of the domain S is associated to exactly one member of the range T. We write $f : S \rightarrow T$ to say that f is a function with domain S and range T. Note the use of a single arrow to distinguish a function from a correspondence. Two or more members of the domain of a function may be mapped to the same image, so $f(s) = f(s')$ is possible. If it does not happen for any two members $s, s' \in S$, we say that the function $f : S \rightarrow T$ is a **one-to-one** function. If for each $t \in T$ there exists $s \in S$ such that $f(s) = t$, we say that the function $f : S \rightarrow T$ is **onto**.

A special set in Calculus is the set of **real numbers,** $\mathbb{R}$. We assume you know that this set contains all integers, rational numbers (which are ratios of integers) and irrational numbers such as $\sqrt{2}, \pi$, and e. An **open interval** is a subset I of $\mathbb{R}$ such that there are two real numbers $a, b \in \mathbb{R}$ so that $I = \{x \mid x \in \mathbb{R}, a < x, \text{ and } x < b\}$. We write such an open interval as (a, b); granted, this is the same notation as for an ordered pair, but it is always clear by the context which one we mean. A **closed interval** is a subset I of $\mathbb{R}$ such that there are two real numbers $a, b \in \mathbb{R}$ so that $I = \{x \mid x \in \mathbb{R}, a \leq x, \text{ and } x \leq b\}$. We write such a closed interval as $[a, b]$. Half-open, half-closed intervals are defined in the obvious manner, based on the open and closed interval concepts.

A.2 Derivatives and Related Notation

Let n be a positive integer and $S \subseteq \mathbb{R}^n$ be a nonempty set. $\mathbb{R}^n$ stands for the Cartesian product of the set of real numbers $\mathbb{R}$ by itself n times, so every member x of S is an n-dimensional vector $x = (x_1, \ldots, x_n)$ with real numbers $x_1, \ldots, x_n$ as its coordinates. Recall that the standard convention is to visualize a vector such as $(x_1, \ldots, x_n)$ in a system of n Cartesian coordinates, as an arrow based in the origin, $(0, \ldots, 0)$ and pointing to $(x_1, \ldots, x_n)$. This enables us to use "vector" and "point" interchangeably. "Visualize" may be a bit too optimistic a term for the case where $n > 3$, but we can get a lot of insight on vectors by the 2- and 3-dimensional pictures that our brains can process.

For any two vectors $x, y \in \mathbb{R}^n$, their **sum** $x+y$ is defined by $x+y \equiv (x_1+y_1, \ldots, x_n+y_n)$. For any real number $t \in \mathbb{R}$ and any vector $x \in \mathbb{R}^n$, the **scalar product** tx is defined by $tx \equiv (tx_1, \ldots, tx_n)$. For any two vectors $x, y \in \mathbb{R}^n$, their difference $x - y$ is defined by $x - y \equiv x + (-1)y$. This is equivalent to $x - y \equiv (x_1 - y_1, \ldots, x_n - y_n)$. For any two vectors $x, y \in \mathbb{R}^n$, the **inner product** $x \cdot y$ is defined by $x_1 y_1 + \cdots + x_n y_n$.

Since we have set $S \subseteq \mathbb{R}^n$ for this section, a function $f : S \to \mathbb{R}$ is a function with n real arguments. If $n = 1$, it is a function of one real argument, the kind of function you encountered in your first Calculus class.

The **Euclidean distance** of two vectors $x \in \mathbb{R}^n$ and $y \in \mathbb{R}^n$ is the positive square root

$$\|x, y\| \equiv \left(\sum_{i=1}^{n} (x_i - y_i)^2 \right)^{1/2}.$$

This comes from applying the Pythagorean Theorem to the Cartesian coordinates of the vector $x - y$.

Given a positive real number ϵ and a vector $x \in \mathbb{R}^n$, the **open ball of radius** ϵ **centered on** x is the set $B_\epsilon(x) \equiv \{ y \mid y \in \mathbb{R}^n, \|x, y\| < \epsilon \}$. If $n = 1$, the open ball becomes an open interval of radius ϵ around x: $(x - \epsilon, x + \epsilon)$.

A function $f : S \to \mathbb{R}$ is **continuous at** $x \in S$ if for every $\epsilon > 0$ there is a $\delta > 0$ such that if $y \in B_\delta(x)$, then $f(y) \in B_\epsilon(f(x))$. A function is **continuous** if it is continuous at every point in its domain.

For the case of one argument, the notion of the **derivative** of a function $f : I \to \mathbb{R}$, where $I \subseteq \mathbb{R}$ is an open interval, at some point $x \in I$, is familiar. It is defined by

$$Df(x) \equiv \lim_{h \to 0} \frac{f(x + h) - f(x)}{h},$$

if this limit exists. The derivative notion can be extended to points on the boundary of closed or semi-closed intervals by taking the appropriate one-sided limit. Many authors write dy/dx or $f'(x)$ for the derivative of f at x (those who write dy/dx first have to let us know that y stands for $f(x)$). The D notation is the most precise and generalizable, and we have adopted it for this book.

If we have a function with more than one real arguments, there are various ways to extend the notion of derivative. We also need a generalization of the open interval notion. These two considerations are related. The h in the definition of the derivative (which authors often write as Δx) is a displacement added to x to reach the amount $f(x + h)$ in the numerator of the definition of the derivative. Clearly, we should only be using h small enough so that $x + h$ is in the domain of f, otherwise the expression "$f(x + h)$" is meaningless. This is why we defined the derivative for a function with an open interval as its domain, and had to make special provisions for half-closed intervals. For any point x in an open interval, there is always some room to move to $x + h$, whether $h > 0$ or $h < 0$, and not leave the interval, provided that h is small enough.

When we have two or more arguments, our function is defined on a space $\mathbb{R}^n$ and in that space a displacement from x to $x + h$ can occur in an infinity of directions. We also need to keep such a displacement within the domain of the function, which means we need a concept of an open set for the n-dimensional space $\mathbb{R}^n$.

A set $S \subseteq \mathbb{R}^n$ is **open** if for each $x \in S$ there exists an $\epsilon > 0$ small enough so that $B_\epsilon(x) \subseteq S$. As you can see if you try some graphical examples, say of a closed and of an open disk in $\mathbb{R}^2$, an open set does not contain the points of its boundary. For any nonempty set $S \subseteq \mathbb{R}^n$, the **interior** of S is the largest open subset of S. We denote the interior of S as int$S$.

We are now ready for our first definition of a derivative for a function with n arguments. Let $S \subseteq \mathbb{R}^n$ be a nonempty open set, let $f : S \to \mathbb{R}$ be a function, and let $v \in \mathbb{R}^n$ be a nonzero vector. The **directional derivative of f in the direction v at $x \in S$** is defined by the following, if it exists:

$$D_v f(x) \equiv \lim_{h \to 0} \frac{f(x + hv) - f(x)}{h}.$$

Here it is understood that we must start with h small enough so that $x + hv \in S$. Because we have assumed S to be an open set, this is always possible (make some pictures to see why).

The most commonly used special case of the directional derivative is the **partial derivative**, which is a directional derivative along a direction parallel to one of the axes in the Cartesian representation of $\mathbb{R}^n$. An equivalent, and probably more familiar definition of the **partial derivative of f with respect to x_i at $x \in S$** is the following, assuming that the limit exists.

$$D_{x_i} f(x) \equiv \lim_{h \to 0} \frac{f(x_1, \ldots, x_i + h, \ldots, x_n) - f(x_1, \ldots, x_i, \ldots, x_n)}{h}. \tag{A.1}$$

A function is **differentiable** if it has a directional derivative in every direction. A differentiable function has every partial derivative at every point in its domain. A function is **continuously differentiable** if it has continuous partial derivatives at every point in its domain.

For a function of n real arguments, we write $Df(x)$ for the row vector of its partial derivatives evaluated at some point x, $(D_{x_1}f(x), \ldots, D_{x_n}f(x))$.

The **second derivative** of a function of one variable is simply the derivative of its derivative. We denote it as $D^2f(x)$ when evaluated at some point x.

A.3 Elements of Mathematical Optimization

Let $S \subseteq \mathbb{R}^n$ be a non-empty set and $f : S \to \mathbb{R}$ a function. A vector x^* is a **maximum** of f on S if for each $x \in S$, $f(x^*) \geq f(x)$. A vector x^* is a **local maximum** of f on S if there is an open ball $B_\epsilon(x)$ such that for each $x \in S \cap B_\epsilon(x)$, $f(x^*) \geq f(x)$. The definitions of **minimum** and **local minimum** are the obvious adaptations of the definitions for maximum and local maximum. Note that if x^* is a maximum of f, it is also a local maximum of f.

Theorem A.1. *Let S be a nonempty subset of $\mathbb{R}^n$ and $f : S \to \mathbb{R}$ a continuously differentiable function. If $x^* \in \text{int}S$ is a local maximum of f, then $Df(x^*) = 0$.*

Another way to phrase the conclusion of this theorem is that every partial derivative of f evaluated at x^* must be zero.

A set $S \subseteq \mathbb{R}^n$ is a **convex set** if for each $x, y \in S$ and each $t \in [0, 1]$, $tx + (1-t)y \in S$. Geometrically, this means that if you connect any two points in the set with a line segment, this segment is contained in the set; the set has "no holes." Let $S \subseteq \mathbb{R}^n$ be a nonempty convex set and let $f : S \to \mathbb{R}$ be a function. We say that f is a **concave function** if for each $x, y \in S$ and each $t \in [0, 1]$, $f(tx + (1-t)y) \geq tf(x) + (1-t)f(y)$. A **convex function** is such that its negative is a concave function (that is, it is a concave function drawn upside down).

Theorem A.2. *Let S be a nonempty subset of $\mathbb{R}^n$ and $f : S \to \mathbb{R}$ a concave function. If there exists a point $x^* \in \text{int}S$ such that $Df(x^*) = 0$, then x^* is a maximum of f.*

We often search for a maximum of a function subject to constraints, such as when we maximize an agent's utility subject to her budget constraint. Let S be a nonempty subset of $\mathbb{R}^n$ and $f : S \to \mathbb{R}$ a function. Let there also be k functions $g_k : S \to \mathbb{R}$, for $k < n$. Consider the problem of finding a maximum of f subject to the k constraints $g_j(x) = 0$ for $j = 1, \ldots, k$. Define for each constraint j a new real variable λ_j, the **Lagrange multiplier corresponding to the jth constraint** and define the **Lagrangean** function by

$$L(x_1, \ldots, x_n, \lambda_1, \ldots, \lambda_k) \equiv f(x) + \lambda_1 g_1(x) + \cdots + \lambda_k g_k(x).$$

Then there is the following very useful theorem, a combination and extension of the previous two. We use it when discussing Lindahl and ratio equilibria later in this appendix.

Theorem A.3. *Let S be a nonempty subset of $\mathbb{R}^n$, $f : S \to \mathbb{R}$ a function, and let there be k functions $g_k : S \to \mathbb{R}$, for $k < n$. If $x^* = (x_1^*, \ldots, x_n^*)$ is a maximum of f subject to the k constraints $g_j(x) = 0$ for $j = 1, \ldots, k$, then there exists a vector $\lambda^* = (\lambda_1^*, \ldots, \lambda_k^*)$ such that $DL(x^*, \lambda^*) = 0$. Furthermore, if f is a concave function and there exist vectors $x^* = (x_1^*, \ldots, x_n^*)$ and $\lambda^* = (\lambda_1^*, \ldots, \lambda_k^*)$ such that $DL(x^*, \lambda^*) = 0$ and the matrix $D_x g(x^*)$ has maximal rank, then x^* is a maximum of f subject to the k constraints $g_j(x) = 0$ for $j = 1, \ldots, k$.*

A.4 Envelope Theorem

Many functions are specified with the use of parameters. If we have a parametrized optimization problem, and if we are interested in examining how the optimal value of the objective function in this optimization problem changes as its parameter changes, Envelope Theorems are very useful. Following Simon and Blume (1994), we state such a theorem. We used it in section 4.5. on page 96.

Theorem A.4. *Let $S \subseteq \mathbb{R}^n$ and $A \subseteq \mathbb{R}$ be nonempty sets, and let $f : S \times A \to \mathbb{R}$ be a continuously differentiable function of $x \in S$ and some choice parameter $a \in A$. Consider the problem of maximizing $f(x, a)$ with respect to x. Let $x^s(a)$ be a solution of this problem. Suppose that $x^s(a)$ is a continuously differentiable function of a. Then it must be that $Df(x^s(a), a) = D_a f(x^s(a), a)$.*

Here, $Df(x^s(a), a)$ stands for the total derivative of $f(x^s(a), a)$ with respect to a, which takes into account the dependence of x^s on a, while $D_a f(x^s(a), a)$ stands for the partial derivative of $f(x^s(a), a)$ with respect to a, which ignores this dependence.

This result can easily be generalized to many parameters.

For an example, consider optimizing some objective function $f(x; a) = ax^2 + a^2 - 2a^2 x$. To find the maximizer, we solve the usual first order condition $D_x f(x, a) = 2ax - 2a^2 = 0$. This gives us the solution $x^s(a) = a$. We would like to examine how the value of the objective function changes as its parameter a changes. We can determine this by plugging the solution $x^s(a) = a$ into the original objective function, such that $f(x; a) = f(a, a) = a^2 - a^3$. The rate of change then for this objective function is $2a - 3a^2$.

The Envelope Theorem allows us to arrive at the same conclusion using fewer steps. The theorem states that $Df(x^s(a), a) = D_a f(x^s(a), a) = x^2 + 2a - 4ax$. Since $x^s(a) = a$, then we have that the rate of change of the objective function given a change in the value of its parameter a is $2a - 3a^2$.

A similar result applies to constrained maximization problems. See Simon and Blume (1994, Section 19.2) for details.

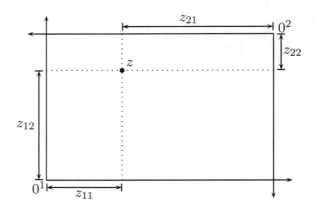

Figure A.1: An Edgeworth Box and an allocation z.

A.5 The Edgeworth Box

There is a very convenient diagram for getting an intuitive idea of an exchange economy. It is called the Edgeworth Box (probably unfairly, but the name has stuck and we will not go into its history here). It works for any exchange economy with two divisible private goods and with two individuals (or with many individuals who belong, in equal numbers, to two types, where individuals of each type have the same preferences and endowments).

We start with two individuals, 1 and 2. We can draw indifference maps of each side-by-side, but that ignores the interaction of the individuals. They interact because they are drawing their consumption amounts of the two private goods from the same source, which is the aggregate endowment of their little economy. Therefore, what one consumes of each good, the other cannot consume.

Think of a rectangle and a point inside it (we interpret "inside" to include the edges). Think of the bottom-left vertex of the rectangle as the origin of the consumption space of person 1, 0^1, and the top-right vertex as the origin of the consumption space of person 2, 0^2. Because the point is in the rectangle, its horizontal coordinates for the two people will add up to the width of the rectangle, and the vertical coordinates for the two people will add up to the height of the rectangle. Figure A.1 illustrates.

It is natural to associate one good with the width of the rectangle and the other with the height. By convention, good 1 is given the width. Now construct a rectangle with width equal to the aggregate endowment of good 1, and height equal to the aggregate endowment of good 2.

In this rectangle, consider a point such as the displayed point z. The coordinates of z viewed from the origin of individual 1 are the amounts of the two goods that 1 consumes at z. Now imagine the box turned around by 180 degrees. From this perspective, the coordinates of z represent the consumption amounts of the two goods of individual 2. You can easily get used to performing this rotation in your imagination, so we display the origin of person 1 in the lower left vertex and leave the rest to you. We display the axes for each individual as protruding outside the box a little, just to remind ourselves that the sides of the rectangle really represent two sets of Cartesian axes.

Any point in the rectangle represents an allocation that uses up exactly the total endowment of each good by giving it to the individuals to consume. With the standard assumption that each individual cares only about the amounts of her own consumption, and not of the other individuals' consumptions, it is easy to draw indifference curves in the box. Just remember that each individual's coordinates are to be read from the appropriate origin. We used the Edgeworth Box in section 1.7 to examine several social choice correspondences.

A.6 Public Good Economies

A.6.1 The Simplest Public Project Model

The simplest useful model of a public good has a group of individuals $\mathcal{I}$ as above, one private good that acts as a stand-in for all private goods and as "money", and one public good of a special kind. This is a public good that can only take two values: 0 or 1. We can think of examples such as building a bridge or installing a statue in a public square. Such public goods, often called public projects, are a good start for our thinking of the issues involved in financing a good with benefit spillovers over many members of the society. We saw this model in action in section 2.4.

A.6.2 Public Goods Models

A large part of the motivation to study incentives in mechanisms came from Paul Samuelson's classic critique of the concept of Lindahl equilibrium for economies with public goods in Samuelson (1954). He pointed out that the artificial markets for personalized public goods that Lindahl envisioned would be a natural breeding-ground for free-riders; this will make more sense in a couple of pages. Naturally, this ensured that public good economies took a prominent place in the economic design literature. For this reason, and because a lot of the material in this section may be unfamiliar to you, we will take our time in describing the domain of public good economies.

We will examine the case of an economy with n private goods and k public goods, and also the commonly studied subcase where $n = 1$. The set of agents is $\mathcal{I}$, as before. Agent i's consumption bundle has two parts: a private good bundle $x_i = (x_{i1}, \ldots, x_{in}) \in \mathbb{R}^n_+$ and a public good bundle $y = (y_1, \ldots, y_k) \in \mathbb{R}^k_+$. Note the absence of an i subscript in the bundle of public goods: by definition, all agents consume each public good in the same amount, the amount that the society produces and makes available to all.[1] The complete consumption bundle of agent i is then $(x_i, y) = (x_{i1}, \ldots, x_{in}, y_1, \ldots, y_k)$. An **allocation** is a vector $z = (x_1, \ldots, x_I, y) \in \mathbb{R}_+^{nI} \times \mathbb{R}^k$. Note again how we have economized on the dimension of the public good part of the allocation, since every agent consumes the same amount of each public good as every other agent.

Agents only hold endowments of the private goods. Think about it for a moment: what would it mean if we had agents who owned some of the public goods? The endowment bundle of agent i is denoted as before by ω_i, but for technical convenience this now equals $\omega_i = (\omega_{i1}, \ldots, \omega_{in}, 0_k) \in \mathbb{R}_+^n \times \mathbb{R}^k$, where 0_k is the vector of k dimensions filled with zeros.

Agents can consume their entire endowments or consume parts of them and contribute the rest to the production of public goods. Exactly how they contribute is specified by the social choice correspondence in effect, but, before we discuss social choice correspondences on this domain, we must specify the technology available to society for the transformation of private good inputs into public good outputs.

The production possibilities available to society are described by a production set $Z \subseteq \mathbb{R}^n \times \mathbb{R}_+^k$. This is a standard production set, meaning that each coordinate of every member of this set is a real number that describes the net output for the corresponding good. When the number is positive, there is more output of that good than is used as input, and the converse if the number is negative. We have restricted the public good coordinates to be non-negative, which is sensible since there are no endowments of the public goods and so no public good can be a net input of the production process. We usually express Z via a cost function for the production of public goods, as we will see below.

An allocation $z = (x_1, \ldots, x_I, y) \in \mathbb{R}_+^{nI} \times \mathbb{R}^k$ is **feasible** if there is a production vector $\zeta \in Z$ such that $\sum_{i \in \mathcal{I}} x_i = \zeta + \sum_{i \in \mathcal{I}} \omega_i$. This requires that it is possible to produce the public good vector y by using some production vector from the production set Z and the aggregate endowment $\sum_{i \in \mathcal{I}} \omega$, and that this production leaves a vector of private goods enough to satisfy the agents' total consumption vector of private goods.

There is a simple graphical device to help visualize public good economies. It is analogous to the Edgeworth box, but much less familiar to economists (although this seems to be less true after each year). It is the *Kolm triangle,* so named in honor of its creator Serge-Christophe Kolm. It is well explained in great detail in Thomson (1999a).

A.6.3 Social Choice Correspondences on Public Good Economy Domains

The study of social choice correspondences in the domain of public good economies builds on general equilibrium theory foundations. Standard general equilibrium theory deals

---

[1]This can be relaxed to the requirement that each agent consumes each public good at an amount no larger than the amount provided socially; we will not examine this case here.

with the interaction of many markets for private goods. In this type of work, general equilibrium theorists, especially in an extensive literature that applies general equilibrium to macroeconomics and finance, usually do not have to worry about which equilibrium notion to apply. Given a private ownership economy e, they study the set of Walrasian equilibria of this economy. Generations of economic theorists have studied this model and its variations which include production and have established many deep results for it.

One of the important problems encountered by general equilibrium theory is that of accommodating externalities. Externalities are present when one agent's choice of an economic variable affects other agents. Perhaps the most commonly studied case is a rather extreme one: a pure public good, which is a good chosen by some governmental authority and is consumed by every agent in the same amount.

A.6.4 Pareto Social Choice Correspondence

The Pareto social choice correspondence has the same basic definition here as for exchange economies: a feasible allocation in an economy with private and public goods is Pareto efficient if there is no other feasible allocation that makes all agents as well off and at least one agent better off. In a classical exchange economy, we saw that an allocation that provides a positive amount of each good to each agent (called an interior allocation) is Pareto efficient if and only if the agents' indifference curves all have the same slope at this allocation. In an economy with private and public goods, things are a little different. We will illustrate the condition that characterizes interior Pareto efficient allocations in the simple domain of economies with one private good and one pure public good. For the most general conditions for Pareto efficient allocations in economies with a finite number of private and public goods, and indeed conditions that apply to all Pareto efficient allocations and not only interior ones, see Conley and Diamantaras (1996).

Paul Samuelson first derived the condition we are now going to explore. Suppose that there is one private and one public good, that all agents have differentiable utility functions and that for every agent i and every allocation $(x_1, \ldots, x_I, y)$, $D_{x_i} u_i(x_i, y) > 0$, in other words, every agent has a positive marginal utility for the private good everywhere. The last part of the assumption is easily justifiable in such a simple model that aggregates all private goods into one. We can imagine that each agent always has some private goods that she would prefer to have in larger quantities, and since all private goods are subsumed in one, more of that good would raise utility at every consumption bundle.

Consider a feasible allocation $z = (x_1, \ldots, x_I, y)$. The **marginal rate of substitution of the public versus the private good** for agent i is defined by

$$MRS_i(z) = \frac{D_y u_i(x_i, y)}{D_{x_i} u_i(x_i, y)}.$$

By our assumption that $D_{x_i}u_i(x_i, y) > 0$, this ratio is well-defined, as there is no division by zero. The marginal rate of substitution measures how much of the private good the agent is willing to give up for an additional unit of the public good. Another good term for the marginal rate of substitution is the **marginal willingness to pay** for the public good.

As Samuelson (1954) described seminally, because all agents consume the same amount of the public good, their marginal willingnesses to pay should be added together to arrive at the society's marginal willingness to pay for the public good. In a Pareto efficient allocation, this should equal the society's marginal cost for the production of the public good. If we denote by $c(y)$ the cost of producing the amount y of the public good and c is a differentiable function with derivative denoted by $Dc(y)$, we can write down the Samuelson condition for a Pareto efficient allocation z as

$$\sum_{i=1}^{I} MRS_i(z) = Dc(y). \tag{A.2}$$

This requires that the sum of all agents' measures of willingness to pay for the public good equals the marginal cost of producing the public good. So it seems that there is no mutual tangency of indifference curves as was the case in the exchange economy domain.

In the Kolm triangle, however, an interior Pareto efficient allocation does correspond to the double tangency we have come to expect from our experience with the Edgeworth box. This is the main reason the Kolm triangle is useful as a representation of a simple economy with a private and a public good.

A.6.5 Lindahl and Constrained Lindahl Social Choice Correspondences

Erik Lindahl (1967), developing ideas of Knut Wicksell (1967), proposed that public good levels be selected by the operation of fictitious markets, one per each combination of an agent and a public good. He assumed that agents would behave as though these markets were competitive, which attracted Samuelson's criticism which we have already mentioned. As we saw in section 6.3., if we are willing to modify Lindahl's idea a little by introducing constrained Lindahl equilibrium, we can implement Lindahl equilibrium in Nash equilibrium. Let us develop the concept of Lindahl equilibrium, starting with the producers of public goods.

Each public good is assumed to be produced by a **bureau**. Bureaus can be publicly owned (as Lindahl envisioned) but they can also be private firms. Each bureau j has a production technology described by a production set $Z_j \subset \mathbb{R}^n \times \mathbb{R}^k$. Since eacu bureau j is assumed to produce only one public good, its production set contains vectors ζ_j with zeroes in the last k coordinates except for the coordinate corresponding to public good j. The aggregate production set of the economy is $Z = \sum_j Z_j$. The bureaus are profit maximizers; each bureau's revenue is determined by multiplying the sum of all the personalized prices $q_{j1} + q_{j2} + \cdots + q_{jI}$ by the amount y_j of output. If the bureaus have any positive profit, it is distributed to the agents in proportion to predetermined shares. Since under constant returns to scale profits are zero at equilibrium, this last rule applies only if we assume a production technology without constant returns to scale. We write π_j for the profit of bureau j.

The agents' budget sets are determined by a feature special to Lindahl equilibrium: each agent faces a specific price for each public good, and, if q_{ij} is the price of public good j to agent i, the agent has to pay a tax equal to $q_{ij}y_j$ toward the cost of producing public good j at the amount y_j. The rest of the agent's budget is determined in the standard way from the endowment and the price vector p of private goods. Agent i's budget depends also on the profits made by bureaus and i's predetermined ownership shares of these profits. Agent i's share of the profits of bureau j is denoted by δ_{ij}. As a result, the agent's budget set is $B_L(\omega_i, p, q_i) = \{(x_i, y_i) \in \mathbb{R}^{n+k}_+ \mid p \cdot x_i + q_i \cdot y_i \leq p \cdot \omega_i + \sum_j \delta_{ij}\pi_j\}$.

Definition A.1. A **Lindahl equilibrium** is a pair of a price vector for private and public goods, $(p_1, \ldots, p_n, q_{11}, \ldots, q_{1k}, \ldots, q_{I1}, \ldots, q_{Ik})$, and an allocation, $(x_1, \ldots, x_n, y)$, such that: (i) each agent i consumes the vector (x_i, y_i) that is rated highest according to i's preferences from i's budget set $B_L(\omega_i, p, q_i)$; (ii) each bureau chooses its production vector ζ_j from the set Z_j so as to maximize its profits; and (iii) the allocation is feasible, so that $y = y_1 = y_2 = \cdots = y_I$ and $\left(\sum_{i \in \mathcal{I}} x_i, y\right) = \sum_j \zeta_j + \sum_{i \in \mathcal{I}} \omega_i$. A **Lindahl allocation** is an allocation such that there exists a price vector so that this price vector and allocation together constitute a Lindahl equilibrium. The **Lindahl social choice correspondence** L_δ assigns to each economy e in a suitable domain the set of its Lindahl equilibrium allocations.

We emphasize that feasibility implies $y = y_1 = y_2 = \cdots = y_I$, ensuring that all the fictional personalized public good consumption levels end up being the same. Note that we use the δ subscript to indicate that the Lindahl correspondence depends on the ownership shares of the agents in the bureaus.

This equilibrium concept overcomes the very serious problems that Walrasian equilibrium faces in the presence of public goods (Thomson, 1999a); these problems include non-existence of equilibrium and Pareto inefficiency of equilibria even when these exist. As summarized in Milleron (1972), Lindahl equilibria exist and yield Pareto efficient allocations in economies with private and public goods under conditions not much more restrictive than those commonly employed for existence results for Walrasian equilibria in economies with only private goods. Lindahl equilibria also have a social stability property: they belong to the core of the economy when production happens under constant returns to scale.

In chapter 3 we saw that the Walrasian social choice correspondence fails to be Maskin Monotonic under the standard assumptions on preferences (recall figure 3.1 and its discussion). The Lindahl social choice correspondence similarly fails to be Maskin Monotonic, we introduce the constrained Lindahl correspondence. Thomson (1999a, page 169) shows this graphically. The constrained Lindahl budget set for any agent i is defined by $B_{CL}(\omega_i, p, q_i) = \{(x_i, y_i) \in \mathbb{R}_+^{n+k} \mid p \cdot x_i + q_i \cdot y_i \leq p \cdot \omega_i + \sum_j \delta_{ij}\pi_j$ and there exists a feasible allocation z of which (x_i, y) is part$\}$. The **constrained Lindahl equilibrium** definition is the same as that of Lindahl equilibrium, but it employs the budget set $B_{CL}(\omega_i, p, q_i)$ instead of $B_L(\omega_i, p, q_i)$. Every Lindahl equilibrium is also a constrained Lindahl equilibrium, and every constrained Lindahl equilibrium allocation is weakly Pareto efficient (this notion was defined on page 23 in subsection 1.7.3 and its definition extends to economies with public goods straightforwardly). In an economy in which all Lindahl equilibrium allocations assign a positive amount of every good to every agent, the set of Lindahl equilibrium allocations is equal to the set of constrained Lindahl equilibrium allocations. We turn now to a detailed example that shows how to find a Lindahl equilibrium.

Example A.1. Consider an economy with one private good, one public good, and two agents. Each agent i has the endowment ω_i of the private good and the quasilinear utility function $u_i(x_i, y) = x_i + a_i \log(y + 1)$. Assume that for each i we have $\omega_i > a_i > 0$ and also that $a_1 + a_2 > 1$. Since there is only one private good, and it has a positive marginal utility for each agent at any consumption bundle, we will use it as the numeraire, therefore we set $p = 1$ and the only prices that we need to track are the personalized prices of the public goods, q_1 and q_2. The technology available for the production of the public good has constant returns to scale and corresponds to the production function $y = f(z) = 1 \cdot z = \omega_1 + \omega_2 - x_1 - x_2$, where we write z for the amount of input of the private good, and the production function itself is the identity function, the simplest linear function possible. In terms of the cost function (which will be handy later when we compute the ratio equilibrium of this economy) the same production technology is expressed as $z = c(y) = y$. In terms of ownership of the bureau, assume that each agent owns δ_i of the bureau, with $\delta_i \geq 0$ for each i and with $\delta_1 + \delta_2 = 1$. In summary, the economy is $e = (u_1, u_2, \omega_1, \omega_2, \delta_1, \delta_2, c)$, with the seven components as specified in this paragraph.

In order to find any Lindahl equilibria that this economy has, we need to set up and solve the utility maximization problems of the two agents, the profit maximization problem of the bureau that produces the public good, and we need to use the conditions that characterize these maximizations together with the feasibility conditions to finally find pairs of allocations and price vectors that are Lindahl equilibria. As it will turn out, this economy only has one Lindahl equilibrium.

The best place to start is profit maximization, as we will need the maximized profit in order to write the budget constraints properly. The bureau that produces the public good is selling the public good to each consumer separately, so it receives the sum $q_1 + q_2$ as the price of its output. The profit then equals total revenue minus total cost: $(q_1+q_2)y - c(y) = (q_1 + q_2)y - y$, since $c(y) = y$ in our simple production technology.

Since the bureau is assumed to act as a price taker, it considers $q_1 + q_2$ as given. The marginal profit, which is the derivative of the profit function with respect to y equals $q_1 + q_2 - 1$. If this exceeds 0, then the bureau will sense that its marginal profit is always positive, and will attempt to produce an infinite amount of the public good y. If the marginal profit is negative, the bureau will produce the smallest possible amount of the public good, zero. So in order to find a non-zero solution to the profit maximization problem, we have to assume that the marginal profit is zero, which means that $q_1 + q_2 = 1$. Note that the bureau cannot ensure this by its choice, as it can only choose y, which has cancelled out when we found the marginal profit. What this exercise tells us is that, if there is to be a Lindahl equilibrium, the requirement of profit maximization means that the personalized prices will have to be set so that their sum equals 1. This is common in any general equilibrium model with a linear production, whether there are public goods in the economy or not. It also implies that the maximized profit is exactly equal to 0, which simplifies the budget constraints of the agents.

Continuing, we need to solve the utility maximization problems of the two agents. The first step is to write down their budget constraints. Consider agent i, for any $i = 1, 2$. The agent's income is the amount received by selling the endowment ω_i at the price of the private good, which we have assumed to be unity, plus the agent's share of the maximized profits of the bureau, which in this case equals $\delta_i \cdot 0 = 0$. Therefore, we will ignore the profit shares δ_i for this example. The same is true for the calculation of Lindahl equilibrium for any economy with constant returns to scale: the profit share coefficients in such an economy do not affect the economy's Lindahl equilibrium. Having concluded that i's income equals ω_i, we can now write i's budget constraint as $x_i + q_i y_i = \omega_i$. Note that we let each agent imagine that he or she gets to choose a personalized amount of the public good to consume. Later on, in applying the feasibility conditions for the Lindahl allocation, we will ensure that $y_1 = y_2$.

We are ready to write down agent i's utility maximization problem. It is to choose x_i and y_i to maximize $x_i + a_i \log(y_i + 1)$, subject to $x_i \geq 0$, $y_i \geq 0$, and $x_i + q_i y_i \leq \omega_i$. To make our life easier, we first note that the budget constraint will always be satisfied as an equality, as if it were not, the agent could attain a higher level of utility by consuming in terms of x_i any unused portion of income. We also ignore the non-negativity constraints for now, subject to checking later that our solutions satisfy them as strict inequalities. With our simplifications, we now have the problem of choosing x_i and y_i to maximize $x_i + a_i \log(y_i + 1)$ subject to $x_i + q_i y_i = \omega_i$. The Lagrangean function for this problem is $L(x_i, y_i, \lambda_i) = x_i + a_i \log(y_i + 1) + \lambda_i(\omega_i - x_i - q_i y_i)$, where λ_i denotes the Lagrange multiplier. The objective function is concave in its arguments, and the constraint is linear, so any solution found by the first-order conditions will be a global maximum. The first-order conditions are as follows, from $DL(x_i, y_i, \lambda_i) = 0$.

$$1 - \lambda_i = 0, \tag{A.3}$$

$$\frac{a_i}{y_i + 1} - \lambda_i q_i = 0, \quad \text{and} \tag{A.4}$$

$$x_i + q_i y_i = \omega_i. \tag{A.5}$$

From the first two, we deduce that

$$\frac{a_i}{y_i + 1} = q_i. \tag{A.6}$$

This allows us to write i's demand function for the public good, which is (assuming that $q_i > 0$, which we must verify before we finish with the example)

$$y_i = \frac{a_i}{q_i} - 1. \tag{A.7}$$

Substituting the demand function for y_i into the third first-order condition, which is the budget constraint, and solving for x_i we find the demand function for x_i, which is

$$x_i = \omega_i - a_i + q_i. \tag{A.8}$$

We are ready to put together the equation system that represents all Lindahl equilibrium conditions for our example economy. The system is as follows.

$$x_1 = \omega_1 - a_1 + q_1, \tag{A.9}$$

$$x_2 = \omega_2 - a_2 + q_2, \tag{A.10}$$

$$y_1 = \frac{a_1}{q_1} - 1, \tag{A.11}$$

$$y_2 = \frac{a_2}{q_2} - 1, \tag{A.12}$$

$$1 = q_1 + q_2, \tag{A.13}$$

$$y_1 = y_2, \quad \text{and} \tag{A.14}$$

$$\omega_1 + \omega_2 = x_1 + x_2 + y_1. \tag{A.15}$$

Note that we could just as well have written y each time y_1 or y_2 appears, as one of the feasibility conditions is $y_1 = y_2$. It may appear that there are too many equations, as we have six unknowns $(x_1, x_2, y_1, y_2, q_1, q_2)$, but one of these equations can be shown to be redundant. One simple way to solve this system follows.

Start with writing y for every y_i instance, and omitting the next to the last equation, which was used up in this substitution. Now use the first two equations in the last one, to obtain

$$y = \omega_1 + \omega_2 - \omega_1 + a_1 - q_1 - \omega_2 + a_2 - q_2 = a_1 + a_2 - q_1 - q_2. \tag{A.16}$$

Use the third and fourth equation of the system to get that $q_1 = (a_2/a_1)q_2$ and also $q_1 = a_1/(y+1)$ and $q_2 = a_2/(y+1)$. Substitute these into equation (A.16) to obtain

$$y = a_1 + a_2 - \frac{a_1}{y+1} - \frac{a_2}{y+1}. \tag{A.17}$$

This yields either $y = 0$ or

$$y = a_1 + a_2 - 1. \tag{A.18}$$

We are hoping that $y > 0$ for a non-trivial equilibrium, so we will take the second solution. As we have assumed at the outset that $a_1 + a_2 > 1$, the second solution, $y = a_1 + a_2 - 1$, is positive. We will examine the $y = 0$ case later.

With the value $y = a_1 + a_2 - 1$, we can now compute the equilibrium values of the personalized prices as follows:

$$q_1 = \frac{a_1}{y+1} = \frac{a_1}{a_1 + a_2}, \qquad q_2 = \frac{a_2}{a_1 + a_2}. \tag{A.19}$$

Using these, we finally find the equilibrium amounts of the private good consumptions:

$$x_1 = \omega_1 - a_1 + \frac{a_1}{a_1 + a_2}, \qquad x_2 = \omega_2 - a_2 + \frac{a_2}{a_1 + a_2}. \tag{A.20}$$

We summarize by saying that a Lindahl equilibrium in this economy has the price vector

$$(p_{L_\delta}(e), q_{1L_\delta}(e), q_{1L_\delta}(e)) = \left(1, \frac{a_1}{a_1 + a_2}, \frac{a_2}{a_1 + a_2}\right)$$

and the allocation

$$(x_{1L_\delta}(e), x_{2L_\delta}(e), y_{L_\delta}(e)) = \left(\omega_1 - a_1 + \frac{a_1}{a_1 + a_2}, \omega_2 - a_2 + \frac{a_2}{a_1 + a_2}, a_1 + a_2 - 1\right).$$

You can check easily that $x_{iL_\delta}(e) > 0$ for each i, given the assumption that $\omega_i > a_i$, and $y_{L_\delta}(e) > 0$ given the assumption that $a_1 + a_2 > 1$, so the non-negativity conditions hold.

We now return to the possible solution for y that is $y = 0$. If this is the equilibrium, then $x_1 = \omega_1$ and $x_2 = \omega_2$, as the agents have nothing to gain by supplying a part of their endowment to produce the public good. You can check that, at least for some specific numbers such as $a_1 = 2$ and $a_2 = 3$, both agents would receive a higher utility at the equilibrium found above than at the putative equilibrium with $y = 0$. As a Lindahl equilibrium must be Pareto efficient, the putative equilibrium, as it is Pareto dominated by the previous one, cannot be a Lindahl equilibrium.

We finally check explicitly that the calculated Lindahl equilibrium satisfies the Samuelson condition for Pareto efficiency, which says that the sum of the agents' marginal rates of substitution between the public and the private good should equal the marginal cost of production of the public good. In our example economy, the marginal cost is by assumption 1. The marginal rate of substitution of each agent i equals the ratio of the agent's marginal utility for y divided by the agent's marginal utility for x. Since the latter is always 1 for quasilinear utility functions, we are left having to show only that the sum of the marginal utilities of y across the agents equals 1 at the Lindahl equilibrium allocation. There are a couple of ways to see this. Perhaps the fastest is by direct substitution. The marginal utility of y for agent i is $a_i/(y+1)$, which equals $a_i/(a_1+a_2)$. Since $a_1/(a_1+a_2) + a_2/(a_1+a_2) = 1$, we are done verifying that the Lindahl equilibrium allocation of this example is Pareto efficient. $\diamondsuit$

The properties of Lindahl equilibrium listed before the example hold in models with constant returns to scale. If one makes the usual assumption of decreasing returns to scale in production (which is not problematic in economies with only private goods) then the Lindahl equilibrium notion has some undesirable properties: It depends on how the profits accruing to the producers of public goods are distributed among the agents, and it no longer always selects allocations in the core (Kaneko, 1977; Wilkie, 1990). Kaneko (1977) responded to these shortcomings by introducing a new equilibrium concept, the *ratio equilibrium,* and Mas-Colell and Silvestre (1989) introduced another class of equilibrium concepts, with the *balanced linear cost share equilibrium* being the most prominent member of this class.

In this situation, where we face a battle of equilibrium concepts, the framework of mechanism theory becomes very useful for organizing our discussion. Such a discussion has important practical implications, since it is possible to design institutions to get economic agents to act according to one specific equilibrium concept, as we show in this book.

We will now describe the technology for the production of public goods in a more specific and natural way than before. Each public good y_j is produced by one production unit, bureau j, from 1 to k. This bureau has a cost function c_j such that $c_j(y_j)$ is the cost in terms of value of private goods required to produce quantity y_j of the public good output. Let us call the domain of these economies $\mathcal{E}_p$.

A.6.6 Ratio Social Choice Correspondence

The *ratio equilibrium* concept is similar to the Lindahl equilibrium, but there are significant differences in conditions (i) and (ii). In (i), each agent i has a budget set that is independent of personalized prices; rather, there is a nonnegative "ratio" for each agent i and each public good j, r_{ij}, and agent i has to pay a tax equal to r_{ij} times the cost $c_j(y_j)$

(not times the amount y_j, as in Lindahl equilibrium). The ratios satisfy the condition $\sum_i r_{ij} = 1$ for all j and are endogenous, playing a role similar to that of the personalized prices of Lindahl equilibrium. As for (ii), each bureau minimizes cost; with no prices for the public goods, it makes no sense to talk of the bureaus' profits. Condition (iii) is as before. This equilibrium is well suited for the case of publicly owned bureaus. The **ratio social choice correspondence** R assigns to each economy e in $\mathcal{E}_p$ the set of its ratio equilibrium allocations.

Kaneko proved that ratio equilibrium allocations are Pareto efficient, in fact, are in the core, for economies with constant as well as with decreasing returns to scale.

Example A.2. Let us calculate the ratio equilibrium for the same economy of example A.1. We will see that for an economy with constant returns to scale, a ratio equilibrium allocation is also a Lindahl equilibrium allocation, and vice versa. The next example shows that this equivalence vanishes when we have decreasing returns in the production of the public good.

For convenience, we repeat here the economy's specification. There are one private good, one public good, and two agents. Each agent i has the endowment ω_i of the private good and the quasilinear utility function $u_i(x_i, y) = x_i + a_i \log(y + 1)$. Assume that for each i we have $\omega_i > a_i > 0$ and also that $a_1 + a_2 > 1$. Since there is only one private good, and it has a positive marginal utility for each agent at any consumption bundle, we will use it as the numeraire, therefore we set $p = 1$. There will be no other prices to track in this example, as the agents pay personalized cost shares instead of amounts based on personalized prices for the public good. The technology available for the production of the public good has constant returns to scale and corresponds to the production function $y = f(z) = 1 \cdot z = \omega_1 + \omega_2 - x_1 - x_2$, where we write z for the amount of input of the private good, and the production function itself is the identity function. In terms of the cost function, the same production technology is expressed as $z = c(y) = y$. The concept of ownership of the bureau is now irrelevant for the agents' budget sets, as the bureau never makes a profit to be distributed, even under decreasing returns to scale, as we will see in the next example.

The bureau's cost minimization problem is already solved for us by having the cost function already specified. Therefore, we proceed to the agents' utility maximization problems. Consider agent i, whose budget constraint is (we do not need the j subscript we used in the definition of ratio equilibrium as there is only one public good):

$$x_i + r_i c(y) \le \omega_i.$$

By the same argument we used in example A.1, we conclude that the inequality sign will not be obtained at the maximization solution. Furthermore, because $c(y) = y$ by assumption, the budget constraint of i is simply

$$x_i + r_i y = \omega_i.$$

But note how this is exactly the same constraint as in A.1! The only difference is the symbol we used for the, exogenous to the agent, quantity that multiplies y. Hence all the work we did in example A.1 is applicable here, with a small change in notation, and we see that in this economy ratio equilibrium and Lindahl equilibrium lead to the same allocations. This equivalence is true for any economy with a finite number of agents, private goods, and public goods, and a linear production technology.   ◇

Example A.3. Now we consider an economy with decreasing returns to scale. Assume there is one private good and one pure public good, and two agents. The endowment of i is ω_i and the utility function of i is $u_i(x_i, y) = x_i + a_i y$, where $a_i > 0$. Production of the public good is subject to decreasing returns, and is represented by the cost function $c(y) = (y)^2/2$. The economy we are considering is $e = (u_1, u_2, \omega_1, \omega_2, c)$, where the five components of e are as specified in this paragraph.

Individual i maximizes $x_i + a_i y_i$ subject to $x_i + r_i c(y_i) \leq \omega_i$; once again, we imagine that i acts as though the amount of public good provided is hers to control, but we will impose later in the feasibility conditions that all the y_i amounts equal each other. The first-order conditions for this utility maximization are:

$$1 - \lambda_i = 0, \tag{A.21}$$

$$a_i - \lambda_i r_i y_i = 0, \quad \text{and} \tag{A.22}$$

$$x_i + \frac{r_i(y_i)^2}{2} = \omega_i. \tag{A.23}$$

From these conditions we find the demand function for the public good to be

$$y_i = \frac{a_i}{r_i}, \tag{A.24}$$

assuming that $r_i > 0$, which we will check before we finish examining this example. Substituting this expression for y_i into the budget constraint, we find the demand for the private good to be

$$x_i = \omega_i - \frac{a_i^2}{2r_i}. \tag{A.25}$$

Combining these demand functions for $i = 1, 2$ and the feasibility conditions $y_1 = y_2 = y$ and $r_1 + r_2 = 1$, we finally find the ratio equilibrium amounts of the goods and ratio levels to be

$$x_{1R}(e) = \omega_1 - \frac{(a_1 + a_2)a_1}{2}, \tag{A.26}$$

$$x_{2R}(e) = \omega_2 - \frac{(a_1 + a_2)a_2}{2}, \tag{A.27}$$

$$y_R(e) = a_1 + a_2, \tag{A.28}$$

$$r_{1R}(e) = \frac{a_1}{a_1 + a_2}, \tag{A.29}$$

$$r_{2R}(e) = \frac{a_2}{a_1 + a_2}. \tag{A.30}$$

To use the social choice correspondence notation, we can write our conclusion as

$$R(e) = \{(x_{1R}(e), x_{2R}(e), y_R(e))\}. \tag{A.31}$$

We can check that this allocation is Pareto efficient. The sum of the marginal rates of substitution is $a_1 + a_2$, while the marginal cost is $y_R(e)$, and the two are equal. Finally, given our assumption that every a_i is positive, the equilibrium ratios r_i are also positive, as we had to check. $\diamond$

It is worth our time to redo this example with Lindahl equilibrium in mind. This will draw attention to a very important property of ratio equilibrium that distinguishes it from Lindahl equilibrium.

Example A.4. Consider the economy of example A.3. In Lindahl equilibrium, the production of the public good is done so as to maximize the profit of the bureau producing the public good. As we know from basic microeconomics, when there are decreasing returns to scale in production, the marginal cost curve slopes upwards and at the profit-maximizing input-output combination there exists positive profit.

In the case of this economy, that means that before we can write down the budget constraints of the agents, we must specify their ownership shares δ_1, δ_2 in the profit of the bureau. Lindahl equilibrium then is seen as less parsimonious than ratio equilibrium. It is not enough to specify all utility functions, endowments, and technology in order to compute a Lindahl equilibrium, although it is enough for ratio equilibrium. We must also specify ownership shares for Lindahl equilibrium.

So let us assume that there are some exogenously given profit shares δ_1, δ_2 such that $\delta_i \geq 0$ for all i and $\delta_1 + \delta_2 = 1$. We are going to find a Lindahl equilibrium that depends on these shares, in addition to all the other aspects of the economy. The Lindahl equilibrium correspondence, for a domain of economies that allow for decreasing returns to scale, should be written as L_δ, to emphasize this dependence; so for a given economy e from such a domain, $L_\delta(e)$ describes the set of Lindahl equilibrium allocations that are based on the particular profit sharing scheme δ. We already used this notation in example A.1, but in this example the δ actually matters.

We start with profit maximization, and we continue to use the same notation as in example A.1. The profit maximization problem for the bureau is

$$\max_{y}(q_1 + q_2)y - \frac{y^2}{2}. \tag{A.32}$$

The first-order condition is

$$q_1 + q_2 - y = 0, \tag{A.33}$$

from which we immediately see that the profit-maximizing level of y is $y = q_1 + q_2$. Because the profit function is a concave function of y, the profit maximum we found is a global one. The profit generated by the profit-maximizing production level of y is $\pi^* = (q_1 + q_2)^2/2$.

The ith agent's budget constraint is therefore $x_i + q_i y_i \leq \omega_i + \delta_i(q_1 + q_2)^2/2$. The agent's utility maximization problem is to choose x_i, y_i to maximize $x_i + a_i y_i$ subject to this constraint. The first-order conditions are

$$1 - \lambda_i = 0, \tag{A.34}$$
$$a_i - \lambda_i q_i = 0, \quad \text{and} \tag{A.35}$$
$$x_i + q_i y_i = \omega_i + \frac{(q_1 + q_2)^2}{2}. \tag{A.36}$$

Using the above conditions for $i = 1, 2$ and the feasibility conditions $y_1 = y_2 = y$ and $\omega_1 + \omega_2 = x_1 + x_2 + (y^2/2)$, we can calculate the Lindahl equilibrium price and allocation vectors. We find that

$$y_{L_\delta} = a_1 + a_2, \tag{A.37}$$

as before, and also that $q_{iL_\delta}(e) = a_i$, $i = 1, 2$, as before. By plugging this information back into the budget constraints, we can now find the $x_{iL_\delta}(e)$ amounts. This step is left for an exercise at the end of the chapter.

Note that, while $y_{L_\delta}(e)$ is equal to $y_R(e)$ from the previous example, the $x_{iL_\delta}(e)$ amounts are not, unless the ownership shares take particular values (this is also part of an exercise). The fact that the same amount of the public good is chosen by the ratio and the Lindahl equilibrium allocations is not surprising, because in these examples we have used a quasilinear specification of utilities. With a quasilinear setup and either utility functions strictly concave in y or a cost function strictly convex in y, there is a unique Pareto efficient level of the public good. Since both Lindahl equilibrium and ratio equilibrium always select Pareto efficient allocations in our domain of economies, it follows that they must select the unique efficient level of the public good. $\Diamond$

A.7 Exercises

Exercise 46: Lindahl Equilibrium Calculation 1

In the economy of example A.1, assume $a_1 + a_2 = 1$. What is the unique Lindahl equilibrium in this case?

Exercise 47: Lindahl Equilibrium Calculation 2

In the economy of example A.1, change the utility of each agent i to be $u_i(x_i, y) = x_i + a_i \log(y + b^i)$ and the marginal cost of the public good to be constant at $c > 0$. What is the unique Lindahl equilibrium in this case? Spell out any additional assumptions required to ensure that the equilibrium has a positive amount of each good, private or public.

Exercise 48: Lindahl and Ratio Equilibrium

In the economy of example A.3, find the private good amounts $x_{iL_\delta}(e)$. Find also the ownership shares δ_1, δ_2 that make these private good amounts equal to the ones of the ratio equilibrium allocation for this economy.

Exercise 49: Ratio Equilibrium Calculation

In the economy of example A.3, change the number of agents to $I > 2$. Calculate the ratio equilibrium allocation.

Exercise 50: Lindahl and Ratio Equilibrium without Quasilinearity

Consider the economy of example A.3. Change the ith agent's utility function to $u_i(x_i, y) = x_i y_i^{a_i}$, where $a_i > 0$, for $i = 1, 2$. Calculate the Lindahl equilibrium allocation and the ratio equilibrium allocation. Does the Lindahl equilibrium allocation now select a level of the public good that depends on the ownership shares? (Hint: Convert the utility functions to their logarithmic form for easier first-order conditions.)

Notation

$\mathcal{I}$ is the set of agents where $\mathcal{I} = \{1, \ldots, I\}$ and an individual agent is denoted by i.

x is the allocation of private goods where $x_i = (x_{i1}, \ldots, x_{in})$ is the consumption bundle (vector) of consumer i. We assume there are n private goods.

y is a vector of public goods where $y_i = y = (y_1, \ldots, y_k)$ is the consumption bundle of every consumer i.

Z is the aggregate production possibilities set for an economy with private and public goods.

ω is the profile of endowments of the individuals in the economy. We write $\omega_i = (\omega_{i1}, \ldots, \omega_{in})$ for agent i's endowment vector, and $\omega = (\omega_1, \ldots, \omega_I)$.

R^i is the preference relation for agent i, such that for any two alternatives x and y, $x \, R^i \, y$ means x is at least as good as y for individual i. A preference profile for all agents is denoted by ρ, where $\rho = (R^1, \ldots, R^I)$.

P^i is agent i's strict preference relation such that for any two alternatives x and y, $x \, P^i \, y$ means that agent i strictly prefers x to y.

I^i is agent i's indifference relation such that for any two alternatives x and y, $x \, I^i \, y$ means that, for agent i, $x \, R^i \, y$ and $y \, R^i \, x$.

$\mathcal{R}$ is the set of all possible complete and transitive preference relations from which R^i is drawn.

$\mathcal{R}^I$ is the set of all possible preference relation profiles $\times_{i=1}^I \mathcal{R}$, subsets of which are considered based on particular restrictions on admissible preferences, such as not admitting indifference.

θ_i is agent i's type. It is private information held by an individual relating to preferences of that individual. The set of possible types for individual i is denoted by Θ_i. A profile of agents' types is $\theta = (\theta_1, \ldots, \theta_I)$. A profile θ is drawn from the set $\Theta = \Theta_1 \times \ldots \times \Theta_I$.

X is the set of possible alternatives from which individuals must make a collective choice.

R is a social welfare functional that aggregates individual preference relations into a society's preference relation $R^i \to R \in \mathcal{R}$.

f is a social choice function that maps each type profile θ from Θ to an alternative in X.

F is a social choice correspondence that that maps each type profile θ from Θ to a set of alternatives in X.

$v_i : X \times \Theta_i \longrightarrow \mathbb{R}$ is individual i's utility function from all aspects of an alternative except the individual's money allocation. Thus, $v_i(x, \theta_i)$ is the benefit that individual i of type $\theta_i \in \Theta_i$ receives from the choice of alternative $x \in X$. Used in quasilinear domains.

$t_i : \Theta \longrightarrow \mathbb{R}$ is a transfer function, $t_i(\theta)$ represents the payment that individual i receives (or pays if it is negative) based on the announcement of types θ, $t = (t_1, \ldots, t_I)$ is a collection of transfers. Used in quasilinear domains.

$u_i(x, t, \theta_i) = v_i(x, \theta_i) + t_i$ is individual i's quasilinear utility function. When we do not have a quasilinear domain, we simply use u_i for the utility function.

(M, g) is a mechanism, where $M = M_1 \times \ldots \times M_I$ is the Cartesian product of the agents' message spaces, and $g : M \to X$ is an outcome function.

Bibliography

Abdulkadiroğlu, A. and T. Sönmez (1999, October). House allocation with existing tenants. *Journal of Economic Theory 88*(2), 233–260.

——— (2003). School choice: A mechanism design approach. *American Economic Review 93*(3), 729–747.

Abreu, D. and H. Matsushima (1992a). Virtual implementation in iteratively undominated strategies: Complete information. *Econometrica 60*, 993–1008.

——— (1992b). Virtual implementation in iteratively undominated strategies: Incomplete information. Princeton University mimeo.

Abreu, D. and A. Sen (1990). Subgame perfect implementation: A necessary and almost sufficient condition. *Journal of Economic Theory 50*, 285–299.

——— (1991). Virtual implementation in Nash equilibrium. *Econometrica 59*, 997–1021.

Alston, R. M. and C. Nowell (1996). Implementing the voluntary contribution game: A field experiment. *Journal of Economic Behavior and Organization 31*, 357–368.

Altman, A. and M. Tennenholtz (2007, May). Incentive compatible ranking systems. Honolulu, Hawai'i: Autonomous Agents and Multiagent Systems Conference.

Anderson, C. M. and L. Putterman (2006). Do non-strategic sanctions obey the law of demand? The demand for punishment in the voluntary contribution mechanism. *Games and Economic Behavior 54*, 1–24.

Andreoni, J. (1995). Cooperation in public goods experiments: Kindness or confusion? *American Economic Review 85*, 891–904.

Arrow, K. J. (1951). *Social Choice and Individual Values*. Cowles Foundation Monograph 12. New York: Wiley.

——— (1979). The property rights doctrine and demand revelation under incomplete information. In M. Boskin (Ed.), *Economics and Human Welfare*, pp. 23–39. New York: Academic Press.

Athey, S. and P. A. Haile (2006). Empirical models of auctions. In R. Blundell, W. K. Newey, and T. Persson (Eds.), *Advances in Economics and Econometrics: Theory and Applications, Ninth World Congress, Volume II*, Number 42 in Econometric Society Monographs, pp. 1–45. Cambridge: Cambridge University Press.

Attiyeh, G., R. Franciosi, and R. M. Isaac (2000). Experiments with the pivot point process for providing public goods. *Public Choice 102*, 95–114.

Austen-Smith, D. and J. S. Banks (2005). *Positive Political Theory II: Strategy and Structure*. Ann Arbor, MI: University of Michigan Press.

Ausubel, L. and P. Milgrom (2002). Ascending auctions with package bidding. *Frontiers of Theoretical Economics 1*(1).

Bagnoli, M. and B. Lipman (1989). Provision of public goods: Fully implementing the core through private contributions. *Review of Economic Studies 56*, 583–602.

Bagnoli, M. and M. McKee (1991). Voluntary contribution games: Efficient private provision of public goods. *Economic Inquiry 29*(2), 351–65.

Baliga, S. and E. Maskin (2003, June). Mechanism design for the environment. In K. Mäler and J. Vincent (Eds.), *Handbook of Environmental Economics*, Volume 1, pp. 306–324. Amsterdam: Elsevier Science/North-Holland.

Barberà, S., M. O. Jackson, and A. Neme (1997). Strategy-proof allotment rules. *Games and Economic Behavior 18*, 1–21.

Bergemann, D. and S. Morris (2005, November). Robust mechanism design. *Econometrica 73*(6), 1771–1813.

Beviá, C., L. C. Corchón, and S. Wilkie (2003). Implementation of the Walrasian correspondence by market games. *Review of Economic Design 7*, 429–442.

Binmore, K. and P. Klemperer (2002). The biggest auction ever: The sale of the British 3G telecom licenses. *Economic Inquiry 112*, C74–C96.

Black, D. (1958). *The Theory of Committees and Elections*. Cambridge: Cambridge University Press.

Blackwell, C. and M. McKee (2003). Only for my own neighborhood?: Preferences and voluntary provision of local and global public goods. *Journal of Economic Behavior and Organization 52*(1), 115–131.

Bolton, P. and M. Dewatripont (2005). *Contract Theory*. Cambridge, MA: MIT Press.

Busetto, F. and G. Codognato (2009). Reconsidering two-agent Nash implementation. *Social Choice and Welfare 32*, 171–179.

Cabrales, A., A. Calvó-Armengol, and M. O. Jackson (2003). La Crema: A case study of mutual fire insurance. *Journal of Political Economy 111*(2), 425–458.

Cabrales, A., G. Charness, and L. C. Corchón (2003). An experiment on Nash implementation. *Journal of Economic Behavior and Organization 51*, 161–193.

Cadsby, C. B. and E. Maynes (1998a). Choosing between a socially efficient and free-riding equilibrium: Nurses versus economics and business students. *Journal of Economic Behavior and Organization 37*, 183–192.

——— (1998b). Gender and free-riding in a threshold public goods game: Experimental evidence. *Journal of Economic Behavior and Organization 34*, 603–620.

Callander, S. and C. R. Plott (2002). Principles of network development and evolution: an experimental study. *Journal of Public Economics 89*, 1469–1495.

Camerer, C. F. (2004). Behavioral game theory: Predicting human behavior in strategic situations. In C. F. Camerer, G. Loewenstein, and M. Rabin (Eds.), *Advances in Behavioral Economics*, Chapter 13, pp. 374–392. Princeton, NJ: Princeton University Press.

Campbell, D. E. (2006). *Incentives: Motivation and the Economics of Information* (2nd ed.). Cambridge University Press.

Carpenter, J. (2007). The demand for punishment. *Journal of Economic Behavior and Organization 62*(4), 522–542.

Carpenter, J. and P. Matthews (2002). Social reciprocity. Technical Report 43, Department of Economics, Middlebury College.

Carter, M. (2001). *Foundations of Mathematical Economics*. Cambridge, MA: MIT Press.

Casari, M. (2007). Emergence of endogenous legal institutions: Property rights and community governance in the Italian Alps. *Journal of Economic History 57*(1), 206–235.

Casari, M. and C. Plott (2003). Decentralized management of common property resources: Experiments with a centuries-old institution. *Journal of Economic Behavior and Organization 51*, 217–247.

Casella, A. (2003). Storable votes. *Games and Economic Behavior 51*, 391–419.

Casella, A., A. Gelman, and T. Palfrey (2003). An experimental study of storable votes. *Games and Economic Behavior 57*, 123–154.

Cason, T. N., T. Saijo, T. Sjostrom, and T. Yamato (2006). Secure implementation experiments: Do strategy-proof mechanisms really work? *Games and Economic Behavior 67*(1), 191–226.

Champ, P. A., R. C. Bishop, T. C. Brown, and D. W. McCollum (2006). Using donation mechanisms to value nonuse benefits from public goods. *Journal of Environmental Economics and Management 33*(2), 151–162.

Chen, Y. (2004). Incentive compatible mechanisms for pure public goods: A survey of experimental research. In C. R. Plott and V. Smith (Eds.), *The Handbook of Experimental Economics Results*. Amsterdam: Elsevier Press.

———— (2005). Dynamic stability of Nash-efficient public goods mechanisms: Reconciling theory with experiments. In R. Zwick and A. Rapoport (Eds.), *Experimental Business Research*, Volume II, Chapter 10, pp. 185–201. Norwell, MA: Kluwer Academic.

Chen, Y. and R. Gazzale (2004). When does learning in games generate convergence to Nash equilibria? The role of supermodularity in an experimental setting. *American Economic Review 94*, 1505–1535.

Chen, Y. and C. Plott (1996). The Groves-Ledyard mechanism: An experimental study in institutional design. *Journal of Public Economics 59*, 335–364.

Chen, Y. and F.-F. Tang (1998). Learning and incentive compatible mechanisms for public goods provision: An experimental study. *Journal of Political Economy 106*, 633–662.

Cheng, A. and E. Friedman (2005). Sybilproof reputation mechanisms. In *P2PECON '05: Proceeding of the 2005 ACM SIGCOMM workshop on Economics of peer-to-peer systems*, pp. 128–132. New York: ACM Press.

Cheng, J. Q. (1998). *Essays on Designing Economic Mechanisms*. Ph. D. thesis, University of Michigan, Ann Arbor, MI.

Clarke, E. (1971). Multi-part pricing of public goods. *Public Choice 11*, 17–33.

Conley, J. P. and D. Diamantaras (1996). Generalized Samuelson conditions and welfare theorems for nonsmooth economies. *Journal of Public Economics 59*, 137–152.

Corchón, L. C. and S. Wilkie (1996). Double implementation of the ratio correspondence by a market mechanism. *Economic Design 2*, 325–337.

Costa-Gomes, M., V. P. Crawford, and B. Broseta (2001). Cognition and behavior in normal-form games: An experimental study. *Econometrica 69*(5), 1193–1235.

Cramton, P., Y. Shoham, and R. Steinberg (Eds.) (2006). *Combinatorial Auctions*. Cambridge, MA: MIT Press.

Crawford, V. (1977). A game of fair division. *Review of Economic Studies 44*, 235–247.

Cremer, J. and R. McLean (1985). Optimal selling strategies under uncertainty for a discriminating monopolist when demands are interdependent. *Econometrica 53*, 345–361.

d'Aspremont, C. and L.-A. Gérard-Varet (1979). Incentives and incomplete information. *Journal of Public Economics 11*, 25–45.

Debreu, G. (1959). *Theory of Value*. New York: Wiley.

Dubins, L. E. and D. A. Freedman (1981). Machiavelli and the Gale-Shapley algorithm. *American Mathematical Monthly 88*, 485–494.

Duggan, J. (1997). Virtual Bayesian implementation. *Econometrica 65*, 1175–1199.

Duggan, J. and J. Roberts (2002). Implementing the efficient allocation of pollution. *American Economic Review 92*(4), 1070–1078.

Dutta, B. and A. Sen (1991). A necessary and sufficient condition for two-person Nash implementation. *Review of Economic Studies 58:1*, 121–128.

Ellingsen, T. and M. Johannesson (2008, June). Pride and prejudice: The human side of incentive theory. *American Economic Review 98*(3), 990–1008.

Falk, A., E. Fehr, and U. Fischbacher (2005). Driving forces of informal sanctions. *Econometrica 73*, 2017–2030.

Falkinger, J. (1996). Efficient private provision of public goods by rewarding deviations from average. *Journal of Public Economics 62*(3), 413–22.

Falkinger, J., E. Fehr, S. Gächter, and R. Winter-Ebmer (2000). A simple mechanism for the efficient provision of public goods: Experimental evidence. *American Economic Review 90*(1), 247–264.

Fehr, E. and S. Gächter (2000). Cooperation and punishment. *American Economic Review 90*, 980–994.

——— (2002). Altruistic punishment in humans. *Nature 415*, 137–140.

Friedman, E., P. Resnick, and R. Sami (2007). Manipulation-resistant reputation systems. In N. Nisan, T. Roughgarden, E. Tardos, and V. Vazirani (Eds.), *Algorithmic Game Theory*, Chapter 27, pp. 677–697. New York: Cambridge University Press.

Gailmard, S. and T. R. Palfrey (2005). An experimental comparison of collective choice procedures for excludable public goods. *Journal of Public Economics 89*, 1361–1398.

Gale, D. (2001). The two-sided matching problem. Origin, development and current issues. *International Game Theory Review 3*(2), 237–252.

Gale, D. and L. S. Shapley (1962). College admissions and the stability of marriage. *American Mathematical Monthly 69*, 9–15.

Gale, D. and M. A. Sotomayor (1985). Some remarks on the stable matching problem. *Discrete Applied Mathematics 11*, 223–232.

Gibbard, A. (1973). Manipulation of voting schemes: A general result. *Econometrica 41*, 587–601.

Glazer, J. and A. Ma (1989). Efficient allocation of a prize—King Solomon's dilemma. *Games and Economic Behavior 1*, 222–233.

Glazer, J. and M. Perry (1996). Virtual implementation in backwards induction. *Games and Economic Behavior 15*, 27–32.

Goeree, J. K. and C. A. Holt (2001). Ten little treasures of game theory and ten intuitive contradictions. *American Economic Review 91*(5), 1402–1422.

Green, J. R. and J.-J. Laffont (1977). Characterization of satisfactory mechanisms for the revelation of preferences for public goods. *Econometrica 45*, 427–438.

Greene, W. H. (2003). *Econometric Analysis. Fifth Edition.* Upper Saddle River, NJ: Prentice Hall.

Groves, T. (1973). Incentives in teams. *Econometrica 41*, 617–663.

Groves, T. and J. O. Ledyard (1977). Optimal allocation of public goods: A solution to the "free rider" problem. *Econometrica 45*, 783–809.

Haeringer, G. and M. Wooders (2007, March). Decentralized job matching. Working Paper, http://idea.uab.es/~r1g/index2.html.

Harsanyi, J. C. (1967). Games with incomplete information played by "Bayesian" players. Part I: The basic model. *Management Science 14*, 159–182.

——— (1968a). Games with incomplete information played by "Bayesian" players. Part II: Bayesian equilibrium points. *Management Science 14*, 320–334.

——— (1968b). Games with incomplete information played by "Bayesian" players. Part III: The basic probability distribution of the game. *Management Science 14*, 486–502.

Harstad, R. M. (2000). Dominant strategy adoption and bidders' experience with pricing rules. *Experimental Economics 3*, 261–280.

Healy, P. J. (2007). Learning dynamics for mechanism design: An experimental comparison of public goods mechanisms. *Journal of Economic Theory 129*, 114–149.

Healy, P. J., J. O. Ledyard, C. Noussair, H. Thronson, P. Ulrich, and G. Varsi (2006). Contracting inside an organization: An experimental study. *Experimental Economics 10*, 143–167.

Heifetz, A. and Z. Neeman (2006). On the generic (im)possibility of full surplus extraction in mechanism design. *Econometrica 74*(1), 213–233.

Hurwicz, L. (1979). Outcome functions yielding Walrasian and Lindahl allocations at Nash equilibrium points. *Review of Economic Studies 143*, 217–225.

Hurwicz, L., E. Maskin, and A. Postlewaite (1995). Feasible Nash implementation of social choice correspondences when the designer does not know endowments or production sets. In J. O. Ledyard (Ed.), *The Economics of Informational Decentralization: Complexity, Efficiency, and Stability.* New York: Springer.

Hylland, A. and R. Zeckhauser (1979, April). The efficient allocation of individuals to positions. *Journal of Political Economy 87*(2), 293–314.

Isaac, R. M., J. M. Walker, and A. W. Williams (1994). Group size and the voluntary provision of public goods: Experimental evidence utilizing large groups. *Journal of Public Economics 54*(1), 1–36.

Jackson, M. O. (1991). Bayesian implementation. *Econometrica 92*(2), 461–477.

——— (1992). Implementation in undominated strategies: A look at bounded mechanisms. *The Review of Economic Studies 59*(4), 757–775.

————— (2001). A crash course in implementation theory. *Social Choice and Welfare 18*(4), 655–708.

————— (2003). Mechanism theory. In U. Derigs (Ed.), *Optimization and Operations Research*, Encyclopedia of Life Support Systems. Oxford: EOLSS.

Jackson, M. O. and H. Sonnenschein (2004, October). Overcoming incentive constraints by linking decisions (extended version). Working Paper, http://www.stanford.edu/~jacksonm/linkinglong.pdf.

————— (2007, January). Overcoming incentive constraints by linking decisions. *Econometrica 75*(1), 241–257.

Jackson, M. O. and S. Wilkie (2005, April). Endogenous games and mechanisms: Side payments among players. *Review of Economic Studies 72*(2), 543–566.

Jackson, M. O., T. R. Palfrey, and S. Srivastava (1994). Undominated Nash implementation in bounded mechanisms. *Games and Economic Behavior 6*, 474–501.

Jehiel, P., M. Meyer-Ter Vehn, B. Moldovanu, and W. R. Zame (2006). The limits of ex-post implementation. *Econometrica 74*(3), 585–610.

Jehle, G. A. and P. J. Reny (2001). *Advanced Microeconomic Theory* (2nd ed.). Boston, MA: Addison-Wesley.

Kagel, J. and A. E. Roth (1995). *Handbook of Experimental Economics*. Princeton, NJ: Princeton University Press.

Kaiser, B. A. (2007, June). The Athenian trierarchy: Mechanism design for the private provision of public goods. *Journal of Economic History 67*(2), 445–480.

Kaneko, M. (1977). The ratio equilibrium and a voting game in a public goods economy. *Journal of Economic Theory 16*, 123–136.

Katok, E., M. Sefton, and A. Yavas (2002). Implementation by iterative dominance and backward induction: An experimental comparison. *Journal of Economic Theory 104*, 89–103.

Kawagoe, T. and T. Mori (2001). Can the pivotal mechanism induce truth-telling? An experimental study. *Public Choice 108*, 331–354.

Kelso, Jr., A. S. and V. Crawford (1982, November). Job matching, coalition formation, and gross substitutes. *Econometrica 50*(6), 1483–1504.

Knuth, D. E. (1976). *Mariages Stables*. Montréal, Canada: Les Presses de l'Universite de Montréal.

Kolm, S.-C. (1972). *Justice et equité*. Paris: Centre National de la Recherche Scientifique.

Krishna, V. (2002). *Auction Theory*. San Diego, CA: Academic Press.

Kugler, T., Z. Neeman, and N. Vulkan (2005). Markets versus negotiations: An experimental investigation. *Games and Economic Behavior 56*(1), 121–134.

Laffont, J.-J. (1987). Incentives and the allocations of public goods. In A. J. Auerbach and M. Feldstein (Eds.), *Handbook of Public Economics*, Volume II, pp. 537–569. Amsterdam: North Holland.

————— (1997). Game theory and empirical economics: The case of auction data. *European Economic Review 41*, 1–35.

Laffont, J.-J. and J. Tirole (1993). *A theory of incentives in procurement and regulation.* Cambridge, MA: MIT Press.

Ledyard, J. O. (1995). Public goods: A survey of experimental research. In J. Kagel and A. E. Roth (Eds.), *Handbook of Experimental Economics.* Princeton, NJ: Princeton University Press.

Lindahl, E. (1919/1967). Die Gerechtigkeit der Besteurung, translated (in part) as "Just Taxation: A positive solution". In R. Musgrave and A. Peacock (Eds.), *Classics in the Theory of Public Finance*, pp. 168–176. London: Macmillan.

Masclet, D., C. Noussair, S. Tucker, and M.-C. Villeval (2003). Monetary and non-monetary punishment in the voluntary contributions mechanism. *American Economic Review 93*, 366–381.

Mas-Colell, A. and J. Silvestre. Cost share equilibria: A Lindahlian approach. *Journal of Economic Theory 47*, 239–256.

Mas-Colell, A., M. Whinston, and J. Green (1995). *Microeconomic Theory.* Oxford: Oxford University Press.

Maskin, E. (1999). Nash equilibrium and welfare optimality. *Review of Economic Studies 66*, 23–38. Working Paper version circulated in 1977.

Matsushima, H. (1988). A new approach to the implementation problem. *Journal of Economic Theory 45*, 128–144.

McKelvey, R. and T. R. Palfrey (1992). An experimental study of the centipede game. *Econometrica 60*(4), 803–836.

Milgrom, P. (2004). *Putting Auction Theory to Work.* Cambridge: Cambridge University Press.

Milleron, J.-C. (1972). Theory of value with public goods: A survey article. *Journal of Economic Theory 5*, 419–477.

Mookherjee, D. and S. Reichelstein (1992). Dominant strategy implementation of Bayesian incentive compatible allocation rules. *Journal of Economic Theory 56*, 378–399.

Moore, J. and R. Repullo (1988). Subgame perfect implementation. *Econometrica 56*(5), 1191–1220.

———— (1990). Nash implementation: A full characterization. *Econometrica 58*(5), 1083–1099.

Moulin, H. (1994). Serial cost sharing of excludable public goods. *Review of Economic Studies 61*, 305–325.

———— (1995). *Cooperative Microeconomics: A Game-Theoretic Introduction.* Princeton, NJ: Princeton University Press.

Muller, E. and M. A. Satterthwaite (1977). The equivalence of strong positive association and strategy-proofness. *Journal of Economic Theory 14*, 412–418.

Myerson, R. B. (1981). Optimal auction design. *Mathematics of Operations Research 6*, 58–73.

———— (1991). *Game Theory: Analysis of Conflict.* Cambridge, MA: Harvard University Press.

Myerson, R. B. and M. A. Satterthwaite (1983). Efficient mechanisms for bilateral trading. *Journal of Economic Theory 29*, 265–281.

Niederle, M., A. E. Roth, and T. Sönmez (2008). Matching and market design. In S. Durlauf and L. J. Blume (Eds.), *The New Palgrave Dictionary of Economics* (2nd ed.). Palgrave Macmillan.

Niederle, M. and L. Yariv (2007, June). Matching through decentralized markets. Technical report, Stanford University. Available at `http://www.stanford.edu/~niederle/DecentralizedMarkets.pdf`.

Osborne, M. J. (2004). *An Introduction to Game Theory*. Oxford: Oxford University Press.

Ostrom, E. (2000). Collective action and the evolution of social norms. *Journal of Economic Perspectives 14*(3), 137–158.

Page, T., L. Putterman, and U. Bulent (2005). Voluntary association in public goods experiments: Reciprocity, mimicry and efficiency. *Economic Journal 115*, 1032–1053.

Palfrey, T. R. (2002). Implementation theory. In *Handbook of Game Theory*, Volume III. Amsterdam: North-Holland.

Palfrey, T. R. and S. Srivastava (1987). On Bayesian implementable allocations. *Review of Economic Studies LIV*, 193–208.

――― (1989). Mechanism design with incomplete information: A solution to the implementation problem. *Journal of Political Economy 97*, 668–691.

――― (1991). Nash implementation using undominated strategies. *Econometrica 59*(2), 479–501.

Pigou, A. C. (1920). *The Economics of Welfare*. London: MacMillan.

Ponti, G. (2000). Splitting the baby in two: Solving Solomon's dilemma with boundedly rational agents. *Journal of Evolutionary Economics 10*, 449–455.

Ponti, G., A. Gantner, D. López-Pintado, and R. Montgomery (2003). Solomon's dilemma: An experimental study on dynamic implementation. *Review of Economic Design 8*, 217–239.

Reny, P. J. (2001). Arrow's theorem and the Gibbard-Satterthwaite theorem: A unified approach. *Economics Letters 70*, 99–105.

Repullo, R. (1987). A simple proof of Maskin's theorem on Nash implementation. *Social Choice and Welfare 4*, 39–41.

Riley, J. G. and W. S. Samuelson (1981). Opimal auctions. *American Economic Review 71*(3), 381–392.

Rondeau, D., G. L. Poe, and W. D. Schulze (2005). VCM or PPM? A comparison of the performance of two voluntary public goods mechanisms. *Journal of Public Economics 89*, 1581–1592.

Rose, S. K., J. Clark, G. L. Poe, D. Rondeau, and W. D. Schulze (2002). The private provision of public goods: Tests of a provision point mechanism for funding green power programs. *Resource and Energy Economics 115*, 131–155.

Roth, A. E. (1982a). The economics of matching: stability and incentives. *Mathematics of Operations Research 7*(4), 617–628.

――― (1982b). Incentive compatibility in a market with indivisible goods. *Economics Letters 9*, 127–132.

――― (1985). The college admissions problem is not equivalent to the marriage problem. *Journal of Economic Theory 36*, 277–288.

――― (2002). The economist as engineer: Game theory, experimentation and computation as tools in economic design. *Econometrica 70*(4), 1341–1378.

——— (2008a, March). Deferred acceptance algorithms: History, theory, practice and open questions. *International Journal of Game Theory 36*, 537–569.

——— (2008b, March). What have we learned from market design? *The Economic Journal 118*, 285–310.

Roth, A. E., T. Sönmez, and M. U. Ünver (2004). Kidney exchange. *Quarterly Journal of Economics 119*, 457–488.

Roth, A. E. and M. A. Sotomayor (1990). *Two-Sided Matching: A study in game theoretic modeling and analysis*. Econometric Society Monographs. Cambridge University Press.

Saari, D. G. (2001). *Decisions and Elections: Explaining the Unexpected*. New York: Cambridge University Press.

Saijo, T. (1988). Strategy space reduction in Maskin's theorem: Sufficient conditions for Nash implementation. *Econometrica 56*, 693–700.

Saijo, T., T. Sjöstrom, and T. Yamato (2007). Secure implementation. *Theoretical Economics 2*(3), 203–229.

Samuelson, P. A. (1954). The theory of public expenditure. *Review of Economics and Statistics 36*, 387–389.

Satterthwaite, M. (1975). Strategy proofness and arrow's conditions: Existence and correspondence theorems for voting procedures and social welfare theorems. *Journal of Economic Theory 10*, 187–217.

Schmeidler, D. and H. Sonnenschein (1978). Two proofs of the Gibbard-Satterthwaite theorem on the possibility of a strategy-proof social choice function. In H. W. Gottinger and W. Leinfeller (Eds.), *Decision Theory and Social Ethics, Issues in Social Choice*, pp. 227–234. Dordrecht, The Netherlands: Reidel.

Schotter, A. (2001). *Microeconomics: A Modern Approach* (Third ed.). Essex, UK: Addison Wesley Longman.

Seabright, P. (2004). *The Company of Strangers: A Natural History of Economic Life*. Princeton, NJ and Oxford: Princeton University Press.

Sefton, M. and A. Yavas (1996). Abreu-Matsushima mechanisms: Experimental evidence. *Games and Economic Behavior 16*, 280–302.

Sefton, M., R. Shupp, and J. M. Walker (2006). The effect of rewards and sanctions in provision of public goods. CAEPR Working Paper.

Serrano, R. (2004). The theory of implementation of social choice rules. *SIAM Review 46*(3), 377–414.

Serrano, R. and R. Vohra (2001). Some limitations of virtual Bayesian implementation. *Econometrica 69*, 785–702.

——— (2005). A characterization of virtual Bayesian implementation. *Games and Economic Behavior 50*(2), 312–331.

Shapley, L. S. and H. Scarf (1974). On cores and indivisibility. *Journal of Mathematical Economics 1*, 23–37.

Shilov, G. and B. Gurevich (1977). *Integral, Measure & Derivative: A Unified Approach*. New York, NY: Dover.

Simon, C. P. and L. Blume (1994). *Mathematics for Economists*. New York: Norton.

Smith, A. (1776/1998). *An Inquiry into the Nature and Causes of the Wealth of Nations.* Washington, DC: Regnery Publishing.

Sönmez, T. (1997, November). Manipulation via capacities in two-sided matching markets. *Journal of Economic Theory 77*, 197–204.

Sprumont, Y. (1991, March). The division problem with single-peaked preferences: A characterization of the uniform allocation rule. *Econometrica 59*(2), 509–519.

Thomson, W. (1996, June). Concepts of implementation. *The Japanese Economic Review 47*(2), 133–143.

—— (1999a, January). Economies with public goods: An elementary geometric exposition. *Journal of Public Economic Theory 1*(1), 139–176.

—— (1999b). Monotonic extensions on economic domains. *Review of Economic Design 4*, 13–33.

—— (2005). Divide-and-permute. *Games and Economic Behavior 52*, 186–200.

Topkis, D. M. (1998). *Supermodularity and Complementarity.* Princeton, NJ: Princeton University Press.

Varian, H. R. (1994). A solution to the problem of externalities when agents are well-informed. *American Economic Review 84*(5), 1278–1293.

Varian, H. R. (2006). *Intermediate Microeconomics: A Modern Approach* (Seventh ed.). New York: W. W. Norton.

Vega-Redondo, F. (2003). *Economics and the Theory of Games.* New York: Cambridge University Press.

Vulkan, N. (2003). *The Economics of E-commerce: A Strategic Guide to Understanding and Designing the Online Marketplace.* Princeton, NJ: Princeton University Press.

Walker, J. M., R. Gardner, and E. Ostrom (1990). Rent dissipation in a limited-access common-pool resource: experimental evidence. *Journal of Environmental Economics and Management 19*, 203–211.

Walker, M. (1981). A simple incentive compatible scheme for attaining Lindahl allocations. *Econometrica 49*, 65–71.

Walras, L. (1874). *Élements d'Économie Politique Pure.* Lausanne, Switzerland: Corbaz. Translated into English by W. Jaffe as *Elements of Pure Economics*, 1954, Orion, New York.

Wicksell, S. (1896/1967). Ein Neues Prinzip der Gerechten Besteurung, translated as 'A New Principle of Just Taxation'. In R. Musgrave and A. Peacock (Eds.), *Classics in the Theory of Public Finance*, pp. 72–118. London: Macmillan.

Wilkie, S. (1990). *Essays in Game Theory.* Ph. D. thesis, University of Rochester, Rochester, NY.

Williams, S. R. (1986). Realization and Nash implementation. *Econometrica 54*, 139–151.

Wilson, R. (2002). Architecture of power markets. *Econometrica 70*(4), 1299–1340.

Wolfstetter, E. (1999). *Topics in Microeconomics: Industrial Organization, Auctions, and Incentives.* New York: Cambridge University Press.

Index